Lecture Notes in Computer Science 2485

Edited by G. Goos, J. Hartmanis, and J. van Leeuwen

T0232078

Springer
Berlin
Heidelberg
New York
Barcelona
Hong Kong
London
Milan
Paris
Tokyo

Andrea Bondavalli
Pascale Thevenod-Fosse (Eds.)

Dependable Computing EDCC-4

4th European Dependable Computing Conference
Toulouse, France, October 23-25, 2002
Proceedings

 Springer

Series Editors

Gerhard Goos, Karlsruhe University, Germany
Juris Hartmanis, Cornell University, NY, USA
Jan van Leeuwen, Utrecht University, The Netherlands

Volume Editors

Andrea Bondavalli
Università di Firenze
Dipartimento di Sistemi e Informatica
Via Lombroso 6/17, 50134 Firenze, Italy
E-mail: a.bondavalli@dsi.unifi.it

Pascale Thevenod-Fosse
LAAS-CNRS
7 Avenue du Colonel Roche, Toulouse Cedex 4, France
E-mail: thevenod@laas.fr

Cataloging-in-Publication Data applied for

Bibliographic information published by Die Deutsche Bibliothek
Die Deutsche Bibliothek lists this publication in the Deutsche Nationalbibliografie;
detailed bibliographic data is available in the Internet at http://dnb.ddb.de

CR Subject Classification (1998): B.1.3, B.2.3, B.3.4, B.4.5, C.3-4, D.2.4, D.2.8,
D.4.5, E.4, J.7

ISSN 0302-9743
ISBN 3-540-00012-7 Springer-Verlag Berlin Heidelberg New York

Springer-Verlag Berlin Heidelberg New York
a member of BertelsmannSpringer Science+Business Media GmbH

http://www.springer.de

© Springer-Verlag Berlin Heidelberg 2002
Printed in Germany

Typesetting: Camera-ready by author, data conversion by DA-TeX Gerd Blumenstein
Printed on acid-free paper   SPIN 10870601   06/3142   5 4 3 2 1 0

Foreword

It was with great pleasure that, on behalf of the entire organizing committee, I welcomed participants to EDCC-4, the Fourth European Dependable Computing Conference, held for the first time in France. The fourth issue of EDCC carried on the traditions established by the previous conferences in this series: EDCC-1 was held in Berlin (Germany) in October 1994, EDCC-2 in Taormina (Italy) in October 1996, and EDCC-3 in Prague (Czech Republic) in September 1999.

EDCC evolved from a merger of tow other conference series at the moment when the Iron Curtain fell. One of these, known as the "International Conference on Fault-Tolerant Computing Systems", was organized during the period 1982–1991, by the German Technical Interest Group "Fault-Tolerant Computing Systems". The other series, known as the "International Conference on Fault-Tolerant Systems and Diagnostics", was organized during the period 1975–1990 in the former Czechoslovakia, Poland, Bulgaria, and the former GDR. The composition of the EDCC steering committee and the organizing committees of the successive issues of the conference have mirrored the East–West unification character of the conference series.

The EDCC conference is becoming a unique meeting point for researchers and practitioners from all over the world in the field of Dependable Systems. It is organized by the SEE Working Group "Dependable Computing" in France, the GI/ITG/GMA Technical Committee on Dependability and Fault Tolerance in Germany, and the AICA Working Group "Dependability of Computer Systems" in Italy. Furthermore, committees of several global professional organizations, such as IEEE and IFIP, support the conference.

Organizations and individuals are becoming increasingly dependent on sophisticated computing systems. Thus, dependability – and all its attributes of reliability, availability, safety, and security, for example – is becoming more and more challenging for every computing system. This growing importance of the field of dependability in everyday life is strongly emphasized by the fact that the European Union has initiated major specific actions on dependability, both in the current 5th Framework Programme on Information Society Technologies, and in the 6th Framework Programme to be launched in a few months.

In September 1999, Toulouse was selected as the conference venue for the 4th conference issue. This beautiful city, situated in the southwest of France, is the capital of the "Midi-Pyrénées" region, the largest French province. Toulouse is a major European center for educational institutions, including universities and several research laboratories covering all spheres of knowledge. A number of industrial companies especially concerned with dependability challenges are located in and around Toulouse: Alcatel Space Industries, Astrium, EADS Airbus, Motorola, Rockwell Collins France, Thales Avionics, etc.

The choice of Toulouse as the October 2002 conference venue gave us the opportunity to organize it in conjunction with the Innovation and Future Technologies Fair, SITEF 2002. This exhibition presents the European Research Programmes, and is structured around the themes defined in the 5th and 6th Framework Programmes which are essential for the economy and jobs in the future: information and communication, health and ecosystem resources, the means required for competitive and sustained growth. Thus, EDCC-4 provided a unique occasion for the participants to visit the SITEF exhibition and initiate or reinforce contacts with both the academic and industrial European communities, in particular, the preparation of the 6th Framework Programme.

Organizing an international conference is never possible without the collective efforts of many people. I had the privilege to work with a group of excellent people, and it is my pleasure to extend to them my sincere thanks for their exceptional work. For lack of space, I cannot draw up the list of all those people who contributed to the successful organization of EDCC-4. But let me mention at least some of them: Andrea Bondavalli (Program Chair), Fabrizio Grandoni (Publication Chair), Vincent Nicomette (Publicity Chair), Felicita Di Giandomenico (Fast Abstracts Chair), the 32 members of the Program Committee, and all the external referees.

The conference received generous financial support from several organizations: the Paul Sabatier University of Toulouse, the French National Centre for Scientific Research, the "Chambre de Commerce et d'Industrie de Toulouse", the French Ministry of Research, and the European Commission. Their support was necessary to offer the participants what we hope was a cordial and unforgettable hospitality. Their help is gratefully acknowledged.

Finally, I would like to thank Springer-Verlag for publishing the conference proceedings in the well-known series of Lecture Notes in Computer Science.

I hope that the conference participants enjoyed both the technical and social programs of EDCC-4, thus confirming the successful continuation of this series.

Toulouse, July 2002   Pascale Thévenod-Fosse

Preface

The European Dependable Computing Conference is in its fourth edition. EDCC is the successor of two European conference series on fault tolerance, dependability, and aspects of testing and diagnosis. One of them, known as the "International Conference on Fault-Tolerant Computing Systems" was organized during the period 1982-1991 by the German Technical Interest Group "Fault-Tolerant Computing Systems". The other series, known as the "International Conference on Fault-Tolerant Systems and Diagnostics", was organized during the period 1975-1990 in the former Czechoslovakia, Poland, Bulgaria, and the former GDR. EDCC-1 was held in Berlin (Germany) in October 1994, EDCC-2 in Taormina (Italy) in October 1996, and EDCC-3 in Prague (Czech Republic) in September 1999; Toulouse (France) was chosen for this fourth edition.

EDCC is organized by the SEE Working Group "Dependable Computing" in France, the GI/ITG/GMA Technical Committee on Dependability and Fault Tolerance in Germany, and the AICA Working Group "Dependability of Computer Systems" in Italy. Furthermore, committees of several global professional organizations, such as IEEE and IFIP, support the conference. EDCC is thus the forum for European researchers in dependability, and is extending towards a world-wide dimension as researchers from all over the world show their interest by choosing EDCC for submitting their manuscripts and presenting their work.

The selection process was very careful. Each manuscript was sent out for review to three PC members plus two external reviewers. Fifty-one submissions from 18 countries were received and the 32 members of the Program Committee and 68 external reviewers returned on time a total of 217 reviews. This made the selection process very comprehensive. The entire process was managed using the START tool. Silvano Chiaradonna of CNUCE-CNR graciously helped with the acquisition, operation, and maintenance of this tool, and for his efforts I feel particularly indebted to him. The committee met in Pisa, Italy for two days in May 2002 to arrange the technical program. A total of 16 papers were selected to appear in the Proceedings. The rest of the technical program was defined to include three panels, a forum for Fast Abstracts to report on very recent work, and a keynote on contemporary topics.

I would like to thank the Program Committee members for their help in putting together the final program. They helped us in many ways right from the beginning, including topic identification, suggesting external reviewers, refereeing, and attending the Pisa meeting in large numbers. I also thank all of the external reviewers for making available their time and their technical knowledge, and the authors of all the manuscripts for their contributions and the timely submissions. Special thanks go to Pascale Thévenod, an enthusiastic and supportive General Chair, Felicita Di Giandomenico, the Fast Abstracts Chair, and Rogerio De Lemos, Jean-Claude Laprie, and Luca Simoncini who led the organization of three panels on interesting and stimulating topics. I would like finally to acknowledge the support of the Steering Committee.

I hope the participants found the conference interesting and stimulating and will continue to contribute to its success in the coming years.

Firenze, July 2002   Andrea Bondavalli

These proceedings were just ready for printing when the sad and terrible news reached the organizers that Jan Hlavicka, member of the Steering Committee of EDCC and the Chairman of the previous EDCC, has gone forever. Jan was not only an outstanding researcher and a devoted professor, but the archetype of a European scientist. He was the initiator of the FTSD conferences held annually from the mid 1970s until 1990. The FTSD conferences were the integrative platform for scientists working in the field of dependability in Central- and Eastern Europe and became one of the roots of the EDCC series. Jan was one of the first to make an effort to integrate scientists both at the regional and at the international levels. We must thank him for the fast integration of our community after the political changes in 1989.

Jan's vision that we have a unique European culture is such an evident truth that we will keep pushing forward to continue the ideas of our late friend.

Throughout his career, he was constantly productive in both research and service to his profession. In short, he was a gentleman and a scholar who will be sincerely missed by all who knew him.

Organization Committee

General Chair

Pascale Thévenod-Fosse
LAAS-CNRS
Toulouse, France

Program Chair

Andrea Bondavalli
University of Firenze
Italy

Fast Abstracts Chair

Felicita Di Giandomenico
ISTI-CNR
Pisa, Italy

Publicity Chair

Vincent Nicomette
LAAS-CNRS
Toulouse, France

Publication Chair

Fabrizio Grandoni
ISTI-CNR
Pisa, Italy

Local Arrangements Chair

Marie-Thérèse Ippolito
LAAS-CNRS
Toulouse, France

EDCC Steering Committee

Algirdas Avizienis, USA
Mario Dal Cin, Germany
Karl-Erwin Grosspietsch, Germany
Jan Hlavicka, Czech Rep.
Andrzej Hlawiczka, Poland
Hermann Kopetz, Austria
Jean Claude Laprie, France

Brian Randell, United Kingdom
Luca Simoncini, Italy
Pascale Thévenod, France
Jan Torin, Sweden
Raimund Ubar, Estonia

Program Committee

Mario Dal Cin
Rogerio De Lemos
Felicita Di Giandomenico
Bernard Eschermann
Paul Ezhilchelvan
Nuno Ferreira Neves
Pedro Gil
Jan Hlavicka
Andrzej Hlawiczka
Karama Kanoun
Johan Karlsson
Jean-Claude Laprie
Erik Maehle
Istvan Majzik
Mirek Malek
Gilles Muller
Ivan Mura

Edgar Nett
Dimitris Nikolos
Fabio Panzieri
Andras Pataricza
Stanislaw J. Piestrak
Peter Puschner
Andre Schiper
Volkmar Sieh
Joao Silva
Luca Simoncini
Janusz Sosnowski
Neeraj Suri
Raimund Ubar
Hélène Waeselynck
Jie Xu

External Referees

A. Amoroso
J. Arlat
A. Avizienis
R. Baldoni
T. Bartha
G. Bauer
C. Bernardeschi
A. Bertolino
C. Bidan
V. Casola
S. Chiaradonna
V. Claesson
A. Coccoli
D. Cotroneo
G. Csertán
M. Cukier
M. Dacier
R. Davoli
Y. Deswarte
R. Dobrin
J.-C. Fabre
A. Fantechi
M. Gergeleit

S. Gnesi
S. Gossens
F. Grandoni
K.-E. Grosspietsch
R. Guerraoui
M. Hiller
G. Horváth
A. Jhumka
M. Kaaniche
K. Kavousianos
A. Kermarrec
M.-O. Killijian
K. Kosmidis
D. Latella
T. Losert
H. Madeira
P. Maestrini
C. Marchetti
P. Marmo
E. Martins
M. Massink
M. Mock
V. Nicomette

R. Obermaisser
M. Paulitsch
D. Powell
B. Randell
J. Richling
M. Roccetti
L. Rodrigues
L. Romano
A. Romanovsky
S. Schemmer
P. Sobe
S. Sommer
W. Steiner
P. Szmala
S. Trikaliotis
D. Varró
H. Vergos
P. Veríssimo
J. WarneP.
G. Zavattaro

Table of Contents

Session 4: Error Detection and Fault Tolerance

Session 5: Experimental Validation

Session 6: Fast Abstracts II

Panel 2: Critical Infrastructure Protection

Session 7: Distributed Algorithms

Panel 3: Towards Information Society Initiative in FP6: Roadmapping Activities in Dependability

Session 8: Real-Time

Use and Misuse of Safety Models in Design

Rene Amalberti

IMASSA, Head Département sciences Cognitives
BP 73, 91223 Brétigny-sur-Orge, FRANCE

Extended abstract. Operator models, or equivalent end-user models have become a standard prerequisite in most man-machine system design. Nowadays, the designer can choose among a great variety of models, e.g., behavioural models and competence models, and these models are available in a large range of granularity from quasi-neuropsychological models of memory to framework models of dynamic cognition. However, despite -or maybe because of- the variety of models, modelling the operator is still a land of contrasts within the industry, with multiple forms and meanings, and as result a feeling persists that these models, which are meant to be useful, are difficult to incorporate into the design process or the operations. This conference focuses on the development and use of cognitive models of human reliability, and tries to understand the biases and limitations of their use in design of safe systems within the industry. It is divided into three sections. The first section details the range of existing cognitive models of human reliability and proposes a classification of these models into four main categories: error production models, error detection and recovery models, systemic models, and integrated safety ecological models. The example of the Aviation Industry shows how difficult it has been in the recent past to incorporate the most advanced of these models into design, even though the same Industry has long complained that such cognitive operators' models were not available. The second section tries to explain the reason for the relative failure. It shows the inter-dependency existing between the category of cognitive model, the safety paradigm, and the strategy for design. Severe drawbacks may occur each time a model is used with the wrong safety paradigm or the wrong strategy for design. It also shows that the more cognitively-based the model is, the less it is incorporated into design. The lack of education in psychology for designers, as well as the lack of a clear procedure for incorporating such models into design, are among the most important factors explaining this lack of success. The third and last section points to the new directions in cognitive modelling to improve the fit between operator modelling and design requirements.

F. Grandoni (Ed.): EDCC 2002, LNCS 2485, p. 1, 2002.
© Springer-Verlag Berlin Heidelberg 2002

On the Effects of Outages on the QoS of GPRS Networks under Different User Characterizations

Stefano Porcarelli[1] and Felicita Di Giandomenico[2]

[1]Computer Engineering Department, University of Pisa
Via Diotisalvi 2, 56126 Pisa, Italy
stefano.porcarelli@guest.cnuce.cnr.it
[2]Istituto di Elaborazione della Informazione, CNR
Via G. Moruzzi 1, 56124 Pisa, Italy
digiandomenico@iei.pi.cnr.it

Abstract. Standard network QoS analysis usually accounts for the infrastructure performance/availability only, with scarce consideration of the user perspective. With reference to the General Packet Radio Service (GPRS), this paper addresses the problem of how to evaluate the impact of system unavailability periods on QoS measures, explicitly accounting for user characteristics. In fact, the ultimate goal of a service provider is user satisfaction, therefore it is extremely important to introduce the peculiarities of the user population when performing system analysis in such critical system conditions as during outages. The lack of service during outages is aggravated by the collision phenomenon determined by accumulated users requests, which (negatively) impacts on the QoS provided by the system for some time after its restart. Then, depending on the specific behavior exhibited by the variety of users, such QoS degradation due to outages may be perceived differently by different user categories. We follow a compositional modeling approach, based on the GPRS and user models; the focus is on the GPRS random access procedure on one side, and different classes of users behavior on the other side. Quantitative analysis, performed using a simulation approach, is carried out, showing the impact of outages on a relevant QoS indicator, in relation with the considered user characteristics and network load.

1 Introduction

GPRS (General Packet Radio Service) is a wireless packet network, standardized by ETSI (European Telecommunications Standard Institute) in recent years, which enhances the GSM (Global System Mobile Communication) system through the introduction of services based on the packet switching technique. These services provide a more efficient use of the radio resources, by accommodating data sources that are bursty in nature, such as Internet applications.

F. Grandoni (Ed.): EDCC 2002, LNCS 2485, pp. 2–18, 2002.

Given its relevance on the market, a number of studies directed to analyze the behavior of GPRS have been and are currently performed to assess its Quality of Service (QoS), or related measures, e.g. [1, 2, 3, 6, 9, 10, 11]. The authors of this paper have been involved in three of them ([6, 9, 10]). In [10], a preliminary analysis of the GPRS under performance and dependability-related indicators has been carried on. In [8], it has been stressed the criticality of the GPRS under availability viewpoint, and a detailed analysis of the effect of outages periods on the system congestion has been carried on. There, however, a simple characterization of the user behavior has been assumed. In fact, the main purpose of the study was to show the impact of users requests accumulated during the outage period on the system quality of service, both during the outage period and in a transient period following the end of the outage. In [6], the focus has been moved on the user's perspective, considering that wireless packet networks, such as GPRS, are intended to support a variety of applications characterized by different features, such as web browsing, file transfer, e-mail services, etc. Different applications have different requirements, which lead users to have different perceptions of the Quality of Service offered by the network. The conducted study, however, did not account for the effects of outages.

Here, we aim at extending and combining the work in [6,9], in order to understand the impact of critical system conditions (outages) on the offered QoS, by including the peculiarities of each class of applications and related users. The purpose is to gain insights on which user's characteristics are mostly influenced in critical system conditions such as during and after outages, so as to help the system designer in devising system configurations that would improve the level of user satisfaction. We mainly focus on the GPRS contention phase for channel reservation, which is the core of the GPRS system from the point of view of availability and congestion, and explore its expected behavior taking into account both operational and unavailability periods. For such "continuously requested" systems, outages do not only imply absence of service, but also accumulation of user requests. Then, at system restart, a higher load (depending on how long the outage was and on the users behavior in accessing the network) has to be processed by the GPRS, thus determining a higher probability of requests collision during some subsequent time interval. This congestion phenomenon is explicitly considered in our analysis, to gain in realism of the derived estimations. When evaluating the measured indicators, the values obtained considering the congestion induced by outages and those referring to a usually simplistic system vision (where no congestion is accounted for at system restart) are compared, in order to understand the extent of the approximation made.

A modeling approach is followed, consisting of two steps. First the GPRS network is modeled, both capturing "normal" system conditions and "abnormal" ones experienced in consequence of outages, as well as the behavior of a few categories of users. Then, the two models are composed to evaluate the combined effects of outages and users characteristics.

The rest of this paper is organized as follows. Section 2 gives an overview of the GPRS architecture. Section 3 describes our assumptions and presents the models of the GPRS and users behavior. In Section 4, two representative scenarios are set up in order to experiment the models, and the obtained results are presented and commented in Section 5. Finally, conclusions are drawn in Section 6.

2   GPRS Overview

As already mentioned in the Introduction, GPRS extends GSM with a more efficient packet switching allocation mechanism. We briefly recall here the main characteristics of GPRS [4,5].

To introduce GPRS in the existing GSM infrastructure, additional elements are needed to provide support for packet switching, namely: *Service GPRS Support Node* (SGSN) and *Gateway GPRS Support Node* (GGSN). The SGSN controls the communications and mobility management between the mobile stations and the GPRS network. The GGSN acts as an interface between the GPRS network and external packet switching networks such as Internet, or GPRS networks of different operators. Between GPRS Support Nodes (i.e., SGSN and GGSN), an IP based backbone network is used. The Base Station Subsystem (BSS) is shared between GPRS and GSM network elements, to maintain compatibility and to keep low the investments needed to introduce the GPRS service. Um, Gb and Gn are the interfaces between the involved sub -systems.

The protocol stack of GPRS is shown in Figure 1.

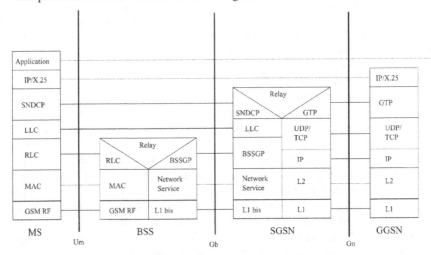

Fig. 1. The ISO/OSI structure of GPRS

The Sub Network Dependent Convergence Protocol (SNDCP) provides functionalities to map different network protocols onto logical link supported by the Logical Link Control (LLC) layer; this last is responsible for moving user data between Mobile Stations (MSs) and the network. The Radio Link Control (RLC) layer allows data transmission across the air interface. The Medium Access Control (MAC) layer controls data transmission in packet oriented mode. The RLC/MAC layer ensures the concurrent access to radio resource among several MSs. Each RLC block is divided in four normal bursts that have the same structure as GSM radio bursts, since GPRS shares the same physical layer as GSM. The GPRS allows several "Logical channels" to share physical channels (called Packet Data CHannel, PDCH) through time division multiplexing. PDCHs are associated with a single time slot of a TDMA frame (Time Division Multiple Access, composed of 8 time slots).

In a cell that directly supports GPRS, a Master PDCH is allocated, to provide control and signaling information to start data transfer both in up-link and in downlink, and to handle the users mobility. The Packet Random Access Channel (PRACH) is one of the logical channels that share the MPDCH; this channel is dedicated to the up-link transmission of channel request. When a mobile station needs to transmit, it has to send a channel request to the network through the PRACH. The access method to the PRACH is based on a *Random Access Procedure*; therefore, collisions may arise among requests by different MSs. Some more details are provided on the GPRS access procedure, since it is the core part of GPRS analyzed in our work. The MSs get the access control parameters (including the number of maximum attempts to transmit, M, and the persistence level, P) by listening to the Packet Broadcast Control CHannel (PBCCH). When the procedure starts, a timer is set (to 5 sec); at the expiry of this timer, the procedure, if still active, is aborted and a failure is reported to the upper layer. The first attempt to send a Packet Channel Request can be initiated at the first possible TDMA frame containing a PRACH. For each further attempts, the mobile station extracts a random value R, and only if R is bigger than, or equal to, the persistence level P the station is allowed to send a Packet Channel Request. After a request is issued, the MS waits for a time, determined on the basis of system parameters S and T. If it does not receive the Packet Downlink Assignment (or a Packet Queuing message) within this time interval, a new attempt is tried, if it is still allowed to make one, otherwise a failure is notified to the upper layer. From parameters S and T, the MS also determines the next TDMA frame, in which a new attempt is possible, should the previous one be unsuccessful and a new attempt still allowed.

Traffic packet data channels, called slave PDCH, are needed in a cell to transport user data and transmission signaling, such as acknowledged and non-acknowledged message. For what concerns data transfer, up-link and down-link channels allocation is completely independent and a MS can operate up-link and down-link data transfer simultaneously.

3   Derivation of the Models for the GPRS and the User Behavior

Our modeling activity is based on the Stochastic Activity Networks (SAN) [7]. SANs, conceived in the early 1980's, are a stochastic extension to Petri nets. Using graphical primitives, SANs provide a high level modeling formalism with which detailed performance, dependability and performability models can be specified relatively easy.

As already discussed in the Introduction, this paper aims at combining and completing previous work ([6, 9]), in order to get a complete view of the impact of outages in GPRS systems when utilized by disparate classes of users. Therefore, in setting up the models for the GPRS and the user behavior, we used our experience acquired in such former studies.

To adhere to more realistic uses of the wireless network system, the adopted users characterization includes:

- users are allowed to issue requests of different sizes, which may take a different number of LLC frames to be transmitted, with different inter-request time intervals. This way, the representation of a population of users requesting service of different kinds is possible (e.g., web-browsing, e-mail);
- users are allowed to set a maximum time interval for their request to be processed by the system (that is, to have the service completed). Should this *user timeout* expire without the completion of the requested service, the user intentionally aborts his connection and waits for some time before issuing a new request. Indeed, this is a reasonable behavior to cope with high traffic load, when the probability of request collision may become too heavy.

Both characteristics at points i) and ii) have been addressed in [6], but in a simplistic system scenario where outage effects are not accounted for. In [9], instead, both of them have been neglected in favor of an elementary user behavior.

In order to account for such user characteristics, we followed a two-step approach in developing the overall model. Firstly, we developed separately the model representing the GPRS network infrastructure, specifically focusing on the random access phase (GPRS_Net Model), and two models capturing the user behavior. Then, such user models are in turn composed with the GPRS_Net Model through the primitives offered by UltraSAN [8], the tool for SAN models resolution.

For the user behavior, we defined two slightly different models, to allow capturing a wider spectrum of user characteristics. One, named Hom_User, models a class of users, inside which users share the same characteristics (*homogeneous* user). Of course, the Hom_User Model has been developed in a parametric way such that it can be customized in accordance with relevant characteristics of the user class under analysis. Through this model, it is possible to analyze separately users accessing the GPRS network through different applications (e.g., the class of users operating web browsing, that of users operating e-mails, etc.). The other, named Het_User, models a class of users inside which users may behave differently (*heterogeneous* user). It allows representing realistic scenarios where, from time to time, the same single user may access the GPRS through a variety of applications, thus making requests of varying size.

We have identified in the *average number of served users per hour* a relevant indicator of the QoS offered by the GPRS system, whose accurate assessment has to include aspects concerning the user behavior. Therefore, the models have been developed to allow quantitative estimation of such measure.

3.1   Model Assumptions

The GPRS_Net Model has been defined under the following assumptions concerning the configuration of the GPRS:

1. only one cell has been taken into account, supporting a constant traffic load. Moreover no "attach" and "detach" procedures, to register and delete users information respectively, are considered in our study;
2. no priority distinction is made among users;

3. the radio channel is considered faultless, meaning that no retransmissions are necessary at the LLC and RLC levels;
4. accounting for the competition between GPRS and GSM traffic is out of the scope of our analysis. Concerning the traffic channels accessible by GPRS, our model supports a maximum of 7 traffic channels;
5. a user is allowed to utilize a single traffic channel to transmit his data frame (multi-slot assignments to a single user are not considered);
6. During an outage the network is completely blocked and the on-going data transmissions are interrupted; such a kind of outage could be caused, for example, by a malfunction in the antenna of the cell itself, which therefore stops to send and receive signals. The outage occurrence follows an exponential distribution, while the repair time is assumed to follow a deterministic distribution.

The first three assumptions have been made for the sake of model simplicity; relaxing them would not invalidate the modeling approach followed, but would add significant complexity to the derived model. The other assumptions are congruent with typical GPRS configurations being currently considered by suppliers.

Concerning the Hom_User and Het_User Models, the following assumptions hold:

1. in accordance with the standard, for each request to be sent a user has to make a number of random accesses to the network equal to the number of LLC frames necessary to complete his request transmission. We assume that, in case of multiple-LLC requests, the user can try the random access for sending the next LLC frame only after the successful transmission of the previous LLC frame;
2. should a user timeout elapse before completing the request transmission, that user does not make a new attempt immediately, but waits for his next inter-request time instant;
3. for the Hom_User model only: users are partitioned in classes; inside the same class, users issue requests of the same size, with the same inter-request rate, and apply the same user timeout;
4. for the Het_User model only: users are grouped in just one non-homogeneous class, inside which users may differ in the length of requests they may issue, in the inter-request time, and in the user timeout.

3.2   The Models

As already stated, our modeling approach consists in combining the basic models relative to: i) the random access to the network, and ii) the user behavior.

The overall model, shown in Figure 2, is obtained by joining the sub-models defined above through the UltraSAN Join operator. Actually two overall models are obtained, in accordance with the usage of the homogeneous user sub-model (Hom_User, Figure 2.a) and of the heterogeneous user sub-model (Het_User, Figure 2.b). Note that in Figure 2.a the multiple boxes labeled Hom_User allow to represent a number of classes of homogeneous users (e.g., the class of users using the e-mail application, that of users using web-browsing, etc.). The Rep operator allows replication of the user sub-model, to properly represent the full population of system users. The places *Served, block,* and *new* are common places among all models.

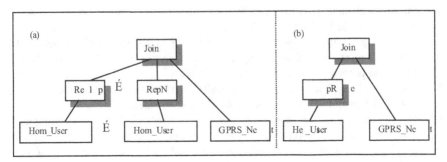

Fig. 2. The composed model

The detailed GPRS_Net Model is shown in Figure 3. The meaning of the main elements is explained in the following:

- A token in the place *Served* represents a request to transmit an LLC frame, successfully accomplished by the network.
- A token in the place *block* represents a blocked request to transmit an LLC frame, either due to exhaustion of the user's assigned attempts to send an LLC frame, or because the timer of the Random Access Procedure accounting for the total contention time fired.
- A token in the place *new* represents a new request to send an LLC frame.
- The block starting with the instantaneous activity *req* and ending with the input gate *control* represents the dynamics of the random access procedure. *req* states the maximum number of attempts a user is allowed to make in sending an Access Burst. It has one case for each possibility; the associated probabilities have been assigned on the basis of network parameters. Tokens in places *ready1*,..., *ready8* represent the number of users allowed to make a maximum of 1,...,8 attempts, respectively. The instantaneous activities *check_p1*,...,*check_p8* model the persistence level. If the user passes the persistence level, he can send an Access Burst and moves into the place *try$_i$*, otherwise he moves into the correspondent place *fail$_i$*. Should a user consume all his assigned attempts to make his request, or should the time-out regulating the maximum allowed time for making a request (set to 5 sec) expire, the user is moved into the place *block*. The place *w5* and the activity *wait_5* take into account those users that haven't been assigned any attempt, because they will always fail the persistence level.
- The instantaneous transition *check_capture* checks, stochastically, if there is a successful receipt of one Access Burst; if yes, a token is placed in *one_accepted*, otherwise in *all_discarded*. A request received correctly is refused only if the queue is full and there is no available traffic channel. The instantaneous transition *who_is_passed* fires when there is a token in *one_accepted* and it allows to choose which level the accepted Access Burst comes from, placing a token in one of the places *p1*,...,*p8* (each Access Burst at each level has the same probability to be the accepted one). The input gate *control* and the activity *control_act* properly update the places recording the re-

sidual tries made available to the other concurrent requests (places *ready1,...,
ready8, try1,...,try8, fail1,...,fail8, wait_a0,...,wait_a7* and *p1,...,p8*).

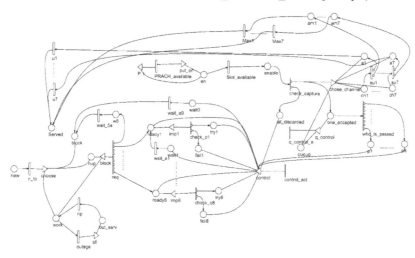

Fig. 3. The GPRS_Net model

- When there is a successful receipt of one Access Burst and there is a free channel (that is at least a free triplet among *ch1-a1-am1,....,ch7-a7-am7*), the output
  gate *choose_channel* puts a token in one of the places *ch1,...,ch7*. The timed
  activities *su1,..., su7* simulate the set-up time of a radio link to send user data.
  The timed activities *Max1,..., Max7* and *u1,...,u7* simulate the data sending time
  for full LLC frame size (1600 bytes) or frame size sampled from a uniform distribution (when an incomplete LLC frame has to be transmitted, i.e., less than
  1600 bytes), respectively. In case all data channels are busy, the request in
  queued by adding a token in the place *queue*, if the queue length allows accommodating the request, otherwise the request is aborted.
- The sub-net enclosing the timed activities *PRACH_available* and
  Slot_available, and the places *en* and *enable*, models the multiframe on the
  MPDCH.
- A token in the place *queue* represents a pending request waiting for up-link
  channel reservation. The input gate *choose_channel* puts a token in the place
  queue if all the available channels are busy. The immediate transition
  q_control_a fires when a channel is released and there are pending requests in
  the queue. When transition *q_control_a* fires, the input gate *q_control* moves a
  token from *queue* to a place *ch$_i$* (*ch1,ch2,..ch7*), corresponding to the available
  channel.

The subnet including Petri net elements *work, rip, outage, all,* and *out_serv* represents the occurrence of outages, and the consequent repair of the system. Specifically:

- A token in the place *work* indicates that the network is operational. The firing of
  the timed activity *outage* triggers the effects of an outage by means of the out-

put gate *all*. This gate simulates the effects of the fault through the inhibition of the immediate activity *req* and the gradual moving of the tokens of the whole net in the place *block*. The firing of timed activity *rip* triggers the repair of the system.

Figure 4 shows the user models. The complete model on the left is the Hom_User model. Replacing the subnet enclosed in the dotted box with the separated subnet in the right part of the figure the Het_User model is obtained.

The Hom_User model is used to represent classes of homogeneous users. It is configurable, so as to adapt to different classes of users, by changing the inter-request time, the number of LLC frames composing each user request and the user timeout. The model description is the following:

- A token in the place *idle* means that the user has no pending service requests. The exponential transition *request* represents the user idle time. The users not in the *idle* state are allowed to take a token from place *Served* or place *block*.
- The exponential transitions *catch* and *catch2* allow to catch a token from the places *Served* (LLC frame successfully transmitted) or *block* (LLC frame not successfully transmitted). The transitions *finish* and *finish2* and places *wait* and *wait2* allow introducing a delay in catching a token from the places *Served* and *block*, respectively: a user can not take a token from place *Served* until the place *wait* is empty (when transition *finish* fires). In the same way, a user can not take a token from place *block* until the place *wait2* is empty.
- Input gates *contr* and *contr2* synchronize all the operations to catch the tokens from places *Served* and *block*. The gate *contr* also controls if the user has finished to transmit all his pending tokens to complete his request (traced in the place *pending*); should this be the case, the user is put back into the idle state, by adding a token in the place *idle*.
- The output gate *send* puts in the place *pending* a number of tokens corresponding to the number of LLC frames the user request consists of.
- The subnet including *start, no_more, count_one,* and *acc_count* represents a timer. Such timer keeps track of the time requirements set by the user; should such timer expire without completing the request sending, the residual operations relative to that request are aborted and the user is put back in the place *idle*. Note that the user who fails to have his request successfully transmitted because of the deadline violation, doesn't know if the failure was due to continuous collisions with other concurrent requests or because the system is experiencing an outage.

The Het_User model differs from the Hom_User one in allowing a user to vary, from one request to the next one, the length of his requests (in terms of number of LLC frames), the inter-request time and the timeout.

- The instantaneous activity *select*, allows to account for varying requests size and inter-request time; it has a case for each possibility allowed to the user. For simplicity, in the represented model they are just two (activated with probability *p* and (*1-p*), respectively), but could be easily extended to a higher number.

- Places *to_req1*, and *to_req2*, represent two possible choices for the inter-request time: short request more frequently or a long request less frequently, respectively. In the first case, the user idle time is modeled by the timed activities *request1* and the number of LLC frames the user request consists of is controlled by the output gate *send1*. Similarly, for the second case the transition *request2* and the gate *send2* are used. Again, the model can be easily extended to include a higher number of possibilities.

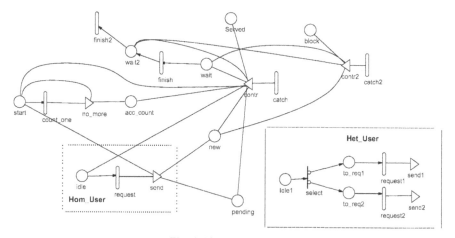

Fig. 4. The user models

4   Settings for the Numerical Evaluation

We approached the resolution of the overall models in Figure 2 through the simulator provided by the UltraSAN tool [8]. In fact, a simulation technique shows appropriate in our context, given the nature of the analyzed measures and the order of magnitude of the expected results.

The analysis focuses on the expected served users per hour, under varying user, load and outages parameters. The purpose is to point out the difference between the evaluation conducted considering the effect of outages at system restart (in terms of the increased collision phenomenon due to accumulated requests during the system downtime), and the usual simplistic vision of an "on-off" system.

Being our study directed to the user viewpoint, in the following experiments we vary the user characteristics, and keep fixed the GPRS configuration. In choosing an adequate configuration, we took advantage of previous work [10], which focused on the performance of GPRS systems: 5 traffic channels (SPDCH) and 3 logical channels (PRACH) are assumed in the following analysis.

Both user models have been considered, thus originating and studying two system scenarios.

In the first scenario, the model Hom_User has been exercised. Specifically, the user population is partitioned into two classes. In the first class, users issue requests fitting in 1 LLC frame, with a shorter inter-request time (10 seconds), while requests issued by the other group require 6 LLC frames, and have a longer inter-request time (120 seconds). The two groups also differ in the maximum time a user is prepared to wait to have his request satisfied before giving up.

Table 1 summarizes the numerical values assigned to such user characteristics for the two classes.

Table 1. User parameters in Scenario 1 and Scenario 2

	SCENARIO 1		
	User characteristics		User requirements
	Inter_request_time	Request size (in LLC frames)	Timeout
class_1	Exponential distribu-tion, $\lambda=1/10$	1 LLC frame	3 sec.
class_2	Exponential distribution, $\lambda=1/120$	6 LLC frame	18 sec.
	SCENARIO 2		
	User Characteristics		User requirements
	Inter_request_time	Request size	Timeout
p	Exponential distribution, $\lambda=1/10$	1 LLC frame	3 sec
(1-p)	Exponential distribution, $\lambda=1/60$	6 LLC frame	18 sec

We are mainly interested in analyzing system behavior under critical conditions; therefore the experiments are conducted under high load situations, from 90% to 110% of the whole system capacity. Users generating such load belong to class_1 and class_2 in a fixed proportion of 50% for each class. Consequently, the total number of users requesting network services varies in accordance with the considered total load.

Outages are first considered of fixed duration (1000 seconds), but of varying frequency (by changing the availability value). Then, in a second experiment, the overall availability is kept fixed, while variations of the duration (and consequently, the frequency) of outages are explored, thus performing a sensitivity analysis to outage parameters. The distributions used to characterize the outage are the deterministic one for the duration, and the exponential one for the frequency.

In the second scenario, the user model Het_User is exploited. Therefore, users are grouped in one, non-homogeneous class. Dynamically, a triplet consisting of a request size, an inter-request time and a timeout are assigned to users waiting for issuing a new request, on the basis of a probabilistic parameter p. Similarly to the previous scenario, two values, 1 and 6 LLC frames, are considered for the request size: with a probability p the request size is 1 LLC frame, and with probability $(1-p)$ it requires 6 LLC frames. Then, the percentage of short and of long requests varies, in accordance with the value assigned to the parameter p. The workload is fixed to 100% of the system capacity. In order to keep it fixed at varying the probability p of choosing a request size, the inter-request time assigned to short requests (1 LLC frame) is 10 seconds, while that associated to longer requests (6 LLC frames) is 60 seconds. The user timeout assumes the same values as in the previous scenario; the bottom of Table 1 summarizes the user characteristics in scenario 2. Outages of fixed duration are considered, but having a variable frequency of occurrence (by varying the system availability).

In all the experiments, results have been determined with 95% confidence interval and a relative confidence interval lower than 10%.

As a final remark on the experiments setup, the selected parameter values are not tied to any specific real application, although short requests may be appropriate for typical web browsing applications while longer ones may fit categories of e-mails or filled forms on the web. Actually, despite the fact that real valued parameters are always preferable than artificial ones when available, studies which compare different situations in a relative way are very useful at system design stage in order to make appropriate decisions (on configurations, mechanisms, etc.), even if based on some arbitrary values. What is recommendable, in such cases, is some sensitivity analysis conducted on a range of values of the most impacting parameters. The value of our analysis stems from this observation, and its utility has to be regarded as a system designer support, rather than in providing absolute final estimations.

5   Numerical Evaluation

This Section presents the numerical evaluation performed solving the SAN model adopting a steady state analysis.

5.1   First Scenario

Two figures summarize the results obtained from experiments based on scenario 1.

Figure 5 depicts the expected number of served users per hour for users belonging to class_1 and to class_2 (part (a) and (b) of the figure, respectively). The measure has been determined at varying values of the GPRS availability, and for two values of the workload (90% and 110% of the system capacity, to explore critical situations from the overload point of view).

In the figure, both the curves relative to the case where outages effects at system restart are accounted for and those in case of a simple "on-off" system are drawn. By comparing these two families of curves, it is immediate to appreciate the extent of the error induced when performing the analysis using the simple model.

Not surprisingly, looking at Figure 5.a, two phenomena are immediately captured. Firstly, there is an over-estimation in the served users when outage effects are not accounted for. Of course, the entity of such over-estimation depends on the availability value; for example, an availability of 0.95 leads to an error of about 10% when the load is 90%, which reduces at growing availability, becoming almost negligible from availability equal to 0.99. In this study, we keep fixed the mean time to repair (MTTR) after an outage occurs (which corresponds to the outage duration). This implies that, for the same load, at system restart the same accumulated requests have to be processed whichever be the availability assumed. However, higher availability means a lower number of outages experienced during the system lifetime, and therefore an enhancement of the evaluated measure. Secondly, all the curves degrade at increasing the system workload, and the error incurred relying on the "on-off" behavior increases.

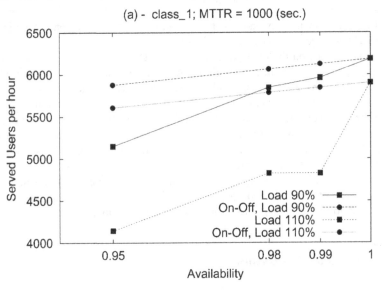

(a) - class_1; MTTR = 1000 (sec.)

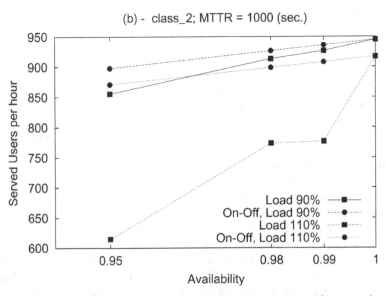

(b) - class_2; MTTR = 1000 (sec.)

Fig. 5. Served users per hour for class_1 users (5.a) and class_2 users (5.b), at varying availability, for two values of the system load

Similar comments apply to Figure 5.b; of course, being the study referred to the class of users issuing less requests of longer size, the derived numbers of served users per hour are significantly lower.

A second experiment in this scenario has been directed to investigate on the impact of different distributions of outages in terms of frequency of occurrence and duration, for a fixed availability value. In fact, availability is an overall system measure that accounts for the total amount of time the system is up in the reference time interval. However, it is expected that different effects are produced on the QoS offered by the system, depending on whether that availability value has been determined by a higher number of shorter duration outages, or by a lower number of longer duration outages. The results are shown in Figure 6, which refers to an availability of 0.98, but where the time to repair the system after an outage (i.e., the outage duration) varies from 500 to 2500 seconds.

From the figure, the following trend is observed: increasing the outage duration, which means decreasing the outage occurrence (being the availability at a fixed value), the expected served users per hour increase. The increase is noticeable in the first part of the figure (from MTTR=500 sec to MTTR=1000 sec, which means halving the number of outages), becoming almost constant in the second part.

Therefore, outages occurring with lower frequency and lasting a longer time have less detrimental effects than more frequent, shorter ones. Note that values relative to class_1 are on the left Y-axis, while those of class_2 are on the right Y-axis.

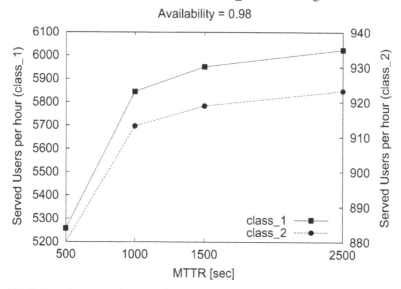

Fig. 6. Served users per hour as a function of outage duration for a fixed availability

5.2   Second Scenario

The results concerning the second scenario are illustrated in Figure 7.

In it, the curves of the difference between the number of expected served users per hour obtained using the simplistic "on-off" model and that accounting for outages are shown. Varying parameters are the probability p of assigning length 1 LLC frame to an issued request, and the availability. The results are shown separately for short and long requests (Figure 7.a and 7.b, respectively).

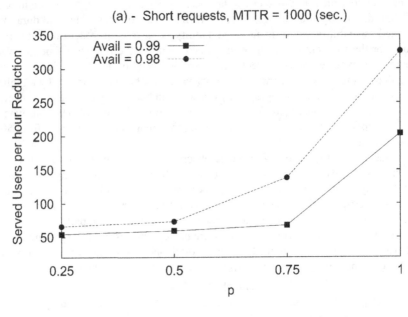

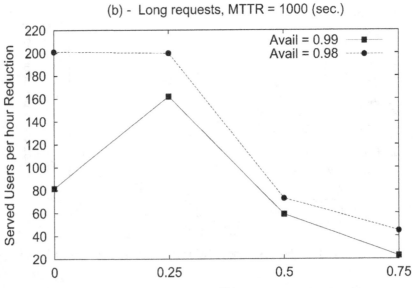

Fig. 7. Reduction in the expected served users per hour without accounting and accounting for outage effects, for short requests (7.a) and longer ones (7.b)

In both parts of the Figure, it can be observed that there is always a reduction in the number of served users per hour when the outage effects are considered, and such reduction is higher when lower availability values are considered. (Note that the MTTR, i.e. the duration of outages, is fixed; therefore lower availability means more frequent outages).

Concerning the variations of the parameter p, the trend is that the highest is the probability of issuing requests of a certain type (between short and long), and the highest is the served users reduction for that type of requests. In fact, in Figure 7.a the highest reduction is in correspondence of $p=1$, which implies all requests are 1 LLC frame. In Figure 7.b, instead, the highest reduction is observed for $p=0$, which means all requests require 6 LLC frames (being $1-p$ the probability of issuing long requests). In this last figure, the point corresponding to p=0 seems to be a singular point, which does not respect this trend. Actually, this behavior could be imputed to the simulation process, since the simulation results of the two values of served users per hour originating this point have not disjoint confidence intervals.

6   Conclusions

This paper has presented a study on modeling and analyzing the effects of outages on the Quality of Service of GPRS network system explicitly accounting for different user behaviors. In fact, we consider that the user viewpoint cannot be neglected in such kind of analysis, being user satisfaction the ultimate goal of system suppliers.

We followed a compositional approach, built on basic sub-models of the network and user behaviors. Combining such basic sub-models, the overall model has been obtained and solved through simulation, in order to make quantitative estimations of a properly identified QoS indicator. The specific user characteristics this paper focuses on are differences in the offered traffic and the possibility to deliberately abort a request after a prefixed time interval. In the developed models, such user characteristics are captured, both during "normal operational" periods of the network, and during outage intervals, when the underlying service is suspended. The QoS indicator selected for the analysis was the expected number of users per hour, a measure that requires accounting for user peculiarities in order to be accurately assessed.

The purpose of this study was to understand the impact of outages on user's characteristics, to better master the system behavior under such critical conditions and to help the system designer in devising satisfactory system configurations. The numerical evaluation and sensitivity analysis carried out, although limited to just a couple of system scenarios, actually point out relevant phenomena and trends.

Of course, extensions of this work would improve the understanding of the phenomena involved in the context. Investigations on the utility of the user timeout to cope with high traffic load and requests collisions at system restart after an outage are currently in progress. Among other directions to explore, we mention the extension of the evaluation campaign to variations of other system and user parameters, the identification and evaluation of additional indicators of QoS and the introduction of other user characteristics, possibly with reference to specific application fields.

References

[1]   M. Ajmone Marsan, M. Gribaudo, M. Meo and M. Sereno, "On Petri Net-Based Modeling Paradigms for the Performance Analysis of Wireless Internet Accesses", in Proc. IEEE PNPM'2001, Aachen, 2001, pp. 19-28.

[2]   G. Brasche and B. Walke, "Concepts, Services and Protocols of the New GSM Phase 2+ General Packet Radio Service," *IEEE Communications Magazine*, August 1997, pp. 94-104.

[3]   J. Cai and D. J. Goodman, "General Packet Radio Service in GSM," *IEEE Communication Magazine*, vol. October 1997, pp. 122-131, 1997.

[4]   ETSI, "Digital Cellular Telecommunications System (Phase 2+); General Packet Radio Service (GPRS); Service Description; Stage 2," GSM 03.60 version 7.1.0 Release 1998.

[5]   ETSI, "Digital Cellular Telecommunication System (Phase 2+); General Packet Radio Service (GPRS); Mobile Station (MS) - Base Station System (BSS) Interface; Radio Link Control/Medium Access Control (RLC/MAC) Protocol," GSM 04.60 version 8.3.0 release 1999.

[6]   S. Porcarelli, F. Di Giandomenico, A. Bondavalli, "Analyzing Quality of Service of GPRS Network Systems from a User's Perspective", to appear in Proc. IEEE Symposium on Computers and Communications ISCC02, Taormina, Italy, July 2002.

[7]   W. H. Sanders and J. F. Meyer, "A Unified Approach for Specifying Measures of Performance, Dependability and Performability," in *Dependable Computing for Critical Applications, Vol. 4: of Dependable Computing and Fault-Tolerant Systems*, (Eds.), Springer Verlag, 1991, pp. 215-237.

[8]   W. H. Sanders, W. D. Obal, M. A. Qureshi and F. K. Widjanarko, "The Ultra-SAN Modeling Environment," *Performance Evaluation Journal, special issue on Performance Modeling Tools*, vol. 24, pp. 89-115, 1995.

[9]   F. Tataranni, S. Porcarelli, F. Di Giandomenico and A. Bondavalli, "Analysis of the Effects of Outages on the Quality of Service of GPRS Network Systems," *Proceedings of the 2001 International Conference on Dependable Systems and Networks*, Göteborg, Sweden, July 2001, pp 235-244.

[10]   F. Tataranni, S. Porcarelli, F. Di Giandomenico, A. Bondavalli and L. Simoncini, "Modeling and Analysis of the Behavior of GPRS Systems," *IEEE 6th International workshop on Object-oriented Real-Time Dependable Systems*, Roma, Italy, 2001, pp. 51-58.

[11]   R.G Addie, M. Zukerman and T. D. Neame "Broadband Traffic Modeling: Simple Solutions to Hard Problems", IEEE Communication Magazine, August 1998, pp. 88-95.

Combination of Fault Tree Analysis and Model Checking for Safety Assessment of Complex System

Pierre Bieber, Charles Castel, and Christel Seguin

ONERA-CERT,
2 av. E. Belin, 31055 Toulouse Cedex, France
{bieber,castel,seguin}@cert.fr

Abstract. Safety assessment of complex systems traditionally requires the combination of various results derived from various models. The Altarica language was designed to formally specify the behaviour of systems when faults occurs. A unique Altarica model can be assessed by means of complementary tools such as fault tree generator and model-checker. This paper reports how the Altarica language was used to model a system in the style of the hydraulic system of the Airbus A320 aircraft family. It presents how fault tree generation and model-checking can be used separately then combined to assess safety requirements.

Introduction

Safety assessment of aircraft systems according to standard as ARP 4754 [12] requires the combination of various results derived from various models. For instance, on one hand safety engineers build fault tree in order to compute minimal cut sets and occurrence probabilities of failure conditions. On the other hand, system designers will use specific languages such as SCADE [15], SABER [3], Simulink [9] to model the system under study in order to perform simulations. Such an amount of modeling languages and models is not easily shared by the different teams involved in the system design and assessment. Moreover, this heterogeneity does not facilitate the result integration.

The Altarica [1] language was designed by University of Bordeaux and a set of industrial partners to overcome such difficulties. Altarica models formally specify the behavior of systems when faults occurs. These models can be assessed by means of complementary tools such as fault tree generator and model-checker.

One issue is now to integrate such a practice into existing safety processes. When can such models be used fruitfully ? At early design stages, in order to assess the first drafts of a system architecture? In latest phases, in order to assess a detailed design? What are the benefits of the available assessment techniques?

We carried out some experiments with the Altarica language and tools in order to assess the validity of some possible answers. We study more specifically the hydraulic system of the Airbus A320 at early stage of design. In this paper, we report how we use the Altarica language to model this system and we present how

F. Grandoni (Ed.): EDCC 2002, LNCS 2485, pp. 19–31, 2002.

fault tree generation and model-checking can be used separately then combined to assess safety requirements.

1   Case-Study: AIRBUS A320 Hydraulic System

1.1   System Description

The role of the hydraulic system is to supply hydraulic power with an adequate safety level both to devices which ensure aircraft control in flight (servocontrols, flaps, ...) and to devices which are used on ground (landing gear, braking systems, ...). In this paper we assume that the hydraulic system is only made of pumps and distribution lines which generate and transmit the hydraulic power to the devices. The actual hydraulic system contains other types of components that we do not consider here such as tanks, valves, gauges, ... There are three kinds of pumps : Electric Motor Pump (EMP) that are powered by the electric system, Engine Driven Pumps (EDP) that are powered by the two aircraft engines and one RAT pump that is powered by the Ram Air Turbine. So some pumps (namely the EDPs) cannot be used on ground when aircraft engines are shut down and the RAT use requires that the aircraft speed is high enough.

To meet safety requirements, this system contains a physical sub-system that is composed of three hydraulic channels : Green, Blue and Yellow. The Blue channel is made of one electric pump EMPb, one RAT pump and a distribution line distb. The Green system is made of one pump driven by engine 1 EDPg and a distribution line distribg. The Yellow system is made of one pump driven by engine 2 EDPy, one electric pump EMPy and a distribution line distriby. Moreover a power transfer unit PTU opens a transmission from green hydraulic power to yellow distribution line and vice versa as soon as the differential pressure between both system is higher than a given threshold.

The physical sub-system is controlled by crew actions and reconfiguration logics that activate the various pumps. The RAT is automatically activated in

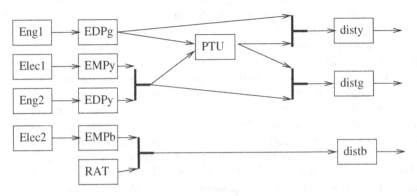

Fig. 1. Hydraulic system structure

flight when the speed of the aircraft is greater than 100 knts and both engines are lost. The EMPb is automatically activated when the aircraft is in flight or on ground when one engine is running. EMPy is activated by the pilot on ground. In the following, we suppose that all other pumps (EDPy, EDPg), the PTU and distribution lines are always activated

1.2 Safety Requirements

AIRBUS follows ARP 4761 [13] recommendations used to define safety assessment process related with airworthiness certification. One step of this process is the definition of a safety requirement document that contains requirements derived from the Aircraft level FHA (Functional Hazard Analysis). For the Hydraulic system we find for instance :

- TotalLoss : "*Total loss of hydraulic power is classified catastrophic*",
- Loss2 : "*Loss of two hydraulic systems is classified major*",
- Loss1 : "*Loss of one hydraulic system is classified minor*",

Quantitative requirement are associated with each of theses requirements, they are the form "*the probability of occurrence of failure condition FC shall be less than* 10^{-N} *per flight hour*" with N=9 (resp. 7 and 5)) if FC is of severity catastrophic (resp. hazardous and major). We also associate qualitative requirements of the form "*if up to N individual failures occur then failure condition FC shall not occur*", with N=2 (resp. 1 and 0) if FC is of severity catastrophic (resp. hazardous or major, minor).

2 Altarica Model

2.1 Altarica Language

An Altarica model of a system consists of hierarchies of components called nodes. A node gathers flows, states, events, transitions and assertions.

```
node block
 flow
  O : bool : out ;
  I, A~: bool : in ;
 state
  S : bool ;
 event
  failure ;
 trans
  S |- failure -> S:= false;
 assert
  O = (I and A~and S);
 extern initial_state = S = true ;
edon
```

- Flows are the visible parameters of the component, whereas states are internal variables. Let us consider a basic component called "block". A block stands for a basic energy provider. It receives two boolean inputs, I that is true whenever the component receives energy, and A that is true whenever the component is activated. It has a boolean output O that is true whenever it produces energy. It has the internal state S, which is true whenever the block is safe. Initially, we assume that S is true.
- Assertions are boolean formulae that state the constraints linking flows and internal states. For instance, the outputO is true whenever the input energy is available (true), the activation order is true and the component state is safe. Assertions are system invariants: they must always be true.
- Transitions describe how the internal states may evolve. They are characterised by a guard (a boolean constraint over the component flows and state), an event name and a command part (value assignation of some state variables). For the block example, an unique transition is considered. It can be taken only if the component is safe (S is true) and the event failure occurs. After this transition, the component is no more safe : S is set to false. This transition models the only failure mode we consider in this paper, i.e. loss of a component.

The whole system node (main node) is built by connecting the basic nodes. Global assertions allow the definitions of the flow connections. For instance, a global assertion states that input flows of a node are output flows of another node. Connections may also be related to events shared by a set of nodes (synchronisation of events). This feature is not used in our example, the interested reader may find more details in [1].

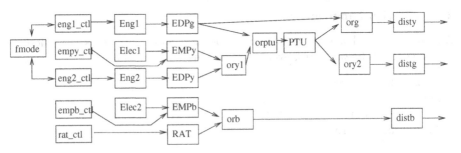

Fig. 2. A320 Hydraulic Model

2.2 Physical Sub-system Model

We model the various Pumps (EDPy, Edpg, EMPy, EMPb, RAT) with "block" nodes, they receive energy from the engines or electric system as input and produce hydraulic power as output. As we do not model aircraft speed we consider that the RAT is always energised. Distribution lines (disty, distg and distb) are also modelled with "block" nodes, they receive hydraulic power as input and produce hydraulic power as output. We suppose that they are always activated. To connect the outputs of two pumps on the input of a distribution line we use an "or" node that is described in the following Altarica code.

```
node or2
 flow
  O : bool : out ;
  I1, I2 : bool : in ;
assert
  O = (I1 or I2);
edon
```

The PTU component is modelled with a combination of an "or" node that merges the hydraulic power produced by yellow and green pumps and delivers it to a "block" node that is always active. So the PTU is able to deliver hydraulic power whenever it has not failed and it receives hydraulic power on I1 (green hydraulic power) or I2 (yellow hydraulic power).

In our study we did not model in great detail the behaviour of dependent systems as *"electric generation and distribution system"* or *"engine system"*. We suppose that each engine acts as a basic block that is always energised. Engines are activated by pilot actions. We suppose that each electric bar (Elec1 and Elec2) acts as a basic block that is always active and is energised if at least one engine is active.

2.3   Control Sub-system Model

The control sub-system model contains models of pilot actions and reconfiguration logic. To control hydraulic system components the pilot or the computers need information about aircraft environment such as the current flight mode. Node flight_mode contains one state variable s_on_ground that is true when the aircraft is on ground and that is false when the aircraft is in flight. Events take_off and land change the value of s_on_ground variable, take_off guard contains the property eng1_A and eng2_A to model the fact that both engines should be activated before take-off. Finally, the value of the s_on_ground internal variable can be observed thanks to the flow on_ground as stated in the assertion part of the node.

```
node flight_mode
 flow
  eng1_A,eng2_A : bool : in ;
  on_ground : bool : out ;
 state
  s_on_ground : bool ;
 event
```

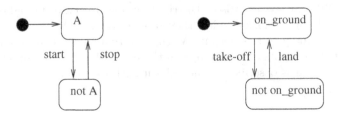

Fig. 3. Flight-mode and engine control models

```
  take_off, land ;
trans
  s_on_ground and eng1_A and eng2_A |- take_off ->
                                              s_on_ground:=false;
  not s_on_ground   |- land -> s_on_ground:=true
assert
  (on_ground = s_on_ground);
  extern initial_state = s_on_ground = true ;
edon
```

An engine is controlled by **eng_cntrl** node that contains state variable s_A that are set to true or false according to pilot actions start and stop. We consider that an engine can only be deactivated on ground if the other engine is activated (i.e. flow **other_A** is true). As previously, flow **A** allows the observation of the corresponding internal state.

```
node eng_cntrl
  flow
  A~: bool : out ;
  on_ground, other_A : bool : in ;
  state
  s_A : bool ;
  event
  start, stop ;
  trans
  not s_A |- start -> s_A :=true;
  on_ground and s_A and other_A |- stop -> s_A := false;
  assert
  (A = s_A);
  extern initial_state = s_A = true ;
edon
```

The EMPy is controlled by **empy_cntrl** node that contains variable s_A. EMPy can be deactivated in flight by pilot action **stop**, it can activated by pilot **p_start** action and it has to be activated on ground by **c_start** action.

```
node empy_cntrl
  flow
   A~: bool : out ;
   on_ground : bool : in ;
  state
   s_A : bool ;
  event
   p_start,c_start, stop ;
  trans
   on_ground and not s_A |- c_start -> s_A :=true;
   not s_A |- p_start -> s_A :=true;
   (not on_ground) and s_A |- stop -> s_A := false;
  assert
   (A = s_A);
  extern initial_state = s_A = true ;
edon
```

There exists two other nodes empb_cntrl and rat_cntrl that control respectively EMPb and RATb.

2.4   Safety Requirement Model

To model safety requirements described in the previous chapter we should first model failure conditions such as "Total loss of hydraulic power". This means that the three distribution lines (green, yellow and blue) output is equal to false. A first approach consists in using formula :

$TotalLoss : \neg distb.O \wedge \neg distg.O \wedge \neg disty.O.$

But this formula fails to describe adequately the failure condition because it could hold in evolutions of the system during a small period and then it would no longer hold as the hydraulic power is recovered due to appropriate activation of a backup such as the RAT for instance. The correct description of the failure condition should model the fact that the hydraulic system is lost permanently or during a period exceeding some allowed amount of time. Hence we use Linear Temporal Logic (see [16]) operators to model a failure condition. For instance, we could use the two following temporal formulae :

$PermanentLoss : \diamond \square Totalloss$

$2TimeStepsLoss : \diamond (TotalLoss \wedge \circ TotalLoss)$

where $\diamond$ is the Future operator, $\square$ is the always operator and $\circ$ is the next operator.

The semantics ot temporal formulae such as $\diamond p$, $\square p$, $\circ p$ can be understood by studying the truth value of p on a sequence of states. Sequence 1 of Figure 4 satisfies formula $\circ p$ in the initial state as p is true in the next state. Sequence 2 of Figure 4 satisfies formula $\diamond p$ in the initial state as there is a state such as p is true in this state. Sequence 3 of Figure 4 satisfies formula $\square p$ in the initial state as p is true in any state. Sequence 4 of Figure 4 satisfies formula $\diamond \square p$ in the initial state as there exist a state such p is true in any subsequent state.

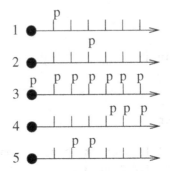

Fig. 4. Linear Temporal Logic models

Sequence 5 of Figure 4 satisfies formula $\Diamond(p \wedge \circ p$ in the initial state as there exist a state such p is true and p is also true in the subsequent state.

Formula *PermanentLoss* models the permanent loss of the hydraulic system it can be read "*eventually the hydraulic power is lost in all future time steps*". Whereas the second formula models the inability to recover hydraulic power in one time step, it could be read "*eventually the hydraulic power is lost during two consecutive time steps*".

So the general form of safety requirements we consider is
$NoPermanentLoss : \Box N\_failures \Rightarrow \neg\Diamond\Box fc$
or is
$No2TimeStepsLoss : \Box N\_failures \Rightarrow \neg\Diamond(fc \wedge \circ fc)$
where fc denotes a non-temporal failure condition formula as TotalLoss and $N\_failures$ is a property that holds in all states of a system such that up to N component failures have occurred. According to the rules of Linear Temporal Logic, these formulae are equivalent to :
$No2TimeStepsLoss : \Box N\_failures \Rightarrow \Box(fc \Rightarrow \circ\neg fc)$
$NoPermanentLoss : \Box N\_failures \Rightarrow \Box\Diamond\neg fc$

3   Safety Assessment

We propose to apply a three steps approach to perform safety assessments based on Altarica models:

1. Generate a fault-tree of the failure condition of interest. The generation is based on the physical sub-system model and the failure condition considered is non-temporal. Analyse the fault-tree in order to extract a set of unexpected failure and activation combinations.
2. Define and check the activation interface. This is a set of properties that eliminate the unexpected combinations found at the previous stage. Use a model-checker to verify that activation properties are enforced by the control sub-system model.

3. Compose the various results in order to prove that safety requirements are met by the global system. This step is performed thanks to a set of inference rules.

In the following sections we show how to use this approach to check safety requirements of A320 hydraulic systems.

3.1 Fault-Tree Generation and Analysis

Altarica fault-tree generator (see [14]) takes an Altarica model as input and an unexpected event, then it generates a fault-tree describing the failure situations that lead to the unexpected event. We use this tool to generate a fault-tree for the non-temporal failure condition (i.e. failure condition without temporal operators) using the Altarica model of the physical sub-system.

Once the fault-tree is generated, we use ARALIA (see [4]) fault-tree analyser to compute the set of prime implicants of the non-temporal failure condition. This gives us a set of combinations of the form :

$$\{c1.failure, c2.failure, ..., \neg c'1.A, \neg c'2.A, ...\}$$

where $c1.failure$ means that component c1 has failed and $\neg c'1.A$ means that $c'1$ is not activated. Each combination implies that the failure conditions occurs. A combination related to failure condition FC is unexpected if it contains less than N failure with N = 2 (resp. 1, 0) if FC is of severity Catastrophic (resp. Hazardous or Major, Minor).

We compute the prime implicants for formula $\neg distb.O \wedge \neg distg.O \wedge \neg disty.O$ that represent the instantaneous total loss of hydraulic system. There are 30 unexpected combinations (i.e. combinations with less than 3 failures) in this set. One combination contains no failure at all : $\{\neg Eng1.A, \neg Eng2.A, \neg RATb.A\}$ that means that when both engines are stopped and the RAT is not activated the three hydraulic systems cannot produce hydraulic power. Six combinations contain only one failure :

- $\{\neg Eng1.A, \neg Eng2.A, RATb.failure\}$,
  $\{\neg Eng1.A, \neg Eng2.A, distb.failure\}$,
  $\{\neg Eng1.A, Eng2.failure, \neg RATb.A\}$,
  $\{Eng1.failure, \neg Eng2.A, \neg RATb.A\}$
- $\{EDPg.failure, \neg EMPb.A, \neg EMPy.A, \neg Eng2.A, \neg RATb.A\}$,
  $\{EDPy.failure, \neg EMPb.A, \neg EMPy.A, \neg Eng1.A, \neg RATb.A\}$

The four first combinations represent situations where both engines are not working (because they are stopped or have failed) and the RAT is not working or the blue distribution line has failed. The two last combinations represent situations where one engine driven pump has failed and the other engine is stopped and electric pumps and RAT are not activated. The 23 remaining combinations contain two failures.

An alternative way to define unexpected combinations can be followed if failure occurrence probabilities are known for each individual components. In this case, we would set the probability of event $c.A$ to 0 and use ARALIA to compute the probability of each combination. Then we would consider as unexpected combination any prime implicant with a probability greater than the probability objective associated with the failure condition.

3.2   Interface Definition and Model-Checking

All the unexpected combinations found at the previous stage contain members of the form $\neg c.A$ meaning that component c has not been activated. Our basic assumptions is that it is the goal of the control sub-system to activate the physical component in a adequate order to avoid the occurrence of unexpected combinations. We propose to define an activation interface, this is a set of properties on $c.A$ variables that eliminate the unexpected combinations. The control sub-system should guarantee these properties.

Finding a good set of activation properties can be difficult. One option is to consider that all components are always active, this trivially eliminates combinations including a member of the form $\neg c.A$. This option does not reflect the actual system where some components are initially stopped and are started when they are needed. Another option is to construct an activation property of the form $\neg unex\_comb$, where $unex\_comb$ is the disjunction of all conjuncts representing an unexpected combination. The conjunct representing combination $\{c1.failure, c2.failure, ..., \neg c'1.A, \neg c'2.A, ...\}$ would be equal to $c1.failure \wedge c2.failure \wedge ... \wedge \neg c'1.A \wedge \neg c'2.A \wedge ...$. Once again, showing that this activation predicate eliminates the unexpected combinations is trivial. The main benefit of this option is that such an activation property could be automatically generated by a tool. But the major drawback of this option is that it does not make a difference between activation properties that should be satisfied by the engine control, the pump control or the RAT control. So we prefer a third option that consists in defining activation properties that are related to one component (EMPy, EMPb, RAT) or to a small set of components (Eng1 and Eng2).

The activation property for the hydraulic system act_ok is defined by the conjunction $act\_engine \wedge act\_EMPy \wedge act\_EMPb \wedge act\_RATb$. Activation properties are of the form $act\_cnd \Rightarrow c.A$: "whenever act_cnd is true component c is activated".

The activation condition of EMPb is that the aircraft is in flight or it is on ground and at least one engine is active.
$act\_EMPb : (\neg on\_ground \vee (on\_ground \wedge (Eng2.A \vee Eng1.A))) \Rightarrow EMPb.A$

The activation condition of RATb is that the aircraft is in flight and both engines are lost.
$act\_RATb : (\neg on\_ground \wedge \neg Eng1.O \wedge \neg Eng2.O) \Rightarrow RATb.A$

The activation condition of EMPy is that the aircraft is on ground.
$act\_EMPy : on\_ground \Rightarrow EMPy.A$

The activation condition of both engines is that the aircraft is in flight.
$act\_engine : \neg on\_ground \Rightarrow (Eng1.A \wedge Eng2.A);$

We use a model-checker to prove that all unexpected combinations are eliminated by the actions of the control sub-system. Altarica is connected to the MEC model checker [2]. We did not use this tool because it has strong limitations on the size of systems that it can handle, a new version of the MEC model-checker that should correct these limitations is under development at University of Bordeaux. In the meanwhile, we used Cadence Lab SMV model-checker [10]. Altarica models are automatically translated into SMV input language. We first prove that activation properties eliminate all unexpected combinations, then we show that activation properties are enforced by the control sub-system model.

Elimination of unexpected combinations should be proved by establishing that the following formula is valid: $\Box(act\_ok \Rightarrow \neg unex\_comb)$. Our first attempt to prove this formula failed, because it was possible that both engines were stopped on ground, and as the aircraft was on ground the RAT would not be activated. So unexpected combination $\{\neg Eng1.A, \neg Eng2.A, \neg RATb.A\}$ could not be not eliminated. To eliminate this combination we have to assume that at least one engine is active, this was established by adding in the guard of the $eng\_cntrl.stop$ action aconstraint related to the status of the other engine.

To check that activation properties are enforced we first attempted to prove that $\Box(act\_ok)$ is valid (i.e. at every time step activation properties hold). But, we failed to prove this property as, due a pilot or automatic logic reaction delay, EMPy can only be started one time-step after the aircraft is on ground. So the correct verification goal is :
$\Box(\neg act\_ok \Rightarrow \circ act\_ok))$ i.e. at every time step, if the activation properties do not hold then they hold at the next time step.

3.3   Result Synthesis

Finally we have to combine the various results we have obtained so far in order to prove that the hydraulic system meets its safety requirements. On one hand we have checked using fault-tree analysis tools that, under the assumption that the unexpected combinations are eliminated, the physical sub-system enforces the non-temporal safety requirements. On the other hand we have proved using a model-checker that the activation properties eliminate the unexpected combinations and the control sub-system guarantees that the activation properties hold.

The synthesis of these verification results is performed thanks to a set of inference rules that preserve the validity of Linear Temporal Logic formulae (see [16]):

- **Necessitation rule** : if non-temporal formula f is valid in any state of the system then $\Box f$ is also valid,
- **Strengthening rule** : if formulae $\Box(g_0 \Rightarrow (f_1 \Rightarrow f_2))$ and $\Box(f_0 \Rightarrow g_0)$ are both valid then formula $\Box(f_0 \Rightarrow (f_1 \Rightarrow f_2))$ is also valid
- **Next rule** : if formulae $\Box(f_0 \Rightarrow (f_1 \Rightarrow f_2))$ and $\Box(\neg f_1 \Rightarrow \circ f_1)$ are both valid then formula $\Box f_0 \Rightarrow \Box(\neg f_2 \Rightarrow \circ f_2)$ is also valid.

We consider that the fault-tree analysis provides a proof that the following non-temporal formula is valid
$\neg unex\_comb \Rightarrow (2\_failures \Rightarrow \neg TotalLoss)$

So, by applying Necessitation rule, we derive that the following formula is valid:

$\square$ $(\neg unex\_comb \Rightarrow (2\_failure \Rightarrow \neg TotalLoss))$

By model-checking we have shown the validity of:

$\square$ $(act\_ok \Rightarrow \neg unex\_comb)$ So by applying Strengthening rule, we obtain the validity of:

$\square$ $(act\_ok \Rightarrow (2\_failures \Rightarrow \neg TotalLoss))$

This equivalent to formula :

$\square$ $(2\_failures \Rightarrow (act\_ok \Rightarrow \neg TotalLoss))$

Finally, we also proved by model-checking the validity of:

$\square$ $(\neg act\_ok \Rightarrow \circ act\_ok)$

By applying Next rule, we show the validity of :

$\square$ $2\_failures \Rightarrow \square(Totaloss \Rightarrow \circ \neg TotalLoss))$

Hence we can conclude that the safety requirement is guaranteed by the hydraulic system.

4 Concluding Remarks

High level languages dedicated to safety analysis usually deal either with static hierarchical view of complex systems, in order to support fault tree analysis (see [8, 7]) or with the dynamic part (see [5] for instance). Altarica language provides high level concepts that allow concise descriptions of both static and dynamic parts of complex systems. We shown how we used these features to model the "static physical part" and the "dynamic control part" of the hydraulic system of the A320 Aircraft.

We explained how each part can be analysed by the most adapted tools, namely a fault tree generator for the static part and a model-checker for the dynamic one. This allows to overcome the limitations of the existing tools. On one hand, the available fault tree generator computes automatically classical static fault trees, that gather all causes of an unexpected event but that do not distinguish the event order. On the other, model-checkers can tackle controllers and event order. Another possibility (see [11] for instance) is to use the model-checker to interactively generate fault-tree. When a model-checker cannot check a formula, it usually computes a counterexamples that shows a scenario leading to a state where the formula does not hold. So a model-checker could be used to find scenarios that are counter-example of the negation of a temporal failure condition. However, the use of a model-checker does not guarantee that all scenarios that cause a failure condition will be found (this problem is studied in ESACS project [6]).

Finally, the proposed approach seems adapted to the assessment of the early definition of a system architecture. Indeed, physical components are first identified during the architecture design. Knowing the safety requirements and the physical features of the architecture, fault tree analysis allows the derivation of requirements that constraint the design of system controllers. Then the designed controllers can be assessed by model-checking. We shown the approach feasibility for the earliest system models, with poor knowledge on failure modes. The experiments are pursued to assess the approach interest and tractability for more detailed models.

Acknowledgements

This work was partially supported by EU GROWTH programme project ESACS (Enhanced Safety Assessment of Complex Systems).

References

[1] A. Griffault A. Arnold, G. Point and A. Rauzy. The Altarica Formalism for Describing Concurrent Systems. *Fundamenta Informaticae*, 34, 1999. 19, 22

[2] P. Crubillé A. Arnold, D. Bégay. *Construction and Analysis of Transition Systems with MEC*. World Scientific Publishers, 1994. 29

[3] Analogy. About saber mixed-signal simulator. http://www.analogy.com/products/simulation/about_saber.htm. 19

[4] Groupe ARALIA. Computation of prime implicants of a fault tree within aralia. *Reliability Engineering and System Safety*, 1996. Special issue on selected papers from ESREL'95. 27

[5] G. E. Apostolakis C. J. Garrett, S. B. Guarro. The dynamic flowgraph methodology for assessing the dependability of embedded software systems. *IEEE systems, man and cybernetics*, 25(5), 1994. 30

[6] ESACS Consortium. Enhanced Safety Assessment of Complex Systems. http://www.cert.fr/esacs. 30

[7] P. Fenelon. Towards integrated safety analysis and design. *ACM Applied Computing Review*, 1994. 30

[8] P. Fenelon and J. MacDermid. Integrated techniques for software safety analysis. In *IEE colloquium on Hazard Analysis*, 1992. 30

[9] MathWorks. The mathworks – simulink. www.mathworks.com/products/simulink/. 19

[10] K. L. McMillan. *The SMV language*. Cadence Berkeley Labs, 1999. 29

[11] G. Staalmarck O. Akerlund, S. Nadjm-Tehrani. Integration of Formal Methods into System Safety and Reliability Analysis. In *17th International System Safety Conference*, 1999. 30

[12] Society of Automotive Engineers. Aerospace recommended practice (arp) 4754, certification considerations for highly integrated or complex aircraft systems. 19

[13] Society of Automotive Engineers. Aerospace recommended practice (arp) 4754, guidelines and methodsfor conducting the safety assessment procees on cibil airborne systems and equipment. 21

[14] A. Rauzy. Modes automata and their compilation into fault trees. *Reliability Engineering and System Safety*, 2002. 27

[15] Esterel Technologies. Scade suite for safety-critical software development. www.esterel-technologies.com/scade/. 19

[16] A. Pnueli Z. Manna. *Temporal Verification of Reactive Systems – Safety*. Springer Verlag, 1995. 25, 29

BPM Based Robust E-business Application Development* (practical experience report)

György Csertán[1], András Pataricza[1], P. Harang[1], Orsolya Dobán[1], Gabor Biros[2], András Dancsecz[2], and Ferenc Friedler[2]

[1] Budapest University of Technology and Economics
Department of Measurement and Instrument Engineering
csertan,pataric,harang,doban@mit.bme.hu
[2] University of Veszprém, Department of Computer Science
biros,dancsecz,friedler@dcs.vein.hu

Abstract. Companies rely more and more on the dependability of their e-business application. E-business systems are, by their nature, heterogeneous, consisting not only of information technology component but also human- and infrastructural resources. Therefore, the assurance of a proper level of dependability has to cover all aspects of the system. In the paper, a Business Process Modeling (BPM) based approach is presented, which uses an extended UML profile to design the business processes to compensate the weaknesses of resources. A fault model describes the typical failure modes of the individual element types. Analysis methodologies well proven in the field of dependable computing are used to assess the dependability of the system and provide a basis for countermeasures against the faults. The paper describes the experiences with a pilot application.

1 Introduction

E-business systems spread more and more. Recently emphasis is shifting towards systems in which a large part of the business flow of a company is implemented in an electronic form. As a result, companies rely increasingly on the Quality of Service (QoS) of their e-business system.

Such an e-business system combines IT components (like computer hardware, application software, intra- and internet), human- (like workers) and infrastructural resources (like production facilities, raw material) into a complete system. Therefore, properties of an e-business system are influenced by all of these components and the QoS of the entire system can only be increased if all of the components are incorporated into a global dependability concept.

Dependability of the IT components is increased mainly by using a high-availability server [7, 9] or a clustering solution. Dependability of the resources is

---

* This work was supported partly by IBM and partly by the Hungarian Ministry of Education under contract No: IKTA 00173/2000.

F. Grandoni (Ed.): EDCC 2002, LNCS 2485, pp. 32–43, 2002.

increased by using more reliable resources (a more reliable production machine, a better trained person). These methods are expensive, especially for SMEs. Therefore, the proper organization of the business processes has to compensate the imperfect dependability of single components. In this paper we present a design approach that provides algorithm based fault-tolerance (ABFT) for electronic business processes. It can be used to increase the QoS of e-business systems.

1.1 Objectives of the Approach

The main objective of the research is to ensure the robustness of e-business services in the heterogeneous and unreliable environment of SMEs by using a proper design approach. The main guideline of our work was the deduction to the well-proven principles and solutions from the field of dependable computing.

The design approach starts with requirement analysis. It is based on Business Process Modeling (BPM), a semi-formal, graphical modeling method that describes corporate resources and activities. We use a combination of the ARIS BPM notation and the UML-BPM profile.

The model is augmented in the next step by adding fault information. Fault modeling aims at describing the local faults and fault propagation of resources and activities in order to be able to evaluate global fault effects and make proper countermeasures. A functional, qualitative fault model is suggested in which faults are grouped, e.g. according to their criticality. Fault modeling is done within the very same notation as BPM by exploiting UML's standard extension mechanism, the stereotypes.

Analysis provides the global fault effects that are interpreted by application experts, who can then decide whether to deal with the local fault leading to the unwanted effect and propose solutions to handle the local fault. The model is modified and re-analyised until its robustness is considered sufficient. This design approach corresponds to the IPSD (interactive, process-oriented systems development) method [2].

The fault tolerance measures are very similar to the ones used in dependable computing: timeout, back-checking, error correction coding, TMR, etc. The application expert and the dependability expert select the proper solution. Further work aims at collecting a library of such measures. This seems to be a realistic goal, since the set of types of activities is limited: user input, output to user, message sending, database access, data calculation, etc.

1.2 Case Study

We implemented a pilot application at our partner Balatontourist (a Hungarian tourism company) to demonstrate and check the practical usefulness of the method. The pilot application covers the management and marketing system of trips organized by the travel agency or by external contractual agents. Part of this application will be used in this paper as a case study.

The aim of the pilot application was to gain experience in using the modeling approach and to collect data during the operation of the system about local faults and the funcioning of fault-tolerance measures. The former results are presented in this paper together with the results of FMEA analysis of the application. The latter results could not be collected because there was no time before the main season to implement the necessary data logging and collection modules. It will be implemented in this season and results are awaited in autumn.

The pilot application interacts with basic product or service providers (external agents, private providers, travel agencies); the headquarter of Balatontourist; and the consumers (external agents, travel agencies, tourists). It provides features for different types of users. Each user type has different rights and possibilities:

Unregistered users can only browse among tours and trips.

Registered users can browse tours and trips, make / modify reservations.

Salesperson can manage reservations (e.g. reserve, cancel, modify), view the participant list, and print vouchers.

Tour operators can manage tours and trips (e.g. create, modify, delete), can assign resources to tips, perform cost and profit calculations, and gain on-line information about current trips (e.g. number of tourists, planned income).

Managers can have statistics about trips, utilization of trips, income and expenditure per salesperson, trip, or tour operator.

The application implements a part of the internal business logic of the company. A larger part deals with selling services (trips) to customers and a smaller part deals with the internal support of tour operators in their work of organizing programs and trips. The following main business processes have been identified during the requirement analysis phase (the case study contains only the trip announcement process):

Searching for tours and trips The application displays the list of trips and their details based on the user-specified time period or tour. Registered users can make reservations for one or more of the listed trips.

User registration The user fills in a registration form and the personal data will be stored in the customer database.

Reservation for trips The user or the salesman can make a reservation by providing the trip data and the necessary additional user data (local address, deposit, etc.).

Reservation management Cancellation of a reservation, modification of a reservation.

Modification of personal user data Registered users can modify the personal data (e.g. name, address, phone number) stored about them in the database.

Acknowledgment of a reservation When the user books a tour the salesman acknowledges his/her reservation.

Tour management Creating a tour, uploading pictures, modifying tour details/descriptions and assignment of resources and suppliers.

Trip announcement The tour operator announces a trip for a tour by specifying the date and time of departure and arrival, the prices for adults and
child, stopping-places, etc.

Trip management The tour operator can allocate the actual resources (bus,
meal, travel guide, etc.), close the registration of a trip, cancel a trip.

Resource management Assignment of resources to tours and particular trips,
modifying capacity and price information, and adding supplier data.

2 Modeling Paradigm

The modeling paradigm of the development approach should be able to:

- describe internal / external resources and the business processes of the company;
- model the relation between resources and processes;
- express dependability and performance parameters of system components;
- include dependability measures to increase system robustness;
- give a common description platform for both IT and economics specialists.

2.1 ARIS and UML-BPM

There are two natural ways to select such a modeling approach: start from
business process design tools [3, 5] and extend them to cover IT systems, or
extend IT CASE notations to represent corporate resources and processes.

BPM arose as a pure illustrative visualization method with an informal semantics. Simulation and limited optimization capabilities were added later. It
uses a small number of elements to model the functions of a company similar
to flow charts. The number of elements becomes too large in complex models,
causing troubles in the understanding. ARIS [3] is one of the most popular BPM
modeling tool used by business architects. It has a well elaborated, but proprietary formalism and its modeling scope is limited mainly to non-IT related
business processes (e.g. accounting, production).

The Unified Modeling Language (UML) is a favorite candidate to serve as
an IT CASE language. It can also be extended to cover non-IT apects. However,
it defines a far too complex notation in order to communicate with non-IT
specialists. Standardized subsets of UML, so called profiles, are used to define
a domain specific subset of the notation. One of them was the withdrawn UML-
BPM profile. It concentrated mainly on the IT related processes of a company,
it was very coarsely defined and it was less expressive than ARIS.

In our work we extended the UML-BPM profile with the elements of ARIS [1].
It was relatively straightforward, since both ARIS and UML-BPM are multi-view
notations, i.e. they are able to describe a given problem from many different
aspects. For example, a person can be seen as an element of a hierarchy of
people. On the other hand, the same person can be seen as a human resource
assigned to an activity.

2.2   The Composite Notation

The notation defines views (sub-models) each of which contain a sub-set of standard UML elements. Please refer to [1] for the detailed, formal description of the notation. The views of the composite notation are (the origin of the view is given in brackets):

Process view (UML-BPM) is a use case diagram that defines the business processes of the company, the users of the system and their relation.

Infrastructure view (UML-BPM) is an object diagram that describes the resources and tangible assets of the company and their mutual relation. Their properties are described by object variables.

Organizational view (ARIS) is a class diagram that describes the organization structure of the company; the organization units and their relations to each other, the persons, roles, jobs, and status within organization units.

Function view (ARIS) is a parametrized class diagram that describes the functions of the company in a hierarchical way; a function-tree contains functions (node) and sub-functions (ancestors of a node). Sub-functions cooperate to realize the function.

Data view (ARIS) is a class diagram that defines the data structures used in the implementation of the functions of the company, i.e. to execute the business processes. It corresponds to an extended entity-relationship model. Entities and entity properties are modeled by classes, relationship types by association classes while relationships are described by class associations and

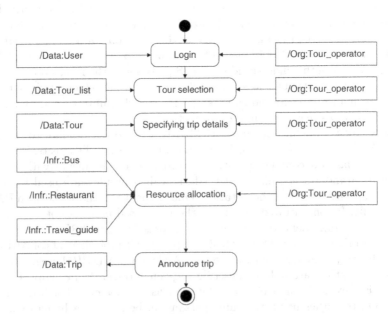

Fig. 1. Control View of the trip announcement process

generalization. Key properties are described by class qualification. Related data is stored in package clusters.

Control view (ARIS) is an activity diagram that describes the dynamics of the business process, and the resources needed for the execution of a given step.

The pilot application was described by one process view, one infrastructure view, one organizational view, one function view, one data view, and ten control views. The extent of the paper does not allow to include all of these views, only the control view (Fig.1.) of the trip announcement process is included.

The process is started by the login of the tour operator (activity `Login`). The required resources are the user database (data resource `Data:User`) and the tour operator (organizational resource `Org:Tour_operator`). Next a tour is selected for "instantiation" (activity `Tour selection`). Required is the list of tours (data resource `Data:Program_list`). Selection is done by the tour operator. Next the details of the program appear and the tour operator extends them (e.g. by date) in order to create a trip. In the next step (activity `Resource allocation`) the tour operator allocates resources to the trip (infrastructure resource `Infr.:Bus, Infr.:Restaurant, Infr.:Travel_guide`). Finally the trip is announced (activity `Trip announcement`) by creating a new resource (data resource `Data:Trip`).

3 Dependability Modeling and Evaluation

Although the proposed BPM notation supports the compact modeling of business processes and the communication between software engineer and economist, a formal notation is needed to analyse the system with mathematical precision. In our approach, the model is transformed (using the method [10]) into dataflow networks (DFN) that serves as the language of analysis. This non-deterministic dataflow programming paradigm [6] is very suitable to describe the aspects of faults, their effects and error propagation at the level of functional units of the business process, i.e. activities, resources. The following tasks can be solved this way concurrently with system design:

- fault simulation,
- test generation,
- testability analysis,
- failure modes and effects analysis (FMEA),
- risk analysis.

3.1 Dataflow Notation

A DFN is a set of nodes that execute concurrently and exchange data items (tokens) over unbounded, unidirectional, FIFO-like, point-to-point communication channels. Nodes represents the components of the system, channels represent

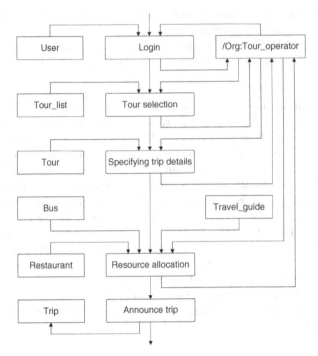

Fig. 2. DFG of the trip announcement process

the communication channels and tokens represent the data passed between the components. The graphical representation of a DFN is a dataflow graph (DFG), nodes of which are drawn as boxes and channels of which are drawn as directed arcs.

Definition 1. *A* dataflow network *DFN is a tuple* (N, C, S) *where:*

> N - *set of nodes*
> C - *set of channels (I-input, O-output, and IN-internal channels)*
> S - *set of states; Cartesian product of node and channel states*

Definition 2. *A* dataflow node *n is a tuple* $(I_n, O_n, S_n, s_n^0, R_n, M_n)$ *where:*

> I_n - *set of input channels*
> O_n - *set of output channels*
> S_n - *set of states*
> s_n^0 - *initial state,* $s_0 \in S_n$
> M_n - *set of tokens*
> R_n - *set of firings,* $r_n \in R_n$ *is a tuple* $(s_n, X_{in}, s_n', X_{out}, \pi)$
> > s_n, s_n' - *states before and after the execution of the firing,* $s_n, s_n' \in S_n$
> > X_{in} - *input mapping,* $X_{in} : I_n \mapsto M_n$
> > X_{out} - *output mapping,* $X_{out} : O_n \mapsto M_n$
> > π - *priority of the firing,* $\pi \in \mathbb{N}$

The meaning of *firing rule* $r_n = (s_n, X_{in}, s'_n, X_{out}, 0)$ is that if node n is in state s_n and $\forall i_n \in I_n$ contains at least the tokens $X_{in}(i_n)$, then r_n can be executed. The execution of r_n removes $X_{in}(i_n)$ tokens from $\forall i_n \in I_n$ and outputs $X_{out}(j_n)$ tokens onto $\forall j_n \in O_n$. After execution the node changes its state from s_n to s'_n.

The dataflow graph of the case study is presented in Fig.2. It describes only the structure of the DFN. It is very similar to the control view, but each resource and activity should appear only once. The description of the announce trip node (n11) is given below as an example for node definition:

node   n11=({trip_details}, {trip_data, finish}, {ok}, ok, {ok}, {r1})
firing   r1=(ok;trip_details=ok;ok;trip_data=ok,finish=ok;0)

The node receives the details of the trip, stores them in the database and finishes the whole trip announcement process. Tokens (ok) describe the fault-free data, since at this step faults are not modeled. The nodes are in fault-free state (ok).

3.2 Fault Modeling

The main idea in the fault modeling is the introduction of the notion of faults at the metamodel level of the BPM notation. Roughly speaking, this is the exact counterpart of the notion of stuck-at faults in gate-level logic testing, which associates faults with signals.

In the case of BPM, faults are associated with resources and activities. The first one models primarily the permanent faults, including those, when a resource is missing. The second category is intended to model transient faults, like those in activities carried out by a human operator.

In its current state the approach does not support modeling of design faults and intentional faults carried out by operators, since this may result a distortion of the entire business flow.

3.3 Dataflow-Driven Dependability Analysis

The qualitative analysis is based on the idea of modeling the fault effects and their propagation similarly to the flow of data in the process model [4, 8]. In the case study tokens representing the data are coloured for instance either as *"correct"* or as *"incorrect"* or as *"missing"*. The faulty behaviour of a node manifests in sending such tokens. Accordingly, the fault states of nodes are similarly grouped into *"sends correct data"* or *"sends incorrect data"* or *"does not send data"*. A set of potential error propagation paths can be estimated by tracing the flow of tokens from the fault site towards the outputs. In the model all potential consequences of a fault are incorporated. At the highest level, this abstraction can help to radically restrict the search space for the origins of failures.

In subsequent steps of analysis a more refined fault model can be used, resulting in a more faithful description of the fault effects. The potential to use

Table 1. Local faults and fault effects in the example

Resource/Activity	Local Fault	Fault Effect
login	does not send data	process hangs (1)
user	does not send data	1
	sends incorrect data	1; wrong access level (0)
tour operator	does not send data	1
	sends incorrect data	0; 1
tour list	does not send data	1
	sends incorrect data	wrong tour selected (2)
tour selection	sends incorrect data	2
tour	does not send data	1
	sends incorrect data	bad trip properties (3)
specifying details	sends incorrect data	3
bus	does not send data	1
	sends incorrect data	3
restaurant	does not send data	1
	sends incorrect data	3
travel guide	does not send data	1
	sends incorrect data	3
resource allocation	sends incorrect data	3
announce trip	does not send data	1
	sends incorrect data	3
trip	does not send data	no data written (4)
	sends incorrect data	3

arbitrary user-defined guiding attributes, colorings of the tokens and propagation rules offer full freedom for the analysis of different user requirements. By adding fault occurrence, fault latency and detection probabilities the model can serve as a starting point for a more detailed dependability analysis.

The dataflow graph of the extended model is unchanged (Fig.2), the nodes are extended in order to cover not only fault-free but also faulty behaviour. The description of the announce trip node (n11) is given below as an example for node definition extension:

node   n11=({trip_details}, {trip_data, finish}, {ok}, ok, {ok}, {r1,r2,r3})
firings   r1=(ok;trip_details=ok;ok;trip_data=ok,finish=ok;0)
         r2=(ok;trip_details=inc;ok;trip_data=inc,finish=inc;0)
         r3=(ok;trip_details=dead;ok;trip_data=dead,finish=dead;0)

The extended behaviour contains the fault-free behaviour. We assume that internal faults do not arise in this activity - the node has only fault-free states (ok). If the details of the trip are incorrect (token inc), incorrect data will be stored in the database and the process finishes. If the activity does not receive

Table 2. Global effects and protective measures in the example

Local Effect	Crit.	Global Effect	Protection
0	1	insufficient authority	
	4	too much authority	
1	2	process dead-lock	process (session) timeout
2	3	trip with wrong data announced	trip check at the end
3	3	trip with wrong data announced	trip check at the end
4	2	no trip announced	data check at the end

the details of the trip (token dead), no data is stored in the database and the process does not finish.

4   FMEA Analysis

In our example, the basic potential of the modeling approach is illustrated by the FMEA analysis of the single selected business process. (In case of multiple processes the paradigm is able to handle even inter-process dependencies. An example see later.)

The first step of analysis was to collect possible local faults of the resources and activities, categorize them according to the fault model and assign fault effects to them. The results of this first step are presented in Table 1. At the first time a reference is given to each fault effect (number in brackects). Subsequent occurences are denoted only by this reference number.

The second step of analysis was to propagate the local fault effects in the system. Local faults manifest as erroneous tokens sent by a node. Communication events of the business process are considered atomic in the sense that communication errors have to be explicitly modeled if necessary by additional DF nodes. This propagation is done by fault simulation.

The DFN can be considered as a network of finite-state machines that can be simulated by discrete event simulation. The simulation is done until the tokens reach the output of the DFN, e.g. the local fault effects propagate until they reach the output. In such case, they result in the failure of the business process that is described by the global effects. The global effects for the case study are described in the 3rd column of Table 2. The numbers in the 1st column refer to the local fault effects in Table 1.

Global in the case study is meant for the trip announcement process. In the pilot application all processes are considered, and global is meant for the whole application. In this case the global effect of fault effect No. 3 could be a tourist who does not get what he paid for (displeased) or a trip with deficit.

If necessary a criticality factor can be assigned to the global effects. It can be the starting point of criticality analysis. The 2nd column in Table 2 shows

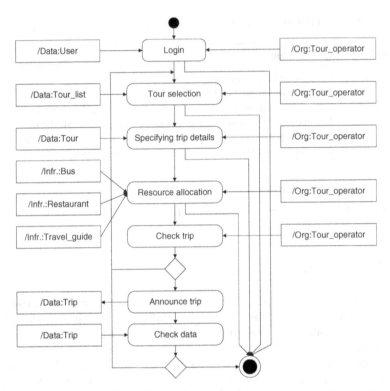

Fig. 3. Control view of the enhanced trip announcement process

a possible grouping of global effects into criticality categories. A trip based on bad data is more critical (3) than not creating the trip at all (factor 2).

The final step of evaluation (not part of FMEA) was to identify fault tolerance measures for the different global effects (failures). It is intended as a solution to improve the dependability of the system. The suggested protection mechanisms are described in the 4th column of Table 2. The interpretation of the 3rd row is the following: if the tour operator does not enter the username and password, the process will wait and hang infinitely. This can be avoided by explicitely finishing the process after a given time if authorization do not occur.

Finally, Fig.3. shows the enhanced trip announcement process that contains the fault tolerance measures listed in Table 2. In the modified process all activities that have an input could also finish the process because of timeout. The details of the trip are presented to the tour operator, who can check them before announcement. Last but not least, there is a check, whether trip data are correctly stored in the database.

5   Conclusions

The experiment (pilot application) showed that modeling paradigms and analysis methods adopted from traditional fields of technical dependability can be used in making e-business systems more robust by providing algorithm based fault-tolerance for the faults of resources.

Our experience shows that the applied fault tolerance measures are simple, logical, many times obvious, but only after the analysis identified the causes of failures by identifying model interdependencies. From the analysis it is clear that counter measures should be applied near to the fault place: tipically at the end of activities and processes.

Acknowledgement

Thanks to Prof. Jie Xu for helping to prepare the final version of the paper.

References

[1] A. Pataricza (editor). BPM Modeling Paradigm to E-business Applications. Technical report, IKTA 00173/2000, 2001. in Hungarian. 35, 36

[2] W. Aalst and K. Hee. *Workflow Management: Models, Methods, and Systems.* MIT Press, 2002. 33

[3] Broad spectrum of solutions for the e-organization. Whitepaper, www.ids-scheer.com, 2001. 35

[4] Gy. Csertán, A. Pataricza, and E. Selényi. Dependability Analysis in HW-SW codesign. In *Proceedings of the IEEE International Computer Performance and Dependability Symposium, IPDS'95,* pages 316–325, April Erlangen, Germany, 1995. 39

[5] A. Helton, E. Zulayabar, and P.J.A. Soper. *Business Process Reengineering and Beyond.* Number SG24-2590-00 in Redbooks. IBM Corp., 1995. 35

[6] B. Jonsson. A Fully Abstract Trace Model for Dataflow Networks. In *Proceedings of the 16th ACM symposium on POPL,* pages 155–165, Austin, Texas, 1989. 37

[7] E. Marcus and H. Stern. *Blueprints for High Availability.* Wiley, 2000. 32

[8] Y. Papadopoulos and M. Maruhn. Model-Based Synthesis of Fault Trees from Matlab - Simulink Models. In *Proceedings of the International Conference on Dependable Systems and Networks, DSN 2001,* pages 77–82, Sweden, 2001. 39

[9] S. Russel, O.L.B. Gonzalez, B.D. Coutere, and D. Furniss. *High Availability Without Clustering.* Number SG24-6216-00 in Redbooks. IBM Corp., 2001. 32

[10] D. Varró, G. Varró, and A. Pataricza. Designing the Automatic Transformation of Visual Languages. *Science of Computer Programming,* To Appear. 37

Solving Agreement Problems with Weak Ordering Oracles*

Fernando Pedone[1,2], André Schiper[2], Péter Urbán[2], and David Cavin[2]

[1] Hewlett-Packard Laboratories, Software Technology Laboratory
Palo Alto, CA 94304, USA
fernando_pedone@hp.com
[2] Ecole Polytechnique Fédérale de Lausanne (EPFL)
Faculté Informatique & Communications
CH-1015 Lausanne, Switzerland
{andre.schiper,peter.urban,david.cavin}@epfl.ch

Abstract. Agreement problems, such as consensus, atomic broadcast, and group membership, are central to the implementation of fault-tolerant distributed systems. Despite the diversity of algorithms that have been proposed for solving agreement problems in the past years, almost all solutions are *Crash-Detection Based* (*CDB*). We say that an algorithm is CDB if it uses some information about the status *crashed/not crashed* of processes. In this paper, we revisit the issue of non-CDB algorithms considering *ordering oracles*. Ordering oracles have a theoretical interest as well as a practical interest. To illustrate their use, we present solutions to consensus and atomic broadcast, and evaluate the performance of the atomic broadcast algorithm in a cluster of workstations.

1 Introduction

The paper addresses the issue of solving agreement problems, which are central to the implementation of fault-tolerant distributed systems. Consensus, atomic broadcast, and group membership are examples of agreement problems. One of the key issues when solving an agreement problem is the choice of the system model. Many system models have been proposed in the past years: synchronous models [8, 12, 13, 4], partially synchronous models [9], asynchronous models with failure detectors [6, 1], timed asynchronous models [7], etc. Despite the diversity of these models, almost all algorithms that have been proposed to solve agreement problems have the common point of being *Crash-Detection Based* (*CDB*). We say that an algorithm is CDB if it uses some information about the status *crashed/not crashed* of processes. Typically, a CDB algorithm contains statements like "**if** p has crashed **then** ..." or "**if** p is suspected to have crashed **then** ..." There is a notable exception to the near universality of CDB algorithms: randomized consensus algorithms [5, 18], which are not CDB.

---

* Research partially supported by the CSEM – Swiss Center for Electronics and Microtechnology Inc., Neuchâtel, and the Swiss National Science Foundation NCCR MICS project.

There are two motivations for this work. The first one is theoretical: it advances the state of the art of non-CDB algorithms, a class of algorithms that has been under-explored. The second motivation is practical: CDB algorithms require tuning of the failure-detection mechanism they use, which has been regarded as a nuisance for a long time [11]. To illustrate the problem, consider a system that wants to react quickly to failures. Since reaction to failures is ultimately triggered by some timer mechanism, such a system should have a very short timeout. However, due to variations in the system load, a short timeout may lead to false failure suspicions. False failure suspicions are problematic because they lead to actions (e.g., selecting a new coordinator) that will increase the system load and degrade performance even further. Of course, one way to reduce false failure suspicions is to increase the timeouts, but then the system no longer has a fast response to failures. By removing the need for failure detection from the algorithms, we eliminate this problem of tuning: non-CDB algorithms operate in the presence of failures just as quickly as they operate in their absence. Given the widespread use of computer clustering — the environment to which our algorithms are best suited, we believe that non-CDB algorithms represent an important paradigm to be exploited in the design of high-performance fault-tolerant systems in the years to come.

The non-CDB algorithms presented in the paper assume an asynchronous system model in which processes may fail by crashing. It is well known that consensus (and other agreement problems) are not solvable in an asynchronous system where processes may fail [10]. To make agreement problems solvable, we extend the asynchronous system with *ordering oracles* (Section 2), which (1) receive queries to broadcast messages and (2) output these messages. The specification of an oracle links the queries to the outputs. The paper defines two ordering oracles: the *k-Weak Atomic Broadcast* oracle (*k*-WAB oracle) where k is a positive integer, and the *Weak Atomic Broadcast* oracle (WAB oracle). Intuitively, our oracles ensure that messages are delivered in the same order from time to time. The k-WAB oracle ensures the ordering property k times. The WAB oracle ensures the ordering property an unbounded number of times.

Section 3 is devoted to consensus: we give two non-CDB algorithms, both requiring the 1-WAB oracle. The first one, called B-Consensus algorithm, is inspired by Ben-Or's randomized consensus algorithm [5] and requires $f < n/2$, where n is the total number of processes and f is the number of faulty processes. The second, called R-Consensus algorithm, is inspired by Rabin's randomized consensus algorithm [18] and requires $f < n/3$.[1] These two algorithms show an interesting resilience/complexity tradeoff: the consensus algorithm inspired by Ben-Or's algorithm has a time complexity of 3δ and $f < n/2$, where δ is the maximum message delay, while the consensus algorithm inspired by Rabin's algorithm has a time complexity of 2δ and $f < n/3$.

---

[1] Contrary to Ben-Or's and Rabin's algorithms, our algorithms solve the non-binary consensus problem.

Our consensus algorithms can be compared to the leader-based consensus algorithms presented in [15]. Although partly similar in structure to ours[2], the consensus algorithms we propose in this paper have a better time complexity. This is because the approach in [15] relies on a leader oracle, that is, an oracle which eventually outputs the same leader process; implementing such an oracle requires a failure detection mechanism. Failure detection is not needed in our algorithms, which are based on weak ordering oracles that match the behavior of current network broadcast primitives, and so, can be efficiently implemented.

In Section 4, we consider atomic broadcast, and we extend our R-Consensus algorithm to an atomic broadcast algorithm. While the R-Consensus algorithm requires the 1-WAB oracle, the atomic broadcast algorithm requires the WAB oracle. The reduction of atomic broadcast to consensus is well known [6]. We consider here a different solution that closely integrates the ordering oracle with the atomic broadcast algorithm. Our new atomic broadcast algorithm has a time complexity of 2δ and requires $f < n/3$. Section 5 discusses some experiments we have conducted to evaluate the performance of the proposed atomic broadcast algorithms, and Section 6 concludes the paper.

2   System Model and Ordering Oracles

2.1   System Model

We consider an asynchronous distributed system composed of n processes $\{p_1, \ldots, p_n\}$, which communicate by message passing. A process can only fail by crashing (i.e., we do not consider Byzantine failures). A process that never crashes is *correct*, otherwise it is *faulty*. We make no assumptions about process speeds or message transmission times.

Processes are connected through quasi-reliable channels, defined by the primitives $send(m)$ and $receive(m)$. Quasi-reliable channels have the following properties: (i) if process q receives message m from p, then p sent m to q *(no creation)*; (ii) q receives m from p at most once *(no duplication)*; and (iii) if p sends m to q, and p, q are correct, then q eventually receives m *(no loss)*.

2.2   Ordering Oracles

Every process has access to an ordering oracle, defined by properties relating queries to outputs. Queries to an oracle are requests to broadcast messages, and outputs of an oracle are messages (that the oracle had to broadcast). More formally, an oracle is a set of oracle histories that satisfy properties relating queries to outputs [2].[3] We introduce the *Weak Atomic Broadcast* oracle,

---

[2] Even though this is not mentioned in [15], similarly to ours, the algorithms in [15] follow the structure of the randomized algorithms proposed by Ben-Or [5] and Rabin [18].

[3] In [2] an oracle is a function that takes a failure pattern F and returns a set $\mathcal{O}(F)$ of oracle histories. This is because the oracles in [2] include failure detectors. We do not consider failure detectors here as our approach does not need them.

defined by queries of the type W-ABroadcast(r, m), and outputs of the type W-ADeliver(r, m), where r is an integer and m is a message. The parameter r groups queries and outputs, i.e., it relates different queries and outputs with the same r value. A Weak Atomic Broadcast oracle satisfies an ordering property (defined below) and the following two properties:

- **Validity:** If a correct process queries W-ABroadcast(r, m), then all correct processes eventually get the output W-ADeliver(r, m).
- **Uniform Integrity:** For every pair (r, m), W-ADeliver(r, m) is output at most once, and only if W-ABroadcast(r, m) was previously executed.

Our oracle also orders the outputs W-ADeliver(r, m). However, not all outputs need to be ordered: we call the property *weak ordering*. To define this property, we introduce the notion of *canonical sequence of queries*, and the notation $first_p(r)$. A canonical sequence of queries, by some process p, is a sequence of queries (1) that starts with the query W-ABroadcast$(0, -)$, and (2) where the query W-ABroadcast$(r, -)$ of p, $r \geq 0$, can only be followed by the query W-ABroadcast$(r+1, -)$. A canonical sequence of queries can be finite or infinite. Given an integer r and a process p, we denote by $first_p(r)$ the message m such that (r, m) is the first pair with integer r that the oracle outputs at p. Using canonical sequences of queries, we define the following ordering properties:

- **Eventual Uniform 1-Order:** If all correct processes execute an infinite canonical sequence of queries, then there exists r such that for all processes p and q, we have $first_p(r) = first_q(r)$.

To illustrate this property, consider three processes p_1, p_2, p_3, executing the following queries to the oracle:

- p_1: W-ABroadcast$(0, m_1)$; W-ABroadcast$(1, m_2)$; W-ABroadcast$(2, m_3)$.
- p_2: W-ABroadcast$(0, m_4)$; W-ABroadcast$(1, m_5)$; W-ABroadcast$(2, m_6)$.
- p_3: W-ABroadcast$(0, m_7)$; W-ABroadcast$(1, m_8)$; W-ABroadcast$(2, m_9)$.

Assume the following prefix of sequences output by oracle at each process (for brevity, we denote next W-ADeliver(r, m) by (r, m)):

- p_1: $(0, m_1)$; $(1, m_2)$; $(0, m_4)$; $(2, m_3)$; $(0, m_7)$; etc.
- p_2: $(0, m_4)$; $(0, m_1)$; $(1, m_5)$; $(0, m_7)$; $(2, m_3)$; etc.
- p_3: $(0, m_4)$; $(0, m_7)$; $(2, m_3)$; $(1, m_8)$; etc.

Here we have $first_{p_1}(0) = m_1$, $first_{p_2}(0) = m_4$, $first_{p_3}(0) = m_4$, etc. The eventual uniform 1-order property holds since we have $first_{p_1}(2) = first_{p_2}(2) = first_{p_3}(2) = m_3$.

We generalize the eventual uniform 1-order property as follows:

- **Eventual Uniform k-Order:** If all correct processes execute an infinite canonical sequence of queries, then there exist k values $r_1, \ldots, r_k$ such that for all processes p, q and for all i, $1 \leq i \leq k$, we have $first_p(r_i) = first_q(r_i)$.

If the oracle satisfies the eventual uniform k-order property, we also say that the oracle *satisfies the ordering property k times*. We can now define our two oracles:

- **k-Weak Atomic Broadcast (k-WAB) Oracle:** Oracle that satisfies *eventual uniform k-order, validity,* and *uniform integrity.*
- **Weak Atomic Broadcast (WAB) Oracle:** A k-WAB oracle, where $k = \infty$.

To summarize, k-WAB oracles satisfy the ordering property k times, while the WAB oracles satisfy the ordering property an infinite number of times.

2.3   Discussion

The idea of the ordering oracles stems from an experimental observation: under normal execution conditions (e.g., small or moderate load) messages broadcast in local-area networks are received in total order with high probability. We call this property *spontaneous total order*. Under high network loads, this property might be violated. More generally, one can consider that the system passes through periods when the spontaneous total order property holds, and periods when it does not hold. Our Weak Atomic Broadcast Oracles abstract this spontaneous total order property.

Figure 1 illustrates the spontaneous total order property in a system composed of a cluster of 12 PCs connected by a local-area network (see Section 5 for details about the environment). In the experiments, each workstation broadcasts messages to all the other workstations, and receives messages from all workstations over a certain period of time. Broadcasts are implemented with IP-multicast (loop-back mode disabled).

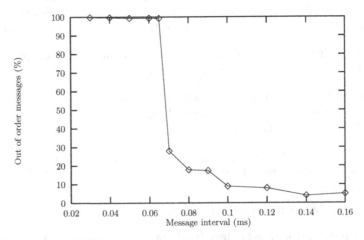

Fig. 1. Spontaneous total order property

Figure 1 shows the relation between the time between successive broadcast calls and the percentage of messages that are received out of order. When messages are broadcast with a period greater than approximately 0.14 milliseconds, IP-multicast implements a WAB oracle with a very high probability (i.e., only about 5% of messages are received out of order).

3   Solving Uniform Consensus with 1-WAB Oracles

3.1   The Consensus Problem

The (uniform) consensus problem is defined over a set of n processes.[4] Each process p_i proposes an initial value v_i, and processes must eventually agree on a common value v that has been proposed by one of the processes. Formally, the problem is defined by the following three properties [6]:

- **Uniform Agreement:** No two processes decide differently.
- **Termination:** Every correct process eventually decides.
- **Uniform Validity:** If a process decides v, then v has been proposed by some process.

In this section we give two algorithms that solve consensus in an asynchronous system augmented with a 1-WAB oracle. The first algorithm, called B-Consensus algorithm, is inspired by Ben-Or's randomized consensus algorithm [5] and the second one, called R-Consensus algorithm, is inspired by Rabin's algorithm [18]. While Ben-Or's and Rabin's algorithms solve the binary consensus problem, where the initial values are 0 or 1, our algorithms solve the general (i.e., non-binary) consensus problem. We present Ben-Or's and Rabin's consensus algorithms in [17], expressed in the same syntactic form as our algorithms.

3.2   The B-Consensus Algorithm

We initially provide an overview of the algorithm and then its description in detail (see Algorithm 1). Similarly to Ben-Or's algorithm, our algorithm requires $f < n/2$ (i.e., a majority of correct processes).

Overview of the algorithm. The algorithm executes in a sequence of rounds, where each round has three stages (see Figure 2, where for clarity messages from a process to itself have been omitted). In the first stage of the round processes ask the 1-WAB oracle to broadcast their estimates to the other processes, and then wait for the first message of the current round output by the oracle.

The second stage is used to determine whether a majority of processes output the same estimate in the first stage. A process first sends its current estimate (updated in the first stage) to the other processes, and waits for the first $n - f$ messages of the same kind. If the $n - f$ messages received contain the same

---

[4] From here on, "consensus" implicitly means "uniform consensus."

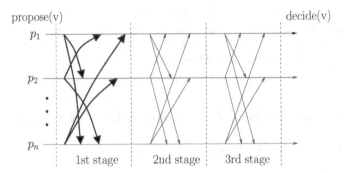

propose(v)   decide(v)

1st stage   2nd stage   3rd stage

Fig. 2. One round of the B-Consensus algorithm

estimate value v, the process takes v as its estimate; otherwise it takes $\perp$ as its estimate. Notice that the majority constraint guarantees that the only possible outcomes of the second stage for all processes is either v or $\perp$.

In the third stage, each process sends its estimate to the other processes and again waits for $n - f$ responses. If the same non-$\perp$ value is received from $f + 1$ processes, the process decides (if it has not yet decided in a previous round) and proceeds to the next round. The algorithm, as it is, requires processes to keep executing even after they have decided. Stopping is discussed in Section 4.

B-Consensus in detail. Algorithm 1 is the B-Consensus algorithm. In each round (lines 6–24), every process p first queries the oracle (line 6), waits for the first answer tagged with the current round number r_p (line 7) and updates its $estimate_p$ value (line 8). Then p sends $estimate_p$ to all in a message of type FIRST (line 9) and waits for $n - f$ such messages (line 10). After updating $estimate_p$, process p sends again $estimate_p$ to all in a message of type SECOND (line 15) and waits for $n - f$ such messages. If $f + 1$ messages received contain a value v different from $\perp$ then p decides v (line 18). After deciding, p continues the algorithm.

Compared to Ben-Or's algorithm, the coin toss has been replaced by an assignment of the initial value to $estimate_p$ (line 23). Notice that while Ben-Or's algorithm solves the binary consensus problem, Algorithm 1 solves the generalized consensus problem with non-binary initial values.

It is easy to see that the validity property holds. The proof of uniform agreement is very similar to the proof of Ben-Or's algorithm, and is given in [17], together with the proof of termination.

3.3   The R-Consensus Algorithm

We now present the R-Consensus algorithm, inspired by Rabin's algorithm. Similarly to Rabin's algorithm, it requires $f < n/3$. As before, we first provide an overview of the algorithm and then present it in more detail.

Overview of the algorithm. The R-Consensus algorithm also solves consensus with a 1-WAB oracle. The algorithm executes in a sequence of rounds divided in two stages (instead of three stages in the B-consensus algorithm). In the first stage, processes use the 1-WAB oracle to propagate their estimates to the other processes, and wait for the first message output by the oracle in the current round. In the second stage, processes send the estimates they received in the first stage and wait for two thirds of replies. If a majority of the values received are the same, the process adopts this value as its current estimate. If all values received by the process are the same, the process decides.

R-Consensus in detail. Algorithm 2 (page 52) is the R-Consensus algorithm. In each round (lines 6–16), just like the B-Consensus algorithm, every process first queries the oracle (line 6), waits for the first answer tagged with the current

---

Algorithm 1 B-Consensus algorithm $(f < n/2)$

1: To execute propose($initVal$):

2:     $estimate_p \leftarrow initVal$
3:     $decided_p \leftarrow false$
4:     $r_p \leftarrow 0$

5: **while** *true* **do**

6:     W-ABroadcast($r_p, estimate_p$)
7:     **wait until** W-ADeliver of the first message (r_p, v)
8:     $estimate_p \leftarrow v$

9:     send (FIRST, $r_p, estimate_p$) to all
10:    **wait until** received (FIRST, r_p, v) from $n - f$ processes
11:    **if** $\exists\, v$ s.t. received (FIRST, r_p, v) from $n - f$ processes **then**
12:        $estimate_p \leftarrow v$
13:    **else**
14:        $estimate_p \leftarrow \perp$

15:    send (SECOND, $r_p, estimate_p$) to all
16:    **wait until** received (SECOND, r_p, v) from $n - f$ processes
17:    **if not** $decided_p$ **and** $(\exists\, \bar{v} \neq \perp$ s.t. received (*second*, $r_p, \bar{v}$) from $f + 1$ processes) **then**
18:        decide $\bar{v}$ {*continue the algorithm after the decision*}
19:        $decided_p \leftarrow true$
20:    **if** $\exists\, \bar{v} \neq \perp$ s.t. received (SECOND, $r_p, \bar{v}$) **then**
21:        $estimate_p \leftarrow \bar{v}$
22:    **else**
23:        $estimate_p \leftarrow initVal$

24:    $r_p \leftarrow r_p + 1$

Algorithm 2 R-Consensus algorithm $(f < n/3)$

1: To execute propose($initVal$):

2:    $estimate_p \leftarrow initVal$
3:    $decided_p \leftarrow false$
4:    $r_p \leftarrow 0$

5: **while** *true* **do**

6:    W-ABroadcast($r_p, estimate_p$)
7:    **wait until** W-ADeliver of the first message (r_p, v)
8:    $estimate_p \leftarrow v$

9:    send (FIRST, $r_p, estimate_p$) to all
10:    **wait until** received (FIRST, r_p, v) from $n - f$ processes
11:    **if** a majority of values received are equal to $\bar{v}$ **then**
12:        $estimate_p \leftarrow \bar{v}$

13:    **if not** $decided_p$ **and** (all values received are equal to $\bar{v}$) **then**
14:        decide $\bar{v}$ {*continue the algorithm after the decision*}
15:        $decided_p \leftarrow true$

16:    $r_p \leftarrow r_p + 1$

---

round number r_p (line 7) and updates its $estimate_p$ value (line 8). Then p sends $estimate_p$ to all in a message of type FIRST (line 9) and waits for $n - f$ such messages (line 10). If a majority of the values received are identical, p updates $estimate_p$. If $n - f$ values received are equal to $\bar{v}$, then p decides $\bar{v}$ (line 14). After deciding, p continues the algorithm. Stopping is discussed in the context of atomic broadcast (Section 4).

Notice that while Rabin's algorithm solves the binary consensus problem, Algorithm 2 solves the generalized consensus problem with non-binary initial values. It is easy to see that the validity property holds. The proof of uniform agreement is very similar to the proof of Rabin's algorithm, and is given in [17], together with the proof of termination.

3.4   Time Complexity *vs.* Resilience

We compare now the time complexity of the B-Consensus and the R-Consensus algorithms in "good runs." In CDB algorithms, a good run is usually defined as a run in which processes do not fail and are not falsely suspected by other processes. Here we define a good run as a run in which, for all correct processes p, q, we have $first_p(1) = first_q(1)$. So, contrary to the definition of good runs in the context of CDB algorithms, a good run can include process crashes.

We measure the time complexity in terms of the maximum message delay δ [2]. We assume a cost of δ for our oracle. In good runs, with Algorithm 1, every process decides after 3δ. Remember that the algorithm assumes $f < n/2$. In good runs, with Algorithm 2, every process decides after 2δ. The algorithm assumes $f < n/3$. This shows an interesting trade-off between time complexity and resilience: 3δ and $f < n/2$ vs. 2δ and $f < n/3$.

These time complexities are similar to the results of consensus algorithms based on failure detectors. For example, the consensus algorithms in [19, 14], based on $\Diamond\mathcal{S}$, have a time complexity of 2δ and assume $f < n/2$; however, the time complexity 3δ for B-Consensus and 2δ for R-Consensus can be achieved in "less favorable" circumstances, that is, in the presence of process crashes.

4 Solving Atomic Broadcast with WAB Oracles

4.1 The Atomic Broadcast Problem

Atomic broadcast is defined by the primitives A-Broadcast and A-Deliver and the following properties:

- **Validity:** If a correct process A-broadcasts message m, then eventually it A-delivers m.
- **Uniform Agreement:** If a process A-delivers m, then all correct processes eventually A-deliver m.
- **Uniform Integrity:** Every message is A-delivered at most once at each process, and only if it was previously A-broadcast.
- **Uniform Total Order:** If two processes p and q both A-deliver messages m and m', then p A-delivers m before m' if and only if q A-delivers m before m'.

Solving atomic broadcast by reduction to a sequence of consensus is well known [6]. We consider here a different solution that closely integrates the ordering oracle with the atomic broadcast algorithm.[5] Our atomic broadcast algorithm is based on Algorithm 2 (considering Algorithm 1 instead leads to a similar solution), and assumes a WAB oracle, which satisfies the ordering property $first_p(r) = first_q(r)$ for an infinite number of rounds r.

Note that the atomic braodcast algorithm in [3], similarly to the algorithm hereafter, is based on prefix agreement. However, the structure of our algorithm is completely different: [3] is based on a variant of consensus.

4.2 Sequences of Messages

We express the atomic broadcast algorithm using message *sequences*. In addition to the traditional set operators, we use the *concatenation* operator $\oplus$ and the *prefix* operator $\otimes$ to handle sequences.

---

[5] When reducing atomic broadcast to consensus, see [6], we get a solution in which the ordering oracle, used in the consensus algorithm, is decoupled from the atomic broadcast algorithm.

– **Concatenation** $s_1 \oplus s_2$: The sequence $s \overset{\text{def}}{=} s_1 \oplus s_2$ is defined as s_1 followed by $s_2 \setminus s_1$, that is, all the messages in s_1 followed by all the messages in s_2 that are not in s_1 (in the same order as they appear in s_2). For example, let $s_1 = \langle m_0; m_1; m_2; m_3; \rangle$, and $s_2 = \langle m_0; m_1; m_4 \rangle$. We have $s_1 \oplus s_2 = \langle m_0; m_1; m_2; m_3; m_4 \rangle$, and $s_2 \oplus s_1 = \langle m_0; m_1; m_4; m_2; m_3 \rangle$.

– **Prefix** $s_1 \otimes s_2$: The sequence $s \overset{\text{def}}{=} s_1 \otimes s_2$ is defined as the longest common prefix of s_1 and s_2. The $\otimes$ operator is commutative and associative. For example, taking s_1 and s_2 as defined above, $s_1 \otimes s_2 = s_2 \otimes s_1 = \langle m_0; m_1 \rangle$. We say that a sequence s is a prefix of another sequence s', denoted $s \leq s'$, if and only if $s = s \otimes s'$. Notice that the empty sequence ϵ is a prefix of every sequence.

4.3   From WAB Oracles to Atomic Broadcast: Version 1

In this section we give a simple version of our atomic broadcast algorithm; we extend it in Section 4.4 with some optimizations.

Overview of the algorithm. The structure of our atomic broadcast algorithm is close to the structure of the R-Consensus algorithm (Section 3.3) and also assumes $f < n/3$. The main difference is that the atomic broadcast algorithm uses sequences of messages instead of single messages. The execution proceeds in rounds; to broadcast a message, process p concatenates the message with a sequence that it keeps locally, denoted *estimate*. Processes send their *estimate* sequence to other processes in the first stage of a round using the WAB oracle, and wait for the first sequence, with the current round number, output by the oracle. In the second stage, processes exchange the estimate sequences output by the oracle in the first stage (possibly with some other messages appended). Each process waits for $n - f$ messages. If all sequences received have a common non-empty prefix, the process A-delivers the messages in the common prefix not yet A-delivered. Then, the process determines the longest prefix among a majority of the sequences received; this prefix, followed by any other messages the process may have received, is the process' new estimate. The process then starts the next round.

The algorithm in detail. Algorithm 3, page 55, is the first version of our atomic broadcast algorithm. Tasks 1, 2 and 3 execute concurrently. Variable r_p (line 2) is the current round number, $estimate_p$ (line 3) contains a sequence of messages broadcast by p or by any other process, and $delivered_p$ (line 4) contains the sequence of messages A-delivered by p, in the order in which they were A-delivered.

   To broadcast a message m, process p appends m to $estimate_p$ (line 6, Task 1). The main algorithm and actual broadcasting of messages is performed by Task 2 (lines 8–20). Task 3 (lines 21–22) ensures the validity property of atomic broadcast. The variable $estimate_p$ is concurrently accessed by Task 1, Task 2, and Task 3; we implicitly assume that it is accessed in mutual exclusion (e.g., using semaphores).

The proof of the algorithm is given in [17]. Correctness follows from the following invariants. Let p and q be two processes:

- If p terminates round r and q is correct, then q terminates round r.
- If p and q terminate round r, either $delivered_p^r$ is a prefix of $delivered_q^r$ or $delivered_q^r$ is a prefix of $delivered_p^r$.
- If p executes round r until the end, and q executes round $r + 1$ until the end, then $delivered_p^r$ is a prefix of $delivered_q^{r+1}$.

Example. Figure 3 shows an execution of Algorithm 3. Processes p_1 and p_3 broadcast m and m', respectively, by appending them to their *estimate* sequence. All processes W-ABroadcast their sequences in the first stage, and p_3 crashes at the beginning of the second stage; nevertheless p_1, p_2 and p_4 W-ADeliver first

---

Algorithm 3 Atomic Broadcast with the WAB oracle ($f < n/3$)—version 1

1: *Initialization*

2:   $r_p \leftarrow 1$
3:   $estimate_p \leftarrow \epsilon$
4:   $delivered_p \leftarrow \epsilon$

5: *To execute* A-broadcast(m):   {*Task 1*}

6:   $estimate_p \leftarrow estimate_p \oplus \langle m \rangle$

7: A-deliver($-$) *occurs as follows:*   {*Task 2*}

8:   **while** *true* **do**
9:     W-ABroadcast($r_p, estimate_p$)
10:    **wait until** W-ADeliver of the first message (r_p, v)
11:    $estimate_p \leftarrow v \oplus estimate_p$

12:    send (FIRST, $r_p, estimate_p$) to all
13:    **wait until** received (FIRST, r_p, v) from $n - f$ processes
14:    $majSeq \leftarrow$ the longest sequence $\otimes_{\{\text{majority of (FIRST}, r_p, v) \text{ received}\}} v$
15:    $estimate_p \leftarrow majSeq \oplus estimate_p$

16:    $allSeq \leftarrow \otimes_{\{\text{all (FIRST}, r_p, v) \text{ received}\}} v$
17:    **for each** $m \in (allSeq \setminus delivered_p)$ **do**
18:      A-deliver m
19:    $delivered_p \leftarrow allSeq$

20:    $r_p \leftarrow r_p + 1$

21: **when** W-ADeliver($-, v$) the second and next messages of any round   {*Task 3*}
22:    $estimate_p \leftarrow estimate_p \oplus v$

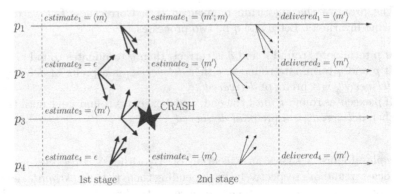

Fig. 3. Execution of the atomic broadcast algorithm

the sequence $\langle m' \rangle$. The estimate of p_1 becomes $\langle m'; m \rangle$, and the estimates of p_2 and p_4 become $\langle m' \rangle$. In the second stage p_1, p_2, and p_4 exchange their estimates. Since all their sequences have m' as a common prefix, they A-deliver m'. In the next round (not shown in the figure), p_1 will W-ABroadcast m again.

4.4   From WAB Oracles to Atomic Broadcast: Version 2

Algorithm 3 has two shortcomings. First, the $estimate_p$ sequence used by processes to store broadcast messages keeps growing: messages are never garbage collected. Second, processes never stop executing the *while loop* (lines 8–20) and, consequently, continue the execution even after all messages A-Broadcast have been A-delivered. To avoid wasting resources, processes should stop executing the *while loop* after all previously A-Broadcast messages have been A-delivered.

The two problems can be solved with small modifications to Algorithm 3. Algorithm 4 is similar to Algorithm 3, but for the underlined lines (14, 16, 19, 21, 23, and 24). To remove messages from $estimate_p$, Algorithm 4 takes advantage of the following property of Algorithm 3: if the first process to A-deliver m does so at round r, then every process that terminates round $r+1$ also A-delivers m. So, at the end of round r, the messages A-delivered in rounds $r' \leq r - 1$ can be discarded from $estimate_p$.

To address the second shortcoming of Algorithm 3, whenever $estimate_p$ is empty at the end of some round r_p at p, process p stops executing the *while* loop (line 8) and waits until either (a) it W-ADelivers some message for the next round (line 24), or (b) some message is included in $estimate_p$ — which may happen if p itself broadcasts a message (line 6) or if p W-ADelivers at line 25 the second or next message of any round. Notice that if p exits the *wait* statement at line 24 by W-ADelivering the first message of round r_p, then p does not wait at line 10, since it has already W-ADelivered the first message of round r_p.

Algorithm 4 Atomic Broadcast with the WAB oracle $(f < n/3)$—version 2

1: *Initialization*

2:   $r_p \leftarrow 1$
3:   $estimate_p \leftarrow \epsilon$
4:   $delivered_p \leftarrow \epsilon$

5: *To execute* A-broadcast(m):   {*Task 1*}

6:   $estimate_p \leftarrow estimate_p \oplus \langle m \rangle$

7: A-deliver$(-)$ *occurs as follows*:   {*Task 2*}

8:   **while** *true* **do**
9:       W-ABroadcast$(r_p, estimate_p)$
10:      **wait until** W-ADeliver of the first message (r_p, v)
11:      $estimate_p \leftarrow v \oplus estimate_p$

12:      send (FIRST, r_p, $estimate_p$) to all
13:      **wait until** received (FIRST, r_p, v) from $n - f$ processes
14:      $majSeq \leftarrow$ the longest sequence $\otimes_{\{\text{majority of (FIRST},r_p,v) \text{ received}\}} \overline{delivered_p \oplus v}$
15:      $estimate_p \leftarrow majSeq \oplus estimate_p$

16:      $allSeq \leftarrow \otimes_{\{\text{all (FIRST},r_p,v) \text{ received}\}} \overline{delivered_p \oplus v}$
17:      **for each** $m \in (allSeq \setminus delivered_p)$ **do**
18:          A-deliver m
19:          $m.round \leftarrow r_p$
20:      $delivered_p \leftarrow allSeq$
21:      $estimate_p \leftarrow estimate_p \setminus \{m \mid m \in delivered_p \text{ and } m.round < r_p\}$

22:      $r_p \leftarrow r_p + 1$

23:      **if** $estimate_p = \epsilon$ **then**
24:          **wait until** W-ADeliver of the first message (r_p, v) **or** $estimate_p \neq \epsilon$

25: **when** W-ADeliver$(-, v)$ the second and next messages of any round   {*Task 3*}
26:      $estimate_p \leftarrow estimate_p \oplus v$

4.5   Time Complexity *vs.* Resilience

If we define time complexity as in Section 3.4, we get the following result. In good runs, our atomic broadcast algorithms deliver messages within 2δ and require $f < n/3$. This result is for an atomic broadcast algorithm inspired by Rabin's algorithm. Similarly, we could have derived an atomic broadcast algorithm from Ben-Or's algorithm, which would have led to a time complexity of 3δ and $f < n/2$. So we have the same "time complexity *vs.* resilience" trade-off as for consensus (Section 3.4).

5   Performance Evaluation

5.1   The Experiments

In order to evaluate our approach, we implemented version 2 of the atomic broadcast algorithm, and compared its performance to a Crash-Detection Based (CDB) algorithm. We chose the atomic broadcast algorithm proposed by Chandra and Toueg [6], along with the $\diamond \mathcal{S}$ consensus algorithm [6]. In the rest of this section, we refer to these algorithms as WABCast and CT-ABCast.

We chose to compare WABCast to CT-ABCast because (a) both algorithms are proved correct in the asynchronous model augmented with some additional assumptions: the WAB oracle (for WABCast) and a $\diamond \mathcal{S}$ failure detector (for CT-ABCast), and (b) in both algorithms, each process proceeds in a sequence of asynchronous rounds (not all processes necessarily execute the same round at a given time). The algorithms differ with respect to the number of crashes they tolerate: WABCast tolerates $f < n/3$ crashes and CT-ABCast $f < n/2$ crashes. In the experiments, we executed the two algorithms with the minimal number of processes that could tolerate one crash, i.e., WABCast with $n = 4$ was compared to CT-ABCast with $n = 3$.

Processes communicate using TCP/IP connections. The WAB oracle is implemented as follows: W-ABroadcast(r, m) results in a UDP/IP multicast of (r, m) to all participants of the algorithm, and the receipt of (r, m) corresponds to W-ADeliver(r, m). In a local area network, UDP/IP multicast datagrams are very much likely to arrive in the same order (see Section 2.3). Notice that WAB-Cast only uses the first W-ADeliver event of a given round r, and works even if the other W-ADeliver events of round r do not occur (message loss).[6]

In the experiment, messages are around 100 bytes. We define the *latency* of an atomic broadcast algorithm as the time between the A-Broadcast(m) event and the first A-Deliver(m) event (these events do not necessarily occur on the same process). In each of our test runs, messages are A-Broadcast by all n processes. The A-Broadcast events follow a Poisson arrival distribution with the same fixed rate on each process. We call the overall rate of A-Broadcast events "throughput". Throughput, given in s^{-1}, is also the average number of messages A-Delivered in a time unit. We ran a lot of test runs with different throughput values, and determined the mean latency in each test run. Our results are plots representing the mean latency (and its 95% confidence interval) as a function of throughput.

The experiments were run on a cluster of 12 PCs running Red Hat Linux 7.2 (kernel 2.4.9). The hosts have Intel Pentium III 766 MHz processors with 128 MB of RAM. They are interconnected by a simplex 100 Base-TX Ethernet hub. The algorithms were implemented in Java (Sun's JDK 1.4.0 beta 2) on top of the Neko development framework [20]. In our environment, we could synchronize the clocks of processes up to a precision of $50 \, \mu s$. This enabled us to determine the latency of the algorithms ($\gg 50 \, \mu s$) rather precisely.

---

[6] The algorithm does not need that these messages are reliably transmitted (Validity property of the WAB oracle, Section 2) because of line 12 of the algorithm.

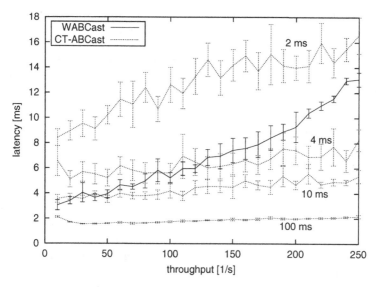

Fig. 4. WABCast vs. CT-ABCast. CT-ABCast was run with a variety of failure detection timeouts.

5.2   Results

Figure 4 depicts the results obtained. CT-ABCast was run with a variety of settings for failure detection: we used timeouts of 2, 4, 10 and 100 ms, respectively, to detect crashes. One can see that WABCast has a higher latency than CT-ABCast at high failure detection timeouts. However, note that this corresponds to "optimal" conditions for CT-ABCast: a case where failure detectors never make mistakes. Moreover, the big advantage of WABCast over CT-ABCast is that the latency of the algorithm does not increase in case of a crash — which is not the case with CT-ABCast: with a timeout of 100 ms, it is possible that the algorithm is blocked for 100 ms after a crash. To achieve similar performances in the case of a crash, CT-ABCast requires an extremely aggressive failure detection mechanism (timeouts of 2 and 4 milliseconds and *"I am alive"* messages sent every few milliseconds). As the two latency curves on the top show, such a failure detection mechanism significantly slows down the CT-ABCAST algorithm in the absence of failures, because (1) failure detection messages load the CPUs and the network, and (2) failure detectors often wrongly suspect correct processes, which increases the cost of the consensus algorithm that is part of CT-ABCAST. With such an aggressive failure detection mechanism, WABCast performs better (except at low throughputs when compared with CT-ABCast with a timeout of 4 ms).

The figure also shows that at high throughputs, the latency of WABCast increases faster than the latency of CT-ABCast as throughput increases. This is because the spontaneous ordering property, on which the oracle of WABCast is based, starts breaking down due to the high number of messages per time unit. The spontaneous total order property breaks down totally at around 400 requests/s, as predicted by Figure 1 (a request generates approximately 16 messages altogether, i.e., approximately 0.15 ms elapse between two messages).

We believe that the performances of the WABCast algorithm may further be improved, e.g., by using UDP/IP multicast for the *send to all* of line 12 in Algorithm 4.

6   Conclusion

From a practical viewpoint, algorithms based on weak ordering oracles do not have to deal with the tradeoffs involved in tuning timeouts. This is a quite interesting characteristic. With CDB algorithms, in order to decide on timeout values, one is faced with the following dilemma: short fail-over time requires short timeouts; to prevent false failure suspicions, timeouts should be long. The "ideal" timeout value is somewhere between the two extremes, and the problem is not only finding it, but also constantly re-adapting to the environment changes that make this ideal value sway back and forth.

From a theoretical point of view, our algorithms derived from Rabin's algorithm have in good runs a time complexity of 2δ and require $f < n/3$, while the corresponding algorithms derived from Ben-Or's algorithm have in good runs a time complexity of 3δ and require $f < n/2$. It would be interesting to understand this trade-off from a more general perspective.

Finally, we are currently extending the atomic broadcast algorithm to efficiently solve generic broadcast [16] using weak ordering oracles.

Acknowledgments

We thank Bernadette Charron-Bost for early discussions about randomized consensus algorithms and ordering oracles, and Matthias Wiesmann for providing us with Figure 1.

References

[1] M. K. Aguilera, W. Chen, and S. Toueg. Using the heartbeat failure detector for quiescent reliable communication and consensus in partitionable networks. *Theoretical Computer Science*, 220(1):3–30, June 1999. 44

[2] M. K. Aguilera, C. Delporte-Gallet, H. Fauconnier, and S. Toueg. Thrifty generic broadcast. In *Proceedings of the 14th International Symposium on Distributed Computing (DISC'2000)*, October 2000. 46, 52

[3] E. Anceaume. A Lightweight Solution to Uniform Atomic Broadcast for Asynchronous Systems. In *IEEE 27th Int Symp on Fault-Tolerant Computing (FTCS-27)*, pages 292–301, June 1997. 53

[4] H. Attiya and J. Welch. *Distributed Computing*. Mc Graw Hill, 1998. 44

[5] M. Ben-Or. Another advantage of free choice: completely asynchronous agreement protocols. In *proc. 2nd annual ACM Symposium on Principles of Distributed Computing*, pages 27–30, 1983. 44, 45, 46, 49

[6] T. D. Chandra and S. Toueg. Unreliable failure detectors for reliable distributed systems. *Journal of ACM*, 43(2):225–267, 1996. 44, 46, 49, 53, 58

[7] F. Cristian and C. Fetzer. The timed asynchronous distributed system model. *IEEE Transactions on Parallel & Distributed Systems*, 10(6):642–657, June 1999. 44

[8] D.Dolev, C. Dwork, and L. Stockmeyer. On the minimal synchrony needed for distributed consensus. *Journal of ACM*, 34(1):77–97, January 1987. 44

[9] C. Dwork, N. Lynch, and L. Stockmeyer. Consensus in the presence of partial synchrony. *Journal of ACM*, 35(2):288–323, April 1988. 44

[10] M. Fischer, N. Lynch, and M. Paterson. Impossibility of Distributed Consensus with One Faulty Process. *Journal of ACM*, 32:374–382, April 1985. 45

[11] R. Guerraoui and A. Schiper. Consensus: the Big Misunderstanding. In *IEEE Proc of the Sixth Workshop on Future Trends of Distributed Computing Systems*, pages 183–188, October 1997. 45

[12] V. Hadzilacos and S. Toueg. Fault-Tolerant Broadcasts and Related Problems. Technical Report 94-1425, Department of Computer Science, Cornell University, May 1994. 44

[13] N. A. Lynch. *Distributed Algorithms*. Morgan Kaufmann, 1996. 44

[14] A. Mostefaoui and M. Raynal. Solving Consensus using Chandra-Toueg's Unreliable Failure Detectors: A Synthetic Approach. In *13th. Intl. Symposium on Distributed Computing (DISC'99)*. Springer Verlag, LNCS 1693, September 1999. 53

[15] A. Mostefaoui and M. Raynal. Leader-based consensus. *Parallel Processing Letters*, 11:95–107, 2001. 46

[16] F. Pedone and A. Schiper. Generic Broadcast. In *13th. Intl. Symposium on Distributed Computing (DISC'99)*, pages 94–108. Springer Verlag, LNCS 1693, September 1999. 60

[17] F. Pedone, A. Schiper, P. Urban, and D. Cavin. Solving Agreement Problems with Weak Ordering Oracles. TR IC/2002/010, EPFL, March 2002. Appears also as Technical Report HPL-2002-44, Hewlett-Packard Laboratories, March 2002. 49, 50, 52, 55

[18] M. Rabin. Randomized Byzantine Generals. In *Proc. 24th Annual ACM Symposium on Foundations of Computer Science*, pages 403–409, 1983. 44, 45, 46, 49

[19] A. Schiper. Early consensus in an asynchronous system with a weak failure detector. *Distributed Computing*, 10(3):149–157, April 1997. 53

[20] Péter Urbán, Xavier Défago, and André Schiper. Neko: A single environment to simulate and prototype distributed algorithms. In *Proc. of the 15th Int'l Conf. on Information Networking (ICOIN-15)*, Beppu City, Japan, February 2001. 58

An Efficient Solution
to the k-Set Agreement Problem*

Emmanuelle Anceaume, Michel Hurfin, and Philippe Raipin Parvedy

IRISA, Campus de Beaulieu, 35042 Rennes Cedex, France
{anceaume,hurfin,praipinp}@irisa.fr

Abstract. In this paper, we present a $\diamond S_x$-based solution to solve the k-Set agreement problem for $f < \frac{n+k-1}{2}$ where f is the maximum number of crashes that can occur and n is the total number of processes. Just as the k-Set agreement problem is a generalization of the consensus problem (at most k different values can be decided), the class of $\diamond S_x$ failure detectors is a generalization of $\diamond S$ failure detectors, where x, the scope of the accuracy property, is the number of processes that do not have to suspect a correct process. We propose a simple protocol based on the following idea: $k - 1$ "privileged" processes directly decide their initial value, while the others ($n - k + 1$ processes) run a 1-Set agreement protocol (i.e., a consensus protocol) to decide on one value. This simple idea enables to tolerate up to $(n + k - 1)/2$ crash failures, and may lead the k-set agreement problem to be solved in only one broadcast. The protocol is decomposed into three modules. Each process executes either 1, 2 or 3 modules. To reduce the scope of accuracy, more processes have to execute the three modules. But, in that case, more messages have to be exchanged. Finally, the proposed solution considers the degree of repetition of the proposed values and takes advantage of a possible high degree of redundancy of one of them.

1 Introduction

In a distributed system, many problems require an agreement on some values among all the processes whenever these processes have to share a view of the computation progress. Atomic commitment, atomic broadcast, and membership are among the most significant agreement problems a designer of distributed applications may have to cope with. All these agreement problems can be reduce to the same basic problem, namely the consensus problem. In this problem, processes propose a value and must unanimously and irrevocably decide on some value that is related to the proposed values. Unfortunately, Fisher, Lynch, and Paterson [8] demonstrated that, whenever the distributed system is both *asynchronous* and prone to *crash failures*, there is no deterministic solution to the consensus problem. Therefore, no agreement problem can be solved in such

---

* This work was supported by the French Ministry of Research - Project GénoGRID
  of the program ACI "Globalization of computer resources and data"

a model. For this reason and for its simplicity, the consensus problem has been the focus of many research works [4, 6, 7, 10, 11, 17].

To circumvent this impossibility result, several approaches have been proposed, and among them, one consists in strengthening the properties characterizing the distributed system. In a seminal paper [4], Chandra and Toueg propose the concept of unreliable failure detectors. An unreliable failure detector is a distributed "oracle" giving (possibly incorrect) hints about which processes may have crashed so far. In an asynchronous system, a failure detector can make mistakes by not suspecting a crashed process, or by erroneously adding a correct process to its list of suspects.

In this paper we focus on a particular class of failure detectors known as $\Diamond \mathcal{S}$ failure detectors, which has been proved to be the weakest class of failure detectors that allows to solve consensus [5]. This class is characterized by the following two properties: (1) *strong completeness*: eventually every process that crashes is permanently suspected by every correct process, and (2) *eventual weak accuracy*: eventually some correct process is never suspected by any correct process. Based on such unreliable failure detectors, several deterministic solutions to the consensus problem have been proposed [4, 11, 17].

From a theoretical point of view, it is impossible to implement $\Diamond \mathcal{S}$ failure detectors in an asynchronous distributed system. Yet, their properties can be approximated by tuning, for example, timeout parameters to the best estimate values [4]. In the worse case, protocols based on $\Diamond \mathcal{S}$ failure detectors may sacrifice their liveness property however they never violate their safety properties. Therefore, the weakest class of failure detectors deserves a lot of attention even if its use imposes an additional requirement regarding the maximal number of tolerated crashes: a majority of processes must be correct. In other words, the maximal number of tolerated crash failures f is such that $f < \frac{n}{2}$, with n the number of processes.

The k-Set agreement problem is a slight and interesting generalization of the consensus problem, that has been introduced by S. Chaudhuri [3]. Similarly to the consensus problem, all the non-crashed processes propose an initial value and execute an agreement protocol to converge to a decision value which is permanently adopted by a non-crashed process when it stops the execution of the protocol. To be valid, a decision value has to be one of the proposed values. The agreement property which characterizes the k-Set agreement problem is more general than the one used in the basic consensus problem. This property states that the number of different decision values is bounded by k. Thus, when the value of k is equal to 1, the decision has to be unanimous. On the contrary, when the value of k is greater, some processes may decide different values, but it is impossible to observe $k + 1$ different processes with pairwise different decision values. Whereas the consensus problem has no deterministic solution as soon as at least one process may crash, the k-Set agreement problem is impossible to solve whenever $k \leq f$ [2, 12]. It has however simple solutions when $k > f$ [3].

Just as k-Set agreement generalizes consensus, a class of weaker failure detectors that generalizes $\Diamond \mathcal{S}$ has been proposed by Yang et al [18] and investigated by Mostefaoui and Raynal [15]. This class of failure detectors is characterized by an accuracy property with a limited scope: the number of processes that have not to suspect a correct process is limited to x $(1 \leq x \leq n)$ [15]. This class is denoted $\Diamond \mathcal{S}_x$, where x is the scope of the accuracy. Note that $\Diamond \mathcal{S}_n$ corresponds to $\Diamond \mathcal{S}$. Investigation of the k-Set agreement problem with unreliable failure detectors with limited scope of accuracy $\Diamond \mathcal{S}_x$ has been first done by Yang et al. [18]. They proved that there is no solution to k-Set agreement with $\Diamond \mathcal{S}_x$ with $x = k$ if $kn \leq (k+1)f$. In the Conclusion Section of [15], Mostefaoui and Raynal conjecture that there is no solution if $f \geq min(n - k\lfloor n/(k+1)\rfloor, k + x - 1)$.

This Paper

In this paper, we propose a $\Diamond \mathcal{S}_x$-based solution to solve the k-Set agreement problem. Outlines of the protocol are as follows. The set of the n processes involved in the k-Set agreement protocol is split into two subsets denoted $\mathcal{P}$ and $\mathcal{U}$. The subset $\mathcal{P}$ contains $k - 1$ pre-determined processes while the subset $\mathcal{U}$ contains $n - k + 1$ other processes. Each process in $\mathcal{P}$ adopts its initial value as a decision value, and broadcasts it to all the processes $p \in \mathcal{U}$. Upon receipt of one of these values, p adopts it and terminates. Clearly, as each process in $\mathcal{P}$ can safely broadcast a decision value without any prior agreement with other processes, one solves the k-Set agreement problem in an absolute minimum amount of time as soon as at least one of the $k-1$ processes of $\mathcal{P}$ has not crashed. Satisfying such a condition seems to be not excessive since in practice, few crashes occur.

Yet, as $f > k - 1$, the processes in $\mathcal{U}$ have to execute in parallel a consensus protocol to get round the possible (premature) crashes of all the processes in $\mathcal{P}$. This execution will possibly generate an additional decision value which is the result of an agreement between the $n - k + 1$ processes. In any cases, at most k decision values are generated by the n processes. The only liveness requirement imposed on the round-based consensus protocol is to terminate when all the processes in $\mathcal{P}$ have prematurely crashed without being able to broadcast their decision values. By weakening the termination property of this protocol, the global resiliency of k-set agreement protocols can easily be increased. We show that the number of tolerated failures f can reach the bound $\frac{n+k-1}{2}$.

Any $\Diamond \mathcal{S}$-based consensus protocol already published in the literature can be chosen to be executed by the processes of $\mathcal{U}$. Within this paper, we propose a modular solution that allows to adapt the number of executed modules to the value of f (and also to the value of x). Specifically, the proposed round-based consensus protocol is structured into three modules called respectively the k-Set agreement module, the source module and the mirror module. Briefly, the k-Set agreement module (where the activity of the processes belonging to $\mathcal{P}$ is distinguished from the activity of processes belonging to $\mathcal{U}$) achieves a reliable broadcast of the decision value. The source module looks like the role acted by the coordinator in a rotating coordinator-based protocol (See for example the one proposed in [4]), whereas the mirror module resembles to the one of a non-coordinator in a rotating coordinator-based protocol. While the first module has to be run by all the processes, a source module is only executed by the processes of $\mathcal{U}$ and the mirror module can be run by any subset of at least $2(f - k + 1) + 1$ processes of $\mathcal{U}$. The number of mirror modules can be tune up to $n - k + 1$. As the number of messages exchanged during a round depends on the number of processes involved in the mirror module execution, decreasing the number of mirrors diminishes the number of exchanged messages and thus improves the message complexity of the algorithm. However, we show in Section 4 that conversely, an increase in the number of mirrors allows to reduce the scope of accuracy x of $\Diamond \mathcal{S}_x$ to $f + 1$, and thus to lower the required quality of the failure detectors.

Additionally, the proposed protocol follows a condition based approach [16] and thus is able to take advantage of a possible redundancy between the proposed values. In particular when processes p_1, p_2, ..., p_{f-k+2} propose the same initial value, the protocol converges quickly to a decision value.

Contributions of this Paper

- We design a very simple and efficient solution to k-Set agreement. In most of the cases, the protocol terminates in an absolute minimum amount of time, namely, the time needed to reliably broadcast a value.
- Second, we sensibly increase the resiliency of previous published solutions. Our solution tolerates up to $f < \frac{n+k-1}{2}$ crash failures. This new upper bound improves the bound proposed by Mostefaoui and Raynal [15] saying that there is no solution to the $\Diamond \mathcal{S}_x$-based k-Set agreement if $f \geq min(n - k\lfloor n/(k+1)\rfloor, k + x - 1)$.
- Third, we show that by splitting a consensus protocol into several modules, one can adjust the number of executed modules to the values f and x. The less the modules you need, the less the number of messages that will be exchanged.
- Finally, we take advantage of the redundancy among the proposed values. Specifically, we show that a simple broadcast of the initial values allows to reduce the number of different proposed values down to $f - k + 2$. A condition-based approach [16] allows to converge quicker to a decision value when the redundancy level is high. This optimization is dynamically and tightly coupled with the traditional timestamp mechanism proposed by Chandra and Toueg to ensure agreement [4].

This paper is organized as follows. Section 2 introduces the computational model, Chandra and Toueg's failure detectors, limited accuracy failure detectors, and the k-Set agreement problem. Section 3 presents our solution to the k-Set agreement problem based on $\Diamond \mathcal{S}_x$. Section 4 exhibits the tradeoff between the number of mirrors and the scope of accuracy x of $\Diamond \mathcal{S}_x$. Section 5 shows the link between a limited scope of accuracy and a reduced number of failure detectors. Finally, Section 6 concludes the paper. Proofs of correctness of the solution can be found in a technical report [1].

2 Asynchronous Distributed Systems and Failure Detectors

The asynchronous model follows the one proposed in [8] and [4].

2.1 The Computation Model

We consider asynchronous distributed systems in which there is no bound on message delay, clock drift, or the time required to execute a step. The system consists of a set of n processes. Every pair of processes is connected by a reliable communication channel, i.e., a channel that does not loose, corrupt, or duplicate messages. Processes are subject to crash failures [13]. If a process ever crashes, we say that it is *faulty*, otherwise it is *correct*.

2.2 Chandra-Toueg's Unreliable Failure Detectors

Chandra and Toueg have defined two types of properties to completely characterize their failure detectors, namely a *completeness property* and an *accuracy property*. A completeness property forces the detection of incorrect processes while an accuracy property restricts the mistakes made with regard to correct processes. In this paper we consider the strong completeness property and the eventual weak accuracy property [4]:

Strong completeness Eventually, every process that crashes is permanently suspected by every correct process.

Eventual weak accuracy There is a time after which some correct process is never suspected by any process.

These properties define the class of *Eventually Strong* failure detectors, also called $\Diamond S$ failure detectors. $\Diamond S$ is the weakest class of failure detectors that allows to solve consensus [5].

2.3 Unreliable Failure Detectors with Limited Scope Accuracy

As noted in the Introduction, a class of weaker failure detectors that generalize $\Diamond S$ (and also S) have been proposed by Yang et al [18] and investigated by Mostefaoui and Raynal [15]. These classes of failure detectors are characterized by an accuracy property with a limited scope: the number of processes that have not to suspect a correct process is limited to x ($x \leq n$). By definition [15], the x-accuracy property is satisfied if there is a set Q of processes such that:

- $|Q| = x$
- There is a correct process $p \in Q$ such that no process $q \in Q$ suspects p.

In this paper we are interested in the eventual x-accuracy property. This property is satisfied if the x-accuracy is satisfied after some finite time. This leads to the class $\Diamond S_x$ which contains all the failure detectors that satisfy the strong completeness and the eventual x-accuracy property. Obviously, when x is equal to n, the class $\Diamond S_n$ corresponds to the class $\Diamond S$ defined in [4].

2.4   The k-Set Agreement Problem

The k-Set Agreement problem has been introduced by Chaudhuri [3]. It is defined by the following three properties:

Termination Every correct process eventually decides on some value
Validity If a process decides v, then v was proposed by some process
Agreement At most k different values are decided by processes

Recall that by taking $k = 1$, we obtain the specification of the consensus problem. As indicated in the Introduction, the k-Set agreement problem is impossible to solve whenever $k \leq f$ [2, 12]. Investigation of the k-Set agreement problem with unreliable failure detector with limited scope of accuracy $\Diamond \mathcal{S}_x$ has been first done by Yang et al. [18]. They proved that there is no solution to k-Set agreement with $\Diamond \mathcal{S}_x$ with $x = k$ if $kn \leq (k + 1)f$. Mostefaoui and Raynal [15] propose a family of protocols that solves the K-set agreement with $\Diamond \mathcal{S}_x$ only when $f \geq min(n - k \lfloor n/(k + 1) \rfloor, k + x - 1)$.

2.5   Practical Interest of the k-Set Agreement Problem

A project called ACI-GénoGRID which is supported by the French Research Ministry aims to provide tools for promoting the use of GRID Computing by a community of biologists. One of the problem addressed within this project concerns the definition of dynamic load balancing strategies. In the proposed solution, tasks are allocated using an agreement protocol that aims to ensure that all the research centers that allow access to their resources share a common view of an efficient allocation of the tasks. Unanimous decisions on the schedule of the computations are preferable. But it is not a strong requirement. If k different decisions are observed within the grid, the consequence is not catastrophic. In the worse case, a same task will be executed by different resources rather than by a single one. Obviously, this waste of time (which occur only from time to time) is a minor drawback compared to the advantages offered by such an approach. We are currently investigating the advantages of using a 2-set agreement protocol (similar to the one proposed within this paper). This approach seems to be a good solution to circumvent partially the lack of scalability of the classical consensus protocols and to obtain predictable response time. Moreover, the definition of $k - 1$ privileged and static processes is a good way to cope with the mobility of many other processes. Privileged processes do not have to know precisely the current composition of the group. They have just to compute locally a valid decision value and to provide it to any process which is temporally a member of the group.

3   An Efficient Solution to k-Set Agreement with $\Diamond \mathcal{S}_x$

This section addresses the k-Set agreement problem assuming that processes are equipped with $\Diamond \mathcal{S}_x$ failure detectors. We present a solution to this problem and then prove its correctness. This solution assumes that $f \geq k$ (indeed, solutions when $f < k$ are easy in an asynchronous system without any additional assumptions [3]).

The protocol we propose is inspired by the solution proposed by Chaudhuri [3] to solve the problem when $f < k$. Briefly, in this solution $f + 1$ predetermined processes (for example, $p_{n-f}, p_{n-f+1}, \cdots, p_n$) broadcast their initial value to the other processes. The other processes wait until they receive one of these values. Any transmitted value is a valid decision value which can be adopted by the processes without violating the agreement property. Using $f + 1$ sources ensures that at least one correct process broadcasts its initial value.

Similarly to this solution, we identify a subset $\mathcal{P}$ of processes, with $|\mathcal{P}| = k-1$. A second subset $\mathcal{U}$ contains the remaining $n-k+1$ processes. Any decomposition that satisfies the above conditions for $\mathcal{P}$ and $\mathcal{U}$ is valid. In this paper, n_k denotes the value $n - k + 1$ (i.e the cardinality of $\mathcal{U}$) and we consider that $\mathcal{P} = \{p_i \mid n_k < i \leq n\}$ while $\mathcal{U} = \{p_i \mid 1 \leq i \leq n_k\}$. All the processes execute the k-Set agreement module depicted in Figure 1. Processes of $\mathcal{P}$ execute lines 3 to 5 of this module whereas processes of $\mathcal{U}$ execute the code within the else clause (lines 7 to 12).

As in the Chaudhuri's algorithm, the processes belonging to $\mathcal{P}$ directly adopt their initial value as a decision value, and broadcast this decision to all the processes of $\mathcal{U}$ (See lines 3, 4 and 5 in Figure 1). Upon receipt of one of these values, the wait condition expires (See line 9 in Figure 1). Then, a process of $\mathcal{U}$ performs a reliable broadcast of the decision value (See lines 10 and 11 in Figure 1) and terminates its execution. Clearly, if among the $k - 1$ processes of $\mathcal{P}$, at least one is correct, then all the correct processes eventually decide and terminate in an absolute minimum amount of time. On the other hand, and contrary to the solution of Chaudhuri, f is supposed to be greater than k or equal to k. Thus in case all the processes in $\mathcal{P}$ crash, the remaining n_k processes cannot decide. To guarantee that all the correct processes decide, we propose to involve the processes of $\mathcal{U}$ into a consensus protocol. For this reason, processes of $\mathcal{U}$ start the execution of either one or two additional modules (See lines 7 and 8 in Figure 1). When all the processes of $\mathcal{P}$ are crashed, at most $f_k = f - k + 1$ processes of $\mathcal{U}$ may crash. The consensus protocol executed by the processes in $\mathcal{U}$ has to terminate only if all the processes in $\mathcal{P}$ have crashed. Indeed, by construction of the protocol, if some of the $k - 1$ privileged processes belonging to $\mathcal{P}$ have not crashed then they eventually succeed in broadcasting a decision message. Therefore, in the design of the consensus protocol, we assume that among the n_k processes in $\mathcal{U}$, at most f_k may crash (all the processes in $\mathcal{P}$ are supposed to be faulty).

The solution we propose to solve the consensus is based on the protocol of Chandra and Toueg [4], and thus relies on the rotating coordinator paradigm [4, 7]. Specifically, it proceeds in asynchronous rounds, each round being coordinated by a particular process, the *coordinator*. This process tries to imposes its values to all the processes involved in the consensus. In the proposed solution, the protocol is structured into two additional modules called respectively the source

Module k-set-agreement$_i$ (executed by p_i such that $1 \leq i \leq n$)
(1)   **if** $(i > n_k)$
(2)   **then**   % $p_i \in \mathcal{P}$
(3)   **for all** u **such that** $(1 \leq u \leq n_k)$ **do**
(4)   send decide(v_i) to the k-set-agreement module of p_u **endo**;
(5)   return(v_i);
(6)   **else**   % $p_i \in \mathcal{U}$
(7)   start module source$_i$(v_i);
(8)   **if** $(i \leq m)$ **then** start module mirror$_i$() **endif**;
(9)   **wait until** a message decide(est) sent by p_j is available;
(10)   **for all** u **such that** $((u \neq i) \wedge (u \neq j) \wedge (1 \leq u \leq n_k))$ **do**
(11)   send decide(est) to the k-set-agreement module of p_u **endo**;
(12)   return(est);
(13) **endif**;

Fig. 1. k-Set agreement module run by p_i

module (see Figure 2), and the mirror module (see Figure 3). Notations s_i and m_i refer to process p_i when executing respectively the source module or the mirror module. As indicated previously, the k-Set agreement module is executed by all the processes (all the processes have to decide). The source module is executed by exactly n_k processes while the mirror module is executed by only m processes with $2f_k + 1 \leq m \leq n_k$. We will see later that the range of possible values for m meets a tradeoff between the scope of accuracy x of $\diamond\mathcal{S}_x$ and the number of messages exchanged during the protocol. On the other hand, the number of sources needs to be equal to n_k to benefit from the accuracy property. In the following, the correct process whose existence is assumed in the accuracy property is denoted p_α. If we consider that p_α is the only correct process of Q such that no process $p \in Q$ suspects p_α, we have to ensure that either p_α belongs to $\mathcal{P}$, or p_α belongs to $\mathcal{U}$ and acts as a source s_α. Therefore the number of sources is fixed and equal to n_k. Of course, if a strongest accuracy property was adopted, namely the *eventual strong accuracy property* which assumes that eventually no correct process is suspected, the number of sources can be reduced down to f_k+1. This possibility is not considered within this paper.

For clarity reasons, the two last modules are first described by assuming that the scope of accuracy x of $\diamond\mathcal{S}_x$ is equal to n, that is, we assume $\diamond\mathcal{S}$. We then augment these modules with the portion of code that transforms the scope of accuracy $x = n$ to $x > f$. Actually, only the mirror module is affected by this transformation.

3.1   Overview of the Chandra Toueg's Protocol

As indicated previously, sources and mirrors implement a consensus protocol which has strong similarities with the protocol proposed by Chandra and Toueg in [4]. Let us denote this protocol by CT. To explain the proposed protocol, we first outline the behavior of the CT protocol.

Like CT, the proposed protocol is based on the rotating coordinator paradigm. Processes proceed in asynchronous rounds, each round being coordinated by a predetermined process, namely the round r is coordinated by the process p_i such that $i = ((r-1) \mod n_k) + 1)$. During a round, the associated coordinator tries to impose a value as the decision value. If the *eventual weak accuracy* property is satisfied, there will be a round during which the associated coordinator will not be erroneously suspected, and this coordinator will succeed in establishing a decision value. Let r be the current round, and p_c the coordinator of r. Each round can be divided into two phases.

In the first phase of round r, each process sends to the current coordinator its own estimation of the decision value. p_c gathers $\lceil \frac{n+1}{2} \rceil$ estimates timestamped with the round at which the processes adopted their estimate. Then p_c selects among these values the one with the greatest timestamp, and sends it to all the processes as a new proposition, say $estimate_{p_c}$.

In the second phase, each process waits for a new proposition from p_c or suspects it to have crashed. If a process receives a proposition from the coordinator, then it adopts it, updates the timestamp associated with its new estimation value by setting it to the current round number r and sends a positive acknowledgment message to p_c. Otherwise (the process suspects p_c), it sends a negative acknowledgment message to p_c. Finally, p_c waits for $\lceil \frac{n+1}{2} \rceil$ replies (positive or negative). If all replies are positive, then p_c reliably broadcasts a request to decide $estimate_{p_c}$.

Note that, at the beginning of both phases, a coordinator waits until it has gathered a majority of information from all the other processes.

3.2   Source Module

The behavior of the source module (see Figure 2) is close to the behavior of the coordinator described in CT with however some modifications that allow mainly to benefit from the redundancy of initial values. More precisely, the proposed protocol does not only take advantage of the redundancy among the proposed values, it also acts in favor of such a redundancy. Therefore, at the very beginning of the consensus (executed by n_k processes), the number of different initial values is reduced down to $f_k + 1$. To achieve this goal, $f_k + 1$ predetermined sources broadcast their initial values to all the mirrors (See line 1 in Figure 2). As all the mirrors wait first until they receive, and adopt, one of the $f_k + 1$ broadcasted values (See lines 1 and 2 in Figure 3), any value exchanged during the consensus between sources and mirrors is necessarily an initial value provided by a source s_i such that $i \leq f - k + 2$ [1]. If all the $k - 1$ privileged processes of $\mathcal{P}$ have crashed, at least one of these $f_k + 1$ predetermined sources is correct and thus is able to broadcast an initial value to the mirrors. Consequently, when all the processes of $\mathcal{P}$ are crashed, no process of $\mathcal{U}$ can remain block due to this additional exchange

---

[1] Note that by imposing these values to be broadcast by predetermined processes, i.e., $s_1, ..., s_{f-k+2}$, one reduces the uncertainty regarding the origin of the eventual decision value. This can be of interest for the upper-layer application.

of initial values. The number of different values ($f_k + 1 = f - k + 2$) depends on the difference between f and k. In particular, when $f = k$, the consensus to be solved boils down to a binary consensus. A condition-based approach [16] allows to converge quicker to a decision value when the redundancy level is high. In the proposed solution, this optimization is dynamically and tightly coupled with the traditional timestamp mechanism proposed by Chandra and Toueg to ensure agreement [4].

Let us now examine our solution in details. First $f_k + 1$ sources broadcast their initial values to the m mirrors (See the discussion above). Then each source enters a while loop (See lines 5-26 in Figure 2). This while loop iterates as long as the master k-Set Agreement module is running (*i.e.*, while no decision is known). It is assumed that all the processes have a priori knowledge that module s_i is coordinator of round i, $i + n_k$, $i + (2n_k)$, and so on. A source module executes only the rounds it has to coordonate. Therefore, the variable r_i managed by a source s_i is initialized to the value i (See line 4 in Figure 2) and increased by n_k every two iterations (See line 24 in Figure 2). For commodity reason, the coordinator of round r is called s_c, just to remind that coordinators run the code of the source module. Like in CT, each round is made of two phases. More precisely, each odd iteration of the source's while loop corresponds to the first phase of a new coordinated round while the following iteration corresponds to the second phase of this round.

In the first phase, s_c waits until it gathers $m - f_k$ estimates sent by the mirrors m_j (*i.e.*, receipt of $m - f_k$ REFLECT($r, 1, -, -$) messages, line 6 in Figure 2). Clearly, because more than f_k mirrors may have crashed, this waiting can be infinite. However, this happens only if some of the $k - 1$ privileged processes are correct. In that case, these (correct) privileged processes have already reliably broadcast their decision value to all the processes in $\mathcal{U}$. On the other hand, if all the $k-1$ privileged processes have crashed, then s_c is guaranteed to receive $m - f_k$ estimates from the mirrors, which ensures its progress within its round. So, upon receipt of such estimates, s_c chooses its new estimate as follows: it first selects the estimate with the highest timestamp. Let ts be this timestamp, and htv be this estimate value. Then it counts the number of times htv appears among the $m - f_k$ received estimates (let $\#htv$ be this number), as well as the number of times htv is timestamped with ts (let $\#ts$ be this number). Obviously, $\#ts \leq \#htv$. Then it selects the most frequent estimate among the $m - f_k$ received estimates. Let mfv be this estimate, and $\#mfv$ be its occurrence number. Of course, htv and mfv can correspond to the same value. In that case, $\#htv = \#mfv$.

In CT, a coordinator tries to decide only during phase2. In the proposed solution, a coordinator can execute the test not only during phase 2 but also during phase 1. The opportunity for a coordinator to decide in its first phase has been presented in [9] where the notions of decider and agreement keepers are used. Clearly, deciding at the very beginning of a round enables sometimes to get round the suspicion of the previous coordinator. If the previous coordinator was not able to decide during phase 2 of round $r - 1$, the new coordinator can execute during phase1 of round r, the same test on another subset of gathered

Module source$_i$ (executed by s_i such that $1 \leq i \leq n_k$)
% Let n_k and f_k be two integers defined as follows:
% $n_k = n - k + 1$ and $f_k = f - k + 1$
Local variables
   r_i % Next round during which the source will be active
   $phase_i$ % phase number equal to either 1 or 2
begin
(1)   **if** $(i \leq f_k + 1)$ **then**
(2)   send init(v_i, i) to all the mirrors
(3)   **endif**;
(4) $r_i \leftarrow i;\ phase_i \leftarrow 1;$
(5)   **while** $(true)$ **do**
(6)   **wait until** $m - f_k$ messages reflect$(r_i, phase_i, \_, \_)$ are available;
(7)   Select reflect$(r_i, phase_i, ts, htv)$ such that ts is the highest timestamp;
(8)   Select reflect$(r_i, phase_i, \_, mfv)$ such that mfv is the most frequent value;
(9)   Let $\#ts$ be the number of occurrence of reflect$(r_i, phase_i, ts, htv)$;
(10)   Let $\#htv$ be the number of occurrence of reflect$(r_i, phase_i, -, htv)$;
(11)   Let $\#mfv$ be the number of occurrence of reflect$(r_i, phase_i, -, mfv)$;
(12)   **if** $((ts = r_i + phase_i - 2) \wedge (\#ts > f_k) \wedge (\#htv \geq m - f_k))$ **then**
(13)   send decide(htv) to the k-set-agreement module of p_i;
(14)   **stop**
(15)   **endif**;
(16)   **if** $(phase_i = 1)$ **then**
(17)   **if** $(\#mfv - \#htv \geq f_k)$ **then**
(18)   send update$(\ r_i\ ,\ mfv\ )$ to all the Mirrors
(19)   **else**
(20)   send update$(\ r_i\ ,\ htv\ )$ to all the Mirrors
(21)   **endif**;
(22) $phase_i \leftarrow 2$
(23)   **else**
(24) $r_i \leftarrow r_i + n_k;\ phase_i \leftarrow 1$
(25)   **endif**;
(26) **endwhile**;
end

Fig. 2. Behavior of a Source Module

information. Whether it decides in phase 1 or phase 2, the decision value is the value htv whose associated timestamp ts is equal either to the previous round number (phase 1) or the current round number (phase 2) (See the first part of the test at line 12 in Figure 2). To decide, this value must have been adopted by at least $f_k + 1$ mirrors during the round ts: $\#ts > f_k$. In other words, more than f_k acknowledgments sent during round ts have to be positive (obviously, the number of mirrors has to satisfy the following constraint: $m \geq 2f_k + 1$). Moreover, the decided value must appear at least $m - f_k$ times among the gathered values: $\#htv \geq m - f_k$. In other words, less than f_k mirrors have kept a different estimation value. If all these conditions are satisfied then s_c adopts htv as decision value, sends a decide message to the k-Set agreement module (line 13 in Figure 2) and stops. Note that the k-Set agreement module (see Figure 1) is necessary to achieve a reliable broadcast of the decision value, and thus has to be executed by all the processes.

If s_c cannot decide, then it will either ends phase 1 and starts the second phase of the current round or ends phase 2 (it updates its round number r to $r + n_k$) and starts the first phase of the next coordinated round.

To finish the first phase, the coordinator has to propose a new estimate value to all the mirrors. In CT, this new estimate is necessarily the value htv. In the proposed solution, we may adopt another value namely mfv if this second value appears really more often than htv among the gathered values. The difference between the occurences of both values has to be greater or equal to f_k. This bound corresponds to the maximal number of values missed while collecting the estimations of the mirrors (See line 6 in Figure 2). As all the missed value may be equal to htv, we priviledge the value mfv if and only if this value is without doubt the most frequent one. Note that proposing mfv as new estimate tends to increase the occurrence number of this particular value and thus to benefit from the redundancy of initial values. Then source s_c sends its new estimate (htv or mfv) to all the mirrors (broadcast of an Update message, lines 18 or 20 in Figure 2) and enters Phase 2.

3.3   Mirror Module

The algorithmic principles that underline the code of the mirror module are very simple and very similar to the one of a non-coordinator in Chandra and Toueg protocol [4]. The only difference (assuming that the scope of accuracy x of $\Diamond S_x$ is maximal, i.e., $x = n$) is that at the very beginning of the code, mirrors wait for an initial value sent by one of the $f_k + 1$ sources, adopt it as estimate, and timestamp it with a value related to the sender's identity of this value. Relating the timestamp of an estimate to its origin ensures that a unique value corresponds to a given timestamp[2].

Then, each mirror enters its round-based protocol (See lines 3 - 25 in Figure 3) . Each iteration of the external while loop corresponds to a new round. Therefore, the round number r and the identity of the new coordinator s_c are re-computed at the beginning of each loop (See line 4 in Figure 3). Then mirror m_i sends its estimate est_i, timestamped with the round number at which it adopted it (ts_i), to the coordinator s_c of the current round r (i.e., invocation of REFLECT($r,1,ts_i,est_i$), line 5 in Figure 3).

Then the mirrors enters a second internal while loop (See lines 6 - 23 in Figure 3). When the variable $state_i$ (initialized to 0 before entering the internal loop) is equal to 2, the mirror is ready to send an acknowledgment (positive or negative) to the current coordinator s_c (See line 24 in Figure 3). If this condition is not satisfied, a mirror m_i waits until either it receives s_c estimate or it suspects s_c (See line 7 in Figure 3). In the former case, it adopts s_c estimate and timestamps this new estimate with the current round number ($ts_i = r$). Its

---

[2] In CT, this property is not satisfied: initially, every estimation is timestamped with 0.

Module Mirror$_i$ (executed by m_i such that $1 \leq i \leq m$)
local variable

est_i	% the mirror's estimation of the decision value
ts_i	% the timestamp associated to the estimation
r_i	% current round number
c	% Identity of the current source
$state_i$	% Depends on the messages sent during the current round
	% 0 : no message has been received nor sent
	% 1 : a Confirmation message has been sent
	% 2 : either an Update message has been received
	% or p_c is suspected by m_i and at least $m - x + k$ mirrors

begin
(1)   **wait until** (a message Init($initial\_est, origin$) is available);
(2) $r_i \leftarrow 0$; $est_i \leftarrow initial\_est$; $ts_i \leftarrow 1 - origin$;
(3)   **while** ($true$) **do**
(4) $c \leftarrow (r_i \bmod n_k) + 1$; $r_i \leftarrow r_i + 1$; $state_i \leftarrow 0$;
(5)   send reflect(r_i , 1 , ts_i , est_i) to the source module of p_c;
(6)   **while** ($state_i < 2$) **do**
(7)   **wait until** ((s_c suspected) **or** (a message update(r_i, est) is available));
(8)   **if** (a message update(r_i , est) is available) **then**
(9) $est_i \leftarrow est$; $ts_i \leftarrow r_i$;
(10)   **if** (($x < n$) $\wedge$ ($state_i = 0$) $\wedge$ ($i \neq c$)) **then**
(11)   send update(r_i , est) to all the mirrors;
(12)   **endif**;
(13) $state_i \leftarrow 2$;
(14)   **else**
(15)   **if** (($x < n$) $\wedge$ ($state_i = 0$)) **then**
(16)   send confirmation(r_i) to all the mirrors;
(17) $state_i \leftarrow 1$;
(18)   **endif**;
(19)   **if** (($x = n$) $\vee$ ($n - x + 1$ messages Confirmation(r_i) are available))
(20)   **then** $state_i \leftarrow 2$;
(21)   **endif**
(22)   **endif**;
(23)   **endwhile**
(24)   send Reflect(r_i , 2 , ts_i , est_i) to the source module of p_c;
(25)   **endwhile**
end

Fig. 3. Behavior of a Mirror Module

acknowledgement will be positive ($r = ts_i$). Otherwise (suspicion of s_c), neither est_i nor ts_i are updated. By keeping ts_i to an old value different from r, m_i indicates to s_c that its acknowledgment is negative. If $x = n$, any mirror exits the internal while loop after only one loop. Then a mirror sends its positive/negative acknowledgment (See line 24 in Figure 3) and starts its next round.

The mirror module as described here above assumed that the scope of accuracy x of $\Diamond \mathcal{S}_x$ spanned the whole system, and thus was equal to n. Let us now present the additional code (mainly located between lines 10 and 20 of the mirror module) necessary to support a limited scope of accuracy. This additional code only concerns the mirror module, which emphasizes (if necessary) the advantage of our structuring into three modules.

Our approach is inspired by the solution proposed by Schiper [17] to limit the impact of incorrect suspicions toward a correct coordinator. When at least one process "falsely" suspects the current coordinator, its negative acknowledgment can prevent the correct coordinator to progress within its round (and thus to possibly decide) (this occurs in most of the coordinator-based protocols). Schiper's solution relies on the idea that a process has to gather $n - f$ suspicions before being allowed to send a negative acknowledgment to a coordinator. We adapt this idea to support a limited scope of accuracy. Recall that limiting the scope of accuracy to x amounts to reduce the number of processes that do not have to suspect some correct process s_α to x. Hence the advantage of limiting the impact of processes that can "falsely" suspect some correct process. Let us now describe how we implement such an idea.

In the worst case, among the x processes that do not suspect s_α, $k-1$ belongs to $\mathcal{P}$ and $n-m-k+1$ are processes of $\mathcal{U}$ that do not act as mirrors. Consequently, at most $n-x$ mirrors may suspect s_α. When some mirror m_i suspects the current coordinator s_c, it informs all the other mirrors about its suspicion (invocation of CONFIRMATION(r), line 16 in Figure 3). To confirm its suspicion (that is, to send a negative acknowledgment to s_c), m_i waits for $n - x + 1$ CONFIRMATION(r) messages. This number of messages is needed to prevent s_α from being "falsely" suspected. Indeed, receiving $n - x + 1$ CONFIRMATION messages guarantees that at least one CONFIRMATION message has been sent by a process belonging to Q (with Q the set containing the x processes as defined in Section 2.3). In that case, s_c cannot be this correct process s_α. By imposing to gather $n - x + 1$ messages, we fix the lower bound on the scope of accuracy x to $f+1$ as introduced at the beginning of the section. Indeed, the maximal number of non crashed mirrors is equal to $m - f_k$ (when all the processes of $\mathcal{P}$ are crashed). Thus we must have $n - x + 1 \leq m - f_k$, leading to $x > f$ when all the processes of $\mathcal{U}$ are mirrors (i.e. $m = n - k + 1$). Note that if it was possible to ensure that Q was included strictly in the set of mirrors then the number of gathered CONFIRMATION messages could be lowered to $m - x + 1$. In that case, we obtain $x > f - k + 1$.

Now, when some mirror m_i receives the estimate of the current coordinator s_c, m_i forwards this estimate to all the other mirrors (invocation of UPDATE (r, est_i) in Figure 3). This forwarding prevents mirrors from an infinite blocking. Indeed, if s_c fails while it is sending its estimate to all the mirrors, some mirror m_k may do not receive s_c estimate and thus sends a CONFIRMATION message to all the other mirrors (because m_k suspects s_c). Now, if less than $m+k-x$ mirrors suspect s_c, then m_k remains blocked forever waiting for enough suspicions to send a negative acknowledgment to s_c. Broadcasting a copy of the received message allows to avoid such a scenario.

Therefore, our solution to limit the scope of accuracy amounts for each mirror to sending only one additional message to all the mirrors regarding the solution when $x < n$ (either an UPDATE message or a CONFIRMATION message).

3.4   Maximal Number of Failures

By construction, if one of the privileged processes $p \in \mathcal{P}$ is correct, it decides and broadcasts its value to all the other processes. In that case, the termination of the consensus executed by the n_k other processes $\in \mathcal{U}$ is no more a requirement. In other words, the termination of the consensus protocol executed by the n_k sources and the m mirrors has to be ensured only if all the processes in $\mathcal{P}$ are faulty and thus possibly crashed. In that case, at most f_k crashes can affect the m mirrors belonging to $\mathcal{U}$. The code executed by a source module requires to gather at least a f_k+1 REFLECT messages (See the condition evaluate at line 12 in Figure 2). If all the processes of $\mathcal{U}$ are mirrors, less than $n_k/2$ are allowed to crash. Consequently, the maximal number of failure has to be less than $(k-1)+n_k/2$ and thus $f < \frac{n+k-1}{2}$. To reach this bound, all the processes of $\mathcal{U}$ have to execute both the source module and the mirror module. Moreover, as indicated previously the condition $x > f$ has to be satisfied. Obviously, the number of tolerated failures can increase when the value of k increases. This improves the limit suggested in [15] where the authors exhibit a strongest condition ($f \geq min(n - k\lfloor n/(k+1)\rfloor, k+x-1)$). As indicated by the authors, an instantiation of their protocol with $k = 1$ can tolerate more failures than an instantiation with $k > 1$. The protocol described within this paper can overcome this limitation. In other words, the value of f can be higher than $n/2$.

4   Number of Mirrors vs. Scope of Accuracy

As the number of messages exchanged during a round depends on the number of processes involved in the mirror module execution, decreasing the number of mirrors diminishes the number of exchanged messages and thus improves the message complexity of the algorithm. Yet, conversely, an increase in the number of mirrors allows to reduce the scope of accuracy of the failure detectors, and thus to lower the quality of the failure detectors (we show that x can be decreased down to $f + 1$). More precisely, the following condition has to be satisfied: $n - x + 1 \leq m - f_k$. Therefore, $(n - m) + f_k < x$. To decrease the value of x, one have to increase the number of mirrors in order to decrease the term $(n - m)$. Consequently, there is a tradeoff between the number of exchanged messages and the quality of the failure detector. When all the processes of $\mathcal{U}$ are mirrors, the protocol, which has been designed to be efficient, requires that $x > f$. Note that this condition is stronger than the condition $x > f - k + 1$ imposed by the protocol described in [15].

5   Reducing the Number of Failure Detectors Modules

When the scope of the accuracy property is less than n, only a subset of the failure detectors exhibits good properties. More precisely, among the n processes, only x do not suspect the source s_α. Now let us define a passive failure detector as a module which always suspects all the sources, whereas active failure detector modules satisfy the completeness and accuracy properties that characterized the class $\diamond S$. Suppose that the x mirrors can be pre-defined and are equipped with active failure detector modules. On the contrary, the other mirrors are equipped with passive failure detector modules. Implementing passive failure detectors is simple and allow to reduce the number of exchanged messages because sources are not required to send any "I-am-alive" message to any passive failure detector module. In such a context, the solution described in this paper will satisfy the termination and agreement properties that characterized the k-set agreement problem if x is greater than or equal to $f_k + 1$. Indeed, the previous requirement, namely $x > f$, can be weakened because none of the privileged processes are equipped with an active failure detector module. Yet as f_k crashes can affect processes equipped with an active failure detector, the condition $x > f - k + 1$ has to be satisfied.

6   Conclusion

In this paper, we have presented a $\diamond S_x$-based solution to solve the k-Set agreement problem. The proposed solution relies on a differentiation of the roles acted by the processes. This enables the protocol to terminate, in most of the cases, in an absolute minimum amount of time, that is the time needed to reliably broadcast a value. Furthermore, we sensibly increase the resiliency of previous published solutions. Our solution tolerates up to $f < \frac{n+k-1}{2}$ crash failures. Finally, we take advantage of the redundancy among the proposed values. Specifically, as the consensus run between the $n - k + 1$ processes has to terminate only when all the $k - 1$ privileged processes have crashed, we show that a simple broadcast of the initial values allows to reduce the number of different proposed value down to $f - k + 2$.

References

[1]   Anceaume E., Hurfin M. and Ph. Raipin Parvedy, An Efficient Solution to the k-Set Agreement Problem. *Technical Report Irisa 1440*, 2001. 65

[2]   Borowsky E. and Gafni E., Generalized FLP Impossibility Results for t-Resilient Asynchronous Computations. *Proc. 25th ACM Symposium on Theory of Computation*, pp. 91-100, 1993. 63, 67

[3]   Chaudhuri S., Agreement is Harder than Consensus: Set Consensus Problems in Totally Asynchronous Systems. *Proc. 9th ACM Symposium on Principles of Distributed Computing (PODC'90)*, pp. 311-324, 1990. 63, 67, 68

[4] Chandra T. and Toueg S., Unreliable Failure Detectors for Reliable Distributed Systems. *Journal of the ACM*, 43(2):225-267, March 1996. 63, 64, 65, 66, 68, 69, 71, 73

[5] Chandra T., Hadzilacos V. and Toueg S., The Weakest Failure Detector for Solving Consensus. *Journal of the ACM*, 43(4):685–722, July 1996. 63, 66

[6] Dolev D., Dwork C. and Stockmeyer L., On the Minimal Synchronism Needed for Distributed Consensus. *Journal of the ACM*, 34(1):77-97, January 1987. 63

[7] Dwork C., Lynch N. and Stockmeyer L., Consensus in the Presence of Partial Synchrony. *Journal of the ACM*, 35(2):288-323, April 1988. 63, 68

[8] Fischer M. J., Lynch N. and Paterson M. S., Impossibility of Distributed Consensus with One Faulty Process. *Journal of the ACM*, 32(2):374–382, April 1985. 62, 66

[9] Hurfin M., Mostéfaoui A. and Raynal M., A Versatile Family of Consensus Protocols Based on Chandra-Toueg's Unreliable Failure Detectors. *IEEE Transactions on Computers*, to appear in 2002. 71

[10] Hadzilacos V. and Toueg S., Reliable Broadcast and Related Problems. In *Distributed Systems*, ACM Press (S. Mullender Ed.), New-York, pp. 97-145, 1993. 63

[11] Hurfin M. and Raynal M., A Simple and Fast Asynchronous Consensus Protocol based on a Weak Failure Detector In *Distributed Computing*, 12(4):209-223, 1999. 63

[12] Herlihy M and Shavit N., The Asynchronous Computability Theorem for *t*-Resilient Tasks. *Proc. 25th ACM Symposium on Theory of Computation*, pp. 111-120, 1993. 63, 67

[13] L. Lamport and M. Fisher. "Byzantine generals and transaction commit protocols", Technical Report 62, SRI International, April 1982. 66

[14] Mostéfaoui A. and Raynal M., Solving Consensus Using Chandra-Toueg's Unreliable Failure Detectors: a General Quorum-Based Approach. *Proc. 13th Int. Symposium on Distributed Computing (DISC'99) (formerly, WDAG)*, Springer-Verlag LNCS 1693, pp. 49-63, (P. Jayanti Ed.), Bratislava (Slovaquia), September 1999.

[15] Mostéfaoui A. and Raynal M., *k*-Set Agreement with Limited Accuracy Failure Detectors. *Proc. 19th ACM Symposium on Principles of Distributed Computing*, pp. 143-152, Portland (OR), 2000. 64, 65, 66, 67, 76

[16] Mostéfaoui A., Rajsbaum S and Raynal M., A Versatile and Modular Consensus Protocol. *Technical Report Irisa 1427*, 18 pages, 2001. 65, 71

[17] Schiper A., Early Consensus in an Asynchronous System with a Weak Failure Detector. *Distributed Computing*, 10(3):149-157, 1997. 63, 75

[18] Yang J., Neiger G. and Gafni E., Structured Derivations of Consensus Algorithms for Failure Detectors. *Proc. 17th ACM Symposium on Principles of Distributed Computing*, Puerto Vallarta (Mexico), pp.297-308, 1998. 63, 64, 66, 67

Novel Approaches in Dependable Computing

Rogério de Lemos

Computing Laboratory, University of Kent at Canterbury, UK
r.delemos@ukc.ac.uk

The complexity of systems and the way they work together will require new approaches for their development and operation, since conventional deterministic approaches may not be sufficient for enabling the provision of services expected from these systems. Several new approaches have emerged recently from different areas, such as, biologically inspired computing, agent technology, and software engineering, just to mention a few. Whether these approaches are able to meet the stringent requirements usually associated with dependable computing is still open to debate. Hence this Panel, which aims to discuss the promises and challenges of novel approaches for dependable computing. Next, in order to set the context of this Panel, some of these approaches are briefly presented.

Biology has been the inspiration of several computational intelligence approaches, such as, neural networks, genetic algorithms, artificial immune systems, etc [3]. The latter in particular, which is now receiving more attention, are adaptive systems inspired by theoretical immunology and observed immune functions, principles and models, which are applied to problem solving [5]. For example, in the context of dependability, the metaphor of the immune system has been initially associated with fault tolerant computing [1], and computer security [7]. Another biologically inspired initiative is autonomic computing, which is being promoted by IBM. The challenge of autonomic computing systems is of building and deploying computing systems that regulate themselves and remove complexity from the lives of administrators and users. Although biologically inspired computational approaches have been successfully employed in several engineering artifacts, they have nevertheless been used with more caution in system that have more stringent dependability requirements [8].

From software engineering, several efforts have been made for providing mechanisms for monitoring and controlling the actual execution of a system through its architectural model, thus allowing self-healing/self-repair of the system at higher levels of abstraction. One of these initiatives relies on extending existing architectural styles by incorporating constraints that capture the desired behavior of the system [4]. Another initiative in this area is based on the explicit representation of the interactions between components in terms of cooperation/coordination connectors that are able to capture different configurations of the system [6, 2].

Planetary computing is another industrial initiative, which is being promoted by HP Labs, and which aims into creating a new model of computing to develop and manage vast IT resources. The goal is to obtain an infrastructure on demand that is scalable, flexible, economical, and always available. At the core of this infrastructure is a data center control system that should be self-monitoring, self-healing and self-adapting.

A major motivation underlying most of the above approaches is the provision of an effective means for these systems to cope with changes at design and run time. The

F. Grandoni (Ed.): EDCC 2002, LNCS 2485, pp. 79-80, 2002.

concerns with design time are related to the ability of building new systems from existing ones without incurring into high development costs. While the concerns with run time are related to the capability of a system to adapting to changes that occur in its operating environment. For both cases, at least for some of the above mentioned approaches, it is assumed that they rely on some learning capabilities. These capabilities should provide the basis for the system employing these novel approaches to adjust its structure/behavior to new needs, without any human intervention. Although the learning capabilities might enable a system to react to unexpected circumstances, it also removes the predictability aspect from its behavior, which is critical on some dependable systems. If this is the case, the question to be asked is whether these learning capabilities can be trusted? If not, how to protect the system against potential undesirable decisions?

Another trend that has been observed in the application of these new approaches is the move from closed to open systems, where the scope of the problem domain is not so clearly identified. Borrowing the IBM slogan that states that "a million enterprises having a billion people using a trillion devices", the issues that need to be raised are whether these new technologies are scaleable, and how these systems should be structured for these new approaches to be effective?

The Panel will discuss these and other issues when describing the potential of novel approaches for building and operating dependable computing systems.

References

[1]   A. Avizienis. "Toward Systematic Design of Fault-Tolerant Systems". *Computer 30(4)*. April 1997. pp. 51-58.

[2]   L. Andrade, and J. Fiadeiro. "Coordination: the Evolutionary Dimension". *Proceedings TOOLS Europe 2001*. Ed. W. Pree. IEEE Computer Society Press. pp. 136-147. 2001.

[3]   P. Bentley. *Digital Biology: How Nature is transforming our Technology*. Headline Book Publishing. London, UK. 2001.

[4]   S.-W. Cheng, D. Garlan, B. Schmerl., J. Sousa, B. Spitznagel, and P. Steenkiste. "Using Architectural Style as the Basis for Self-repair". The Working IEEE/IFIP Conference on Software Architecture 2002. Montreal, Canada. August 2002. (to appear).

[5]   L. N. de Castro, and J. I. Timmis. Artificial Immune Systems: A New Computational Intelligence Approach. Springer-Verlag. 2002.

[6]   R. de Lemos. "Describing Evolving Dependable Systems using Co-operative Software Architectures". *Proceedings of the IEEE International Conference on Software Maintenance (ICSM'02)*. Florence, Italy. November 2001. pp. 320-329.

[7]   S. Forrest, S. A. Hofmeyr, and A. Somayaji. "Computer Immunology". *Communications of the ACM 40(10)*. 1997. pp. 88-96.

[8]   K. Frith, and R. Ellis. "Artificial Intelligence – Genuine Hazards?" *Safer Systems: Proceedings of the Fifth Safety-critical Systems Symposium*. Brighton, UK. February 1997. Eds. F. Redmill, and T. Anderson. Springer-Verlag. London, UK. pp. 79-95.

An Immune System Paradigm for the Design of Fault Tolerant Systems

Algirdas Avizienis

A. Avizienis and Associates Inc.
2711 Washington Avenue, Santa Monica, CA 90403 U.S.A.
aviz@cs.ucla.edu

An in-depth assessment of the implementation of fault tolerance in contemporary "off-the-shelf" computing systems [1] leads us to conclude that hardware defenses are not adequately exploited for the assurance of dependability. In the search for a fundamentally better solution we have looked at the self-protection (i.e., fault tolerance) mechanisms of the human being. We use two analogies [2]: (1) the body is analogous to hardware; and (2) the cognitive processes of the mind are analogous to software. The immune system of the body is a major protective mechanism that is completely independent of the cognitive processes. It functions from conception until death of the body and protects the body of an unconscious or sleeping human equally well as that of a conscious one.

The solution that we have proposed is to insert into a given "host" computing system a hardware subsystem that is analogous to the immune system of the human body [3]. We call this approach to building dependable systems the "immune system paradigm" (ISP). The ISP is a set of design principles for a software-independent and fully fault-tolerant implementation of the FTI.

To develop the ISP we identify the key properties of the human immune system and from them derive the attributes that the FTI must have in order to satisfy the analogy with the immune system. There are four attributes of the immune system that are especially relevant [4]:

1. It functions (i.e. detects and reacts to threats) continuously and autonomously, independently of cognition.
2. Its elements (lymph nodes, other lymphoid organs, lymphocytes) are distributed throughout the body, serving all its organs.
3. It has its own communication links – the network of lymphatic vessels.
4. Its elements (cells, organs, and vessels) themselves are self-defended, redundant and in several cases diverse.

The properties that the FTI must possess to justify the immune system analogy are:

1. The FTI consists of hardware and firmware elements only.
2. The FTI is independent of (requires no support from) any software of the host platform, but can communicate with it and support its recovery.
3. The FTI supports (provides protected decisions algorithms for) multichannel computing of the host platform, including diverse hardware and software channels to provide design fault tolerance for the host platform.

F. Grandoni (Ed.): EDCC 2002, LNCS 2485, pp. 81-83, 2002.
© Springer-Verlag Berlin Heidelberg 2002

4. The FTI is compatible with (i.e., protects) a wide range of host platform components, including processors, memories, supporting chipsets, discs, power supplies, fans and various peripherals.
5. Elements of the FTI are distributed throughout the host platform and are interconnected by their own autonomous communication links.
6. The FTI is fully fault-tolerant itself, requiring no external support. It is not susceptible to attacks by intrusion or malicious software and is not affected by natural or design faults of the host platform.

An FTI that possesses the above attributes and supports host platforms that use Intel's P6 family of processors has been described in [3]. It is a generic, hierarchical, fault-tolerant (f-t) hardware infrastructure that serves as a software independent innermost defense for error detection and recovery of a platform that may also employ various other fault tolerance and security techniques.

The hierarchical structure within the FTI is as follows: an f-t set of S^3 (Startup, Shutdown, Survival) nodes protects an f-t set of M (Monitor) nodes, which in turn protects f-t A (Adapter) and D (Decision) nodes that are connected to and protect the components (C-nodes) of the host platform (see figures 2 and 4 of [3]). A new concept that is being explored is a "hierarchy of infrastructures:" an FTI is installed within each chip of the host platform, another FTI protects one board, and still another FTI protects the entire platform. The on-chip FTI performs the A-node and D-node functions for the board FTI, while the board FTI does the same for the platform FTI. The principal constraint in developing a hierarchy of FTIs is the need for dedicated and protected communication links within each FTI and between FTIs. This constraint makes the further extension of FTI hierarchy to clusters and LANs of platforms relatively costly to implement.

The goal of the Immune System Paradigm is to use hardware more extensively and more effectively than it is being done currently in providing fault tolerance for very dependable high-performance platforms. A benefit of the FTI is the ability to simplify higher-level defenses that require software participation. The presence of an effective FTI simplifies the error detection and recovery requirements for system software.

In concluding we predict that adoption of the FTI in platform designs will lead to a better structured and more cost-effective overall dependability assurance architecture, since the other levels of protection will be supported by hardware that is missing in today's designs.

References

[1]   A. Avizienis and R. Avizienis. An immune system paradigm for the design of fault-tolerant systems. Presented at Workshop 3: Evaluating and Architecting Systems for Dependability (EASY), in conjunction with DSN 201 and ISCA 2001, Goteborg, Sweden, Jul 1, 2001. Available at: http://www.crhc.uiuc.edu/EASY/easy01-program.html.
[2]   A. Avizienis. Toward systematic design of fault-tolerant systems. Computer, 30(4)51-58. April 1997.

[3]   A. Avizienis. A fault tolerance infrastructure for dependable computing with high-performance COTS components. In Proceedings Of the Int. Conference on Dependable Systems and Networks (DSN 2000), June 2000, pp. 492-500.

[4]   G.J.V. Nossal. Life, death and the immune system. Scientific American, 269(33)52-62, September 1993.

Security and Survivability of Large Scale Critical Infrastructures

John Bigham

Electronic Engineering, Queen Mary, University of London
john.bigham@elec.qmul.ac.uk

At the heart of a large complex critical infrastructure (LCCI) such as an electricity distribution or telecommunications network, is a management network consisting of a number of interconnected computers running server, database, monitoring and control software. This management network is vulnerable to attacks because it is often connected to a number of IP networks as well as to the public telephone network, switches, routers and remote terminal units interfacing with sensors. Operator mistakes and malicious insiders can also damage the management network and the system.

Guardians of LCCIs need to monitor and protect the system at a number of different levels. The CEC funded project Safeguard project plans to build agent system components to manage this. Low-level agents will build up models of the normal operation of the software and data in their local environment. These will communicate with higher-level agents with an overview of the system that will build up or use a model of normality within a broader context. Once an abnormality has been detected, a response to protect the network will be carried out. Low-level agents will initiate a fast protective response at a local level, while high-level agents will be responsible for a more sophisticated diagnosis of the problem and a system-wide response.

1 The Objectives of the Safeguard System

What Safeguard will try to do is to construct a unified system architecture (across different LCCIs that can manage the resources so as to robustly provide the services offered. This will consist of) dynamic components that can observe the world and can perform actions that change the allocation of resource or inform third parties. These dynamic components can be at different levels of abstraction and will co-operate with each other. The general architecture of the Safeguards agents is illustrated in the figure 1. Each agent is comprised of several intelligent components with different roles (c.f. striker or defender) and must co-operate to fend off chance circumstances and deliberately hostile acts. Interaction between agents is through the co-ordination layers in the agent. Here the agents are shown located at each control centre, though the architecture is not yet decided. Different components will have different roles and components communicate within the layers of the agent. An aim of the project is to find a solution that fits the requirements of the domains, which is scaleable and is dependable, and not just one that corresponds to an over simplified structure.

F. Grandoni (Ed.): EDCC 2002, LNCS 2485, pp. 84-85, 2002.

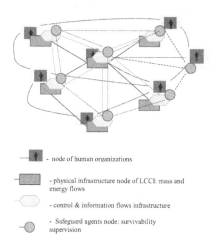

- node of human organizations

- physical infrastructure node of LCCI: mass and energy flows

- control & information flows infrastructure

- Safeguard agents node: survivability supervision

Fig. 1. An illustration of networked layers of a LCCI with the SAFEGUARD agency layer

There are two important kinds of action that can compromise the system and that Safeguards must detect

1. Intrusion attacks and system failures: This includes prevention of intrusion attacks on the software of the controllers and prevention and detection of other malfunctions of the controllers (either by hardware failures in actuators or software bugs in the controlling software) of the system at all layers. This not only includes the controllers in the physical layer of the system, but also attacks on and other mishaps associated with the configuration and reconfiguration management software. In the telecom domain attacks and failures on the latter are considered more likely and potentially more damaging than attacks on individual element control software because of their scope. Also many response mechanisms already exist for failures in the physical layer, though perhaps not yet for those caused by attacks on the element controlling software.
2. Unexpected behaviour due to modifications to the management and control software when service or structure changes: Software in large systems is continually changing and mechanisms to flag errors and to give indicators of unusual conditions are essential

The availability of expert knowledge in the management of attack detection, resource reallocation, failure mitigation etc. is needed. It is not our intention, for example, to replace existing diagnostic mechanisms for the network, but to design and develop a system of agents that can interface with existing (legacy) software, each with different but coordinated roles, that together ensure the survivability of the system. For example, an in house diagnostic system could be wrapped in an agent wrapper so that it also can communicate with the SAFEGUARD agent that has a diagnostic role.

An Architectural Approach to Fault Treatment in Critical Infrastructures

José Luiz Fiadeiro

ATX Software S.A. and LabMOL–University of Lisbon
Alameda António Sérgio 7 – 1 C, 2795-023 Linda-a-Velha, Portugal
jose@fiadeiro.org

1   On the Challenges Raised by Critical Infrastructures

Critical infrastructures, as information-intensive systems that support vital functions of our modern society (telecommunications, financial services, transports, energy supplies, etc). are becoming particularly vulnerable to failure. They are often built over unreliable networks of heterogeneous, fragile platforms. They perform critical missions that make them vulnerable to attacks. These are also systems that, individually, are becoming ever more complex and, globally, ever more interdependent.

Fault treatment for this kind of systems requires new levels of flexibility and responsiveness. Due to the critical nature of the services that they support, such infrastructures cannot stop their operation when a fault arises. They can tolerate a certain degree of downgraded service for a certain period, but they need to ensure a minimal set of properties while the original services are not fully restored. For this purpose, they need to be able to react automatically to the occurrence of faults and reconfigure themselves to adapt to the new situation in which they need to operate, making use of the available resources.

2   Separating Computation, Coordination and Configuration

The need to operate, in "real-time", with "surgical" precision for limiting the impact of the treatment, in contexts of increasing interdependency, requires a clear separation of concerns to be enforced in the way we model and manage such systems. We propose a three-layered architecture that separates what we consider to be the key concerns involved in this problem: computation, coordination and configuration.

The first separation, that between computation and coordination, is enforced by modelling explicitly the interactions that exist in the system as first-class entities – architectural connectors that we call coordination contracts. These connectors coordinate the way the components that reside in the computation layer interact. The latter correspond to "core" entities of the domain that provide basic services that, usually, cannot be "repaired" because they are performed by "black-boxes". By externalising all interactions as connectors, it becomes possible to circumscribe treatment of faults occurring at the level of a component to the connectors through which it interacts with the rest of the system. Basically, because it is often impossible to find a component

F. Grandoni (Ed.): EDCC 2002, LNCS 2485, pp. 86-87, 2002.

that performs "equivalent" services, we see fault treatment as consisting of searching, within the available resources, components that offer alternative services, even if in a downgraded mode, and establishing the connectors that can adapt them to the expectations of the components with which they are required to interact.

This model supports the means for fault treatment to be performed through dynamic reconfiguration, in run-time, without interruption of service. For this process of reconfiguration to be able to be programmed, leading to self-adaptive and self-healing, we propose a third architectural layer consisting of entities that can react to events and act on the configuration, which are treated, again, as first-class citizens.

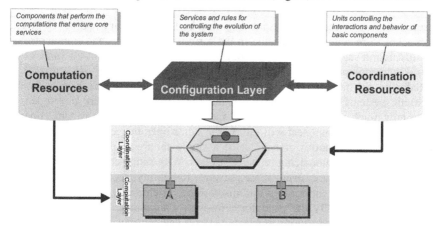

3   Agent and Objects Have Been Promising the Same...

Interaction in most agent-based models is, like for object-oriented systems, based on *identities* in the sense that, through clientship, objects interact by invoking specific methods of specific objects (instances) to get something specific done. As a result, systems become too rigid to support the levels of agility that are required for fault treatment in critical infrastructures: any change on the collaborations that an object maintains with other objects needs to be performed at the level of the code that implements that object and, possibly, of the objects with which the new collaborations are established. On the contrary, being based on external connectors, our proposal models interactions in a service-oriented approach, i.e. interconnections are established on the basis of the description of what is required, thus decoupling the "what one wants to be done" from the "who does it". This is why faults can be treated in ways that are not intrusive on the rest of the system, thus ensuring increased levels of agility and responsiveness.

This does not mean that our architectural approach cannot be deployed over object-oriented platforms: it can, and we have even provided a proof of concept over Java. What is important is that the methodological approach and corresponding conceptual model is based on a service-oriented architecture as described. More information on this architectural approach can be found in www.atxsoftware.com.

Biologically Inspired Fault-Tolerant Computer Systems

Andy Tyrrell

Bio-Inspired Architectures Laboratory, Department of Electronics
University of York, YO10 5DD, UK
amt@ohm.york.ac.uk

Researchers have recently begun investigating both evolutionary and developmental approaches to reliable system design in the form of Embryonics and Immunotronics. This discussion suggests a completely new approach to creating fault-tolerant systems that takes inspiration from biology.

Reducing the failure probability and increasing reliability has been a goal of electronic systems designers ever since the first components were developed. No matter how much care is taken designing and building an electronic system, sooner or later an individual component will fail. For systems operating in remote environment such as space applications, the effect of a single failure could results in a multi-million pound installation being rendered useless. With safety critical systems such as aircraft the effects are even more severe. Reliability techniques need to be implemented in these applications and many more. The development of fault tolerant techniques is driven by the need for ultra-high availability, reduced maintenance costs, and long life applications to ensure systems can continue to function in spite of faults occurring.

Nature has achieved levels of complexity that far surpass any man-made computing system, and phenomenal robustness: in the trillions of cells that make up a human being, faults are rare, and in the majority of cases, successfully detected and repaired. This level of reliability is remarkable.

In any living being, every one of its constituent cells interprets the DNA strand allocated in its nucleus to produce the proteins needed for the survival of the organism, independently of the particular function it performs. Which part or parts of the DNA are interpreted will depend on the physical location of the cell with respect to its neighbours.

Embryonics (*embryonic electronics*) is inspired by the basic processes of molecular biology and by the embryonic development of living beings. By adopting certain features of cellular organization, and by transposing them to the two-dimensional world of integrated circuits, properties unique to the living world, such as *self-replication* and *self-repair*, can also be applied to artificial objects (integrated circuits). Self-repair allows partial reconstruction in case of a minor fault, while self-replication allows complete reconstruction of the original device in cases where a major fault occurs.

The aim of Embryonics is to transport these basic properties to the 2-dimensional world of cellular arrays using specifically designed FPGAs as building blocks. In any embryonic system, every one of its FPGA-based cells interprets a configuration register allocated in its memory, independently of the particular logic function it

F. Grandoni (Ed.): EDCC 2002, LNCS 2485, pp. 88-89, 2002.

performs. Which configuration register is interpreted will depend on the co-ordinates of the cell determined by those of its neighbours. Embryonic cellular arrays share the following properties with their biological counterparts.

To increase still further the potential reliability of these systems, inspiration has also been taken from biological immune systems – Immunotronics. The acquired immune system in humans (and most vertebrates) has a mechanism for error detection, which is simple, effective and adaptable.

Artificial immune systems take their inspiration from the operation of the human immune system to create novel solutions to problem solving. Although still a relatively new area of research, the range and number of applications is already diverse. Computer security, virus protection, anomaly detection, process monitoring, pattern recognition, robot control, and software fault tolerance are some of the applications artificial immune systems are being applied too. One important feature links all of these applications – they operate in a software domain. Our approach demonstrates that artificial immune systems can also exist in the hardware domain.

The early history of the theory of self-replicating machines is basically the history of John von Neumann's thinking on the matter. Von Neumann's automaton is a homogeneous two-dimensional array of elements, each element being a finite state machine. In his historic work, von Neumann showed that a possible configuration of his automaton can implement a universal constructor able to build onto the array any computing machine described in a dedicated part of the universal constructor, the tape. Self-replication is then a special case of construction, occurring when the universal constructor itself is described on the tape. Moreover, von Neumann demonstrated that his automaton is endowed with two major properties: construction universality, the capability of describing on the tape and building onto the array a machine of any dimension, and computation universality, the capability of describing and building a universal Turing machine.

May be we should look towards biology and back to von Neumann to consider how we can manage such huge complexities in our computing systems and still place our lives in their hands.

Test Set Embedding Based on Phase Shifters*

Maciej Bellos[1,3], Dimitri Kagaris[2], and Dimitris Nikolos[1,3]

[1] Computer Engineering & Informatics Dept.
University of Patras, 26500 Greece
bellos@ceid.upatras.gr
[2] Electrical & Computer Engineering Dept.
Southern Illinois University, Carbondale, IL 62901, USA
kagaris@engr.siu.edu
[3] Computer Technology Institute
3 Kolokotroni St., 262 21 Patras, Greece
nikolosd@cti.gr

Abstract. In this paper we present a new method for designing test pattern generators (TPG) for the embedding of precomputed test sets. The proposed TPG is based on the use of an LFSR and phase shifters and produces the exact test set. The proposed TPG compares favorably, with respect to test application time and/or hardware overhead, to the already known approaches.

1   Introduction

Built-In Self Test, BIST, is being increasingly used today to test large and complex ICs. BIST structures consist of three components: a Test Pattern Generator which produces and applies the test vectors to the circuit under test (CUT), a Test Response Compactor which compacts the test responses of the CUT to a signature and the BIST controller, which generates the necessary control signals and compares the signature of the CUT with the expected one.

Several BIST schemes have been proposed so far which can be classified into two general categories: test-per-scan and test-per-clock [1]. In the test-per-scan scheme a complete or partial scan path is serially filled by the TPG, while in the test-per-clock scheme a new test vector is applied to the CUT at each clock cycle. In this paper we consider only test-per-clock BIST schemes. BIST schemes can also be classified to pseudorandom [1], pseudoexhaustive [1] and deterministic, according to the type of the test patterns they generate.

A deterministic scheme takes into account deterministic test patterns and generates a test set that will contain these patterns among others. There are different ways of

* This research was partially supported by the Public Benefit Foundation "Alexander S. Onassis" via its scholarships program and by the Research Committee of Patras University within the framework of K. Karatheodoris scholarships program.

F. Grandoni (Ed.): EDCC 2002, LNCS 2485, pp. 90-101, 2002.
© Springer-Verlag Berlin Heidelberg 2002

generating the above deterministic test patterns. The simplest way is by using ROMs [2, 3], in which the deterministic test patterns are stored. However, this approach imposes a significant area overhead. A solution to this problem is to use weighting logic [4-6], mapping logic [7, 8], mixed mode BIST [9-11] and test set embedding [12-15].

In this paper we address the problem of test set embedding for test-per-clock BIST schemes. Test set embedding is defined as follows: given a test set T, produce a sequence of test vectors such that every test vector of T appears in the produced sequence. In this work we try to reproduce the given test set T in *minimum* time, that is, in n clock cycles where n is the number of vectors in T. A trivial way to do this is to store the patterns in a ROM, but the overhead of this approach is generally large. In this paper, we propose a new mechanism that requires less overhead than a ROM. The mechanism consists of an LFSR combined with an exclusive-OR, XOR, circuitry whose function is similar to that of Phase Shifters. Phase Shifters were originally introduced (see [16, 17]) in the context of pseudorandom TPG in order to reduce the correlation of the bit sequences produced by successive stages of an LFSR when that LFSR is used to feed multiple scan chains. In our scheme, the phase shifters are used for a different purpose: the goal is to produce appropriate shifts of the LFSR's m-sequence (characteristic sequence) so that every column of the given test matrix T coincides with the n first bits of some shifted version of the m-sequence, where n is the number of vectors in T.

The remaining of the paper is organized as follows: Section 2 describes the main idea of our approach, the proposed algorithm and how the test-per-clock scheme can be implemented targeting either at-speed testing of the CUT or hardware minimization. Section 3 presents the experimental results and Section 4 concludes.

2   Proposed Method

In this section we first describe the main idea of the proposed method. Then we provide an algorithm that implements our method and show how our method can be applied targeting either at-speed testing of the CUT or hardware overhead minimization.

2.1   Main Idea

The method proposed in this work uses an LFSR along with a number of Phase Shifters in order to reproduce a given test set T. In fact a Phase Shifter is a tree consisting of XOR gates. The overall architecture is depicted in Figure 1.

The main idea of our method is based on the following two facts:

1. *Every* column of a given test matrix can be shown to be a subsequence of the m-sequence of some LFSR of appropriate length and characteristic polynomial. In the worst case, for a test matrix with dimension n times w, where w is the pattern bit length, all w columns of the matrix are bound to be subsequences of the m-sequence of any LFSR with primitive characteristic polynomial of degree n. (It is assumed, of course, that $w < 2^n - 1$.)

2. Shifting the m-sequence of an LFSR by any desired number k of positions can be achieved by XOR-ing together the bit sequences from an appropriate group of LFSR cells. This is the "Shift-and-Add" property of the m-sequences, according to which the sum of any m-sequence M and a cyclic shift of itself produces another cyclic shift of the m-sequence M.

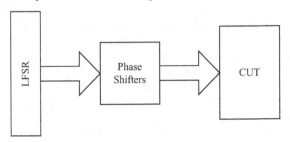

Fig. 1. Proposed architecture

These two facts are used as follows: assume that we have found an LFSR of appropriate length and characteristic polynomial so that each column of the test matrix T occurs as a subsequence of the m-sequence of the LFSR. Let p_j be a position at which column j, $1 \leq j \leq w$, occurs in the m-sequence (each column may occur in more than one positions in the m-sequence). Using now the "Shift-and-Add" property, we can shift the bit sequence of the corresponding LFSR stage by a number of places as determined by p_j and the index of the LFSR stage in order to "synchronize" all these occurrences, i.e. to make them start appearing at the corresponding LFSR stages at the same clock cycle. The individual shifts can be achieved by using for each column a Phase Shifter that will provide the appropriate shifted version of the m-sequence.

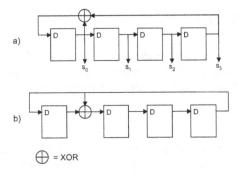

Fig. 2. a) Type I (external XOR) LFSR and b) its dual structure

For example, suppose that the given test matrix T is:

$$T = \begin{bmatrix} 1 & 0 & 1 & 1 & 0 \\ 1 & 1 & 0 & 1 & 0 \\ 0 & 0 & 0 & 0 & 0 \\ 1 & 0 & 1 & 0 & 1 \end{bmatrix}$$

Suppose also that we use an external XOR (or Type I) LFSR, that is an LFSR where all the feedbacks drive the inputs of a multi-input XOR gate or, equivalently, a tree of XOR gates, with the characteristic polynomial $p(x) = x^4 + x^3 + 1$ (Figure 2.a). If the initial state of the LFSR is 1000, then from the leftmost stage (s_0) of the LFSR we get the following m-sequence:

$$s_0 = 1\ 1\ 1\ 1\ 0\ 1\ 0\ 1\ 1\ 0\ 0\ 1\ 0\ 0\ 0$$

We observe that Column 1 (c_1) appears as a subsequence 2 cycles after the initial state, Column 2 (c_2) appears as a subsequence 10 cycles after the initial state and so on. We can use a Phase Shifter for each column, which will produce such a cyclic shift of the above m-sequence that the first bits of all columns can be produced simultaneously, at exactly the same clock cycle. In this manner test set T can be produced in just 4 clock cycles. In order to construct a Phase Shifter for each column, we have to determine the appropriate group of LFSR stages to be XOR-ed together for obtaining the desired shifting. The outputs of those LFSR stages will be referred to as "taps". A fast method for obtaining the taps has been given in [17]. This method, given a phaseshift value (k), provides fast computation of the Phase Shifter inputs. For the sake of completeness we restate this algorithm.

Algorithm 1 [17]
Step 1. Given an n-bit type I LFSR determine its dual structure.
Step 2. Initialize the dual LFSR to the value 10...0.
Step 3. Simulate the dual LFSR for $2^n - 1 - k$ clock cycles.
Step 4. The locations of ones in the resulting content of the dual LFSR point to the positions of taps that must feed the inputs of the Phase Shifter. Then, the output of the Phase Shifter will be a k-bit left cyclic shift of the reference m-sequence.

The dual of the LFSR of Figure 2.a is given in Figure 2.b. Then, using Algorithm 1 in the above example, we obtain the following taps s_i for each column c_i:

c_1: s_0, s_2 and s_3
c_2: s_1 and s_2
c_3: s_0, s_1 and s_3
c_4: s_0 and s_2
c_5: s_3

Each of the above groups of taps creates a XOR network whose outputs synchronize the m-sequence shifts so as to produce the desired test set, namely T.

2.2   Test Set Embedding Algorithm

Our algorithm uses as input a test matrix T and it examines it column-wise. Before feeding the algorithm with the test matrix, we can preprocess it in certain ways that will improve the results obtained from our algorithm.

From the above example it is clear that the area required for the implementation of the phase shifters can be reduced by reducing the columns of test matrix T. This obviously can be achieved by eliminating constant columns and substituting possible groups of identical or complementary columns by one column. Let T' be the new test matrix. The constant columns are eliminated since they can be easily produced by means of a constant-zero or constant-one source. In case the test matrix contains don't cares, Xs, then if a column contains Xs and defined bits of the same value (1 or 0), this column is considered to be also a constant one. Test sets provided for the detection of only the hard to detect faults contain usually many Xs.

It is obvious that for a test matrix consisting of a test set that detects all the faults of a circuit a constant column does not exist. However, if the test is split into two or more subsets (consequently a column is split to two or more parts), then there could be a subset that would have a constant part of a column, even though the whole column is not constant. This idea indicates another preprocessing step, which is to rearrange the vectors of the test matrix in order to create columns, which have blocks of continuous '1' and '0'. The rearrangement of the vectors in the test matrix is done in the following way. We choose an arbitrary column and we arrange the vectors so as to have a block of zeros followed by a block of ones. Then we consider only the rows corresponding to the block of zeros and we recursively perform the previous step. This is also done for the block of ones. The recursion stops when the blocks created for each column drop below a user defined threshold, which is usually dictated by the size of the subsets.

Having preprocessed the test matrix we now must consider the size of the LFSR. The number of rows in the test matrix as well as the maximum number of defined bits in a column impose limitations on the minimum number of LFSR stages that will be used. If the number of rows in the test matrix is n then an n-bit LFSR is sufficient, since it can produce 2^n-1 different states, which will appear in the m-sequence. However, by using a LFSR with one stage less, that is n-1, we can find in the resulting m-sequence $2^{n-1}-1$ different combinations of n-1 bits and consequently (by appending, e.g., a '0') the same number of n-bit combinations. The latter number is enough since by complementing these combinations we can get all the needed n-bit combinations except for the two that contain only ones and only zeros. It is obvious that the n-1 bit LFSR cannot produce a sequence of n contiguous 1s or 0s since this would lead the LFSR to be stuck in the all ones or all zeros state respectively. However this is not a problem, since constant columns have been eliminated from the test matrix. In a similar fashion, we can use a smaller LFSR if the Xs in the test matrix limit the maximum number of defined bits in each column to m, which is smaller than n. Theoretically an even smaller LFSR can be used, however for test sets with a relatively small number of rows the possibility of finding such an LFSR becomes small.

As mentioned earlier, by splitting the test into two or more phases we can have some constant columns. This also can increase the probability of finding complementary or identical columns, since their size is now smaller. Consequently the LFSR needed is reduced at least to half the original size which can possibly reduce the size of the XOR networks, needed to implement the shifts, at least to half. However, a set of multiplexers will be needed since now a column may be driven from different XOR networks.

Having discussed the above, the following simple algorithm provides a solution to the embedding of a given test set.

Algorithm 2. Test Set Embedding

Step 1. Perform constant, identical and complementary column elimination.

Step 2. Compute the weights, that is the number of defined bits, of the resulting columns and sort them according to the weights in descending order.

Step 3. Determine the size of the LFSR that will be used. The size can be either the maximum number of defined bits minus one or a value given by the user.

Step 4. Perform pattern matching and record the possible phaseshifts required for each column in a group. The taps associated with each phaseshift are determined by the use of a dual LFSR, as described in Algorithm 1.

Step 5. From each column's group choose one phaseshift so as to minimize the area required.

Step 6. Repeat Steps 4 and 5 as many times as the number of parts the test matrix was split into.

In the above algorithm the only part that needs to be refined is Step 5, the procedure that chooses the phaseshifts. In Step 4 a group of possible phaseshifts has been recorded. In Step 5 we first find the column with the bigger weight, that is the column with the largest number of defined bits. In case more than one columns have the same weight we choose one arbitrarily. The next step of the procedure searches the group of the examined column for the phaseshift with the fewest inputs, that is the phaseshift that will need the fewest XOR gates for its implementation. After this first step the procedure examines each group of phaseshifts starting from the group corresponding to the column with the next bigger weight. The target is to find a phaseshift that will impose the smallest area increase compared to the other phaseshifts of the group. This can be achieved by first calculating the number G of 2-input XOR gates that are needed to implement the phaseshift. Then, we examine if this phaseshift exhibits common taps with a phaseshift already chosen. The common taps are translated to a gate count which is then subtracted from the initial gate count G. This is done until there are no other common taps with other phaseshifts or all the taps of the examined phaseshift are used. The value in G contains the estimated area that the examined phaseshift adds. Obviously we choose the phaseshift that will have the smallest value in G.

The above algorithm along with the preprocessing steps was implemented in C language.

2.3   Application Schemes

The proposed method can be implemented in two different ways depending on whether at-speed testing of the CUT or hardware minimization is targeted. In the first case, shown in Figure 3.a, a distinct k-bit LFSR is used along with the Phase Shifters and in test mode the n multiplexers pass the produced test patterns to the input register. Figure 3.b shows the second case, where during test mode the LFSR is created by using k of the n existing flip-flops of the input register. The k flip-flops drive the Phase Shifters whose each output drives one input of each 2->1 multiplexer. The other input of the multiplexers is driven by the outputs of the flip-flops of the input register. Therefore the circuit under test (CUT) is driven in normal mode by the input register and in test mode by the outputs of the phase shifters.

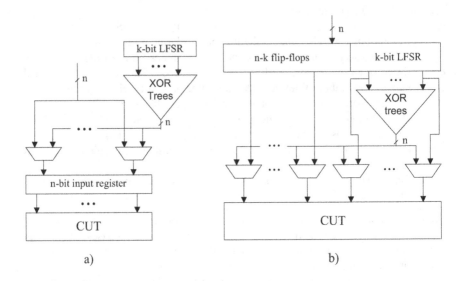

Fig. 3. Proposed approaches: a) Scheme I, Distinct LFSR, b) Scheme II, Embedded LFSR

It is obvious that the first approach, when the delay through the XOR tree is smaller or equal to the delay through the CUT, can perform at-speed testing as opposed to the second approach where the Phase Shifters are placed between input register and the CUT. However, the second approach requires less hardware for its implementation since instead of k extra flip-flops it needs k multiplexers in order to modify during test mode a part of an existing register to an LFSR.

3   Experimental Results

In this section we provide experimental results for two kinds of test sets:

- The first kind regards test sets that target the detection of the random pattern resistant or hard faults.
- The second kind regards test sets that detect all the faults of a circuit.
- The test sets used in our experiments concerned the ISCAS 85 benchmark circuits.

3.1   Test Sets for Hard Faults

The test sets used as inputs to our tool are the same with the test sets used in [12, 13]. Therefore our experimental results can be easily compared with those found in [12, 13], where a number of counter schemes are used to perform test set embedding. We also compared our method with the case of using a ROM to store the test vectors. The ROM also uses a counter in order to produce the addresses of the vectors, therefore the area imposed by the counter was also taken into consideration. The data stored in the ROM represent the test matrix that was obtained after the preprocessing steps presented in Section 2. The test matrix obtained was used in our method as well.

We used our tool to produce the Phase Shifter structures that are needed to perform the required phaseshifts of the m-sequence of the LFSR used. A number of experiments were carried out, examining different combinations of LFSR stages and number of phases. Since the test sets used are relatively small, in most cases the vectors are produced in one phase and the size of the LFSR is one smaller than the maximum number of specified bits in a column.

In Table 1 we provide experimental results regarding the clock cycles needed for embedding the given test set. Columns 2S, 2C, 2P and τ'RC correspond to the counter based schemes described in [13] while scheme 1C is described in [12]. We observe that all the counter schemes require a large number of clock cycles, compared to the test set size, in order to embed the given test set and in some cases it may be impractical, for example circuits c1355 and c6288. On the other hand, our method and the ROM approach apply the test patterns in the minimum possible number of clock cycles.

Table 1. Required clock cycles regarding hard fault test set embedding

Circuit	Test Matrix	1C	2S	2C	2P	τ'CR	ROM	Proposed
c432	6 x 36	125	92	125	92	13	6	6
c499	14 x 41	22,064	17,002	9,230	14,243	46	14	14
c880	11 x 60	29	20	19	20	13	11	11
c1355	12 x 41	1.2×10^8	8×10^7	4×10^7	7.8×10^7	9,012	12	12
c1908	14 x 33	1169	670	665	876	121	14	14
c3540	22 x 50	970	930	883	942	79	22	22
c5315	7 x 178	62	55	50	55	19	7	7
c6288	36 x 32	9.8×10^7	6.8×10^7	1.7×10^7	6.9×10^7	702,013	36	36

The circuits derived from our method were synthesized using the Leonardo Spectrum® synthesis tool from Mentor Graphics Corp. We used the sample ASIC XCL05U library (0.5μm) provided with the tool and we optimized the circuits with respect to area. The approach implemented was the one depicted in Figure 3.a), i.e. a distinct LFSR was used. We also synthesized the counter-based scheme presented in [12] which requires the less area among the other counter based schemes described in [13], while for the ROM-based scheme we assumed that a bit requires area equal to 0.25 of a gate equivalent (GE) [18]. Finally, the address counter needed for the ROM-based approach was optimized for area and added to the area of the ROM array. The results are shown in Table 2.

From the results of Table 2, we observe that in half the cases our scheme requires on average 55% less area than the counter-based scheme. Comparing now the proposed scheme with the ROM-based approach, we observe that our scheme imposes less area overhead in all, except for one (c1908), cases, clearly indicating its superiority. Furthermore, in cases where long test times are prohibited, the counter based schemes cannot be applied, unless a ROM is also used (τ'RC). In the latter case our scheme is still superior in terms of clock cycles needed, while the area required is expected to be significantly smaller.

Table 2. Hardware overhead (GEs) regarding hard fault test set embedding

	1C	ROM	Proposed method		Comparisons	
Circuit	Area	Area	Phases	Area	1C vs Proposed	ROM vs Proposed
c432	27.4	20.5	1	14.8	85.14%	38.51%
c499	63	70.8	2	43.2	45.83%	63.89%
c880	18.6	36.8	1	30.8	-39.61%	19.48%
C1355	116.4	104.8	3	70.6	64.87%	48.44%
C1908	45.2	56.8	1	60.2	-24.92%	-5.65%
C3540	41.4	100.1	2	86.6	-52.19%	15.59%
C5315	23.6	25.75	1	19	24.21%	35.53%
C6288	116.4	302.6	4	211.8	-45.04%	42.87%

3.2   Test Sets for all Faults

The full test sets used for the second type of the experiments were produced by using the ATALANTA ATPG tool [19]. These test sets do not contain any undefined bits and therefore contain a quite small number of test vectors. However, the amount of test vectors for each test set is such that partitioning into phases was essential and was accompanied by the preprocessing steps of Section 2. We implemented both schemes of the proposed method (Figures 3.a and 3.b) and we used the same synthesis tool and implementation library as in the experiments carried out for the hard fault test sets.

The methods given in [12, 13] are based on the manipulation of the large number of don't cares appearing in the test sets for the hard to detect faults. They cannot be used in the case of fully compacted test sets that target all the faults of the CUT. Therefore in this case we do not compare our method with the ones given in [12, 13].

In the case that a compacted test set detects all the faults of a circuit, two methods can be used [14, 15] apart from the proposed and the ROM based method. In [14] the number of cycles needed to apply the test patterns is $2s(n^2+n)$ where n is the number of primary inputs and s is the number of seeds used for the twisted ring counter (TRC). A lower bound of the number of clock cycles required by [14] is given in Table 3 using the values of s given in [20], since the authors of [14] confess that for the ISCAS 85 circuits their method requires more seeds than that of [20]. Table 3 also shows the clock cycles when a ROM is used and the clock cycles when our method is applied. We observe that our method is far more efficient than [14] with respect to the required number of clock cycles. The hardware overhead of [14] is smaller than that of our method, however the test application time is more than 1000 times larger.

The method proposed in [15] is interesting, however does not present experimental results, so we will compare it with our method only qualitatively. In [15] the number of phases is equal to $\lceil v/n \rceil$, where v is the number of the test vectors, n is the number of the CUT's inputs and $\lceil X \rceil$ denotes the smallest integer that is greater than or equal to X. For each one of the phases a new ALFSM or an ALFSM with reconfigurable feedback functions is required. Furthermore, the number of cells in the ALFSM is always equal to n, whereas in our method it is usually significantly smaller. Therefore, we expect the hardware required for the implementation of this method to be larger than that of our method.

Table 3. Required clock cycles regarding full test set embedding

Circuit	[14]	ROM	Proposed
c432	>42624*	48	48
c499	>79212	52	52
c880	>139080	49	49
c1355	>141204	85	85
c1908	>150348	111	111
c2670	>6433596	100	100
c3540	>244800	143	143
c5315	>1911720	112	112
c6288	>12672	27	27
c7552	>6372288	178	178

* >f: a number of clock cycles larger than f

In Table 4 we compare our schemes against the ROM based scheme with respect to hardware overhead in gate equivalents (GEs). From this table we observe that the area required by the proposed scheme is smaller in all of the examined circuits. The difference becomes larger for test sets with a lot of vectors and a lot of inputs, as we can see from c2670, c5315 and c7552 where the area savings are over 50%.

Table 4. Hardware overhead (GEs) for full test set embedding

Circuit	Test Matrix	ROM	Scheme I	Scheme II	I vs ROM	II vs ROM
c432	48 x 36	457	381.8	338.4	19.70%	35.05%
c499	52 x 41	557.6	455	413.6	22.55%	34.82%
c880	49 x 60	760.8	573.2	534.4	32.73%	42.37%
C1355	85 x 41	901.85	685.6	650	31.54%	38.75%
C1908	111 x 33	946.35	708.8	672.8	33.51%	40.66%
C2670	100 x 233	5855	3506.4	3472.6	66.98%	68.61%
C3540	143 x 50	1822.9	1406.4	1377.8	29.61%	32.31%
C5315	112 x 178	5013	3284.4	3249.8	52.63%	54.26%
C6288	27 x 32	236.4	209.6	197.4	12.79%	19.76%
C7552	178 x 207	9246.9	5670	5636	63.08%	64.07%

4   Conclusions and Future Work

We have presented a new method, which can reproduce a given test set. To achieve the latter, the method uses an LFSR and a number of Phase Shifters that produce cyclic shifts of the LFSR's m-sequence. The outputs of the Phase Shifters produce cyclic shifts of the LFSR's m-sequence in a way that when the test procedure starts at each clock cycle a test vector of the test set will be produced. The method can be used in a mixed mode BIST environment when the given test set targets random pattern resistant faults leaving the rest of the faults to be detected by other means of test pattern generation circuits. It can also be used as a standalone mechanism when the given test set detects all the faults of the circuit. In this case the method does not require a structural model of the circuit and therefore is suitable when targeting test pattern generation for Intellectual Property (IP) cores. In both cases the hardware overhead imposed is smaller than other approaches while the number of cycles needed to reproduce the test vectors is optimal.

We are currently working to improve the basic scheme in directions such as finding a heuristic for the separation of the columns of the test matrix into groups and driving the columns of each group by a distinct LFSR or applying a superset of the test set in order to minimize the hardware overhead.

References

[1]   Abramovici, M., Breuer, M. A. and Friedman, A. D., Digital Systems Testing and Testable Design. New York: Computer Science Press, 1990.

[2]   Agarwal, V. K. and Cerny, E., "Store and Generate Built-In Testing Approach", Proc. Int'l Symp. Fault-Tolerant Computing, pp. 35-40, 1981.

[3]   Dandapani, R., Patel, J. and Abraham, J., "Design of Test Pattern Generators for Built-In Testing", Proc. Int'l Test Conf., pp. 315-319, 1984.

[4]   Brglez, F., Gloster, G. and Kedem, G., "Built-in Self-Test with Weighted Random Pattern Hardware", Proc. IEEE Int'l Computer Design, pp. 161-166, 1990.

[5]   Reeb, B. and Wunderlich, H.-J., "Deterministic Pattern Generation for Weighted Random Pattern Testing", Proc. European Design & Test Conf., pp. 30-36, 1996.

[6]   Kapur, R., Patil, S., Snethen, T. J. and Williams, T. W., "Design of an Efficient Weighted Random Pattern Generation System", Proc. IEEE Int'l Test Conf., pp.491-500, 1994.

[7]   Touba, N. A. and McCluskey, E. J., "Synthesis of Mapping Logic for Generating Pseudo-Random Patterns for BIST", Proc. IEEE Int'l Test Conf., pp.674-682, 1995.

[8]   Wunderlich, H.-J. and Kiefer, G., "Bit-Flipping BIST", Proc. of IEEE Int'l Conf. on Computer Aided Design (ICCAD), pp. 337-343, 1996.

[9]   Kalligeros, E., Kavousianos, X., Bakalis, D. and Nikolos, D., "On-the-Fly Reseeding: A New Reseeding Technique for Test-Per-Clock BIST", JETTA, Vol. 18-3, pp. 315-332.

[10]   Chakrabarty, K. and Das, S. R., "Test-Set Embedding Based on Width Compression for Mixed-Mode BIST", IEEE Trans. Instrumentation and Measurement, Vol. 49, No. 3, pp. 671-678, Jun. 2000.

[11]   Chakrabarty, K., Murray, B. T. and Iyengar, V., "Built-In Test Pattern Generation for High-Performance Circuits Using Twisted-Ring Counters", Proc. 17th IEEE VLSI Test Symp., pp. 22-27, 1999.

[12]   Kagaris, D., Tragoudas, S. and Majumdar, A., "On the Use of Counters for Reproducing Deterministic Test Sets", IEEE Trans. Comp., Vol 45, No. 12, pp. 1405-1419, Dec. 1996.

[13]   Kagaris, D. and Tragoudas, S., "On the Design of Optimal Counter-Based Schemes for Test Set Embedding", IEEE Trans. CAD, Vol. 18, No. 2, pp. 219-230, Feb. 1999.

[14]   Swaminathan, S. and Chakrabarty, K., "On Using Twisted-Ring Counters for Test Set Embedding in BIST", JETTA, Vol.17, No. 6, pp. 529-542, Dec. 2001.

[15]   Lew Yan Voon, L. F. C., Dufaza, C. and Landrault, C., "BIST Linear Generator Based on Complemented Outputs", Proc. IEEE VLSI Test Symposium, pp. 137-142, 1992.

[16]   Bardell, P. H., "Design Consideration for Parallel Pseudorandom Pattern Generators", JETTA, Vol. 1, No. 1, pp. 73-87, 1990.

[17]   Rajski, J., Tamarapalli, N. and Tyszer, J., "Automated Synthesis of Phase Shifters for Built-In Self-Test Applications", IEEE Trans. CAD, Vol. 19, No. 10, pp. 1175-1188, Oct. 2000.

[18]   Huang, L. R., Jou, J. Y. and Kuo, S. Y., "Gauss-Elimination-Based Generation of Multiple Seed-Polynomial Pairs for LFSR", IEEE Trans. CAD, Vol. 16, No. 9, pp. 1015-1024, Sept. 1997.

[19]   Lee, H. K. and Ha, D. S., "ATALANTA: An efficient ATPG for compbinational circuits", Dept. of Elect. Eng., Virginia Polytechnic Inst. and State Univ., Blacksburg, VA, USA, Tech. Rep. 93-12, 1993.

[20]   Hellebrand, S., Reeb, B., Tarnick, S. and Wunderlich, H.-J., "Pattern Generation for a Deterministic BIST Scheme", Proc. of IEEE Int'l Conf. on Computer Aided Design (ICCAD), pp. 88-94, Nov. 1995.

Reset–Driven Fault Tolerance*

João Carlos Cunha[1,2], António Correia[2], Jorge Henriques[2],
Mário Zenha Rela[2], and João Gabriel Silva[2]

[1] Dep. Eng. Informática e Sistemas, Instituto Superior de Engenharia de Coimbra
3030 Coimbra, Portugal
jcunha@isec.pt
[2] CISUC/Dep. Eng. Informática, Universidade de Coimbra
3030 Coimbra, Portugal
{scorreia,jh,mzrela,jgabriel}@dei.uc.pt

Abstract. A common approach in embedded systems to achieve fault–
tolerance is to reboot the computer whenever some non-permanent error
is detected. All the system code and data are recreated from scratch,
and a previously established checkpoint, hopefully not corrupted, is used
to restart the application data. The confidence is thus restored on the
activity of the computer. The idea explored in this paper is that of uncon-
ditionally resetting the computer in each control frame (the classic read
sensors → calculate control action → update actuators cycle). A stable–
storage based in RAM is used to preserve the system's state between consecutive cleanups and a standard watchdog timer guarantees that a reset
is forced whenever an error crashes the system. We have evaluated this
approach by using fault-injection in the controller of a standard temperature control system. The experimental observations show that the
Reset–Driven Fault Tolerance is a very simple yet effective technique to
improve reliability at an extremely low cost since it is a conceptually
simple, software only solution with the advantage of being application
independent.

1 Introduction

The correct functioning of embedded computing systems is essential to modern
civilization. We depend on a myriad of embedded computing devices from chips
inside credit cards and mobile phones, to automatic teller machines (ATM's) and
traffic controllers. We can now carry our medical record in a credit card-like media or use contactless tickets in public transportation services. A digital camera
has now more memory and processing power than a five-year-old desktop computer. Luxury cars carry a full network linking some tens of microcontrollers to
handle from comfort to safety-critical features such as ABS. Everywhere we can

* This work was partially supported by the Portuguese Foundation for Science
and Technology under the POSI programme and the FEDER programme of
the European Union, through the R&D Unit 326/94 (CISUC) and the project
PRAXIS/P/EEI/10205/1998 (CRON).

find an embedded system that silently fulfils its role in our technologically driven societies.

The need for fault-tolerance in such small embedded computing systems is demanding due its growing importance. However, such systems pose a formidable challenge to dependability: they are a case on their own due their small dimensions, low power available, trimmed-down hardware and the mandatory requirement to maintain costs low. Any additional cent in consumer electronic devices may prevent a product economic feasibility. Therefore, the use of hardware redundancy is not an option.

The main class of computer faults are transients: voltage fluctuations, electromagnetic interference, heat, moisture, all contribute to the generation of such faults. Only a minority of faults are permanent, thus the common approach of "fixing" most computing systems by simply resetting them. Such transient misbehavior can also be attributable to the software, namely unexpected interactions between correct modules or unexpected inputs from its environment. It is virtually impossible to identify clearly if a transient fault has been caused by hardware or software. Nevertheless, what is clear is that the number of transients is much larger than permanent failures and its share is rising due to the increasing complexity of software and the smaller geometries and lower power levels of integrated circuits [15], [17].

In this paper we propose a novel approach that provides a simple and yet very effective solution for this class of applications: by resetting systematically the computer to flush any latent errors from it's internal state, we guarantee a state cleanup before every new control cycle is started. The main memory is used as a stable-storage medium to preserve the relevant data across reset boundaries. This approach avoids the need to pack a delicate and complex set of fault-tolerance techniques into resource scarce computing systems. It is a very low cost solution since it is a conceptually simple software-only operation. Moreover, it is not application dependent. Some studies on software rejuvenation [8] have a similar approach to deal with software aging. When software continuously executes for long time, some error conditions such as memory leaks, memory fragmentation, broken pointers, missing scheduling deadlines, etc., accumulate and eventually lead to system failure. This approach involves resetting the system periodically and then starting with clean internal states, thus flushing latent software errors.

This paper is organized as follows: in the next section, we discuss how the traditional fault-tolerance approaches are applicable to small embedded computing systems. In section 3, the details of using Reset–Driven fault tolerance are presented. In section 4, the results from the experimental evaluation of this approach through fault-injection are presented and discussed. The paper concludes with an overview of the proposed technique and discussion of the work currently underway.

2   Fault-Tolerance in a Resource Scarce Environment

Redundancy is the key to achieve fault-tolerance. If systems had strictly the resources required to fulfill their intended functional goals, they could not handle the additional tasks required to cope with the abnormal circumstances that result from the occurrence of faults. Redundancy can be hardware, software or time. In small scale systems there is a short supply of any of them: due to the economic, space and power constraints hardware cannot be added, software uses scarce RAM, FLASH-RAM or ROM silicon space. Depending on the application, time may be the only slack resource available; due to the physical-world inertia these systems spend most of their time idle. Slow clock rates are mandatory whenever power consumption is critically restricted such as in mobile devices. Nevertheless, at least a minimum hardware redundancy devoted to fault-tolerance is required: in case a permanent fault occurs, the system should be brought into a safe-state (if one exists), so that at least its outputs do not produce random or dangerous results: in furnaces the heating is turned off, elevators automatically go down to the nearest floor, valves in tanks are seldom left unchanged, and alarms are set. In case of failure, the outputs are brought to these default values. A "redundant" hardware component that can be found in every controller system is the ubiquitous watchdog timer. This is a timer set to trigger a reset on the target controller if it is not refreshed in a predefined time interval. This last resort mechanism detects system hang-ups.

Software redundancy can also be used to detect the occurrence of errors if the system is able to continue after recovery and/or reconfiguration. However, traditional software techniques such as recovery blocks [13] and N-version [2] are inadequate to handle hardware transients: there is no need to have alternate or multi-version code since the software is assumed correct. Moreover, budgetary constraints as well as memory-size limitations prevent such approaches: they are usually reserved for high critical applications. For the class of systems under consideration, software correctness is assumed since the applications are normally not very demanding.

The designer or even the system at run-time can also use a measure of quality of service to trade-off hardware or software redundancy vs. time [9]. Instead of having extra space resources to recover from an error in time to produce the correct result, it may produce an imprecise result in a fast way (e.g. simply maintaining the previous result) while recovering. In face of the above-referred constraints, in practice small embedded systems are restricted to use behavioral error detection mechanisms such as checking the reasonableness of the results produced or coding checks (CRC's, checksums, parity). These are low overhead techniques that pay off the error coverage they provide. It is in such resource scarce environments that the Reset–Driven fault tolerance (RDFT) approach, described in the next section, can best be applied.

3   Reset–Driven Fault Tolerance

We illustrate the RDFT approach using a real-time control system application as example. This is because if RDFT can handle the constraints of such systems it can also be applied to a broader class of applications. However, it must be clear that some characteristics of continuous control systems may not apply to discrete applications. We shall discuss such differences where applicable.

3.1   System Model

Our model considers real-time control systems based on periodic tasks executed cyclically. A real-time clock produces a signal at some predetermined time interval T_s (or sampling period), enabling the controller to read the sensors, compute the control actions, and write them into the actuators (Figure 1). The sampling period must be such that the controller gets feedback from the process at a rate that enables control with the required quality of service. This period is thus dependent on the characteristics of the controlled process, namely its time constants.

During this time, a set of operations must be executed: the process outputs $y(t)$ are converted $y(k)$ by the analogue/digital converters and read by the controller; the controller receives the desired setpoint $r(k)$ and computes the control action $u(k)$; the control action is converted $u(t)$ by the digital/analogue converters and written into the actuators. The control action values are kept active in the actuators until they are updated in the following control cycle.

The main limitations to the timely fulfillment of these tasks are the processing power of the controller computer and the complexity of the control algorithm. However, in most feedback control systems, the control algorithm is very simple and, with the surplus processing power of current controllers, idle times above 80% are common. This model is general enough to describe applications from temperature controllers to anti-locking brakes, including most process control performed in industrial plants.

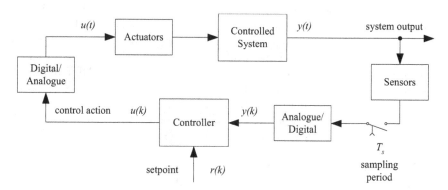

Fig. 1. Block diagram of a periodic real-time control system

3.2   Failure Tolerance in Continuous Control Systems

There is an important behavioral characteristic that pertains to most real-world entities, in particular feedback control systems, that can be used advantageously for fault-tolerance purposes: such systems must be actuated at regular intervals to follow the prescribed state-space trajectory. If the controller computer fails, it produces wrong, late or missing control actions. However, since feedback control algorithms are designed to compensate for external disturbances that the controlled process may suffer, many of the wrong control actions are also compensated for by those algorithms so that no particular fault-tolerance mechanism is needed to handle them. This is possible because the controlled process does not collapse instantaneously due to its physical inertia (mechanical, chemical, etc.), giving the algorithm time to recover. This inertia, known as grace-time[10], is not an exceptional behavior, but rather an intrinsic characteristic of a large number of physical systems. In [5] and [16] it has been showed that feedback control algorithms can indeed compensate for many computer malfunctions, not just disturbances affecting the controlled process. The fail-silent model [11] would flag as failures very many situations where the system in fact does not suffer any negative impact at all. Essentially, for these types of systems, the fail-silent model lacks the notion of time (a single erroneous controller output is not significant, only a sequence of erroneous outputs is) and fails to take into account the fact that the natural inertia of the controlled process filters out short-lived disturbances. If we are able to do a quick recover from a controller failure, avoiding a long sequence of erroneous control actions, there is a high probability that the system could tolerate such controller failure. It must be clear, however, that this grace-time is heavily application dependent and can only be used according to the dynamics of the physical system under control.

Whenever we are not dealing with a continuous application, this "error filtering" by the application may not apply. For example, the control of a bottle-filling conveyor is clearly event driven. What matters is whether a bottle is between two sensors, whether the conveyor is moving or not, etc. Fortunately, discrete-event applications have their own characteristics that heavily simplify the error detection. Such event-driven systems are modeled by state transitions, so a state-flow checking can easily detect wrong paths/transitions performed (the destination state can always check whether it has been correctly reached). In fact, such systems are usually programmed as a large transition table whose correctness can be dynamically checked. Thus, while discrete applications are distinct from continuous applications, that does not prevent the use of the RDFT approach. Another point to be stressed is that in many applications the process state is often irrelevant. All that matters is the data state: given the appropriate inputs and a piece of code the computing system can produce the correct outputs. In such systems the data state, not the process state is the critical asset to be preserved from faults. This reasoning does not apply only to transactional systems, but also to many real-time applications. An example: in a running vehicle the throttle control task may be killed and restarted. As long as the restarted task can access its predecessor's state and the throttle valve output follows the pre-scribed state trajectory, it is not relevant whether a task or its clone is running.

3.3   Periodic Controller Reset

The previous sections show that: i) in most systems the only available resource may be time; ii') a continuous process physical inertia can be used to filter transient erroneous or missing outputs from the controller as long as correct control is resumed shortly, or ii") the discrete nature of an application provides an effective reasonableness check; and iii) the data state is often the relevant asset to be preserved from faults.

The reasoning behind Reset–Driven fault tolerance is conceptually very sim-ple (see Fig. 2): after the execution of every control cycle (read sensors, compute control actions, update actuators), the system state variables are written into a stable storage, the controller is reset and, after restarting, the state variables are restored from stable storage. The controller then stays idle until the next control cycle or external event. In the sections that follow, we shall analyse the continuous case in more detail.

The controller state variables are usually composed of the previous control actions and an historic of process output (or differences to the setpoint values). The matrixes used in the control algorithm that were obtained by means of auto-tuning and the process calibration values should also be saved on stable storage.

To preserve the system state across reset boundaries, we need a stable mem-ory. In face of the application domain, it can only be based on RAM or FLASH–RAM due to the timing constraints. Stable memory has been described and evaluated in a previous paper [6] and is based on the use of the built-in memory protection mechanisms of the processor itself (so that no dedicated hardware is required) underlying the use of replicated robust data structures protected by means of a CRC (cyclic redundancy check). Such stable-storage mechanism can resist hardware and software failures, and guarantees the atomicity of reads and writes. It is clear that without the preservation of the data state this approach would not be feasible. Thus, if a corruption of the stable memory were detected,

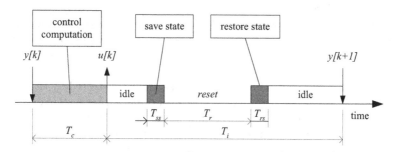

Fig. 2. Reset–Driven controller steps and timings

there would be no other way around but flag a general system failure and jump into a (possible) safe-state.

The whole RDFT approach can therefore be described as a sequence of steps:

i. **Control computation** – When an external or internal event triggers a new iteration of the control loop, the task associated with the required action starts its execution, by reading any inputs (e.g. from the process sensors). The system converts these values into a usable format (e.g. from a 12-bit format into a floating-point), and executes the code associated with the action to be performed, by making use of any additional internal data (e.g. the previous iteration state). The result is again converted to a suitable format (e.g. 12-bit format) and sent to the actuators.

ii. **Save state** – The state variables and any constants that were initialised in run-time (e.g. during process calibration or self-tuning) are written into a stable storage.

iii. **Reset** – The controller reset may be triggered either by software or by hardware. In the first case the control software makes a call to a reset procedure. If the controller fails by hanging and delays its restart, the watchdog timer eventually resets the system. This guarantees that in any case the reset will be applied and that the system will be ready for the next control iteration. As is clear, the hardware reset period must be synchronized with the control loop, in order not to reset the controller while it is executing the control computation.

Two different reset types can be applied: hot or cold reset. In a cold reset, the computer system is fully restarted and all data is initialised. The computer is brought to the same state as in a normal power up. In a hot reset, the system just refreshes the code and data, and starts executing from the system starting point. Code and data refreshing can be made by copying their image from a fixed memory location or another non-volatile memory into RAM, while checking its integrity by checksumming. In either case, the controller system needs to distinguish a refreshing reset from an error-induced reset or from the initial power-up, i.e. if it is in control of a process. This can be done by storing an identifier ("magic number") at a known address in non-volatile storage, such as the CMOS memory in the computer boards where the BIOS stores configuration data.

iv. **Reboot and restore state** – After restarting, the system restores all data structures from stable storage and the watchdog timer is initialized. It then detects that a refreshing reset has happened and becomes idle until a new iteration begins. This idle time can be spent either in a low-power mode or used to run diagnosis tests.

v. **Error-induced reset** – In the case that an error is detected by the intrinsic error-detection mechanisms (e.g. a processor or operating system exception), the system is immediately reset, either hot or cold. If the system hangs, the watchdog timer triggers the reset. It then follows the previously explained steps to reboot and restore state. However, when it detects that this is not a refreshing reset, it restarts immediately the control computation. If the control action from the previous iteration has already been sent to the actuators, the controlled process would probably receive two control actions in the same sampling period. If not, the process would probably receive the control action from the current sampling period later than usual. In either case, this sporadic situation does not usually induce any meaningful disturbances to the controlled process.

This last description deserves an additional comment: we are consenting a controller to fail, either by outputting an erroneous value or by disrespecting the time constraints. However, for embedded control systems, the distinction between the computer and the application is somehow blurred, since none can be though without the other. This means that the pair controller + controlled process should not be viewed separately. Thus, we should only consider as a failure an error that is observable outside of this pair (e.g. the driver feels that the engine is not running smoothly). In fact, for a large number of embedded applications, internal errors are not observable so, for every practical purpose, they never occurred.

If an error occurs during reset, it may abort and be restarted again, in which case the error is flushed; the system cannot hang since the WDT is always active. On the other hand, the system may restart in an erroneous state, maybe with latent errors. This situation is not different from a "typical" latent error: it will be either detected by the integrity checks or flushed in the next reset. Whenever such an error is detected, the system is restarted immediately. If errors lead to successive restarts, we are in the presence of permanent faults to which this approach is not adequate (e.g. if the error corrupts the code or data image). Anyway, as long as the error does not generate a new output, the previous values are maintained. Of course, the outputs can always be brought into a default safe–state through dedicated hardware if the criticality of the application requires it.

3.4   Timing Analysis

The proposed approach requires that there is enough time to reset and restart the controller. Considering the sampling period T_s and the computation time T_c, the system stays idle for $T_i = T_s - T_c$ in every control cycle. The Reset–Driven approach can thus be used if the time to reset the controller (T_r) plus the time to save (T_{ss}) and restore (T_{rs}) the system state fits within the idle time, that is:

$$T_r + T_{ss} + T_{rs} < T_s - T_c \tag{1}$$

- The **sampling period** (T_s) depends upon the time constants of the controlled process. A time constant is a measure of the time taken by the controlled process to respond to a change in input or load [3].
- The **computation time** (T_c) is dependent on the performance of the processing unit and on the complexity of the control algorithm. Control algorithms for feedback control systems are often based on PID (Proportional, Integral and Derivative) algorithms, due to its ability to control almost any

sort of linear physical processes. This control algorithm usually consists on a few lines of code in a high-level language. It is thus very common to have a large fraction of processing time being used by the idle task or in low-power mode. Discrete applications, represented by a set of state-machines are even less demanding in processing power since such systems states are usually programmed through a simple table lookup.

- The **time to save and to restore the system state variables** (T_{ss}, T_{rs}) does not usually represent a significant amount of time, since state variables normally sum up to a few tens of bytes. In real-time embedded systems it is unthinkable to use any sort of disk based stable storage, and thus data is stored in non-volatile memory, like battery-backup RAM, or FLASH-RAM.
- The **time to reset the controller** (T_r) is mainly dependent on the time for integrated circuits to reset. The advantage of using a hot instead of a cold restart derives from this physical constraint. By using a hot restart, we achieved a restart time (T_r) of about 50 milliseconds on a standard PC.

On error-free situations, the control action is sent to the actuators after T_c time from the start of the control iteration. If an error occurs and causes an error-induced reset, the control action sent to the process after restart may present different timings:

- If the reset occurs before the control action from the current iteration has been sent to the actuators (i.e., occurs before the end of T_c), then the control action is output within a maximum delay from the start of the control iteration of $T_c + T_r + T_{rs} + T_c$. If this time exceeds the sampling period T_s, then the current iteration failed to update the process actuators, and thus the control action from the previous iteration is still valid to the process. As already explained, this situation does not usually cause any significant disturbance to the system.
- If the reset occurs after the control action from the current iteration has been sent to the actuators (i.e., occurs after the end of T_c), then if the controller is able to restart and recalculate the control action before the following iteration ((*reset moment* $+ T_r + T_{rs} + T_c < T_s$), the process would receive two control actions in the same cycle. If not, the process would receive the control action in the following iteration, with a maximum delay from the start of the iteration of $T_r + T_{rs} + T_c$ (this is the case when the error occurs at the very last moment in the control cycle). In these situations, an erroneous control action could have been delivered to the process. Again, this sporadic controller failure is usually tolerated by the system.

4   Experimental Validation

We have used a physical process and a PC-based controller to validate the Reset–Driven control approach. We have prepared the controller to reset in every control cycle and injected a comprehensive set of hardware transient faults in the main functional units of the CPU and in memory. The physical process chosen was a hot-air blower, a standard thermal control process widely used in control systems research and education.

4.1   The Experimental Setup

The main elements of our experimental setup are depicted in Fig. 3. The hot-air blower process is being controlled by a controller computer that receives the process outputs from its sensors, computes the control action, and writes it in the process actuators. A second computer is also receiving the process outputs in order to monitor its behavior. The fault-injection experiments are managed by a third computer, connected to the controller computer, where faults are actually injected.

Process Description. The hot-air blower is a standard control process that represents the generality of thermal processes, such as furnaces, industrial boilers or air conditioning devices. We have used the laboratory process PT326 [12]. Its functioning is simple: a centrifugal fan blows air over a heating element and into a tube, having a thermocouple placed at its end. The control action, which determines the power to apply to the heater element, is written by the controller into the DA (digital/analogue) converter in a 12-bit format. This value is then converted into a DC voltage in the range 0 to 10 volts and supplied to the process actuator. The process sensor outputs the air temperature in the form of a voltage in the range -10 to $+10$ volts (corresponding approximately to a temperature in the range 26° to 60°C), and the AD (analogue/digital) converter makes this value available for the controller in a 12-bit format. Based on the time constants of the process, we have chosen a sampling period (T_s) of 70 milliseconds. Although representative of general thermal processes in terms of control theory, this PT326

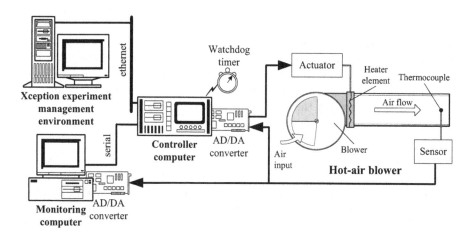

Fig. 3. Experimental setup

has a very small inertia, and thus its time constant is very small, in comparison e.g. to furnaces or boilers. This characteristic makes particularly difficult to apply the Reset–Driven approach to this process, since the sampling period (T_s) is small, leaving a very short time to reset the controller (T_r).

The System Model. The hot-air blower PT326 is a non-linear process with a pure time delay, which depends on the distance between the thermocouple and the heating element, and on the air flow rate. The process can be described as a first order system by the following equation:

$$y(k) = a.y(k-1) + b.u(k-d) \tag{2}$$

where $y(k)$ is the system output at discrete time k, $u(k)$ is the the input, a and b are constants that characterize the process and d is the time delay in sampling periods. We have used a traditional PID control algorithm, since this kind of control is widely used due to its simplicity and ability to regulate most industrial processes with dissimilar specifications. A PID controller is described by the following equation:

$$u(k) = u(k_1) + q_0.e(k) + q_1.e(k_1) + q_2.e(k_2) \tag{3}$$

where $e(k)$ is the control error, defined by the difference between the reference and the process output $(e(k) = r(k) - y(k))$, and q_0, q_1 and q_2 are the PID parameters. In our experiments, we have used $q_0 = 0.17$, $q_1 = 0.09$, and $q_2 = 0.002$, obtained by means of a pole placement method [1].

The Controller Computer. The controller computer is a standard 90MHz Intel Pentium based PC-board with 8M of RAM. The control application is running on top of SMX© (Simple Multitasking Executive) [14], a COTS real-time kernel from Micro Digital, Inc. If any error is detected by the intrinsic error detection mechanisms of the system, such as processor exceptions or operating system checks, the normal procedure is to immediately reset the system. A standard watchdog timer card is responsible to reset the system if it hangs. We have measured the time (T_c) to read the input ports from the AD/DA card, calculate the control action and write the results into the output ports of the same card, and got values no greater than 1.5 milliseconds (input and output took most of this time).

Stable Storage. We have used a RAM-based stable storage [6] to collect the data that should survive resets. This data is composed of the state variables from the control algorithm, the process status, the setpoint generator, and on constant values obtained from the process calibration. If the control matrixes were obtained by means of self-tuning (which is not the case in our experiments), these should also be saved on stable storage. Nevertheless, we have also saved them. In total, we have placed 120 bytes of data in stable storage. Every data structure written in stable storage has a 16-bit CRC appended to it. Our stable storage mechanism follows each write with a simple correctness verification: the CRC is recalculated and, if wrong, the write is repeated. Writes are also performed in an atomic way, by using two separated memory regions. Only after the write in the first memory region succeeds, a copy of the data is written in the second memory region and checked again. Only then does the write to the stable memory commit. At each system restart following a reset, data is recovered from stable storage and, if any corruption is detected by means of the CRC verification, it is alternatively recovered from the copy in the second memory region. The time to save the system state variables (T_{ss}) was measured to be no greater than 200 microseconds, and the time to restore the system state variables (T_{rs}) was less than 450 microseconds.

Controller Reset. From the above measurements and calculations, we have obtained the following figures for our system: the sampling period (T_s) is 70 milliseconds, the maximum computation time (T_c) is 1.5 milliseconds, and the maximum time to save and restore the system state variables $(T_{ss}$ and $T_{rs})$ is, respectively, 0.2 and 0.45 milliseconds. This means, from Equation (1), that we have a maximum time to reset the system (T_r) of 67.85 milliseconds. Some PC hardware components have long reset delays, well above 100 milliseconds, which make cold reset unfeasible in our system. We have thus adopted the hot reset approach in this target system. The reset may be triggered by a software call (just after state storage), by the CPU exception handlers, or by the kernel error handling routines. The watchdog timer is also able to trigger reset by means of a non-maskable interrupt. The hot reset procedure follows a series of steps, namely:

i. The caller type (software call, exception ID, etc.) is stored in CMOS memory.
ii. The processor is switched from protected into real mode and the control flow jumps to the starting address of the BIOS (address F000:FFF0).
iii. After performing the system test, the BIOS calls the operating system kernel, that was previously loaded into a fixed memory area, which initialises its structures and switches into protected mode.
iv. It then copies an image of the operating system and control application, also in main memory, to another memory area where they will run. This data is tested for corruption by means of a checksum.
v. When the control application is called, it begins by resetting the watchdog timer and restoring the system state variables.

All these steps take no longer than 51.5 milliseconds, thus below the 67.85 milliseconds of idle time available.

4.2   Experiment Definition

Our experiments consisted on the injection of more than 7500 transient faults in the controller's CPU and memory.

The Fault Injection Tool. The disturbances internal to the controller were produced using RT–Xception [7], the real-time version of the Xception tool [4]. This version adds to the original Xception the benefit of not having almost any *probe effect*, i.e., it induces a negligible and bounded time overhead on the target application. RT–Xception had to be adapted for the Reset–Driven approach, since it has to preserve its state during resets. This is done transparently to the application.

The Fault Model. We have injected transient bit flips, affecting only one machine instruction and one processor functional unit at a time (Registers, Integer ALU, Floating-point ALU, Data bus, Address Bus, and Memory Management Unit). Some faults were also injected in main memory (code and data areas). Only one bit was affected by each fault. The faults were time triggered so that they occurred randomly at any point during the execution of the program. In order to speed-up the experiments, the probability to inject faults while running the idle task has been reduced by using a spatial trigger located at the beginning of the iteration programmed to start the time trigger after a random number of times. Then, the time trigger starts the fault-injection after a random time, set to fall inside the execution of the controller code. We have also injected faults aimed specifically to the state variables and constants. The previous experiments described in [5] have shown that those faults have the greatest impact on the controller behavior.

Outcome Classification. Feedback control systems are usually designed to follow a reference path (*setpoint*). Due to external disturbances, inexactnesses of the process model and other environment variables, the system outputs are expected to show some deviations from the specified setpoint. It is thus normal to specify a valid state-space region around the setpoint, based in performance requirements. Even so, going out of the valid state-space does not necessarily have catastrophic consequences, provided the process outputs return to this region within a maximum delay. We have thus classified the outcomes of the experiment with the PT326 process as:

- Tolerated (benign) – even if an erroneous output is produced, the air temperature stayed inside the valid state-space region. This includes also errors that simply vanished without being detected and without producing erroneous outputs;
- Out of valid state-space – the temperature left the valid state-space region, but re-entered it within a maximum specified delay;
- Collapsed – the temperature left the valid state-space region for longer than the maximum delay.

We have defined a setpoint as presented in Fig. 4, and monitored the process outputs under normal conditions (without fault-injection). Due to the time the air takes to cross the tube from the actuator until the sensor, the process outputs present a constant delay to the setpoint of about 770 milliseconds (11 control iterations). The valid state-space region was thus defined with a tolerance of 1 volt (about 1.7°C) to the setpoint, with a delay of 11 iterations:

$$y(k) < r(k-11) + 1 \ and \ y(k) > r(k-11) - 1 \qquad (4)$$

The collapse condition occurs if the process output violates the valid state–space region for more than 10 iterations (700 milliseconds). The experiments were limited to 240 iterations (16.8 seconds), which complete a full setpoint cycle.

Since we are injecting faults in the controller computer, we cannot have any confidence on its information about the process behavior. We have thus used a second computer (the *Monitoring computer* in Fig. 3) to collect the process outputs. We only had to synchronize it with the controller computer, so both could get data from the process at roughly the same time. We used a serial connection for this synchronization and for data transmission at the end of each injection run.

4.3   Experimental Results

Baseline: Non-Reset–Driven Controller. We have started by testing the hot-air blower controller without making use of the Reset–Driven approach. The whole system is as the Reset–Driven case, including the storage of data and constants in stable storage in every control iteration. Note that this means that we are using as baseline a system with a non-negligible amount of fault-tolerance mechanisms. Only if an error is detected, does the controller reset and recover by restoring the data in stable storage. Thus, the only difference is that this

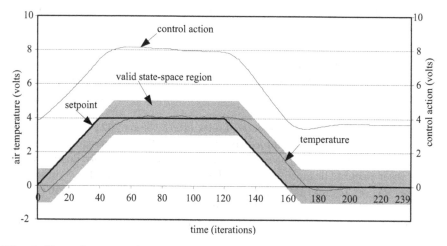

Fig. 4. Error-free experiment, presenting the setpoint, control action, process temperature and valid state–space region

Table 1. Behavior of the baseline controller under fault injection (number of faults)

Fault location	Injected faults	Tolerated	Out-of-valid state-space	Collapsed	Detected
Constants	200	182	3	15	2
State variables	300	293	0	7	37
Memory (code)	500	500	0	0	14
Memory (data)	500	500	0	0	6
Random	824	824	0	0	275
Total	2324	2299	3	22	334

controller does not compulsory reset at each control iteration. We have injected 2500 faults in different targets, such as the controller constants and state variables, code and data memory, and randomly on the CPU functional units (some random faults were not injected because the trigger conditions weren't met). The results are presented in Table 1.

As expected from our previous work [5], faults affecting constants and long-lasting state variables have a significant impact on the process behavior. From the 500 faults injected in constants and state variables, the controller output left its valid state-space region 25 times, and only in 3 cases it later re-entered this region within 10 iterations. In the remaining 22 cases it collapsed. From the 2324 effectively injected faults, 334 were detected by a CPU exception, an operating system assertion or the watchdog timer. Recovery performed well in all cases but one, in which the process did collapse. In the other 21 cases of collapse, no error was ever detected. The zero cases of misbehavior for the memory and random faults are consistent with the observations in previous studies and can be explained by the intrinsic redundancy present into the compiled code.

A Reset–Driven Controller. We have then simply introduced a call to reset in every control cycle, after storing data in stable storage, and injected the same set of faults as in the previous experiment. The results for this Reset–Driven controller are presented in Table 2.

The number of effectively injected faults (1541 versus 2324 before resetting the system) illustrate a most interesting point of RDFT: errors that become latent and would later affect the system when activated are simply flushed whenever a reset occurs. It must be stressed that in our testbed the "window" of injection was set to fall inside the execution of the controller code, not the idle time. Nevertheless, the number of effectively injected faults has decreased significantly since many faults timed-out the trigger during reset, and thus were simply flushed. This is the preventive face of RDFT: errors that would sum up and later affect the system are now cyclically cleared. In no case (versus the 3 without reset) has the system left its valid region and later returned. It can also

Table 2. Behavior of the Reset–Driven controller under fault injection (number of faults)

Fault location	Injected faults	Tolerated	Out-of-valid state-space	Collapsed	Detected
Constants	129	129	0	0	2
State variables	172	169	0	3	36
Memory (code)	334	334	0	0	20
Memory (data)	322	322	0	0	3
Random	584	584	0	0	197
Total	1541	1538	0	3	258

be observed that in only 3 cases (versus the 22 observed before) has the process deviated outside its valid state-space region, leading to collapse. The 3 faults that lead to this situation where injected in the state variables. This means that a corrupted state was saved undetected (e.g. a wrong readout was saved and the subsequent control iterations where "compensating" for a deviation that never occurred). These observations are very interesting in that they illustrate clearly what can be the main problem of the RDFT approach: if a corrupted state is saved, RDFT may be ineffective. That's why the main effort in using RDFT can be devoted to prevent corrupted checkpoints. These figures are remarkable if we consider the simplicity of the solution. The cost/benefit makes this a very interesting approach to a large number of applications whose criticality does not require the highest levels of dependability only achievable through more costly sophisticated techniques.

Tolerating Corrupted Checkpoints. Our previous research has shown that constants and long-lasting state variables are particularly vulnerable to corruption. In the 3 cases presented in the section above it was the corruption of such variables that lead the process to collapse. In the experiments that follow we evaluated the robustness achieved by additional protection into these data structures by performing integrity tests before its reutilisation in later control iterations. To perform such integrity tests, we kept the state variables from the previous control loop, recalculated the new values and verified if they matched the current state variables. Although these tests seem quite generic since they just reuse the control algorithm, they are not: they require a deep knowledge of the code that calculates the control action, the internals of the drivers that convert the data received/sent from/to the process, and the setpoint generator, if one exists. The results of this new fault-injection experiment are shown in Table 3.

Note that the number of injected faults has risen again, since the executing time has almost doubled. We did not include the faults that would have been injected during reset (they were simply flushed). No misbehavior was ever ob-

Table 3. Behavior of the Reset–Driven controller with state protection (number of faults)

Fault location	Injected faults	Tolerated	Out-of-valid state-space	Collapsed	Detected
Constants	188	188	20	0	29
State variables	297	297	0	0	61
Memory (code)	485	485	0	0	10
Memory (data)	492	492	0	0	4
Random	810	810	0	0	262
Total	2269	2269	0	0	366

served: neither the system has left its valid state-space or later collapsed. This does not mean that if a larger number of faults were injected they would not occur; simply they are unlikely enough so that none was observed in these experiments. We must stress a point that is not apparent from these figures: the effort to achieve the results depicted in Table 3 was extremely high. The effectiveness of the integrity tests could only be achieved by systematically injecting faults, inspecting the execution trace and analysing the reasons behind each error. This was a complex, highly sophisticated and time consuming task. Moreover, it was clear that for every new application everything must be restarted from scratch. This effort emphasized the main advantage of the Reset–Driven approach versus several behavior-based error-detection techniques. The former is absolutely application independent and can be applied to almost every application as long as the processing time requirements are met. Even if the later techniques provide good error coverage, it must be stressed that since they are not automatable, a lot of effort must be used to "tune" the error detection techniques to the application at hand.

5   Conclusions and Future Work

In this paper we propose a novel approach to achieve fault-tolerance based on systematically resetting the computing system after every output produced, and restarting with a refreshed state. This action can be viewed as a fault removal procedure, since it effectively aims at preventively removing any latent faults or errors, thus avoiding a system failure in the future. This approach is mostly applicable to small embedded systems which involve short startup times that would not be feasible, for example, with workstations whose complex hardware and software require long reboot times. The experimental observations show that the Reset–Driven fault-tolerance approach is a very simple yet effective technique to improve dependability at an extremely low cost since it is a conceptually simple, software only solution with the advantage of being application independent.

We are now studying the applicability of this approach in a networked environment. If the target system uses a network connection or other heavy communication protocol, the RDFT may be hard to implement. In experiments not described in this paper we noticed that after reset the peer nodes tried to communicate with the restarting node, which somehow confused the protocols. This delay made restarting very time consuming (several seconds). This forced us to communicate only through a serial channel with a strict token protocol so that spurious characters sent/received during restart where simply discarded. A parallel port could also be used. Several solutions are being considered, namely "hiding" that a reset is occurring but preserving locally the communication channel state; another possibility is to decouple the processing and physical world interface from the communication hardware (e.g. using an autonomous network card).

There is a large number of ubiquitous small embedded computer systems whose criticality does not justify the cost of the more sophisticated error detection techniques. However, their dependability requirements may not be achieved by the simpler, most traditional approaches. We think that's where the Reset–Driven Fault Tolerance can be very cost-effectively used.

References

[1] Åström, K. J., Hägglund, T.: PID Controllers: Theory, Design, and Tuning. Second edition. Instrument Society of America (1995) ISBN 1–55617–516–7   112

[2] Avizienis, A., Kelly, J. P. J.: Fault Tolerance by Design Diversity: Concepts and Experiments. IEEE Computer, Vol. 17. No. 8, August (1984) 67–80   104

[3] Bennet, S. Real-time Computer Control – An Introduction. Second edition, Prentice Hall Series in Systems and Control Engineering, M. J.Grimble ed. (1994)   109

[4] Carreira, J., Madeira, H., Silva, J. G.: Xception: A Technique for the Experimental Evaluation of Dependability in Modern Computers. IEEE Transactions on Software Engineering, February (1998) 125–135   114

[5] Cunha, J.C., Maia, R., Rela, M.Z., Silva, J. G.: A Study on Failure Models in Feedback Control Systems. International Conference on Dependable Systems and Networks, Goteborg, Sweden (2001)   106, 114, 116

[6] Cunha, J. C., Silva, J. G.: Software-Implemented Stable Storage in Main Memory. Brazilian Symposium on Fault-Tolerant Computing, Florianópolis, Brazil (2001)   107, 112

[7] Cunha, J.C., Rela, M. Z., Silva, J. G.: Can Software-Implemented Fault-Injection be used on Real-Time Systems? 3rd European Dependable Computing Conference, Prague, Czech Republic (1999)   114

[8] Huang, Y., Kintala, C., Kolettis, N., Fulton, N. D.: Software Rejuvenation: Analysis, Module and Applications. 25th International Symposium on Fault Tolerant Computing Systems (1995) 381–390   103

[9] Jahanian, F.: Fault-Tolerance in Embedded Real-Time Systems. Hardware and Software Architectures for Fault Tolerance, Michel Banâtre and Peter A. Lee Eds. Springer-Verlag (1994)   104

[10] Kopetz, H.: Real-Time Systems: Design Principles for Distributed Embedded Applications. Kluwer Academic Series in Engineering and Computer Science, John A. Stankovic ed. (1997)   106

[11] Powell, D., Veríssimo, P., Bonn, G., Waeselynck, F., Seaton, D.: The Delta–4 Approach to Dependability in Open Distributed Computing Systems. International Symposium on Fault Tolerant Computing Systems, Tokyo (1988) 106

[12] Process Trainer PT326. Feedback Instruments Limited. http://www.fbk.com 111

[13] Randell, B.: System Sructure for Software Fault–Tolerance. IEEE Transactions on Software Engineering, Vol. SE–1, No.2, June (1975) 220–232 104

[14] SMX Simple Multitasking Executive. http://www.smxinfo.com 112

[15] Somani, A. K., Vaidya, N. H.: Understanding Fault Tolerance and Reliability. IEEE Computer, April (1997) 45–50 103

[16] Vinter, J., Aidemark, J., Folkesson, P., Karlsson, J.: Reducing Critical Failures for Control Algorithms Using Executable Assertions and Best Effort Recovery. Int. Conference on Dependable Systems and Networks, Goteborg, Sweden (2001) 106

[17] Yurcik, W., Doss, D.: Achieving Fault-Tolerant Software with Rejuvenation and Reconfiguration. IEEE Software, July/August (2001) 48–52 103

Towards Dependability Modeling
of FT-CORBA Architectures

István Majzik * and Gábor Huszerl

Department of Measurement and Information Systems
Budapest University of Technology and Economics
Magyar Tudósok krt. 2., H-1117 Budapest, Hungary
{majzik,huszerl}@mit.bme.hu
http://www.mit.bme.hu/

Abstract. The paper presents techniques to support the dependability modeling and analysis of distributed object-oriented applications that are designed according to the Fault Tolerant CORBA (FT-CORBA) specification. First the construction of a high-level dependability model is described. It is based on the architecture of the application and allows the analysis of the fault tolerance strategies and properties that are directly supported by the standard infrastructure. Then a technique to construct a refined dependability model is presented. It exploits the detailed behavioral model of the object responsible for replica maintenance. The UML statechart of this object is transformed to a stochastic Petri net that forms the core of the dependability model. In this way the designer is allowed to utilize the full power of statecharts to construct models of application-dependent replication strategies and recovery policies.

1   Introduction

The need for distributed object-oriented systems has led to the development of middlewares that allow the interaction of objects regardless of their specific platforms and implementation languages. The Common Object Request Broker Architecture (CORBA) is such a middleware standardized by the Object Management Group (OMG). CORBA defines the basic mechanisms for remote object invocation through the Object Request Broker (ORB).

Fault Tolerant CORBA (FT-CORBA) is a general framework for CORBA-based systems that need fault tolerance (FT) [1]. Applications ranging from small, embedded systems to wide area communication networks can utilize the infrastructure defined in the standard and implemented by commercial CORBA providers [2].

In FT-CORBA, single point of failures caused by single objects are avoided by replicating the server objects on a group of hosts. Clients can invoke the

---

* This work has been partially supported by the Hungarian Ministry of Education under contract FKFP 0103/2001.

F. Grandoni (Ed.): EDCC 2002, LNCS 2485, pp. 121–139, 2002.

methods of these replicated objects transparently. The creation and maintenance of replicated objects is provided either by the predefined Fault Tolerance Infrastructure (infrastructure-controlled FT) or directly by the application
(application-controlled FT).

In the case of infrastructure-controlled FT, the availability of a group of replicated objects is determined by a set of properties assigned to the infrastructure.
Among others, the initial number of replicas, the minimum number of replicas,
the fault monitoring interval and granularity are properties that have to be set
carefully to keep the costs at low level and at the same time provide the availability required by the application. In the case of application-controlled FT, the
designer of the application is fully responsible for the replica maintenance including activation, recovery and reconfiguration. Application-specific strategies
can be elaborated to satisfy requirements that cannot be met by the common
implementation of the infrastructure.

The complexity of the standard and the lack of mechanized dependability
analysis are, among others, obstacles to the widespread use of FT-CORBA. The
designer needs support to select the property values of the infrastructure or
to construct optimal application-controlled FT strategies. The comparison of
solutions, the estimation of the effects of selected property values and the identification of dependability bottlenecks can be supported in the design phase by
the construction and analysis of dependability models. Stochastic dependability
models using Markov chains or Petri nets (PN) can provide numerical availability figures as well as the sensitivity of system-level measures to the component
property values.

The paper presents techniques that support the dependability modeling and
analysis of FT-CORBA applications. First the creation of an architectural dependability model in the form of a stochastic Petri net is described. It allows
the early analysis of infrastructure-controlled FT strategies. This approach is
a relatively straightforward adaptation of the methods proposed in previous
works [3]. Then a technique to construct a refined dependability model is presented that utilizes the detailed behavioral models of the objects responsible for
replica maintenance. The UML statechart models of the replication managers
are transformed to a stochastic Petri net that forms the core of the dependability model. In this way a designer is allowed to utilize the full power of statecharts (including event processing and state hierarchy) to construct models of
application-dependent replication strategies, repair and recovery policies. In this
way the same model is used both for model-based dependability analysis and for
(automatic) code generation.

The paper is structured as follows. Section 2 presents the basics of the FT-
CORBA specification, Section 3 gives an overview of interesting trends in dependability modeling. Our approach is outlined in Section 4. The analysis of the
effects of the standard properties of the FT infrastructure and the construction of
the architectural dependability model are detailed in Section 5. The refinement
of this high-level dependability model is introduced in Section 6. The approach
is illustrated by examples in Section 7.

2   FT-CORBA

In FT-CORBA, fault tolerance is provided by entity redundancy (i.e. replication of server objects on different hosts of a distributed system), fault detection and error recovery. The fault model assumes object crash failures: in the case of an error the server object will not provide any response to the clients and will not return to normal operation until an explicit recovery. There is no protection against commission faults and correlated faults.

The client objects should not be aware of the fact that the server objects are replicated (replication transparency) and should not be aware of a failure or recovery of a server replica (failure transparency). The transparent connection between the client and the server replicas is the responsibility of the ORB of the client. In FT-CORBA both time redundancy (retry) and spatial redundancy (invoking alternative servers) are allowed. The Interoperable Object Group Reference (IOGR) used by the client ORB may contain either the profiles of the server replicas or the profiles of gateways (that can be used e.g. to implement ordered and reliable multicast in the case of active redundancy).

The redundant server objects belong to *object groups*, and several object groups can be managed together in a *fault tolerance domain* (FTD). The fault tolerance infrastructure (FTI) of a domain consists of several objects as follows

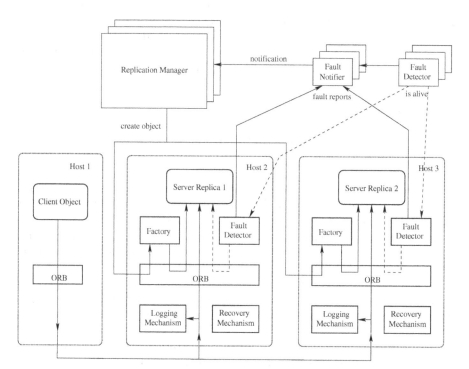

Fig. 1. The architecture of the FT-CORBA redundancy structure

(Figure 1). The creation and maintenance of the object replicas is provided by the *replication manager* (RM). The replica objects are continuously monitored by *local fault detectors* that are deployed on each host. If an object fails then the local fault detector reports the error to the *fault notifier*. The fault notifier filters and analyzes the incoming error reports and sends a notification to the RM and to other registered objects. The local fault detectors are monitored by a *global fault detector* that detects when a local fault detector is not available (e.g. if the host fails). In order to increase availability, the objects of the FTI can be replicated as well.

In the case of the infrastructure-controlled style, it is the responsibility of the RM to maintain the necessary number of replicas. When it receives a notification about the crash of a replica, then it can initiate the recovery of that replica (by utilizing the logging and recovery mechanisms implemented in the object group) or it can remove the replica from the object group and create a new one (by invoking a factory object that is deployed on the selected host). In the case of application-controlled style, the application is responsible for the maintenance of the replicas, by using the services offered by the fault detectors and notifiers, factory objects and partially by the RM.

The reliability and availability of an object group (from the point of view of a client) is determined by a set of properties associated with the group. These properties are summarized in Table 1. They can be set when the object group is created and they can be modified later at run-time. Default values can be assigned to the FT domain or to the type of the server objects.

It has to be emphasized that FT-CORBA standardizes the interfaces and responsibility of the FTI, but does not fix the internal implementation of the mechanisms like logging, recovery and group communication.

3   Background

The literature of dependability evaluation presents several useful ideas that have to be followed in our work.

It is commonly accepted that the results of dependability analysis are especially important in the *early design phase* when decisions among architectural alternatives have to be made and dependability bottlenecks have to be found. In this phase dependability evaluation based on analytical modeling deserves particular attention [4, 5]. The dependability model constructed in the early design phase needs to be *refined hierarchically* as new design information and decisions will be available [6].

In general-purpose architectures the separation of architectural and service concerns is a valuable idea. The architectural failure modes can be mapped separately to service degradation levels interesting to the end-users of the architecture [7].

To allow automated dependability model generation instead of manual modeling, the construction of the dependability model should be based on *engineering modeling languages* and *automatic model transformations* [8]. Results described

Table 1. Fault tolerance properties

Property name	Values and role
ReplicationStyle	STATELESS, WARM_PASSIVE, COLD_PASSIVE or ACTIVE replication.
MembershipStyle	Application controlled (MEMB_APP_CTRL) or infrastructure controlled (MEMB_INF_CTRL) addition or removal of replicas.
ConsistencyStyle	Application controlled (CONS_APP_CTRL) or infrastructure controlled (CONS_INF_CTRL) logging and recovery of replicas.
FaultMonitoringStyle	PUSH ("I am alive") or PULL ("ping") style monitoring of the replicas.
FaultMonitoringGranularity	MEMB (each replica), LOC (each location) or LOC_AND_TYPE (each replica type per location) is monitored.
FaultMonitoringInterval	Interval of time between successive monitoring requests and the corresponding timeout.
Factories	The list of objects that create or delete replicas.
InitialNumberReplicas	Number of replicas when the group is created.
MinimumNumberReplicas	The number of replicas that must exist to provide the service.
CheckpointInterval	Time period between successive checkpoints.

in [3, 9] show that it is possible to augment CASE environments based on UML with automatic tools that generate dependability models in the form of Petri nets. The method of analyzing redundancy management in distributed object-oriented systems is introduced in our workshop paper [10].

4   The Modeling Approach

4.1   Guidelines

First we construct an architecture-based dependability model that takes into account the components and properties of the FTI without requiring the detailed behavioral models of its objects and mechanisms. The standardized structure and properties of the FTI allow us to construct the model and quantify the effects of the alternative values and deployment choices.

Then we will support the refinement of the architectural dependability model by focusing on the behavior of the objects of the FTI, especially the (application-specific) replication manager. We elaborate how a refined model of the RM can be constructed and integrated with the architectural model.

Since the RM contributes directly to maintenance and fault management, i.e. it receives the error messages and decides on the recovery and/or creation of new replicas, its behavior determines how the failures of replicas may lead to a system failure. Accordingly, it influences the *structure* of the system-level dependability model. (The analysis of the refined behavior of the components that implement the application functions can contribute to the assignment of more precise dependability attributes like failure rate and latency time.) In general, the careful and purposive selection of the key components to be refined (like the RM in our case) helps to avoid model complexity problems while still keeping the faithfulness of the dependability model at a high level.

The dependability of an object group is modeled and analyzed from the point of view of a client application. In this view the mapping from the failures of server replicas (i.e. the architectural failure modes of the object group) to the client (i.e. the service level) is performed by the FT-CORBA compliant ORB of the client. This way the dependability model consists of 3 layers: the hardware layer (hosts), the server replica layer (including maintenance by the FTI) and a layer of mapping from replica failures to the service required by the client.

The dependability model is constructed on the basis of the UML model of the FT-CORBA application. This decision is straightforward since UML can be considered as the standard description language of object-oriented systems. In the case of the architectural model, we utilize the package, class and object diagrams. During the refinement, we process the statechart diagrams of the selected objects.

The formalism of the dependability model is timed Petri nets (TPN), more precisely Stochastic Reward Nets (SRN) [11]. Dependability measures can be specified by using reward functions. We utilize the outstanding modeling power (e.g. guards assigned to transitions) and the sophisticated solution tools available [12, 13]. In certain cases (e.g. in the case of exponential transition firing times) analytic solution is possible, otherwise simulation has to be performed.

4.2   Assumptions

We adopted the following assumptions during the construction of the dependability model:

1. In the basic model, only crash failures of hosts and server replicas are taken into account. (In Section 5.6, we will include extensions to resolve this restriction.) The effects of the failures of the underlying components of the ORB, the internal logging/recovery mechanisms and group communication should be expressed by the replica failure rates.
2. A crash failure of a host results in immediate crash failures of the objects deployed on that host. The recovery of a replica is always successful except for the case of a host failure.
3. In the case of the infrastructure objects of the FTI, it is assumed that there is no software fault. They may crash due to host failures only. Moreover, we simplify the dependability model by not modeling the maintenance of the replicated FTI objects in detail (it is not specified in FT-CORBA, but may follow the same ideas as that of the server replicas). An implicit recovery is assumed if the host they are deployed on is in healthy state.

4. Conditions specific to the retry mechanism of the client (i.e. expiration time of requests and request duration policy) are not covered. Similarly, continuous heartbeating of the server objects by the clients is not modeled (since it is quite rarely implemented due to high communication costs).
5. We assume that the property values of the object groups are not changed at run-time. They have to be assigned to domains (as default) or to server types (object groups).

4.3   UML Modeling

The dependability model is constructed mechanically on the basis of the UML model of the FT-CORBA application. To help in identifying the roles and properties of the objects of the FTI, we introduced the following conventions.

Each fault tolerance domain is grouped into a separate package stereotyped as ≪FTD≫. It contains the predefined objects of the FTI (each identified by a stereotype like ≪replication_manager≫, ≪fault_notifier≫ and ≪fault_detector≫) and embedded packages (with stereotype ≪OG≫) containing the objects of the replica groups. The initial configuration is modeled by an object diagram. Deployment relations can be modeled by a deployment diagram or by links with stereotype ≪deployed_on≫.

In FT-CORBA, the standardized properties of a replica group are defined as common types. The values are accessible through the PropertyManager interface of the RM. Instead of relying on a particular implementation, we assign the properties to the packages of the domain and/or group as UML tagged values. The tag name is the same as the property name, and the value is one of the values defined in the FT-CORBA specification (see Table 1). The values assigned to an object group override the ones assigned to the FT domain. Additional parameters that are not specified in the FT-CORBA will be introduced in the sequel when the dependability submodels are described.

5   The Architectural Dependability Model

The clear interfaces and the separation of the tasks of the different components of the FTI allow a straightforward architectural dependability modeling. The modules (submodels) of the dependability model correspond to the objects (including the objects of the FTI) and to the dependability-related processes like fault activation, error propagation, fault management and recovery. The standard properties of FT-CORBA are mapped to the parameters of the submodels.

5.1   Server Replicas, Hosts and Infrastructure Objects

Each replica is represented by a subnet consisting of TPN places corresponding to the possible states of the object from the point of view of the availability and recoverability of its service. These places will also form the interface towards the other subnets of the model. We distinguish five states (places) as Table 2 shows.

Table 2. States of a replica

State	TPN place	Role
Initial state	I	The replica was not created yet (but its factory is capable to create it).
Primary replica	HP	The replica is primary and its service is available.
Backup replica	HB	The replica is backup and working correctly.
Recoverable failure	SF	The replica is crashed but it is recoverable.
Non-recoverable failure	C	The replica is crashed and it is not recoverable (due to the failure of its host).

Each replica of the initial configuration (as derived from the UML object and deployment diagrams) is represented by a separate subnet. In these subnets either place HP or HB is marked. Additionally, a subnet is created for each host that is capable of running a replica but does not have any replica deployed in the initial configuration. (This information can be derived from the UML model by recognizing the Factory objects corresponding to that replica type on a given host.) In this case place I of the subnet is marked.

The deployment of primary and backup replicas depends on the Replication-Style property. If its value is ACTIVE, then all replicas are primary ones, state HB is unnecessary. If its value is COLD_PASSIVE or WARM_PASSIVE, there is a single primary replica and the others are backup.

Hosts are represented by subnets consisting of two places: H (healthy state) and C (crashed).

According to Assumption 3, the infrastructure objects of the FTI are modeled in a simplified way: each object is represented by a pair of places H (healthy) and C (crashed). The factory objects need not be modeled separately, since we take into account that the creation of objects is not possible in the case of a host failure.

5.2   Fault Activation and Error Propagation

Fault activation subnets are created for each host and each object. Due to Assumption 1, fault activation is modeled by a timed transition with a single parameter characterizing the (hardware or software) failure rate (UML tagged value FR).

Deployment relations and links in the object model initiate error propagation. The failure of a host results in an immediate failure of all objects deployed on it (Assumption 2). The corresponding subnet is depicted in Fig. 2(a). Links among objects of different types indicate communication that may result in error propagation. Besides the direction of the propagation, which is the reverse of the direction of the link, here another parameter, the propagation probability (UML tagged value PP) is introduced. It is mapped to the probability of TPN transitions of the subnet as shown in Fig. 2(b).

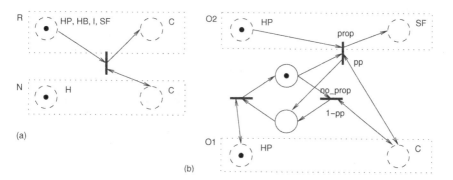

Fig. 2. Modeling error propagation from a host N to a replica R (a) and from object O1 to object O2 (b). Interface places are depicted by dashed lines

In the case of infrastructure objects, failure (repair) of the host results in the failure (healthiness, respectively) of the object (Assumption 3).

The repair of a host is an explicit (external) repair, which is not maintained by the FTI. Accordingly, it is characterized by a repair rate (UML tagged value RR), and represented in the model by a timed transition from place C to H.

5.3   Fault Management

Fault management includes fault detection (performed by the fault detectors) and fault notification (performed by the fault notifiers). Fault handling depends on the following conditions:

- Failure of a replica is detected only if the replica is monitored by a local fault detector on its host. In FT-CORBA, it is possible that only representative replicas (one per host or one per type and host) are monitored. This condition can be derived from the deployment diagram (in accordance with the property FaultMonitoringGranularity).
- Failure of a host is detected only if the local fault detector of the host is monitored by at least one global fault detector. (The host failure report is to be generated by a global fault detector, since in the case of host failures the local fault detectors will also fail.)
- The fault report triggers an action of the RM only if at least one fault notifier and at least one RM are available.

These conditions can be combined to form a Boolean expression on the existence and healthiness (state H) of the mentioned infrastructure objects. Boolean expressions can be represented in Petri nets in two ways. In simple nets, the subnets corresponding to AND and OR gates can be constructed explicitly as shown in [14]. In higher level nets, transitions can be assigned enabling conditions that can refer to (simple functions over) markings.

5.4   Replica Maintenance

Replica maintenance includes recovery and reconfiguration of replicas. Here we assume a common implementation, since the standard does not specify the mechanisms but implicitly suggests a "common practice" that is behind the interfaces.

In the architectural dependability model the tasks of replica maintenance are modeled by subnets consisting of timed PN transitions. All of them are conditional on the fault management, i.e. they are enabled in the TPN only if the conditions described in the previous subsection hold.

In the case of passive replication, the subnets and the additional conditions can be defined as follows:

- Recovery of a replica. If a software fault occurs, then the replica is recovered and it becomes a backup. It is modeled by a timed transition from SF to HB, its parameter is the recovery rate (UML tagged value RR).
- Activation of a new primary replica. This subnet is a timed transition from HB to HP. The need for a new primary replica is represented by a separate place *activate_primary*, which is another input place of this transition. Activation is required if a primary replica fails either due to a host failure (propagation subnet from place HP to C) or due to a propagated software failure from another object or due to a local software failure (subnets from place HP to SF). Each of these three subnets inserts a token in place *activate_primary*.
- Creation of a new backup replica. This subnet is a timed transition from I to HB. The need for a new backup replica is represented by a separate place *create_backup*, which is input place of this transition. Creation of a new backup is required if either a backup fails due to a host failure (subnet from HB to C) or a backup will become primary and the previous primary cannot be recovered to be a backup. This latter case results if the primary fails due to a host failure (propagation subnet from state HP to C) or due to a host failure right after a software failure (propagation subnet from SF to C). Each of these subnets inserts a token in place *create_backup*.

  The time required to perform the fault handling is dominated by the property FaultMonitoringInterval. Additional time required for recovery (replay of logged messages, proportional with CheckpointInterval) and creation of a replica (by a factory) can be estimated by the designer. Cold and warm passive replication can be distinguished by the time required for recovery and activation.
- Shutdown of all replicas. This subnet consists of two immediate transitions from place HP to I and from HB to I. These transitions fire only if the number of working replicas falls below MinimumNumberReplicas (in this case all replicas will be shut down). It happens if the number of replicas being in state C becomes higher than the number of hosts capable of running a replica minus MinimumNumberReplicas. This enabling condition can be expressed by a Boolean function on the markings of places C. If the transition from HP to I (HB to I) fires then a token will be inserted in place *activate_primary*

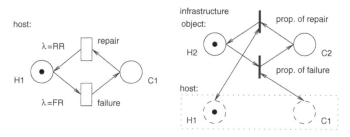

Fig. 3. Subnets corresponding to a host (H1, C1) and an infrastructure object (H2, C2)

(*create_backup*, respectively). These tokens will trigger the re-creation of the object group as soon as the number of replicas in state C will decrease (due to the repair of hosts). In order to avoid loops in the TPN, the creation of a new backup is enabled only if the shutdown condition does not hold.

At this point, the composition of subnets can be summarized.

In the case of hosts and infrastructure objects, the composition of the simplified subnets is presented in Fig. 3.

The composition of the subnets corresponding to server replicas depends on the replication style. In the case of passive replication (COLD_PASSIVE or WARM_PASSIVE ReplicationStyle), the structure of the composition is shown in Table 3. The model in case of active replication (ACTIVE ReplicationStyle) can be derived from this one by taking into account that all replicas are primary ones. The structure of the model is presented in Fig. 4.

5.5   Client Failover

The client failover strategy determines the behavior of the client ORB when it does not receive the requested service. The ORB can retry the call or invoke alternative servers. FT-CORBA specifies that the client ORB must not fail until it has tried to reach the server object replicas through all profiles available in the IOGR. From the point of view of the client, several mechanisms of FT-CORBA are transparent: Transient failures are tolerated by the retry mechanism; the ORBs of the clients and servers provide mechanism to update the IOGR and thus discover newly created or activated replicas.

The client failover subnet maps the failures in the object group to the failure of the service for the client. According to the observations above, the condition of the failure of the service can be expressed by a simple Boolean expression: The service fails if there is no available (i.e. healthy) primary server replica. Accordingly, the failover subnet is a PN representation of a fault tree consisting of a single AND gate. As soon as a primary server replica becomes healthy, the client service will be correct. This effect is modeled by the dual counterpart of the above fault tree bounded with the original one [14]. The service is represented

Table 3. Composition of subnets (passive replication)

Subnet	From	To	Firing conditions	Action (token to)
Recovery	SF	HB	Fault management	
Activation	HB	HP	Fault management, activate_primary	
Creation	I	HB	Fault management, create_backup, no shutdown condition	
Shutdown	HP	I	Fault management, min. number of replicas	activate_primary
Shutdown	HB	I	Fault management, min. number of replicas	create_backup
Propagation	HP	C	Host failure	activate_primary, create_backup
Propagation	HB	C	Host failure	create_backup
Propagation	SF	C	Host failure	create_backup
Propagation	I	C	Host failure	
SW failure	HP	SF		activate_primary
Propagation	HP	SF	Object failure	activate_primary
Propagation	C	I	Host repair	

by a pair of places OGH and OGC, the server replicas are interfaced to the fault tree through places HP and the other states (that are equivalent from the point of view of the failover condition).

5.6   Possible Extensions

The FTI is specified to handle crash failures only. Commission faults (when an object generates incorrect results) are also interesting for the designer. An anticipated extension of FT-CORBA is the ACTIVE_WITH_VOTING ReplicationStyle that can protect against these faults. To cover commission faults in the dependability model, the following extensions are necessary: An additional failure state CF has to be inserted in the submodels of the replicas. This state is reached from state HP by a timed transition parameterized with a distinguished *commission failure rate*. This state is not detected by the FTI (until it changes to crash failure), but it leads to a failure of the service. The failover subnet has to be modified accordingly.

Error latency can be modeled by distinguishing an error state (in stateful hosts and objects) that may lead to the failure state by a timed transition. Transient faults can be modeled by implicit repair (transition from the error state to the healthy state.) The subnets that cover these extensions are practically the same as the subnets introduced in [3].

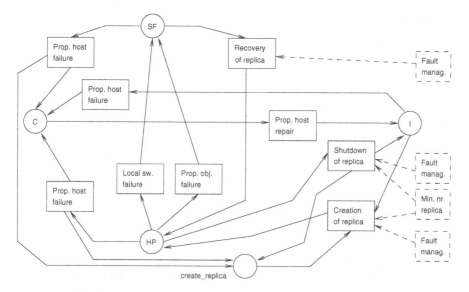

Fig. 4. Composition of subnets for active replication (conditions are drawn by dashed line)

6 Refinement of the Architectural Dependability Model

The subnets of replica maintenance presented in the previous section assume a typical, common behavior of the RM. Dependability modeling can support the evaluation of specialized maintenance when the vendor of the FTI implements a specific strategy in the RM or the designer implements application-controlled maintenance (by setting MEMB_APP_CTRL and CONS_APP_CTRL style and by replacing the RM with her own implementation).

In both cases, the detailed behavior of the (new) RM has to be made available in the form of a UML statechart diagram. This statechart model is processed in order to replace the initial subnets presented in Section 5.4 with the specific ones.

There is no doubt that the behavior of the RM has crucial effects on the availability of the object group, and the RM has the most sophisticated behavior in the FTI. To be able to model its activities, it seems to be mandatory to support the following features of UML statecharts:

- State hierarchy. An RM handles several object groups in an FTD. State hierarchy including concurrent substates is a natural way to model the maintenance of independent groups.
- Event processing. In the distributed environment of an FT-CORBA application, the failure reports from fault detectors and the messages of the RM towards the factories and replicas manifest themselves as events. The temporal relations of these events determine when a faulty replica is recovered, how

Table 4. Dependability-related events in an FT-CORBA architecture

Event	From	To	Handler	Action/meaning
c_i	RM	Factory	create_object()	Create a replica
d_i	RM	Factory	remove_object()	Remove a replica
r_i	RM	Replica	set_state()	Initiate recovery
p_i	RM	RM	set_primary_member()	Set the primary replica
s_i	Fault notifier	RM	push_structured_event()	Replica failed
f_i	Fault notifier	RM	push_structured_event()	Host failed
h_i	Fault notifier	RM	push_structured_event()	Host repaired

many replicas are maintained, where a new replica is created, what is the condition of object removal etc. The basic events and the standard handler functions of FT-CORBA are listed in Table 4.

We have elaborated the model transformation from UML statecharts to Petri nets with timing and stochastic extensions [15]. This transformation will be utilized to generate the specific subnets of replica maintenance. Note that the statechart model of the RM describes only dependability-related behavior, no application-specific functional details are included. Thus, there is no need to filter out irrelevant states or transitions.

In the following, we shortly introduce the model transformation and then define how the subnet (generated automatically from the statechart of the RM) can be integrated with the other subnets.

6.1   From UML Statecharts to Stochastic Petri Nets

Our transformation supports UML statecharts including event processing and state hierarchy. The following restrictions apply: Actions generate events only, events do not have parameters, and history states are not allowed. Since the transformation was detailed in [15], we summarize only the properties that are important from the point of view of the current application.

The event queue that connects the state machine with its environment can be parameterized to be a FIFO queue or a set (non-deterministic selection of events). Both implementations use the same TPN interface. Each type of event is represented by a separate place. Tokens representing events from the external subnets are inserted in these places. Similarly, the output tokens (events from the RM) are inserted in another set of places.

The semantics of timed transitions is again parameterized: The designer is able to choose among three implementations regarding the policy of transition selection and firing. The stochastic parameters of transitions correspond to the tagged values associated with the UML transitions. In this way time delay or duration of actions can be modeled.

The behavior of the resulting TPN satisfies the requirements defined in the UML semantics. The priority relations, the step semantics and the evaluation of guard conditions are all taken into account and represented by specific constructions in the TPN. By using the transformation, the statechart model of the RM can be mapped to a TPN (SRN) representation with event processing and stochastic parameters corresponding to the UML model.

6.2   Composition of the Subnets

The subnet generated from the statechart model of the RM is integrated with the other subnets of the architectural dependability model by utilizing the event processing mechanism. It means that the state changes of the replicas are "translated" to events. However, to simplify the model, the relatively simple fault monitoring (is_alive_() calls) and the communication between fault detectors and fault notifiers (push_structured_fault() calls) are not mapped to events. Instead, the logic conditions of event transmission are represented in the model.

In the architectural dependability model, the state changes and the maintenance subnets were integrated by using local conditions and two interface places. Instead of these places, now the places corresponding to the events will be used. The propagation subnets (see Table 3 and Fig. 4) remain unchanged. Tokens representing the events will be generated and processed as follows:

- Recoverable failure (transition to state SF) of replica i results in an event s_i if the replica is monitored by a healthy local fault detector, and at least one of the fault notifiers is healthy.
- Failure (transition to state C) of host j results in an event f_j if at least one of the global fault detectors is healthy, and one of the fault notifiers is healthy. The repair of the host results in event h_j on the same conditions.
- Recovery of a replica, activation of a new primary replica and creation of a new backup replica are enabled if the corresponding event from the RM is present (event r_i, p_i and c_i, respectively). The interface places *activate_primary* and *create_backup* are replaced by the places corresponding to events p_i and c_i for each replica. The conditions of fault handling are not modeled here (since they are involved in the generation of the failure reports). The assumption that replicas are created/activated immediately on a randomly selected host is resolved; the location, time and order of occurrence now depends on the RM.
- The subnet representing the shutdown of replica i is replaced by a simple immediate transition that is enabled when a corresponding event d_i is present. Using the above mentioned input events, it is the responsibility of the RM to keep track of the changes in the system and account for MinimumNumberReplicas.

7   Examples

We present two simple examples just to illustrate the kind of analysis that can be performed.

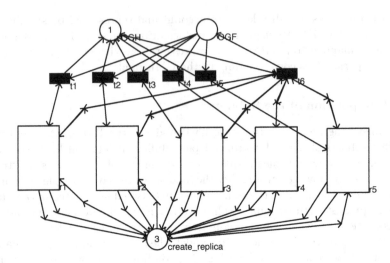

Fig. 5. Structure of the example network (the five subnets correspond to the replicas)

The first example is an active redundant system that consists of 5 hosts (all capable of running a replica) and initially 3 primary replicas. If a replica fails then a new one is created on a randomly selected host that has no active replica.

The architectural dependability model of the system was constructed (Fig. 5). Various parameter settings and the corresponding steady state unavailability (i.e. 1-Availability) of the service of the object group are presented in Table 5. The FaultMonitoringGranularity was varied by changing the number of hosts on which the replica is monitored, assuming a static deployment of fault detectors.

This dependability model was refined by replacing the replica maintenance subnets by a subnet which was generated from the UML statechart model of a non-standard RM implementing a "lazy" recovery strategy. This RM initiates the creation of a new replica as soon as a hardware failure is detected, but delays the recovery from software faults until the failures of at least 2 (or 3) replicas are reported by local fault detectors. In this case the recovery of all failed replicas is performed in parallel.

The core of the UML statechart model of the RM is sketched in Fig. 6. Note that the first 5 parallel regions of the statechart keep track of the states of the hosts. The presentation of the sixth region (the maintenance control) is simplified in the Figure by parameterizing the transitions. Here $1 \leq i,j \leq 5$, $i \neq j$. The analysis of the dependability model showed that the strategy is effective only if InitialNumberReplicas>3.

One of the lessons learnt during these experiments is the following. The statechart-based modeling of the behavior of an RM is cumbersome if we apply the restrictions that events can not have parameters and internal variables are not allowed in the UML model. (Thus, the only way to keep track of the changes

Table 5. Analysis results. Parameter values are set as follows: replica FR=1, RR=100; host FR=0.1 and RR=10, all distributions are exponential. Unavailability is the mean number of tokens in OGF

InitialNumberReplicas	1	2	3	4
Unavailability	9.89E-3	1.23E-4	1.25E-6	<1.0E-8
FaultMonitoringInterval	0.01	0.02	0.1	1
Unavailability	1.25E-6	6.81E-6	7.62E-4	1.07E-1
FaultMonitoringGranularity	1	2	3	4
Unavailability	1.96E-2	3.79E-4	8.45E-6	1.18E-6

in the controlled system is the use of guards referring to the active states of parallel regions.) The extension of the transformation from UML statecharts to Petri nets without these restrictions is a matter of our future work.

8   Conclusion

We showed in this paper that the design of FT-CORBA applications can be supported by mechanical dependability analysis. In the early stage of the development an architectural dependability model can be constructed that is based on the standard properties and mechanisms of FT-CORBA. In this stage, the designer is able to evaluate the effects of the architectural choices on the system availability. We showed that this model can be refined in subsequent design phases when the detailed behavior (in the form of UML statecharts) of the objects responsible for replica maintenance is available. The designer is able to "try out" various replica maintenance strategies, find design errors and select the most optimal strategy from the point of view of system availability. Comparison of solutions can be effectively supported, while numerical results have to be validated in subsequent design phases.

The model transformation from UML statecharts to SRN is a powerful technique to support the hierarchical refinement of the initial dependability model. It has an additional advantage that the dependability will be evaluated on the basis

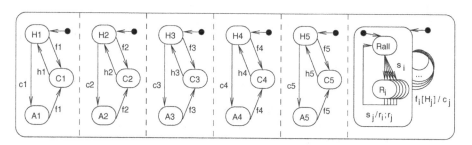

Fig. 6. Statechart of the RM with delayed recovery

of the same model that will be used for the (automatic) code generation. However, the complete transformation of a detailed statechart model of an entire application is impracticable. To avoid model complexity problems, only those objects should be selected that contribute to the core of the replication, membership, consistency and fault management mechanisms. Applications based on FT-CORBA are good candidates for this kind of hierarchical analysis since the standard defines the responsibilities of the objects and provides clear interfaces among them.

References

[1] Object Management Group: Fault tolerant CORBA. CORBA 2.6, Chapter 25 formal/01-12-63, OMG Technical Committee, http://www.omg.org (2001) 121

[2] Eternal Systems Inc.: Eternal embedded edition. Product description, http://www.eternal-systems.com/products (2001) 121

[3] Bondavalli, A., Majzik, I., Mura, I.: Automated dependability analysis of UML designs. In: Proc. 2nd IEEE Int. Symposium on Object-Oriented Real-Time Distributed Computing (ISORC'99), Saint Malo, France (1999) 139–144. 122, 125, 132

[4] Popstojanova, K. G., Trivedi, K. S.: Architecture based software reliability. In: Proc. Int. Conf. on Appplied Stochastic System Modeling, Kyoto, Japan. (2000) 124

[5] Nelli, M., Bondavalli, A., Simoncini, L.: Dependability modelling and analysis of complex control systems: An application to railway interlocking. In: Proc. EDCC-2, Springer Verlag (1996) 93–110. 124

[6] Betous-Almeida, C., Kanoun, K.: Dependability evaluation - From functional to structural modeling. In: Proc. SAFECOMP 2001, Springer Verlag (2001) 239–249. 124

[7] Rabah, M., Kanoun, K.: Dependability evaluation of a distributed shared memory multiprocessor system. In: Proc. EDCC-3, Springer Verlag (1999) 42–59. 124

[8] Bondavalli, A., Dal Cin, M., Latella, D., Majzik, I., Pataricza, A., Savoia, G.: Dependability analysis in the early phases of UML based system design. International Journal of Computer Systems - Science & Engineering 16 (2001) 265–275. 124

[9] Bondavalli, A., Majzik, I., Mura, I.: Automatic dependability analysis for supporting design decisions in UML. In: Proc. Fourth IEEE Int. Symposium on High Assurance Systems Engineering (HASE'99). (1999) 64–71. 125

[10] Huszerl, G., Majzik, I.: Modeling and analysis of redundancy management in distributed object-oriented systems by using UML statecharts. In: Proc. Workshop on Software Process and Product Improvement, the 27th EUROMICRO Conference, Warsaw, Poland. (2001) 200–207. 125

[11] Muppala, J. K., Ciardo, G., Trivedi, K. S.: Stochastic reward nets for reliability prediction. Comm. in Reliability, Maintainability and Serviceability 1 (1994) 9–20. 126

[12] Ciardo, G., Muppala, J., Trivedi, K. S.: SPNP - stochastic Petri net package. In: Proc. IEEE 3rd Int. Workshop on Petri Nets and Performance Models (PNPM'89), Kyoto, Japan (1989) 142–151. 126

[13] Allmaier, S., Dalibor, S.: Panda - Petri net ANalysis and Design Assistant. In: Tools Descriptions, 9th Int. Conf. on Modeling Techniques and Tools for Computer Performance Evaluation (Tools'97), St. Malo, France (1997) 126

[14] Malhotra, M., Trivedi, K. S.: Dependability modeling using Petri-nets. IEEE Transactions on Reliability **44** (1995) 428–440. 129, 131

[15] Huszerl, G., Majzik, I.: Quantitative analysis of dependability critical systems based on UML statechart models. In: Proc. Fifth IEEE Int. Symposium on High Assurance Systems Engineering (HASE'2000). (2000) 83–92. 134

Experimental Evaluation of the Unavailability Induced by a Group Membership Protocol

Kaustubh R. Joshi[1], Michel Cukier[2], and William H. Sanders[1]

[1] Coordinated Science Lab., Dept. of Electrical and Computer Engineering, and
Dept. of Computer Science, University of Illinois
Urbana IL 61820, USA
{joshi1,whs}@crhc.uiuc.edu
[2] Dept. of Materials and Nuclear Engineering, University of Maryland
College Park MD 20742, USA
mcukier@eng.umd.edu

Abstract. Group communication is an important paradigm for building highly available distributed systems. However, group membership operations often require the system to block message traffic, causing system services to become unavailable. This makes it important to quantify the unavailability induced by membership operations. This paper experimentally evaluates the blocking behavior of the group membership protocol of the Ensemble group communication system using a novel global-state-based fault injection technique. In doing so, we demonstrate how a layered distributed protocol such as the Ensemble group membership protocol can be modeled in terms of a state machine abstraction, and show how the resulting global state space can be used to specify fault triggers and define important measures on the system. Using this approach, we evaluate the cost associated with important states of the protocol under varying workload and group size. We also evaluate the sensitivity of the protocol to the occurrence of a second correlated crash failure during its operation.

1 Introduction

Group communication is an important paradigm for building dependable distributed systems. Reliable system designers often use the dependability-related properties of group communication systems (GCS) to make claims about the dependability of their own applications. This makes the verification and assessment of these properties an important endeavor. Consequently, formal specification and verification of GCS properties is a very active area of research [28, 12, 22, 17]. Work has also been done on automated construction of such specifications from source code [19]. These techniques have generally lacked the ability to assess the performance of GCS implementations. However, the performance of GCS components can have a significant impact on a system's dependability properties. For example, applications that require a virtual synchrony model [4] force the GCS to block communication when membership changes occur. This blockage can cause a loss of availability of some or all components in the system, thus reducing its overall dependability. Thus, the performance of the group membership component has a direct impact on dependability. The degree of this impact depends not only on the protocols and algorithms used, but also on the actual implementation.

That observation leads to the necessity of experimental evaluation of the dependability-related performance characteristics of group membership protocols to complement formal verification. Although there has been some work on evaluation of group communication protocols [21, 26], the primary focus has been on performance of message-ordering and delivery protocols. In this paper, we present an experimental evaluation of the blocking behavior of a widely used group membership protocol. Our evaluation sheds light on how the availability of the system is affected under varying operating conditions. We use the Ensemble GCS as the basis for our experiments.

Ensemble [27] is a popular group communication system developed at Cornell University. It was written in the OCAML dialect of the ML language so that it would be amenable to automated proof checking [16]. Ensemble communication stacks have a modular structure and are built up of several layers of micro-protocols stacked on each other. Ensemble allows applications to specify which micro-protocol layers to use in their stacks, thus allowing applications to choose group properties. Layers implement several message-ordering properties, group membership properties, and virtual synchrony. The Ensemble group membership protocol supports member addition and removal as well as partition merging, failure detection, and suspicion sharing. We use a stack that provides membership properties, virtual synchrony, and a sequencer-based total-ordering protocol. We treat events that cause membership changes in the system as faults, because they cause the system to go into an undesired (blocking) state, and we treat the group membership protocol as the fault tolerance mechanism. Consequently, we use the technique of fault injection [1] to exercise the Ensemble membership protocol and subsequently perform distributed measurements on the system to evaluate blocking time.

A large body of work exists on both fault injectors for networked systems [24, 9, 11, 13] and fault injection, including some work on fault injection of group communication systems [2, 10]. However, past injection efforts have concentrated either on assessment of statistical dependability metrics such as coverage [2, 25, 8], or on fault removal [10]. The problem of assessing blocking behavior for a distributed system such as Ensemble poses significant new problems. First, since this evaluation aims to get an insight on system availability under specific conditions, statistically driven fault triggers (such as those in [23]) cannot be used. Due to the distributed nature of the membership protocol, fault triggers based on local state of nodes [9] are also unable to represent all the configurations in which faults may be injected. Second, due to the need to compute a global measure such as the blocking time for the entire group, a facility for distributed measurement and measure specification is needed. The topic of distributed system measurement and performance evaluation has been considered in the literature [3, 20].

However, we are not aware of any past work that has combined the use of fault injection with distributed measurements to assess dependability characteristics of a real system.

To solve both problems, we use a novel global-state-based fault injection technique. The technique involves abstracting the operation of each node in the group by a state machine. A global state for the entire system is defined in terms of the local states of the nodes. Fault triggers are expressed in terms of this global state. Measurements of local state changes are taken, and combined to form a timeline of global state changes on which measures can be defined. We use Loki [6], a fault injector that supports global-state-based fault triggers and measure estimation, to conduct our experiments. This approach enables the injection of faults precisely in interesting states and the subsequent collection of fine-grained measures of the system.

As a case study, this paper presents a detailed state machine specification of the operation of the Ensemble group membership protocol, provides insight into its operation, and quantifies, via experimental results, the cost of group membership operations. In addition, this work serves as a real-life demonstration of how global-state-based fault injection coupled with distributed measurement can be used to assess the performance of complex distributed systems. In doing that, we also demonstrate how highly layered event-driven protocol structures may be modeled using state machines and how the resulting global state-space can be used to define scenarios for fault injection and to specify system measures. Finally, the results of experimentation provide insight on how the performance of the group membership service of a GCS can affect its availability.

2   Methodology and System Model

This section describes the fault injection methodology and fault models we use for this study. The target of the fault injection is the Ensemble group membership protocol, which can only exist in, and be exercised by, an application that instantiates the Ensemble stack. Hence, this section also describes the application we use to drive the Ensemble stack.

Global-State-Based Fault Injection Methodology Our methodology involves abstracting the parts of the distributed system that are to be measured by a collection of state machines; one for each node. The global state of the system is then defined as the collection of the states of these state machines. The fault triggers consist of the name of the node on which to inject the fault, and a boolean expression on the global state which, when true, triggers the fault. During experiment execution, the Loki fault injector is used to track the state machine states, and record state-transition-event occurrence times using the local clocks of the nodes. This requires that the application be instrumented to notify Loki of local events that cause state transitions. Since the Loki runtime only exports a C interface, we wrote a C-ML wrapper for this interface, so that notifications could be done natively from the Ensemble stack. After the experiments are conducted, the local transition times are combined into a global execution trace called the *global timeline*, which contains occurrence times of all state transition events that occurred in the system as measured by a single "global clock". Loki uses an offline clock synchronization algorithm to generate the global timeline [7], and hence the physical clocks of the hosts used for the experiments need not be synchronized. Measures are defined in terms of the global state [5], and are computed using the global timeline.

Fault Model In this case study, we treat the group membership protocol as a fault tolerance mechanism and seek to evaluate it as such. Hence, we do not consider faults, such as message corruption, delays, and packet loss, that have been traditionally used for fault-injecting communication systems [10], and restrict ourselves to the "faults" that the membership protocol is designed to handle.

The events that trigger the membership protocol are node crashes, network partitions, node joins and departures, and the merging together of different groups. However, a network partition is handled as a series of node crashes. Nodes leaving the group are removed through the same protocol used for crash failures, except that there is no crash detection timeout involved. Also, node joins are implemented as the merging of two groups: the primary group, and a singleton group consisting of just the new member. Hence, the crash failure and node join events are representative of all membership change events, and the fault model for this study is restricted to these events. Due to space limitations, we present results only for crash failure injections. The experimental results for node joins can be found in [18].

Application Model One of the most important characteristics of an application for a group communication system is the message workload it generates, and this is the only characteristic we consider. The message workload is specified in terms of the length, type (point-to-point or broadcast), and generation times of the messages generated. In our experiments, we consider 100-byte-long fixed-sized broadcast messages. We model the application message generation process at a single node (the workload) by a Poisson process with parameter λ, which is varied in different studies. Hence, to drive the experiments, we wrote a simple ML application that instantiates an Ensemble stack, and generates the Poisson workload once a group of a specified sized has formed. The application uses the compatibility application interface provided by the Ensemble distribution [15] and runs on a standard virtual synchrony stack with the sequencer-based total ordering protocol included.

3   State Machine Abstraction

This section presents the methodology used to construct a state machine abstraction of the group membership protocol, and then presents the resulting Loki state machine. Since we are not aware of a complete description of the

Ensemble group membership protocol in the literature, we also briefly describe the protocol itself, to help the reader better understand the results.

3.1   Methodology for State Machine Construction

Construction of a state machine to represent the temporal behavior of a highly layered, event-driven stack like Ensemble is difficult due to a lack of order between layer executions [16] and the simultaneous existence of multiple event flows in the stack. Existing specifications have either not considered the interaction between layers [14], or not captured the temporal behavior of the protocol [17]. One approach would be to model each layer in isolation, and compose the resulting state machines. However, such a composition must be guided by a functional model of the protocol behavior (such as [17]) to constrain the state-space explosion that results due to the large number of layers. Since only non-functional measures (such as blocking time) are of interest for this study, we avoid the need for a functional model by using a novel approach based on "event chains."

An external event to incorporate into the model (e.g., a crash failure) is first chosen, and an event chain is constructed for it. An *event chain* is a directed graph in which the vertices represent inter-layer or external events and the edges represent direct causal relationships between the events. An incoming event at a layer may generate several outgoing events, and, conversely, an outgoing event at a layer may be generated as a result of several incoming events. Event chains represent the temporal behavior of the inter-layer protocol that is composed of events bouncing back and forth within the stack. Each edge in the event chain is assigned a weight, which is the time between the generation of the parent message and the generation of the child. Since the actual durations of these times are not known beforehand, the weights represent relative timing constraints only. The event chains for the group membership protocol were generated by reverse-engineering the source code.

A state machine description of the blocking behavior of the protocol is obtained by computing the critical path between the initial event in which we are interested (crash failure, node join) and the event that finally causes the group to unblock. The *critical path* between two vertices in an event chain is the maximum weight path between them. The edges on this critical path represent possible states in the state machine model. Since the number of edges in our critical path were large (more than 50), several adjacent edges of the same type were merged to form the states in the state model. The type of an edge (and thus its corresponding state) depends on the reason for the time delay associated with it. These reasons can include processing time within layers (represented by unshaded states in the state machine in Figure 1), time spent in application callbacks (the doubly circled states), and time spent waiting to receive a message from another node (the shaded states).

In order to incorporate an additional external event into a state machine, e.g., a second crash failure during the operation of the protocol, we examined the event chain for the event to be added, and determined, for each state of the original state machine, whether the events in the new event chain would

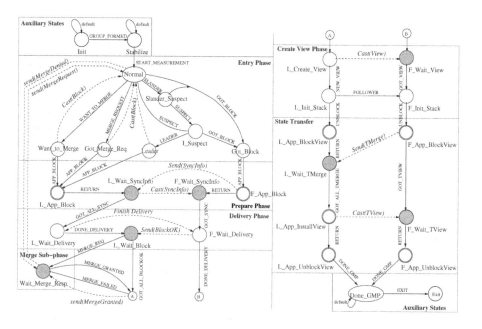

Fig. 1. State Machine for the Group Membership Protocol

cause additional blocking. If they did, and the reason for additional blocking was represented by a state other than the one currently under consideration, an edge was introduced between the two states.

3.2 State Machine Specification

The Ensemble group membership protocol can be decomposed into multiple phases. Figure 1 presents the state machine that describes the protocol operation in response to a single fault at a level of abstraction appropriate for this study. In the figure, solid transitions represent the local event notifications at each node that cause state changes. The dashed lines represent actual communication between the Ensemble stacks on different nodes (typically between the leader and followers). States with names prefixed by L (F) represent states that only the leader (followers) of a group may enter. To model the effects of multiple fault injections, additional transitions beyond those shown in the figure are needed. A description of the state machine for multiple crash failures can be found in [18]. Since node joins are not presented in this paper, the state machine description ignores the states and transitions related to the partition merge protocol.

Auxiliary states are not part of the protocol, but track the execution of the protocol stack until the conditions are right for fault injection and measurement. The `Init` state on the top left of Figure 1 is the initial state, and is held until the formation of a group of the required size. Once the group has formed, the node starts message transmission. However, before fault injection or measurement can be done, any startup transients need to be removed. This is done by causing the state machine to wait in the `Stabilize` state and ignore application notifications (via the `default` event) until a specified number of initial messages have been exchanged. Once this is done, the state machine transitions into the `Normal` state, and fault injection and measurement can be done from then on. After the group membership protocol has completed, the state machine transitions into the `Done_GMP` state shown in the bottom right-hand side of Figure 1. Any further application notifications are ignored by the state machine. In this manner, we ensure that for every run, exactly one instance of the group membership protocol is evaluated.

The *Entry Phase* is when Ensemble initiates the membership protocol due to a triggering event. The state machine models this for crash failures and partition merges. Crash failures are detected by a stack through either a timeout (suspect) mechanism or a slander message from another node. When a crash is detected, the state machine eventually transitions into the `I_Suspect` state, in which the node determines if it is the leader of the group. If it is, the state machine transitions to the `Leader` state, in which the node sends a *Block* message to the other nodes in the group. When a follower node receives a block message, it transitions to the `Got_Block` state regardless of its current state. At that point, all the nodes in the system execute the *Block* application callback (represented by the `L(F)_App_Block` states), informing the application of an impending group block. When this callback returns, no new messages can be sent until the completion of the group membership change. The time spent in an application callback is application-dependent. Our application does nothing in the callbacks, and hence represents the best-case blocking time.

The *Prepare Phase* begins when the application returns from the *Block* callback. It consists of an agreement protocol in which the nodes in the group agree upon a *consistent* set of messages that must be delivered in the current view to preserve virtual synchrony. The `L_Wait_SyncInfo` state on the leader represents the time spent by the leader waiting for each follower's version of the virtual synchrony information (sent when the follower returns from the *Block* callback). The `F_Wait_SyncInfo` state represents the time each follower then waits for the leader to send out a consistent version of the virtual synchrony information in a *SyncInfo* message. The dissemination of virtual synchrony information to the group marks the end of the prepare phase.

In the *Delivery Phase*, nodes in the system deliver outstanding messages from the set agreed upon in the Prepare Phase. The `L_Wait_Delivery` and `F_Wait_Delivery` states represent the time spent by the leader and followers, respectively, in delivering messages (represented by the *Finish Delivery* message exchange). Once a follower finishes its message delivery, it sends a *BlockOK* message to the leader. The `L_Wait_Block` state of the state machine represents the time spent by the leader waiting to receive *BlockOK* messages after it has finished its own message delivery. At the end of `L_Wait_Block`, no messages in transit exist anywhere in the system, and the group is said to be *totally blocked*.

The *Create View Phase* begins when the leader enters the `L_Create_View` state of the state machine. This state represents the time spent by the leader in creating a new view, which it broadcasts to the group. The time in the `F_Wait_View` state represents the time spent by each follower waiting for the new view. When a node has a copy of the new view, it creates a new stack. The `L(F)_Init_Stack` states of the state machine represent the time required for this operation.

The *State Transfer* phase is present in some configurations of Ensemble, and is initiated after the creation of a new stack. It implements a protocol that enables applications to agree on a common state for the new view. Although state transfer is not part of the core group membership protocol, the group is blocked during its execution, and hence we model this protocol in our blocking behavior model. In this protocol, the stack at each node requests application state via the *BlockView* application callback (the `L(F)_App_BlockView` states), and the followers send their versions of this state to the leader via a *TMerge* message. The leader waits for *TMerge* messages (in the `L_Wait_TMerge` state), and on receiving them asks the application to compose them into a single state via the *InstallView* callback (the `L_App_InstallView` state). The single state is sent to all the followers (which wait for it in state `F_Wait_TView`) via a *TView* message. All nodes install this common state via the *Unblock* callback (represented by the `L(F)_App_UnblockView` states), and henceforth the group is unblocked.

4   Fault Triggers

Our evaluation of the group membership protocol as a fault tolerance mechanism seeks to quantify two properties of the protocol. The first is its performance under varying system conditions, while the second is its robustness to the occurrence of additional faults during its operation. Quantification of the first property can be achieved by injecting a single fault when the system is in the normal state, and parameterizing the experiments by workload and message size. Quantification of the second property requires injection of an additional fault into the system while it is recovering from the first fault. This second set of experiments is parameterized by the global state of the system at which the second "correlated" fault is to be injected. The performance metric in both cases is the blocking behavior of the group, which is computed by measuring overall group blocking time and per-state holding times in blocking states. In the trigger specifications, nodes are identified by their names, which are NodeFail, $Node_1, Node_2, \ldots, Node_n$. All nodes execute the same application and are tracked by the same state machine (the one shown in Figure 1 augmented with transitions to account for multiple crashes). NodeFail is the node used to inject the first crash failure.

For the single-fault experiments, a single crash failure is injected into the node NodeFail when a group of the proper size has formed and each state machine has transitioned to the **Normal** state of the state machine. The fault method for crash failures simulates a crash by generating a segmentation failure exception. The fault trigger for single crash failures is defined on node NodeFail simply as:

$$(Node_1 : Normal) \wedge \ldots \wedge (Node_n : Normal) \wedge (NodeFail : Normal) \mapsto CrashFault$$

For the correlated fault experiments, exactly two faults are injected in every experiment. The first fault is injected when all nodes are in their Normal state, just as for the single-fault experiments, and hence uses the trigger shown above. The second fault is then injected when the system is recovering from the first crash, and is in certain global states. Since faults can be either crash failures or node joins, four combinations of injections are possible. Of these, only Crash-Crash and Merge-Crash injections are valid, because Ensemble disallows group merges during membership changes. We have explored only the Crash-Crash scenario, but the techniques are equally applicable to the Crash-Merge scenario.

Although the trigger for the second crash failure depends on the exact global state in which the fault is to be injected, a recurrent theme is injecting a leader or follower when it is in one of a set S of local states, and no other injections have been done. If the injection is to be done in a leader, S will contain only leader states ($\mathcal{L}$) whose names have the prefix L_. Since any node in a system can be a leader, fault triggers must be installed on each node in the system. These triggers must be temporally synchronized; i.e., after a leader has crashed, the same trigger should not be invoked a second time in the new leader elected by the group. This is ensured by checking that when the fault is injected, no nodes except NodeFail have crashed. When injecting a follower, S will contain only follower states ($\mathcal{F}$) that have the prefix F_. We define the set function $L(S) : 2^{\mathcal{F}} \mapsto 2^{\mathcal{L}}$, which returns the subset of leader states ($\mathcal{L}$) that the leader of a group could be in when a follower is in one of the S states. When a follower is being injected, fault triggers need to be installed only on two nodes, since at-least one of them must be a follower. The triggers must be spatially synchronized (i.e., only one of the triggers injects the fault in a given experiment, even if both nodes are followers). This is ensured by having one of the two nodes inject a fault only if the other node is in one of the leader states ($L(S)$). Note that neither temporal nor spatial synchronization can be done without a knowledge of the global state. The fault triggers that satisfy the above conditions are the following:

Leader Crash Injections
$\forall i = \{1, \ldots, n\}$, At Node$_i$:
(Node$_i$: state $\in S$) $\wedge \neg$(Node$_1$: CRASH) $\wedge \ldots \wedge \neg$(Node$_n$: CRASH) $\mapsto$ CrashFault
Follower Crash Injections
At Node$_1$: (Node$_1$: state $\in S$) $\mapsto$ CrashFault
At Node$_2$: (Node$_1$: state $\in L(S)$) $\wedge$ (Node$_2$: state $\in S$) $\mapsto$ CrashFault

State Selection Using the general fault triggers described above, we now compute the smallest set of local states that need to be targeted (with a second crash failure) for completeness. A node crash impedes the progress of the protocol whenever the rest of the group waits for a protocol message from the crashed node. If the execution path of a node is split into intervals delimited by the times at which it transmits protocol messages, then it is necessary to target each interval at least once, since the blocking of different outgoing messages may each have a unique impact on the group. Also, each interval is representative of all the states within that interval, since a node can affect others only through outgoing messages. Hence, injecting *only one* state in the set of states (S) that represent each interval is enough to obtain *representative behavior* for all states. However, this does not mean that the response of the system to a crash at any instant is *identical* to the response to a crash elsewhere in the same interval, since other factors in the protocol (such as expiration of timeouts) are sensitive to the exact crash time. The dotted edges in the state machine in Figure 1 represent the protocol messages, and the states between successive outgoing messages represent the intervals. For example, the *Send(BlockOk)* and *Send(TMerge)* protocol messages delineate an interval that contains the `F_Wait_View`, `F_Init_Stack`, and `F_App_BlockView` states. The intervals used for the correlated fault injection experiments are shown below in terms of S and $L(S)$ (format is $S \mapsto L(S)$):

$\{Leader\}, \{L\_Wait\_SyncInfo\}, \{L\_Create\_View\}, \{L\_Wait\_TMerge, L\_App\_InstallView\} \mapsto \phi$

$\{Got\_Block\} \mapsto \{Leader, L\_App\_Block, L\_Wait\_SyncInfo\}$

$\{F\_Wait\_Delivery\} \mapsto \{L\_Wait\_Delivery, L\_Wait\_Block\}$

$\{F\_Init\_Stack, F\_App\_BlockView\} \mapsto \{L\_Init\_Stack, L\_App\_BlockView, L\_Wait\_TMerge\}$

5   Measures

For this study, group blocking time and contributions of individual local states to this time are the measures of interest. We define blocking times for two versions of the membership protocol. The version that includes the application state transfer function (Section 3.2) is called the *Base Protocol*, and the version without it is called the *Core Protocol*. The blocking times for the Core Protocol can be obtained by treating the state transfer phase as non-blocking and as a part of the application. The last states in which applications are allowed to transmit are the `L(F)_App_Block` states of the Entry Phase. The group unblocks in the `L(F)_App_BlockView` states for the core protocol and in the `L(F)_App_UnblockView` states for the base protocol. Hence, the sets B_{base} and B_{core} of blocking states in the base protocol and the core protocol, respectively, are defined as follows:

$B_{core} = \{L\_Wait\_SyncInfo, L\_Wait\_Delivery, L\_Wait\_Block, Wait\_Merge\_Resp, L\_Create\_View,$
$\quad L\_Init\_Stack, F\_Wait\_SyncInfo, F\_Wait\_Delivery, F\_Wait\_View, F\_Init\_Stack\}$

$B_{base} = B_{core} \cup \{L\_App\_BlockView, L\_Wait\_TMerge, L\_App\_InstallView,$
$\quad F\_App\_BlockView, F\_Wait\_TView\}$

For a given set of blocking states B, we define the *Total Group Blocking Interval* as that interval of time during which all the nodes in the group are blocked. During that period, no messages can originate anywhere in the system. The length of this interval is $t_{total}(B)$, where $B \in \{B_{core}, B_{base}\}$. The *Partial Group Blocking Interval* is defined as that interval of time during which a non-empty subset of the nodes are blocked. The length of this interval is $t_{partial}(B)$. The intervals for the core protocol start at the same time as the corresponding intervals for the base protocol. However, a total interval is properly contained within its corresponding partial interval, because nodes enter and leave the protocol at different times due to variations in message delay, speed, load, and protocol characteristics. The difference between the start times of the partial and total interval of the base (or core) protocol is called the *preblock stagger*, and represents the maximum blocking time spent by a group member waiting for other nodes to start the protocol. It is upper-bounded by $t_{partial}(B_{core}) - t_{total}(B_{core})$.

To compute the blocking intervals, a predicate is defined on the global state of the system such that the predicate is true when the system is blocked. Application of this predicate to the global timeline for an experiment yields a predicate timeline that is a Boolean-valued function of time. The interval for which this predicate timeline is true gives the blocking interval, and the time for which it is true gives the blocking time. The predicates for the partial group blocking interval $Block_{partial}(B, t)$ and the total group blocking interval $Block_{total}(B, t)$ are defined as follows:

$$Block_{partial}(B, t) = \exists x \in \{Node_1, \ldots, Node_n\} \text{s.t.} \bigvee_{s \in B}(x : state(t) = s)$$

$$Block_{total}(B, t) = \forall x \in \{Node_1, \ldots, Node_n\}, \bigvee_{s \in B}(x : state(t) = s)$$

The contributions of individual states to the blocking time are expressed as the ratio of the average individual-state blocking time to the overall blocking time. The group blocking time used is dependent on the state being considered. Computing this measure for a state s requires multiple predicates: one for each node in the system. Each predicate is defined as $Block_{partial|total}(B, t) \wedge (Node_i : state(t) = s)$. The measure is then the average ratio of the duration of time each predicate is true to the requisite group blocking time.

In the experiments of Section 6, it was observed that the crash detection timeout interval dominated the results. Using the Loki measures language, we were able to analytically factor this timeout interval out of a blocking time. We did so by first computing the time interval between the first SUSPECT event after the second crash failure injection, and the event just prior to that SUSPECT event. This is the interval when the protocol does nothing while waiting for a timeout, and its overlap with the group blocking time interval gives the contribution of the timeout to the group blocking time. That overlap is subtracted from the group blocking time to remove the effects of the timeout.

6   Experimental Results

This section presents the experimental results of our fault injection for both single and correlated crash failure injections. The node join results are not presented here. The testbed used consisted of 12 identical hosts (1GHz Pentium-III with 256MB RAM) running Redhat Linux 6.2. We used a bytecode version of Ensemble 1.20 compiled with the OCaml 3.02 compiler. Each application node was started on a separate host. The results for single fault injections are divided into studies with varying workload and varying group sizes. After we conducted experiments, we observed that message blocking depended on whether or not the first crash was a leader. For leader crashes, the group cannot deliver any messages during the crash detection timeout period. For follower crashes, the issue is more subtle. Hence, we have filtered out experiments in which the first crash was a leader, and present measures for follower crashes only.

Single Crash Failure with Varying Workload During these experiments, a crash failure was injected in a group of a fixed initial size of five nodes, and the workload rate parameter λ (Section 2) was varied from 1 message/sec to 10,000 msgs/sec.

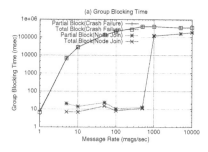 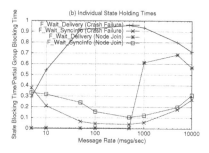

Fig. 2. Blocking Times for a Standard Stack with Varying Workload

Figure 2(a) shows the resulting total and partial blocking times for the base protocol. Corresponding results for a node join in a group of four nodes are also shown for the sake of comparison. It is seen that for low message rates, the blocking time for crash failures is five orders of magnitude higher than that for node joins, even though the protocols are not very different. Node join blocking time also suddenly increases for high message rates; after an investigation that we will not detail here, we found that that was due to the lack of a negative acknowledgment mechanism in the merge protocol. Addition of such a mechanism would be a minor modification to the protocol.

To analyze the extraordinarily large blocking times for crash failures, we plotted the ratios of the time a node spent in each blocking state to the partial group blocking time. Figure 2(b) shows these ratios for the F_Wait_Delivery and F_Wait_SyncInfo states for crash failures. The ratios for node joins are also shown for the sake of comparison. It is seen that for message rates up to 500 msgs/sec, the F_Wait_Delivery state forms a significant fraction of the time spent blocking for crash failures, but not for node joins. This reflects a problem with message delivery in the presence of crash failures. An examination of the global timelines revealed that messages were being blocked and buffered by the flow control layer for most of the Normal state because of interactions with the failure detection mechanism. The Ensemble flow control layer *MFlow* employs a credit-based scheme for broadcast traffic that bounds the number of undelivered messages. While that does bound buffer sizes in the reliable delivery layer, nodes quickly run out of credit after a crash due to the lack of message acknowledgments from the crashed node. Subsequent transmissions are buffered by the flow control layer for almost the entire duration of the failure detection timeout period, causing a large backlog of messages that must be delivered in the delivery phase and resulting in large blocking times.

One solution is for the flow control layer to prevent the application from transmitting when it runs out of credits. After some investigation, we found that Ensemble does provide a new application interface (different from the one we used) that does that. However, this solution is not ideal from an availability standpoint, because it causes the group to be blocked for almost the entire

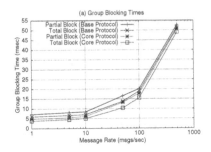 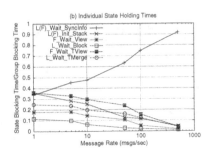

Fig. 3. Single Crash-failure Injection With Varying Workload (Without Flow Control)

crash detection timeout interval. Alternatively, the credits available to each node can be increased such that there are enough to sustain message delivery at the expected workload throughout the crash detection timeout period. However, doing so couples flow control settings with the timeout interval and expected workload; that is undesirable, since the flow control settings should depend only on network and host capacities. A flow control scheme that takes into account the timeout interval when setting a bound on the maximum number of undelivered messages, but limits the instantaneous rate of traffic according to network and host characteristics, seems more suitable for high-availability applications.

To ensure that further results were not dominated by flow control layer effects, the remaining experiments were conducted without a flow control layer in the stack. If message traffic is kept low enough that the flow control layer would not have blocked any messages during failure-free operation, this configuration is equivalent to having a flow control scheme that does not block messages during a crash detection timeout period, and buffers unacknowledged messages. Hence, we restricted workload message rates to a maximum of 500 messages per second per node. Figure 3(a) shows the total group blocking times for the core and base protocols for follower crash failures under a varying workload. The difference between the total blocking times for the base and core protocols is the time taken for application state transfer. It is seen that the blocking times for crash failures increase linearly with increasing message rate and that all four curves are fairly close to each other. This indicates that the preblock stagger time (Section 5) is low. Figure 3(b) shows the contributions of individual states to the overall blocking time for those individual states that contribute significantly. The holding times for the state transfer protocol states (F_Wait_TView and L_Wait_TMerge) are expressed as fractions of the base protocol partial block time, while the other times are expressed as fractions of the core protocol partial block time. It is seen that at low rates, a node spends around 35% of its blocking time in the state transfer protocol. The L(F)_Wait_SyncInfo states are the largest consumer of the remaining time (the core protocol blocking time). Those states are also responsible for most of the increase in overall blocking time with

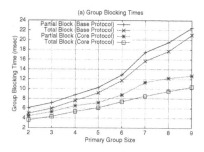
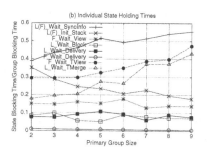

Fig. 4. Single Crash-failure Injection With Varying Group Size (Without Flow Control)

increasing workload. At 500 msgs/sec, the state transfer protocol consumes only 5% of a node's blocking time, while the L(F)_Wait_Sync_Info states consume over 85%.

An investigation of this phenomenon revealed that most of the time spent in the L(F)_Wait_SyncInfo states was because virtual synchrony information sent by followers at the beginning of the F_Wait_SyncInfo state wasn't reaching the leader quickly enough. That, in turn, was due to processing going on within one of the layers in the leader's stack; that processing was preventing the single-threaded leader stack from reading the network for new messages. The troublesome processing turned out to be the garbage collection of unacknowledged messages sent to the crashed node. This garbage collection was initiated when the crashed node was declared as Failed at the beginning of the L_Wait_SyncInfo state, and was a result of removing the flow control layer and thus allowing message delivery during the crash timeout period. However, note that the penalty of additional garbage collection is much smaller than the penalty of restricting message flow during the timeout interval, as demonstrated in the earlier experiments. This phenomenon points to a trade-off. When a crash failure occurs, a flow control layer may either block messages from being transmitted to any member in the group until the failure is resolved, or allow transmission to live members of the group but face the issue of maintaining and disposing of potentially large unacknowledged message buffers. The former approach guarantees bounded buffers and garbage collection times, but sacrifices availability of the entire group during the crash detection timeout period. Additionally, if the messages that have been blocked need to be buffered by the application anyway, that approach buys nothing. The latter approach increases the availability of the system, but can place on the communication stack the burden of maintaining and disposing of buffers that may be as large as the product of the maximum throughput of the system and the crash detection timeout interval.

Single Crash Failure with Varying Group Size During these experiments, the message rate was fixed at a rate of 10 msgs/sec. Our intention was to keep it low to minimize the garbage collection effects explained earlier, while still ensuring enough load that we did not evaluate a trivial case. The initial group size was varied from 3 nodes to 10 nodes, and a single crash failure was injected. The resulting group blocking times are shown in Figure 4(a). It is seen that all the blocking times increase linearly with group size. The total blocking times for both the base and core protocols are close to their corresponding partial blocking times indicating that the preblock stagger is low. Hence, nodes are not blocked for too long waiting for other nodes to enter the protocol. Figure 4(b) shows the contributions of the individual states to the blocking times. As before, the contributions of the two state transfer protocol states are expressed as fractions of the base protocol partial blocking time, while the contributions of other states are expressed as fractions of the core protocol blocking time. The increasing ratios for the L_Wait_TMerge and F_Wait_TView states demonstrate that the state transfer protocol is more sensitive to increasing group size than the core protocol is; this is probably due to the fact that the cost of totally ordered message delivery (required in the state transfer protocol) is higher than the cost of unordered message delivery (which is used in the core protocol). The time the leader spends collecting state information from the followers (L_Wait_TMerge) increases more rapidly than the time followers wait to receive a reply from the leader (F_Wait_TView). The reason is that an increasing number of nodes implies increased synchronization costs, whereas the time required to compose a global state remains more or less constant.

Of the remaining part of the blocking time, the percentage contribution of the L(F)_Init_Stack states reduces with increasing group size, reflecting a near constant stack initialization time. The percentage contributions of all the other states, except the L(F)_Wait_SyncInfo states, remain fairly constant with group size, indicating that they are all equally sensitive to group size. The percentage contributions of L(F)_Wait_SyncInfo states, however, show a modest increase with increasing group size. The reason is that as group size increases, the total message traffic in the system increases, because of the constant workload at each node; hence, the increase in the L(F)_Wait_SyncInfo state holding time is due to the effects of garbage collection (as described before). It could be argued that this garbage collection time is an artifact of the flow control scheme (or the lack thereof), and hence should not be considered as part of the blocking time. However, the alternative would have been to conduct experiments with no workload, which, in addition to not being realistic, would also not exercise the virtual synchrony layers at all. If desired, the effects of the garbage collection time can be analytically removed using the same technique (see Section 5) that is used for removing the effects of timeout intervals in the correlated fault experiments.

Correlated Fault Experiments The correlated fault experiments evaluated the result of injecting two crash failures into the protocol, with the second one injected in the states described in Section 4. The initial group size was fixed at 5 nodes, and the message rate was set to 10 msgs/sec. The crash detection timeout was set to 5 seconds. Figure 5(a) presents the resulting group blocking times. The labels on the X axis denote the state in which the second fault was injected. It can be seen that blocking times were dominated by the crash detection timeout,

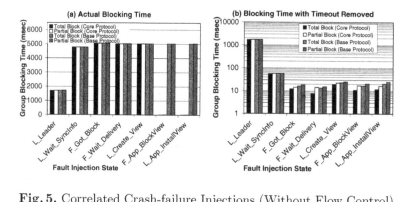

Fig. 5. Correlated Crash-failure Injections (Without Flow Control)

with three exceptions. The blocking times for the core protocol were low when faults were injected into the **F_App_BlockView** and **L_App_InstallView** states because the definition of the core protocol does not include the state transfer protocol that these states are a part of. Using the same argument, the injection of a crash in the **Leader** state to prevent the leader from sending a *Block* message should have left the blocking times unchanged from the single-fault experiments. The only result should have been a doubling of the crash detection timeout period. However, this is not what happened. To investigate this phenomenon, we removed the effects of the timeout as described in Section 5, thus representing an idealized scenario of instant crash detection. The resulting group blocking times are shown in Figure 5(b). Comparing these times to the group blocking times for a single crash with a workload of 10 msgs/sec (Figure 3(a)), we see that a correlated fault injected in most states causes only a modest (10% to 100%) increase in blocking time over a single fault injection. The two exceptions are the **Leader** state and the **L_Wait_SyncInfo** state, for which blocking times are unusually high. An examination of the global timelines revealed that the reason is the sequencer-based total ordering protocol. The protocol works by having followers unicast broadcast messages to the leader, which then sequences and broadcasts these messages to the group. When the leader crashes before the group is blocked, any subsequent broadcast messages sent to the leader are not delivered and are buffered by their senders. When the members learn of the leader failure, they broadcast the buffered messages to the rest of the group. This burst transmission of accumulated messages from all members of the group causes the membership protocol to take longer than usual to complete. This phenomenon is the cause of the high blocking times for correlated injections in the **Leader** state and the **L_Wait_SyncInfo** state. This problem does not arise when the leader crashes after the group has blocked, because new message transmissions cannot be generated in a blocked group. However, it is easy to solve the problem by explicitly notifying the application to stop sending broadcast messages when the unicast flow control layer has run out of credits. Since the new

Ensemble application interface has support for explicit flow control notification, this modification should be trivial to implement.

7 Conclusions

This paper has presented the use of a novel fault injection methodology based on global state to experimentally evaluate the blocking characteristics of the group membership protocol of the Ensemble GCS. Through this case study, we have shown how the notion of global state can be made precise through the construction of local state machines, and how fault triggers defined on this global state can be used to elegantly specify and coordinate the injection of faults into a distributed system. We have also shown how global measures on the system can be specified using a global-state timeline, and shown the importance of these measures in bringing out subtle timing characteristics of the distributed application. Thus, global-state-based fault injection is shown to have the potential to be an invaluable technique for dependability and performance assessment as well as testing of distributed systems.

The resulting evaluation has quantified group membership blocking characteristics for the Ensemble system. This data can be useful for designers of applications built on top of the Ensemble system to evaluate the dependability of their applications. Our work has also demonstrated that the choice of a flow control scheme in a GCS can be a very important factor in determining the availability of the entire system. This, along with other insights presented in this paper, can be useful to the designers of group communication systems. In conclusion, our work highlights the role of experimental evaluation as a technique that is complementary to formal verification in the design of highly dependable distributed systems.

Acknowledgment

This material is based on work supported by the National Science Foundation under Grant No. 0086096. Any opinions, findings, and conclusions or recommendations expressed in this material are those of the author(s) and do not necessarily reflect the views of the National Science Foundation. The authors would also like to thank Ryan Lefever for providing technical feedback and Jenny Applequist for helping improve the readability of this work.

References

[1] J. Arlat, M. Aguera, L. Amat, Y. Crouzet, J. C. Fabre, J. C. Laprie, E. Martin, and D. Powell. Fault injection for dependability validation: A methodology and some applications. *IEEE Trans. on Software Eng.*, 16(2):166–182, Feb. 1990. 141

[2] J. Arlat, M. Aguera, Y. Crouzet, J. Fabre, E. Martins, and D. Powell. Experimental evaluation of the fault tolerance of an atomic multicast protocol. *IEEE Trans. on Reliability*, 39:455–467, Oct. 1990. 141

[3] D. Bhatt, R. Jha, T. Steeves, R. Bhatt, and D. Wills. SPI: An instrumentation development environment for parallel/distributed systems. In *Proc. of the 9th Int'l Parallel Processing Symp.*, pages 494–501, 1995. 141

[4] K. P. Birman. *Building Secure and Reliable Network Applications.* Manning, 1996. 140

[5] R. Chandra, M. Cukier, R. M. Lefever, and W. H. Sanders. Dynamic node management and measure estimation in a state-driven fault injector. In *Proc. of the 19th IEEE Symp. on Reliable Distrib. Systems*, pages 248–257, Oct. 2000. 143

[6] R. Chandra, R. M. Lefever, M. Cukier, and W. H. Sanders. Loki: A state-driven fault injector for distributed systems. In *Proc. of the Int'l Conference on Dependable Systems and Networks (DSN-2000)*, pages 237–242, Jun. 2000. 142

[7] M. Cukier, R. Chandra, D. Henke, J. Pistole, and W. H. Sanders. Fault injection based on the partial global state of a distributed system. In *Proc. of the 18th IEEE Symp. on Reliable Distrib. Systems*, pages 168–177, Oct. 1999. 143

[8] M. Cukier, D. Powell, and J. Arlat. Coverage estimation methods for stratified fault-injection. *IEEE Trans. on Computers*, 48(7):707–723, Jul. 1999. 141

[9] S. Dawson, F. Jahanian, T. Mitton, and T. L. Tung. Testing of fault-tolerant and real-time distributed systems via protocol fault injection. In *Proc. of the 26th Int'l Symp. on Fault-Tolerant Computing (FTCS-26)*, pages 404–414, Jun. 1996. 141

[10] S. Dawson and F. Jahanian. Probing and fault injection of dependable distributed protocols. *The Computer Journal*, 38(4):286–300, 1995. 141, 143

[11] K. Echtle and M. Leu. The EFA fault injector for fault-tolerant distributed system testing. In *Proc. of the IEEE Workshop on Fault-Tolerant Parallel and Distrib. Systems*, pages 28–35, 1992. 141

[12] Fekete, Lynch, and Shvartsman. Specifying and using a partitionable group communication service. In *PODC: 16th ACM SIGACT-SIGOPS Symp. on Principles of Distrib. Computing*, 1997. 140

[13] S. Han, K. G. Shin, and H. A. Rosenberg. DOCTOR: An integrated software fault injection environment for distributed real-time systems. In *Proc. of the Int'l Computer Perf. and Dependability Symp.*, pages 204–213, 1995. 141

[14] M. Hayden. *Ensemble Reference Manual.* Cornell Univ., 1997. 144

[15] M. Hayden. *Ensemble Tutorial.* Cornell Univ., 1997. 143

[16] M. Hayden. *The Ensemble System.* PhD thesis, Comp. Sci., Cornell Univ., 1997. 141, 144

[17] J. Hickey, N. Lynch, and R. van Renesse. Specifications and proofs for Ensemble layers. In *Proc. of the Fifth Int'l Conference on Tools and Algorithms for Construction and Analysis of Systems (TACAS'99)*, Mar. 1999. 140, 144

[18] K. R. Joshi. *A Global-State Based Approach to Evaluation of Unavailability caused by Group Membership.* M. S. thesis, Univ. of Illinois, 2002. To be published. 143, 145

[19] C. Kreitz, M. Hayden, and J. Hickey. A proof environment for the development of group communication systems. In *Automated Deduction - 15th Int'l Conference on Automated Deduction. Proc.*, pages 317–332, Jul. 1998. 140

[20] F. Lange, R. Kroeger, and M. Gergeleit. JEWEL: Design and implementation of a distributed measurement system. *IEEE Trans. on Parallel and Distrib. Systems*, 3:657–671, Nov. 1992. 141

[21] S. Mishra and Wu. Lei. An evaluation of flow control in group communication. *IEEE/ACM Trans. on Networking*, 6(5):571–587, Oct. 1998. 141

[22] G. Neiger. A new look at membership services. In *Proc. of the Fifteenth ACM Symp. on Principles of Distrib. Computing*, pages 331–340. May 1996. 140

[23] D. Scott, N. Speirs, Z. Kalbarczyk, S. Bagchi, J. Xu, and R. K. Iyer. Comparing fail-silence provided by process duplication versus internal error detection for a DHCP server. In *Proc. of Int'l Parallel and Distrib. Processing Symp.*, Apr. 2001. 141

[24] D. T. Scott, B. Floering, D. Burke, Z. Kalbarczyk, and R. K. Iyer. NFTAPE: A framework for assessing dependability in distributed systems with lightweight fault injectors. In *Proc. of IEEE Int'l Computer Perf. and Dependability Symp.*, pages 91–100, 2000. 141

[25] D. T. Scott, M. C. Hsueh, G. Ries, and R. K. Iyer. Dependability analysis of a commercial high-speed network. In *Symp. on Fault-Tolerant Computing*, pages 248–257, 1997. 141

[26] P. W. Uminski, M. R. Matuszek, and H. Krawczyk. Experimental evaluation of PVM group communication. In *Recent Advances in PVM and MPI. 4th European PVM/MPI Users' Group Meeting. Proc.*, pages 57–63, 1997. 141

[27] R. van Renesse, K. P. Birman, M. Hayden, A. Vaysburd, and D. A. Karr. Building adaptive systems using Ensemble. *Software - Practice and Experience*, 28(9):963–979, 1998. 141

[28] R. Vitenberg, I. Keidar, G. Chockler, and D. Dolev. Group communication specifications: A comprehensive study. Tech. report CS99-31, Comp. Sci. Inst., The Hebrew Univ. of Jerusalem and MIT Tech. Report MIT-LCS-TR-790, Sep. 1999. 140

UMLinux – A Versatile SWIFI Tool

Volkmar Sieh and Kerstin Buchacker

Institut für Informatik 3
Friedrich Alexander Universität Erlangen-Nürnberg, Germany
{volkmar.sieh,kerstin.buchacker}@informatik.uni-erlangen.de

Abstract. This tool presentation describes UMLinux, a versatile framework for testing the behavior of networked machines running the Linux operating system in the presence of faults. UMLinux can inject a variety of faults into the hardware of simulated machines, such as faults in the computing core or peripheral devices of a machine or faults in the network connecting the machines. The system under test, which may include several machines, as well as the fault- and workload run on this system are configurable.

UMLinux has a number of advantages over traditional SWIFI and simulation tools: speed, immunity of fault-injection and logging processes from the state of the machine into which the faults are injected and binary compatibility with real world data and programs.

1 Introduction

This tool presentation describes UMLinux, a framework capable of evaluating the dependability behavior of networked machines running the Linux operating system in the presence of faults. The Linux operating system is usually employed in networked server environments, for example as web- or mailserver.

The tool uses software implemented fault injection (SWIFI) to inject faults into a simulated system of Linux machines. The simulation environment is made available by virtualization, i.e. by porting the Linux operating system to a new "hardware" — the Linux operating system! Due to the *binary compatibility* of the simulated and the host system, any program that runs on the host system will also run on the simulated machine.

A process paired with each simulated machine injects faults via the `ptrace` interface. This interface allows complete control over the traced process, including access to registers and memory as well as to arguments and return values of input/output operations. Possible faults include hardware faults in computing core and peripheral devices of a single machine as well as faults external to machines, such as faults in external networking hardware.

The tool will be used in the European DBench Project [6] for dependability benchmarking of Linux systems.

The rest of the paper is structured as follows. Section 2 gives a short overview of the main advantages of UMLinux over traditional SWIFI and simulation tools. Section 3 gives an outline of the different parts of the tool. Information about the

F. Grandoni (Ed.): EDCC 2002, LNCS 2485, pp. 159–171, 2002.
© Springer-Verlag Berlin Heidelberg 2002

configuration of the simulated hardware is found in Sect. 4. Section 5 explains how to inject faults using UMLinux. Section 6 describes an example experiment. The final section outlines a tool demonstration. For information about the implementation of UMLinux please refer to [2].

2   Advantages of UMLinux

Since the issues and problems in implementing a software injection tool at the operating system level as well as the technical details of UMLinux have been treated in [2, 8, 17] this tool presentation will concentrate on the user perspective of UMLinux. UMLinux has advantages over pure simulation and SWIFI tools or virtualization software, because it combines all three — simulation, SWIFI and virtualization. To our knowledge, there is currently no other such tool available worldwide.

[2] gives a short overview of a number of available simulation and SWIFI tools, including VHDL-based simulation ([9, 18]), CrashMe [4], Fuzz [13], FERRARI [10], MAFALDA [14], a fault-injector based on the ptrace interface [16], FIAT [1], Xception [3], and Ballista [11].

UMLinux differs from the SWIFI and simulation work named in the previous paragraph in several important aspects. It *combines* SWIFI with a simulation approach and therefore offers all the possibilities of the former. Since we simulate the hardware at a relatively high level, the simulation is unusually fast (slowdown is less then one order of magnitude). Using SWIFI together with a simulated machine has the advantage, that once set up, no user interaction is required.

When using a SWIFI tool to inject faults into the operating system of the machine the tool is actually running on, the faults may also affect the integrity of the tool and cause erroneous results to be logged. In addition, automating testing is difficult, since the machine must usually be rebooted manually when the operating system crashes or hangs and test results may be lost. In UMLinux, on the other hand, the faults are injected into a simulated machine and the fault injection software is not in any way dependent on the integrity of this simulated machine. The integrity of the host machine is in no way affected by the faults injected into the simulated machine. Since the fault injection code is separated from the code for the simulated machine and runs as a separate process, undesired interference and intrusion of the fault injection code on the simulated machine is avoided. Additional capabilities *not* offered by other simulation or SWIFI techniques include fault injection into a system of networked machines.

When using a simulation to represent a real world system, the most important question is, how closely does the simulation mimic the behaviour of the real world system? And inversely, how closely will the real world system follow the behaviour of the simulation in the presence of faults? UMLinux machines can run unmodified real world binaries and can directly use disk images of real world machines. This means that almost the complete software and data part of a UMLinux machine is identical to that of a real world machine. The differences are in the hardware and the closely hardware related software parts (drivers).

These are the same differences you encounter when you install the same software onto two machines with slightly different hardware (e.g. harddisks, cdroms, motherboard from different manufacturers). The difference in behaviour between UMLinux and a real world machine is therefore no greater than the difference in behaviour between two real world machines with slightly different hardware.

In this and the following sections, the term *host* will always be used to designate the physical machine including its operating system. The terms *virtual* or *user mode (UM)* will be used interchangeably when the simulated machine and operating system or processes running on this simulated machine are being referred to. [2] lists a number of available virtualization tools, including Bochs [19], SimOS [15], Simics™ [20], Plex86 [12], VMware™ [21], Virtual PC™ [5], User Mode Linux (UML) [7].

To be able to inject a variety of faults precisely at the targeted fault locations, it is necessary to know in detail, how the simulated hardware is implemented. For the commercial products Simics™, VMware™ and Virtual PC™ the source code is not available to us. Therefore we decided not to use them as the core of our fault injection tool. For performance reasons we also did not want to use the tools with processor emulation (Bochs, SimOS). We did not consider using Plex86 as it is still in an experimental phase.

At first sight, the UML described in [7] has a number of similarities with the user mode port of Linux we present in this paper. When taking a closer look, major differences become clear. The first big difference is, that UML [7] does not yet implement kernel memory protection. This will cause differences in behaviour to a real Linux kernel, when user processes write into the kernel memory space maliciously or due to an injected fault. In a real Linux kernel, illegal access of kernel memory space by a user process will usually crash the user process, whereas the kernel memory remains intact. In UML — because of the missing kernel memory protection — the kernel memory will also be corrupted. Therefore, to make UMLinux behave like a real Linux, we have implemented kernel memory protection. Another major difference is, that in [7] a design decision was made, to map *every* UML process onto a *separate* process in the host system. From the latter follows, that parts of the information any operating system must keep for each process will not be kept by the UML kernel, but by the kernel of the host system. Of course, information kept by the host kernel will not be affected by faults injected into the virtual main memory of the UML kernel, with the result, that injected memory faults cannot affect all processes (as would be the case in a real world system). In our UMLinux implementation the simulated machine (including its operating system and all the processes running on it) is therefore implemented as a *single* real process.

3   Overview of UMLinux

The tool consists of several interacting processes. An abstract view of the tool is shown in Fig. 1. This tool presentation describes UMLinux from a user's perspective. The technical and implementation details have already been presented

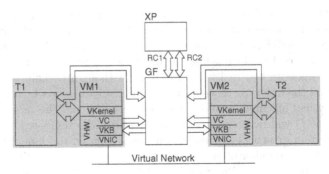

Fig. 1. Tool overview

in [2, 8, 17]. The figure shows the processes of the tool when two virtual machines (VM1 and VM2) are started. Each virtual machine is paired with its tracer (T), which is also the fault injector. Every box is a single process on the host. The processes making up a VM-T pair (shaded background) must run on the same host, but other than that there is no restriction. If several physical hosts are available, it is convenient to balance the load by starting VM-T pairs on different hosts. The close interaction of the tracer and the virtual machine is symbolized in the figure with a wide arrow.

The narrow arrows show how the graphical frontend (GF) interacts with the virtual machines. The output of each virtual console (VC) is sent to the frontend, where it can be viewed, saved or fed into Expect (XP), an automatic control program, as necessary. The frontend (or Expect) can simulate users sitting in front of the virtual machines typing away at the keyboard, since the virtual keyboard (VKB) is taking input from the frontend. The frontend must be started to use the UMLinux, whereas Expect is optional and need only be started when running prepared experiments without human interaction. The frontend can switch between the virtual machines, so a single instance is sufficient to control a complete virtual system under test consisting of several virtual machines. Expect opens a remote control connection (RC) to the frontend for every virtual machine to be controlled. Expect is configured from a file.

Fig. 2 shows a screenshot of the graphical user frontend. Two machines have been started. The window in the middle shows a UMLinux machine which is just booting. Due to a fault-injection induced crash in the previous run, a file system check is forced. The bottom window shows another UMLinux machine just being installed with the installation routine of an out-of-the-box Debian Linux.

4   Configuring the Virtual Hardware

We group the hardware into the three main categories *computing core, peripheral hardware* and *external hardware*. All information about the virtual hardware of a single machine is gathered in a single directory.

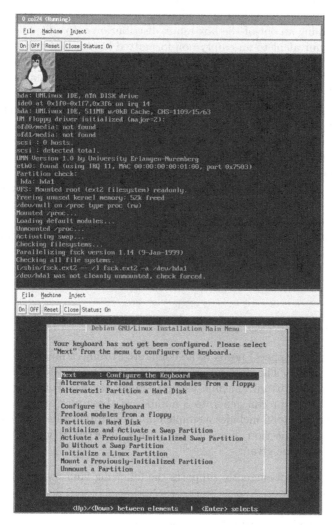

Fig. 2. Screenshot of the UMLinux user frontend

UMLinux makes no changes to the way processes use the CPU, i.e. there is no simulated CPU, instead the real CPU is accessed directly. Thus it is not possible to configure the CPU. The memory management unit (MMU) is implemented using system calls which allow to map files into certain address ranges in main memory. It is always the same and cannot be configured. UMLinux simulates random access memory (RAM) with a memory-mapped file, the size of which is the size of the UMLinux machine's "physical RAM". It can be configured freely within the limits posed by the real hardware available on the host machine.

Peripheral devices mainly include storage devices, but also input/output devices and network interfaces. Block devices, such as harddisks, floppy and cdrom drives are implemented as files. The contents of these "harddisk-files" can be created by installing an out-of-the-box Linux-distribution onto a file filled with only zeroes (the equivalent to an empty non-formatted harddisk of a certain size). It is also possible to create an image from a partition of a real harddisk and use it directly. Files implementing cdroms are simply image-files of real cdroms. It is also possible to access the cdrom of the host machine. The same holds true for floppy-drives. The number and size of the disks available to the virtual machine can be configured freely within the limits posed by the real hardware available on the host machine.

The console and keyboard device are not configurable.

The number of ethernet interfaces is configurable (the standard Linux kernel supports up to 16 interfaces). The number of free ports available on the host machine is usually large enough (there are up to 2^{16} ports on any machine running the IP protocol) to not pose a limit, even if several UMLinux machines are running on the same host. The networking hardware and routing setup is implemented by a separate process, called UM networking process (UMNP), which is configurable. When UMNP is running, the virtual machines are transparently integrated into the the local area network to which the host machine is attached.

5   Injecting Faults

The frontend (or Expect) needs to be configured to inject faults when a virtual machine is started. The description of the faults to be injected, the *fault load*, is configured per virtual machine using a simple textfile. For a large series of experiments, a script can generate a number of these files automatically. The graphical user frontend includes a simple fault description editor which supports interactive fault injection. For each fault to be injected at least the following information must be given:

Location: The tool currently supports the following fault locations:
  - RAM
  - CPU registers
  - Blockdevices (harddisks, cdroms, floppy-drives, etc.)
    - failure of a number of consecutive bytes
    - device inaccessible
  - Network interfaces
    - inability to send
    - inability to receive

Type: The fault type may currently be one of
  - permanent
  - duration
  - transient

Activation Time: This is the time (in seconds, ≥ 0) at which the fault becomes active in the system. $t = 0$ is the time at which the virtual system boots.

Following the hardware categories defined in Sect. 4 we define fault types of the same categories, i.e. computing core faults, peripheral faults and external faults. For the first two categories, the following sections explain, what additional information is needed to fully describe those faults. External faults include power failures or failures of external networking hardware such as cables or switches. We are currently working on implementing these type of faults.

For technical information explaining *how* the faults are injected, please refer to [2].

5.1 Computing Core Faults

Computing core faults include RAM, MMU and CPU faults.

RAM faults include transient bit-flip and permanent stuck-at faults. In addition to the information listed at the beginning of this section, a RAM fault is defined by

Address: A valid address in the virtual machine's physical RAM (must fall on a word-boundary).
Bit: The number of the bit which flips (between 0 and 31, where 0 is the least and 31 is the most significant bit of the word).

CPU faults include transient bit flips or permanent stuck-at faults in registers. An effect may be instructions skipped or wrong branches taken. In addition to the information listed at the beginning of this section, a CPU fault is defined by

CPU-Number: The number of the CPU. This is always 0 for single-processor machines and ranges between 0 and the number of CPUs less one on multi-processor machines.
Register: A valid register of an Intel CPU (e.g. eip, eax, eds, esp).
Bit: The number of the bit which flips (between 0 and 31, where 0 is the least and 31 is the most significant bit of the register).

Faults injected into the computing core will affect both the UM kernel and all UM user processes on the given virtual machine, just as would be the case on a real machine.

5.2 Peripheral Faults

The following paragraphs treat peripheral faults.

In addition to the information listed at the beginning ot this section, a *block-device fault* is defined by

Device: A valid Linux block-device name, e.g. hda (IDE master on first controller, usually harddisk containing boot partition), hdc (IDE master on second controller, usually cdrom), fd0 (first floppy).
First Byte: (only for byte-wise failure) The number of the faulty byte.

Number of Bytes: (only for byte-wise failure) The number of faulty bytes following the first byte.

An active fault does not necessarily have to have an effect on the operating system at all, for example, when the blocks including the defect bytes on the harddisk are never accessed. If these blocks are accessed, the fault is noticed by the operating system, but unless the blocks contain data important to the operating system (such as filesystem information), there may be no further visible effects.

In addition to the information listed at the beginning of this section, a *network interface fault* is defined by

Device: A valid Linux network interface name such as eth0, eth1.

Injecting permanent faults into peripheral devices does not incur a significant overhead, since the virtual machine is stopped at entry and exit of every system call anyway, so that the tracer can redirect the system call to the UM kernel if necessary [2]. Additionally, only those system calls implementing UMLinux device drivers need to be examined more closely when peripheral faults are active. Those system calls redirected into the UMLinux kernel need not be manipulated to inject peripheral faults.

6   Example Experiment

This sections describes a simple example experiment to show how to use UMLinux. The general setup of the example system is the following:

System under test:
> DNS: domain name-server running bind.
> DB_WWW: web and database-server running Apache and MySQL. This virtual machine was equipped with two harddisks, one containing the operating system and binaries (HD1), the other containing the database and HTML-pages for the webserver (HD2). The contents of the database were generated automatically and consist of timestamped records each with a primary key. Two different databases were used. One contained about 2.7 million entries (DB1), the other started out empty and was filled and emptied again during the testrun (DB2).

Network: The virtual machines were connected by a virtual local network.

Processor, memory, harddisk and network faults were injected into DB_WWW.

The workload was generated by Perl-scripts running on an additional virtual machine (CLIENT). Two different workloads were used.

WL1 : 230 SELECT statements made via the webinterface accessing records evenly distributed throughout the database.

WL2 : A series of 100 INSERT, followed by 150 SELECT and 100 DELETE statements (all randomly generated and submitted via the webinterface) was repeated twice on different record sets.

The record sets to be read and written by the client were prepared in advance and known to the client, such that the client was able to recognize a faulty record returned by the server.

Four different experiments were conducted, one for each type of fault, as described in the following list. The results are summarized in the next paragraphs. The results were extracted from client logfiles.

Memory Faults: The faultload was a single transient bitflip of a randomly chosen bit in a randomly chosen byte of memory between 0 and 32MB. An equal percentage of runs was made with activation times of 150, 200 and 250 seconds. The workload and database used were WL2 and DB2. 282 single runs were conducted.

Processor Faults: The faultload was a single transient bitflip of a randomly chosen bit in a randomly chosen register. An equal percentage of runs was made with activation times of 150, 200 or 250 seconds. The workload and database used were WL2 and DB2. 447 single runs were conducted.

Harddisk Faults: The faultload consisted of permanent failures of 2000 consecutive blocks on the harddisk (HD2) containing the data. The activation time was 200, the start block was randomly chosen on the harddisk. The workload and database used were WL1 and DB1. 726 single runs were conducted.

Network Faults: The faultload consisted of transient failures of the network device of DB_WWW. Both send and receive failures with durations from 5 to 40 seconds (with step of 5) were injected, with activation time being 150 seconds. The workload and database used were WL2 and DB2. 109 single runs were conducted.

The server's behavior was viewed from the client's point of view and the errors observed were therefore classified into the following categories

- faulty response (faulty record data)
- delayed response
- server error response (SER)
- server crash or hang

The item SER corresponds to the HTTP-server returning some kind of error message, such as a "page not found" message or error messages from the database server which are passed on to the client via the HTTP-server. The last item is a server crash or hang from the clients point of view, i.e. the client is unable to evoke a response from the server until the end of the testrun. Not all of these possible behaviors were observed for each type of fault injected.

The memory faults injected had no immediately visible effect on the server. We believe this is due to the fact that only a single fault was injected per testrun.

We also did not try to target sensitive parts of the memory explicitly, since (apart from the memory location of the kernel) it is not possible to tell a priori where i.e. the database- or webserver executables are located in memory at a certain time during the testrun. This behavior has also been observed on real machines with a defect RAM, were the only visible errors occurring once in a while were some defect files on the harddisk (the reason for this being the fact that Linux buffers disk I/O, so a memory fault in one of the I/O buffers will affect what is written to disk).

Figure 3 shows the percentage of different types of behavior observed in the example setup for the processor and harddisk faults. For 86.1% of the testruns injecting processor faults, the client could not observe a faulty server behavior. For the 23.9% of testruns with observable faulty behavior, the distribution is shown in the left part of Fig. 3. It is possible for several different errors to occur during a single testrun. The client completely lost connection with the server and could not regain it during this testrun (35.7% of the faults). For the client it is impossible to tell, whether the lost connection is due to an operating system crash of the server or crash of the webserver daemon only. In 40.0% of the errors observed, the server returned an error message, saying, that it could not insert the data into the database. In 22.1% of the cases no error message but a faulty record were returned. In the last 2.1% the web server returned the message, that it was unable to connect to the database.

Harddisk faults, since confined to HD2, could not affect the operating systems or database- and webserver binaries. Accordingly the clients never lost connection to the webserver, instead the webserver returned error messages when the data the client requested was inaccessible. Of the testruns performed, 77.8% terminated without errors. The percentages of the errors observed in the other 22.2% of the testruns are shown in the right part of Fig. 3. In about a quarter of the cases the web server returned an HTTP 404 "page not found" error, the rest of the time faulty records were returned without any error messages.

The experiment shows, that the worst case, i.e. undetectable errors, happens in, as we believe, a non-negligible percentage of the testruns. In the experiment setup, the clients knew which response to expect from the server and could therefore identify the faulty records returned. This is usually not the case in a real world system.

Network faults only led to delayed server responses being observed by the clients. This is due to the fact, that the HTTP-exchange between client and server is layered on the fault-tolerant Transmission Control Protocol (TCP). The latter hides the retransmissions occurring due to the network failure from the application layer and the client only records a higher response time. The durations of the network faults were obviously not long enough to lead to TCP-timeouts. The response times are sometimes much higher than the actual fault duration. This is due to the backoff and retry mechanism of TCP, which backs off for an increasing amount of time after an unsuccessful retry before trying again to connect.

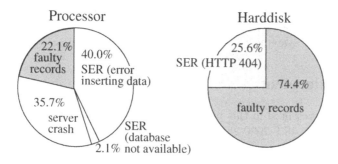

Faulty runs: 23.9%   Faulty runs: 22.2%

Fig. 3. Results of the experiments (faulty runs only)

7   Tool Demonstration

The graphical user frontend of UMLinux is better suited for presentation than the automatic experiment controller. We can show how to inject faults into one or more running UMLinux machines interactively using the graphical user frontend. The effect of some faults can be experienced directly by logging onto the UMLinux machines and checking their behaviour with some commands. To view network faults, for example, set up two UMLinux machines each doing a `ping` to the other machine and then inject a network fault into the network interface of one machine. Flipping a bit in the program counter of the CPU will usually instantly panic the kernel. To view harddisk faults, running a lengthy search or copy over the complete harddisk while injecting the fault will trigger the output of a lot of error messages.

We can present UMLinux to a larger audience using a beamer and a prepared series of interactive fault injections using the frontend. A small audience could sit down in front of a few laptops running UMLinux and examine the frontend themselves or log onto a UMLinux machine to do a few tests.

Conclusion and Outlook

UMLinux is already a versatile tool for testing and fault injection and fully operational.

We are currently working on improving the simulation of the virtual hardware with the aim, of having to change as little as possible in the original Linux operating system to port it to our virtual hardware. We have already implemented VESA graphics hardware, IDE-Controller, real time clock, APIC, mouse and keyboard which can be accessed with the original Linux drivers. We are working on doing the same for the network interface.

We are currently implementing are medium scale experiment using the Linux Virtual Server [22] as a web frontend to a database to see how UMLinux scales for testing larger systems.

Acknowledgement

The research presented in this paper is supported by the European Community (DBench project, IST-2000-25425).

References

[1] J. Barton, E. Czeck, Z. Segall, and D. Siewiorek. Fault injection experiments using FIAT. *IEEE Transactions on Computers*, 39(4):575–582, 1990. 160

[2] K. Buchacker and V. Sieh. Framework for testing the fault-tolerance of systems including OS and network aspects. In *Proceedings Sixth IEEE International High-Assurance Systems Engineering Symposium*, pages 95–105, 2001. 160, 161, 162, 165, 166

[3] J. Carreira, H. Madeira, and J. G. Silva. Xception: Software fault injection and monitoring in processor functional units. In *5th International Working Conference on Dependable Computing for Critical Applications*, pages 135–149, 1995. 160

[4] G. J. Carrette. Crashme. http://people.delphi.com/gjc/crashme.html, 1996. 160

[5] Conntectix Corporation. Virtual PC. http://www.connectix.com/, 2001. 161

[6] DBench - Dependability Benchmarking (Project IST-2000-25425). Coordinator: Laboratoire d'Analyse et d'Architecture des Systèmes du Centre National de la Recherche Scientifique, Toulouse, France; Partners: Chalmers University of Technology, Göteborg, Sweden; Critical Software, Coimbra, Portugal; Faculdade de Ciencias e Technologia da Universidade de Coimbra, Portugal; Friedrich-Alexander Universität, Erlangen-Nürnberg, Germany; Microsoft Research, Cambridge, UK; Universidad Politechnica de Valencia, Spain. http://www.laas.fr/DBench/, 2001. 159

[7] J. Dike. A user-mode port of the Linux kernel. In *5th Annual Linux Showcase & Conference, Oakland, California*, 2001. 161

[8] H.-J. Höxer, K. Buchacker, and V. Sieh. Umlinux - a tool for testing a linux system's fault tolerance. In *LinuxTag 2002, Karlsruhe, Germany, June 6-9, 2002*, 2002. 160, 162

[9] E. Jenn, J. Arlat, M. Rimen, J. Ohlsson, and J. Karlsson. Fault injection into VHDL models: The MEFISTO tool. In *Proceedings of the 24th IEEE International Symposium on Fault Tolerant Computing*, pages 66–75, 1994. 160

[10] G. Kanawati, N. Kanawati, and J. Abraham. FERRARI: A tool for the validation of system dependability properties. In *Proceedings of the 22th IEEE International Symposium on Fault Tolerant Computing*, pages 336–344, 1992. 160

[11] N. Kropp, P. J. Koopman, and D. P. Siewiorek. Automated robustness testing of off-the-shelf software components. In *Proceedings of the 28th IEEE International Symposium on Fault Tolerant Computing*, pages 230–239, 1998. 160

[12] K. Lawton. Plex86. http://www.plex86.org/, 2001. 161

[13] B. P. Miller, D. Koski, C. P. Lee, V. Maganty, R. Murthy, A. Natarajan, and J. Steidl. Fuzz revised: A re-examination of the reliability of UNIX utilities and services. Computer Science Technical Report 1268, University of Wisconsin-Madison, 1995. 160

[14] M. Rodríguez, F. Salles, J. C. Fabre, and J. Arlat. MAFALDA: Microkernel assessment by fault injection and design aid. In *3rd European Dependable Computing Conference*, pages 208–217, 1993. 160

[15] M. Rosenblum, S. A. Herrod, E. Witchel, and A. Gupta. Complete computer simulation: The simos approach. *IEEE Parallel and Distributed Technology*, Fall, 1995. 161

[16] V. Sieh. Fault-injector using UNIX ptrace interface. Internal Report 11/93, IMMD3, Universität Erlangen-Nürnberg, 1993. 160

[17] V. Sieh and K. Buchacker. Testing the fault-tolerance of networked systems. In U. Brinkschulte, K.-E. Grospietsch, C. Hochberger, and E. W. Mayr, editors, *International Conference on Architecture of Computing Systems ARCS 2002, Workshop Proceedings*, pages 37–46, 2002. 160, 162

[18] V. Sieh, O. Tschäche, and F. Balbach. VERIFY: Evaluation of reliability using VHDL-models with integrated fault descriptions. In *Proceedings of the 27th IEEE International Symposium on Fault Tolerant Computing*, pages 32–36, 1997. 160

[19] Source Forge. Bochs IA-32 Emulator Project. http://bochs.sourceforge.org/, 2001. 161

[20] Virtutech Inc. simics. http://www.simics.com/, 2001. 161

[21] VMware Inc. VMware. http://www.vmware.com/, 2001. 161

[22] W. Zhang. Linux virtual server for scalable network services. In *Ottawa Linux Symposium 2000*, 2000. 170

A Methodology for Dependability Evaluation of the Time-Triggered Architecture Using Software Implemented Fault Injection

Astrit Ademaj

Vienna University of Technology, Real-Time Systems Group
Treitlstr. 3/182-1, A-1040 Vienna, Austria
ademaj@vmars.tuwien.ac.at

Abstract. Fault injection has become a valuable methodology for dependability evaluation of computer systems. Software implemented fault injection is used because of the relative simplicity of injecting faults. In this paper we present a methodology for assessment of the error detection mechanisms of the Time-Triggered Architecture (TTA) bus structure by emulating hardware faults using software implemented fault injection. The TTA is an architecture for distributed embedded safety-critical real-time applications which have high dependability requirements. At the core of the architecture is the time-triggered communication protocol TTP/C running on a dedicated communication controller. In the TTA fail-silence is a main concern, thus high error detection coverage with small error detection latency is required. Temporal intrusiveness of the software fault injector is measured and analyzed. A fault injection tool set for use in experimental assessment of newer chip implementations of the TTPC communication controller, is developed.

1 Introduction

Fault-tolerant real-time systems are being applied more and more in complex and critical applications in automobile control (brake-by-wire or steer-by-wire) and aircraft avionic (fly-by-wire). Such critical applications impose high dependability requirements. Even a small temporal failure of the embedded computer system can lead to catastrophic consequences. The Time-Triggered Architecture is an architecture for distributed embedded safety-critical real-time applications. At the core of the architecture is the time-triggered communication protocol TTP/C running on dedicated communication controllers. A prototype microprogrammable version of a TTP/C-C1 [18] controller chip was designed and implemented during EU-founded ESPRIT OMI project TTA [22]. The objectives of our work are to determine the error detection coverage of the TTA in a realistic application scenario by emulating hardware faults using software fault injection, to locate weaknesses in the architecture and to search for and evaluate design alternatives to correct these weaknesses. We focus on not introducing intrusiveness on the target system. Another concern of our work is the reusability

F. Grandoni (Ed.): EDCC 2002, LNCS 2485, pp. 172–190, 2002.

of the experimental setup for different silicon implementations of the dedicated TTP/C-controller [19].

Fault injection is a widely used technique for dependability estimation of fault-tolerant systems in the prototype stage and for the validation of systems that are in the final stage. Software implemented fault injection (SWIFI) methods are used to inject software faults and to emulate hardware faults in memory and CPU registers [7, 10, 23]. The error detection mechanism on the MARS system (an earlier prototype version of the TTA architecture) were evaluated by using SWIFI [6] and by using three physical fault injection techniques [11].

In this paper we present a methodology for software implemented fault injection for dependability evaluation of the TTA, which uses an application specific integrated circuit (ASIC) as the TTP/C communication controller. The process of fault injection goes through the following steps:

- Analysis of the target system
- Defining fault model.
- Defining fault distribution over location and time
- Implementation of the fault injector, having in mind constrains that the target system introduces.
- Measuring the worst case execution time (WCET) of the fault injection code
- Developing a monitoring system
- Performing experiments and
- Analysis of obtained results

During the process of execution of fault injection experiments one implementation bug in the clock synchronization algorithm was detected. Slightly-off-Specification failures described in Section 4 are one of the most important results of this work.

2   Target System and Experimental Setup

A TTA system consist of a system of n nodes (called TTP nodes), which are interconnected by two broadcast channels, denoted as *channel 0* and *channel 1*. The nodes access the replicated bus according to a Time Division Multiple Access (TDMA) scheme. Each node in the system has a unique transmission slot, which is specified in the static data structure of the TTP/C controller called Message Description List (MEDL) [12]. All protocol activities are periodically repeated in TDMA rounds, while application activities are periodically repeated each cluster cycle, which is multiple of one TDMA round.

A TTP node (Figure 1) consists of a TTP/C communication controller, Communication Network Interface (CNI) and a host controller. The TTP/C protocol runs on the TTP/C communication controller, whereas the application run on the host controller. The CNI is a data exchange interface between the application (host) layer and the protocol (communication) layer of a TTP/C node. The CNI consists of:

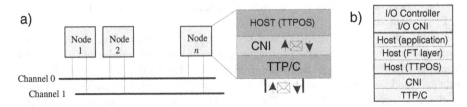

Fig. 1. a) TTA bus architecture b) TTP node structure

Status Area - contains current status of the TTP/C protocol (read only from host).

Control Area - contain host control information for the TTP/C controller.

Message Area - contain messages exchanged among the nodes.

A set of interconnected and synchronized TTP nodes is denoted as TTP cluster. Each node is equipped with a local bus guardian [21]. The bus guardian is an autonomous subsystem of a TTP node, which protects the communication channels from temporal transmission failures. It enables the node to transmit only within the node transmit window. It has a separate oscillator to prevent temporal coupling with the communication controller and to prevent common mode failures.

The TTA is based on the single-fault assumption, which states that a single physical fault in any of its constituent parts (nodes, bus) should not impact the operation of the system [12]. Error detection mechanism (EDM) in TTA can be classified into 4 classes:

- EDMs of the TTP/C Protocol (PROT)
- Built-In Self Test mechanism of the TTP/C communication controller (BIST),
- Time Triggered Operating System (executed on the host controller) EDMs (TTOS),
- Host controller hardware EDMs (HOST) include the error detection mechanism of the host controller such as, zero division, address error, etc.
- application end-to-end EDMs.

Different EDMs can be implemented at the host level and they are application specific. End-to-end EDMs can by implemented by adding end-to-end message checksum at the application layer, or by performing double task execution, triple task execution or double task executions with reference check (DERC). In DERC setup each application task is executed twice. First it performs reference check, i.e., the application task is executed with given specified input values and it is checked whether it delivers the expected output values (which are calculated off-line). If the application task passes the reference check it is executed with real input data.

The structure of the current implementation of a TTP node is presented in Figure 1.b. The TTP/C protocol runs on the dedicated controller TTP/C-C1 [18]. The CNI is implemented with a dual ported RAM and is the same silicon as the TTP/C-C1 controller. The host controller (a Motorola MC68360 microcontroller) has three software layers: the time-triggered operating system (TTPOS), the *fault-tolerant layer* (responsible for reading/writing redundant messages from/to the CNI) and the application layer. The I/O controller (a Motorola MC68376 microcontroller) is responsible for reading/setting sensor/actuator values. The I/O CNI is also a dual ported RAM used for message exchange between the I/O and the host controller. The hardware set-up for the fault injection experiments consists of a cluster with four active TTP nodes and one passive monitoring node:

- The fault injection node (FI-node) - the device subjected to fault injection.
- The golden node is the exact replica of the FI-node.
- The comparator node compares the messages received from the FI and the golden node.
- The additional node is required for the correct function of the TTP/C protocol clock synchronization algorithm [12].
- The monitoring node collects all the messages (frames) on the redundant busses and sends them to a personal computer. This node is passive, i.e. it does not send any frames.

Brake-by-wire (BBW) control system is used as application workload. BBW is a distributed simulation program designed by Volvo Technological Development. One TDMA round consists of 4 slots whereas one cluster cycle consists of two TDMA rounds.

3   Fault Model

The objective of the software fault injection is to emulate physical faults in the components of the target system. Transient bit flip faults are considered to be the most common physical faults in computer systems. This model is in accordance with most SWIFI tools [7, 8, 10], with the studies at NASA - JPL laboratory [15], and with works presented in [3, 5].

Permanent faults are easy to emulate only in the program's code segment (faults need to be injected only once). To emulate a permanent fault in the data space, the fault injector should corrupt the memory location every time that memory location is written. Thus, emulating permanent fault in the data space or registers requires the execution of fault injection code after every write operation into the memory location or register. This takes a relatively high timing overhead and makes the emulation of permanent faults not suitable when the system under test is a real-time system [9]. Emulation of permanent faults is suitable at pre-run time (targeting static configuration data and program code space).

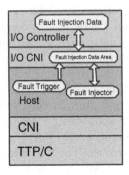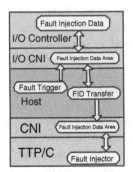

Fig. 2. Fault Injection scenarios for the host and the TTP/C controller fault injection

In this work we consider transient hardware faults, which are injected into the communication and the host controller. Fault injection is performed at runtime. Since the aim of this work is to validate the TTA architecture, we focus on the validation of the TTP/C protocol and on the validation of the design and implementation of the dedicated communication controller TTP/C-C1 [18]. The TTP/C protocol code is stored in the flash memory and upon restart it is downloaded into the RAM denoted as instruction memory, and executed from there. Emulating transient bit flip faults in the instruction memory changes the protocol code and therefore enables the fault injector to emulate transient bit flips in the TTP/C protocol code.

3.1 Fault Location

Target of fault injection experiments are two subsystems, the communication controller TTP/C-C1 (CNI, registers and instruction memory) and the host controller MC68360 (CNI, host controller RAM). Therefore, we have two fault injection scenarios. Since we intend to use the same SWIFI tool to validate other implementations of the TTP/C communication controller, the memory addresses and/or registers are user-definable as target locations for fault injection. Fault injection target locations (list of memory addresses and registers) are stored in the I/O controller. On request of the host controller the I/O controller delivers the fault injection address and the bit to be flipped. We denote this data structure as the fault injection data - FID. The fault injection process proceeds systematically over the list of predefined memory addresses and registers.

Fault injection in the host controller proceeds in the following three steps: i) the host puts a request for FID to the I/O controller, ii) the I/O controller sends the FID data back, increases the counter pointing at the FID list and clears the request, iii) the host reads the FID data and performs the fault injection.

Fault injection in the communication controller proceeds in the following four steps: i) the host puts a request for FID into the I/O controller, ii) the I/O controller sends the FID data back, increases the counter pointing at the FID

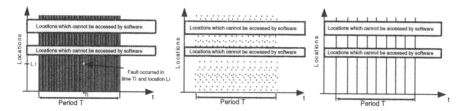

Fig. 3. a) Perfect fault distribution b)uniform random c) Discrete

list and clears the request, iii) the host reads FID data from the I/O CNI and stores them in a part of a CNI (Fault Injection Data Area, Figure 2), which is not used by the application, iv) the communication controller reads the FID from the CNI and performs the fault injection.

3.2   Fault Distribution

A perfect fault injector would be a fault injector which is able to inject faults over the entire range of memory locations and over the entire duration of program execution. If the target system is a real-time system (where tasks are executed periodically) the perfect fault injector should be able to inject faults over one period of the program execution (Figure 3.a). In this case all possible faults which may occur in the locations that are accessible by software are tested. Since the experiments could run for years, it is not reasonable to have such a fault injector. Rather then injecting faults over whole program execution the fault injector should inject faults with a uniform random distribution over a specified location range and execution time window (Figure 3.b). This fault injection mechanism can be implemented by using a timer interrupt service routine (with the highest priority) or another (internal/ external) interrupt with the accompanying interrupt service routine. This method requires no modification of the application but requires a hardware timer or a hardware external trigger with an interrupt service routine.

If the target system has no available resources to achieve this mechanism, the code insertion technique can be used, i.e., instructions are added to the target program, which performs fault injection before a particular instruction is executed. Locations to insert the fault injection should be chosen in order to try to uniformly distribute faults over one period of the program execution time. If the target architecture uses a static scheduling algorithm, then the fault distribution using code insertion technique will be discrete in the time domain (Figure 3.c). Since the TTP/C-C1 controller [18] does not have a hardware timer with programmable timer interrupt or any another interrupt with an interrupt service routine, we use the code insertion technique. The TTP/C protocol uses a static scheduling algorithm. Almost all TTP/C protocol activities are periodically repeated every slot, and they are fully repeated every cluster cycle, while application tasks are periodically repeated every cluster cycle (period T). As

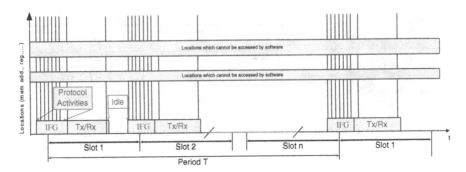

Fig. 4. SWIFI fault distribution

shown in Figure 4, the protocol activities are concentrated in the so-called *inter frame gap* (IFG) time intervals and in the transmit/receive routines. IFG is the time interval between two successive transmissions. Using a uniform discrete fault distribution over the time might result in fault injection experiments, which are performed when the controller is idle. The effects of these injected faults will impact the target system after the controller enters the activity intervals. If two or more injections are performed during the idle time interval, this will lead to replication of the same experiments. Therefore, injections are targeted towards those areas and times representing the resources used by a particular algorithm (routine) or representing a specific program execution point.

A criterion to choose the insertion points is described as follows. All significant algorithms of the TTP/C protocol are selected (clock synchronization, protocol acknowledgment, clique avoidance, etc.) in a set denoted as Alg. The fault injection code is inserted at the beginning and at the end of each algorithm from the set Alg. The logic behind the decision to place the fault injection code before each algorithm is to influence all possible input parameters, which are used by a particular algorithm. Since the injection targets all possible locations (memory addresses and registers) we are sure that all input parameters from a specific algorithm, say alg_1, are influenced by fault injection. The reason for inserting the code right after an algorithm is to influence the output results of each algorithm. If alg_1 is scheduled before algorithm alg_2, the fault injection code placed at the end of the alg_1 influences the output results of alg_1 (for example locations from L_n to L_m) and also influences the input parameters of alg_2 (for example locations form L_i to L_j). The fault injection code can be also inserted in the middle of an algorithm (or in some places within an algorithm) in order to influence the intermediate results. If the input parameters of an algorithm are influenced due to the fault injection, that will have impact on intermediate results as well (not in the same way if the experiments directly change intermediate results). Therefore the fault injection code is inserted only at the beginning and at the end of the chosen algorithms. We shall also have in mind that the number of experiments to be executed should be finite and reasonable. By reasonable number of experiments we mean that the number of executed experiments multiplied by the time needed to perform one experiment should be equal to the time planned to perform all experiments. The fault injection code is placed within the transmit and receive-routines, in order to impact the transmission/reception of the application messages to/from the bus.

Different versions of protocol codes with inserted fault injection code in one of the algorithms are created off-line. One of the protocol versions is stored in the TTP/C controller and the fault injection experiments are executed. In the next fault injection campaign, the next version of the protocol is stored and the fault injection experiments are executed. The execution of the fault injection code takes place after a predefined number of TDMA rounds from the node startup. Using the same logic, the same fault distribution is used in the host controller. Several versions of the host application are created off-line and at each host application version the fault injection code is inserted at the beginning and at the end of application and *fault-tolerant layer* tasks. The fault injection proceeds over all target locations defined by the user. One of the applications is stored in the host controller and the fault injection experiments are executed. In the next fault injection campaign, the next application is stored in the host controller and the fault injection experiments are executed.

3.3   Intrusiveness

The main disadvantage of the software fault injection tools is the problem of temporal intrusiveness. In order to circumvent the problem of temporal intrusiveness, different ways to implement a fault injector have been analyzed. For example the fault injection code could be inserted in time-slices when the processor is idle. In this case, one can assume that the probe effect is eliminated. However, this method has a disadvantage that the fault injector is limited to inject faults only during specific time intervals. In some cases this can lead to ineffective fault injection experiments.

Intrusiveness in the Host Controller. One possibility of avoiding the temporal intrusiveness is to change the execution schedule in order to reserve the system resources for the fault injector and the monitoring task (see Section 4). The TTA uses static scheduling and since we are not testing a particular application but the architecture as a whole, a change in the static schedule of the particular workload application does not change the system behavior. At the host controller the fault injector task and the monitoring task have their own resources.

Intrusiveness in the TTP/C Controller. The code which performs the fault injection is denoted as the fault injection code (agent). To analyze whether the execution of fault injection code in the TTP/C controller changes the timing behavior of the system, a *nop-loop* task (a program that executes only *nop*-operations) is inserted instead of the fault injection code. The execution time of the nop-loop task is equal to worst-case-execution-time (WCET) of the fault injector code. After insertion of the nop-loop task we have observed no change on the behavior of the system. The logical explanation is that the system has a static schedule and there is enough idle time for inserting a fault injection code. This analysis is done with the TTP/C protocol code. Let's analyze a system that has a set of periodic tasks denoted as t, which are executed periodically with a period of T time units. The $t_{WCET} = T - \Delta T$, where ΔT represents the processor idle time. The fault injector code is denoted as fi. In order to comply with its deadline the WCET of inserted fault injector code should satisfy the condition $t_{WCET} + fi_{WCET} < T$ which implies that the WCET of fault injector code should be less than ΔT ($fi_{WCET} < \Delta T$). If a real fault (no fault injector code is inserted in the program) causes an extension of the execution time of t for ΔTe, no change of the system behavior will occur if the extension $\Delta Te \leq \Delta T$. No change would be observed also if a real fault caused the extension of $\Delta Te \approx \Delta T$. If the same fault is injected, which causes t_{WCET} to extend for $\Delta Te \approx \Delta T$ and if fi_{WCET} is on the same order of magnitude of the ΔT, the t will miss the deadline because the $t_{WCET} + \Delta Te + fi_{WCET} > T$. In this case the real fault would not cause a deadline violation but the injected fault will violate the deadline of t. The probe effect would be negligible if $fi_{WCET} \ll \Delta T$ or if the fi_{WCET} is less than the jitter of the workload output [9]. In current implementation of the TTP/C protocol the tolerated jitter of a sending frame is less than $1\mu s$. The measured WCETs of a set of implemented fi tasks for the TTP/C controller are between the $0.55~\mu s$ and $1.1~\mu s$. For investigation of a special case of fault injection, we use a simple fi agent which injects fault only in one specific memory address or register and has the WCET equal to $0.55~\mu s$. No monitoring code is inserted in the TTP/C controller (see Section 4).

4   Monitoring System

A fundamental decision that must be made before the fault injection is deployed is the issue of how the monitoring will take place. In our environment we use both monitoring alternatives: nonintrusive and intrusive [17]. The nonintrusive part of the monitoring system is the monitoring node. It forwards all messages transmitted on the redundant busses to a personal computer. The monitoring allows the visualization of the messages sent in the redundant buses. The intrusive method adds new code to the program under test, which collects the data that we are looking for. The occurrences of errors and state changes in the TTP/C controller are reported in the CNI. The content of CNI is readable from the host controller therefore events in the TTP/C controller can be monitored by an intrusive monitoring task running on the host controller. Thus, a monitoring task is implemented only at the host controller, which has the function of monitoring events in TTP/C and also in the host subsystem. If an error is detected by error detection mechanisms in the TTP/C controller, the TTP/C controller triggers an interrupt in the host controller and sets the corresponding error status bit in the CNI. The interrupt service routine in the host controller reads the status bits, calculates the difference (in slots) between the slot when the fault was injected and the current slot (the slot in which the error is detected), and sends this data through a serial communication line to a personal computer.

Fail silent violation in the time domain occurs if a frame sent from a faulty node collides with a frame sent by another node. If a frame collision occurs, both nodes lose the membership bit in the membership vector [12] and perform restart. Each TTP node has the actual view of which node is currently active (operating) in the cluster. These informations are stored in the membership vector, which consists of a vector of n bits, where n is the number of nodes in the cluster. If a node excluding the fault injection node loses its membership during the fault injection experiments, it is an indication that fail propagation has occurred (a faulty node should not affect the operation of non-faulty nodes). *Fail silent violation in the value domain* is detected by comparing the application messages transmitted from two replica nodes (fault injection and golden node). If there is a mismatch a fail silence violation in value domain has occurred and the comparator node sends the information about the occurrence of fail silent violation via a serial line to the PC (the resources for monitoring are reserved during the design of the workload application). In this case the differences of the internal state of the subsystems are not observed, only the differences on external *events* are observed.

An additional monitoring system in all nodes has been implemented, which is capable to record each significant state transition in local nodes. The interpretation of monitoring data requires a priori knowledge of the TTA system. The monitoring data, (a couple of bytes for each TDMA-slot) are saved in a ring buffer in each node. Storing internal state data into a buffer implies a relatively low time overhead. If an error occurs in one of the nodes, the faulty node and the other nodes in the cluster send the content of their own ring buffer via serial communication line to PC. Sending the content of ring buffers via serial communication to PC is very time consuming, but this is done after an error has occurred i.e., the time no longer plays any role. This monitoring system is referred later on in the paper as subsystem monitoring.

We classify five different scenarios which may occur during the execution of fault injection experiments:

- The injected fault affects the operation of the FI node, an error is detected and the FI node becomes fail silent.
- The injected fault does not affect the operation of the FI node, the fault has not been activated or has been masked.
- The FI node continues operation but delivers faulty messages in value domain.
- The FI node sends at wrong point in time.
- A frame sent from FI node is correctly received by some nodes, and rejected as invalid frame by other nodes, this is called a Slightly-Off-Specification (SOS) failure.

SOS failures can occur at the interface between the analog and the digital world. The specification for a node requires that every correct node must accept input signals if they are within a specified receive window of a parameter in frequency and/or voltage [13, 16]. Each individual node will have a slightly different receive window. If an erroneous node produces an output signal (in time or value) slightly outside the specified window, some nodes will correctly receive this signal, while others might fail to receive it. Such a scenario will result in an inconsistent state of the distributed system. An SOS fault is a variant class of Byzantine faults [14].

5 Results

Fault injection experiments are divided into two sets. The first set of experiments is focused on finding out, whether it is possible to provoke fail silence violation in the time domain by injecting single faults (bit-flip). In the second set of fault injection experiments we focus on finding fail silence violations in value domain and on determining the error detection coverage of the Time-Triggered Architecture EDM without using any end-to-end error detection mechanisms.

Fail Silence Violations (FSV) in the Time Domain. In this set of experiments 1.508.976 experiments were executed. Only 16.35 % of injected faults have triggered errors. The rest of the injected faults are either not activated or masked. Each frame of a TTP node sends the same frame on two channels. A frame is received as a correct frame, if one of the frames sent on the redundant channels is received correctly. The possibility of masking of a single bit flip error is high (as can be seen from the results). Each fault injection target location is being tested several times during the execution of fault injection in different points in time within two TDMA rounds. No cases of frame collisions in the bus are observed. A detailed analysis of some experiments has shown that the frame collisions have been avoided by the bus guardian of the local node. Since the aim of this campaign was to *search* for fail silent violation in the time domain no detailed description of results is given.

Slightly-Off-Specification Failures. Different cases of the SOS failures in the time domain have been observed during the execution of the fault injection from the fist campaign. A frame sent from a node is received as correct frame at the receiver node, if the frame is received within the specified receive window of the receiver node. Each individual node will have a slightly different receive window, but this difference should not be higher than the precision Π [12]. The clock synchronization algorithm assures that the nodes remain synchronized within a specified precision Π. An example of the SOS is presented in Figure 5. Due to a fault injection, a timer register of the TTP/C controller was affected at $t1$ point in time, forcing the clock of the node to speed-up slowly. The frame sent from the faulty node (node 4) at $t2$ point in time is close to the limits of the receive window of the receiver nodes. The slowest node in the cluster (node1), will receive the frame sent by the faulty node slightly outside its receive window and reject it as an invalid frame. Other nodes receive the frame sent from the faulty node as a valid frame. After $t2$ point in time the slowest node in the

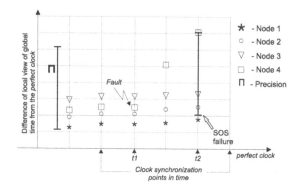

Fig. 5. SOS scenario

cluster (node 1) has inconsistent view of the actual global cluster state from other nodes in the cluster. A TTP/C frame consists of the message sent followed by the CRC calculated over the message to be sent and over local view of the global state of the cluster (including membership vector) of the sender node. At the receiver node the CRC is calculated over the received message and over the receiver's local view of the global state of the cluster (including the content of the membership vector). After $t2$, the frame sent from node 1 will be received as incorrect frame at other nodes because of the different CRC (which results from the different membership vector), and thus node 1 will be expelled from the membership of the receiver nodes. Node 1 *realizes* that it is not consistent with the majority of the nodes in the cluster and will become fail silent [12]. This is a typical case of fault propagation. A faulty node makes a non faulty node to become fail silent. SOS failures violate the fault hypothesis of the TTP/C protocol. A detailed description of observed cases of SOS failures is given in [1]. No SOS failures in the value domain have been observed during the execution of SWIFI experiments as the fault injection mechanism is orthogonal to this dimension. Value SOS failures might be observed if the power supply of a node is influenced.

A bug in the implementation of the clock synchronization algorithm of the protocol microcode for the TTP/C-C1 controller was found during the execution of first set of experiments. This improper implementation allows the node to become SOS faulty when the node performs external clock synchronization [12]. Details of this problem are given in [2]. The clock synchronization problem and other cases of SOS failures are analyzed using subsystem monitoring (Section 4).

Fail Silence Violations (FSV) in the Value Domain. Fail silence violations in the value domain are detected by comparator node by comparing the messages received from fault injection node and from the golden node, which is the replica of the fault injection node. In the experiments, in which fail silence violations in the value domain occur, no errors are detected by the faulty node, thus the output of experiments from that node is NO ERROR. In this set of experiments, several different fault injection campaigns performing 651.796 experiments in total, targeting different locations were executed. Error detection latency (EDL) is the time difference between the instant when a fault is activated (error triggered) and the instant when the error is detected by an EDM. We measure the error detection latency with the number of TDMA slots. For example, the TTP/C EDMs take two TDMA slots to detect an error in a node if the node receives incorrect frames because of an error in the receiver subsystem [12]. If the error detection latency is measured with the absolute time units, different EDL values will be observed if experiments are executed in two different applications with different TDMA slot durations. Since we do not have any mechanism to check for fault activation time, the EDL is measured as the difference between an injected fault and the detected error. This will lead to overestimation of EDL values. The Results of SWIFI experiments are classified depending of different target locations.

TTP/C-C1 Register File. The target of the fault injection was the TTP/C-C1 register file. The TTP/C-C1 controller has 64 word registers used to store intermediate results of the TTP/C protocol. The fault injection code was inserted into the TTP/C protocol code.

Table 1: Fault injection into the TTP/C-C1 register file

EDM		Detected Errors	5,075	99.88%
PROT	3,751	SOS	0	0.00 %
BIST	1,287	FSV Value	6	0.12 %
TTPOS	37	Error Triggered	5,081	35,80 %
NO ERROR	9,117	EDL (Min/Max)	0/7 TDMA Slots	
Total	14,192	Average EDL	1.04 TDMA Slots	

TTP/C-C1 Hardware Registers. In this campaign of experiments the target of fault injection were hardware registers of different functional units (timer unit, CRC, Tx/Rx unit, etc.) of the TTP/C-C1 controller. The fault injection code was inserted into the TTP/C protocol code. Faults were injected at different slots within two TDMA rounds. In this campaign 8 cases of SOS were observed.

Table 2: Fault injection into the TTP/C-C1 hardware registers

EDM		Detected Errors	1,918	99.58%
PROT	231	SOS	8	0.40 %
BIST	1,164	FSV Value	0	0.00 %
TTPOS	523	Error Triggered	1,926	31.70 %
NO ERROR	4,156	EDL (Min/Max)	0/12 TDMA Slots	
Total	6,074	Average EDL	1.4 TDMA Slots	

TTP/C-C1 Instruction Memory. In Table 3, experiments with the instruction memory of the TTP/C controller are presented. The TTP/C protocol code is stored in a flash memory and upon restart it is downloaded into the RAM of the TTP/C-C1 controller denoted as instruction memory.

Table 3: Fault injection into the TTP/C-C1 instruction memory

EDM	No. of Exp.	Detected Errors	46,261	97.68%
PROT	24,943	SOS	6	0.01 %
BIST	17,841	FSV Value	1092	3.31 %
TTPOS	3,477	Error Triggered	47,359	9,32 %
NO ERROR	461,483	EDL (Min/Max)	0/24 TDMA Slots	
Total	507,744	Average EDL	3.66 TDMA Slots	

The TTP/C protocol code is executed from the instruction memory. Emulating transient bit flip faults in the instruction memory changes the program code space of the TTP/C protocol. The TTP/C protocol line codes except the lines of code that perform fault injection, were target of fault injection. The number of not activated and masked errors is high (462581/507774) 90.84%. Fault injection experiments are executed at run-time i.e. only the part of the protocol code running in the application [12] state were affected by fault injection. The TTP/C protocol code profiling (an analysis of the TTP/C microcode at VHDL level) has shown that 30% of the protocol code lines are executed during the application state. The rest of the code is executed during the download state (download process of configuration data) and during the initialization state [12]. This is the reason why such a low number of injected faults has been activated. In this campaign of experiments 6 cases of SOS failures were observed.

TTP/C CNI. The fault injection code was inserted into the TTP/C protocol code. The target of fault injection was the CNI. The number of fail silence violations in the value domain is (1568/34112) 4,59% if all fault injection experiments are considered, or 52.01% if only the fault injection experiments that have triggered errors are considered. 91.16% of the experiments resulted in NO ERROR detected. This high number experiments with no errors detected is due to the masking of faults because of the redundancy of the messages (redundant messages are sent/received in two redundant channels).

Table 4: Fault injection into the CNI performed from TTP/C-C1 controller

EDM	No. of Exp.	Detected Errors	1,447	47.99%
PROT	1,158	SOS	0	0.00 %
BIST	30	FSV Value	1,568	52.01 %
TTPOS	259	Error Triggered	3,015	8.84 %
NO ERROR	32,665	EDL (Min/Max)	0/10 TDMA Slots	
Total	34,112	Average EDL	2.98 TDMA Slots	

Host CNI. In this campaign of experiments the fault injection code was inserted into application and fault tolerant layer tasks. Faults are injected in all slots of the cluster cycle. Target of the fault injection was the CNI.

Table 5: Fault injection into the CNI performed from host controller

EDM	No. of Exp.	Detected Errors	1,096	61.99%
PROT	896	SOS	0	0.00 %
BIST	0	FSV Value	672	38.01 %
TTPOS	200	Error Triggered	1,768	4.40 %
NO ERROR	39,032	EDL (Min/Max)	0/7 TDMA Slots	
Total	40,128	Average EDL	1.62 TDMA Slots	

Host RAM. In this campaign of experiments the fault injection code was inserted into application and fault tolerant layer tasks. The fault injection was triggered at all different sending slots. Target of the fault injection was the RAM memory of the host controller (MC68360). Performing fault injection experiments in the RAM of the host controller, affects the operation of the application tasks, the fault tolerant layer tasks, and the time-triggered operating system.

Exchange of messages among the nodes in a cluster proceeds as follows:

Table 6: Fault injection into the host controller RAM

EDM	No. of Exp.	Detected Errors	1,780	67.01%
PROT	604	SOS	0	0.00 %
HOST	514	FSV Value	876	32.99 %
TTPOS	662	Error Triggered	2,656	5.35 %
NO ERROR	47,766	EDL (Min/Max)	0/4 TDMA Slots	
Total	49,546	Average EDL	0.76 TDMA Slots	

t_1 Host of a sender node performs calculations for a message to be sent (m_{s1}).

t_2 Fault tolerant layer task writes the content of m_{s1} in the CNI.

t_3 TTP/C communication controller of the current sender node reads the m_{s1} from the CNI, computes CRC and transmits the message in its sending slot.

t_4 TTP/C communication controller of a receiver node calculates the CRC of the received frame and stores the content of the received message in the CNI.

t_5 Fault tolerant layer task of the receiver node reads the content of the CNI and stores the result in the variable say m_{r1}.

t_6 Host of the receiver node reads the m_{r1} and performs further calculations.

The TTP/C protocol assures the fail silence in the value domain from the t_3 point in time until t_4 point in time. If a fault occurs prior to t_3 at the sender node (in RAM and/or CNI Message Area where the content of message m_{s1} is stored) or after the t_4 at the receiver node (in RAM and/or CNI Message Area where the content of received message m_{r1} is stored) there is a high probability that a fail silence violation in value domain will occur. Therefore the number of observed fail silence violations in the value domain is high in the set of experiments with the CNI and the host RAM. To achieve fail-silent behavior in the value domain, it is necessary to deploy end-to-end error detection mechanism at the application level.

SWIFI experiments have been performed in the predecessor of the TTA, the MARS system [6]. The hardware configuration setup is similar to the work in [11, 6], but the main differences between the MARS and the TTP nodes are in hardware (ASIC controller in the TTP node) and software components. Therefore the software fault injection tools implemented in MARS are not applicable for TTP nodes. MARS nodes have been implemented using different hardware components. In the actual implementation, a TTP node uses an ASIC controller TTP/C-C1 [18] as a communication controller. Because of the different hardware implementation the results with TTA nodes differ from the results with the MARS nodes. SWIFI experiments presented in [6] are performed in MARS application with three different end-to-end error mechanisms (no end-to-end error detection mechanism, message checksum, and double task execution plus message checksum) in order to estimate the error detection coverage of the MARS architecture. In the work presented in [6] faults are injected at the pre-run time (target of fault injection were the code and data segment of two workload applications) and at the run-time (target of fault injection were application messages with the aim of evaluating the limits of the application level error detection mechanisms). In our work we concentrate on the validation of the TTA architecture as a whole. The target of the fault is the code and data space of the TTP/C protocol macrocode, registers file and hardware registers of the of the TTP/C communication controller, CNI (data exchange interface between the host and communication controller), and the host controller executing an application without any end-to-end error detection mechanisms.

6 Bus Guardian Implementations

From the obtained results, it has been concluded that the weakness of the current implementation of the TTA with bus interconnection structure are SOS failures. An SOS fault occurs because of the change in the timer parameters of a node and because of the imperfect synchronization of the nodes in the distributed system. As one SOS failure may occur because a bit flip in one of the timer registers, the probability of the occurrence of an SOS is not negligible. An SOS-faulty node causes the non-faulty nodes in the cluster to have inconsistent view of the distributed system, and forcing non-faulty node to become fail silent. Therefore the SOS failure violates the fault hypothesis of the TTPC protocol. In a TTA system node system the bus guardian (BG) protects the bus from the babbling-idiot failures [21]. In the role of protecting the bus, the bus guardian should also prevent the occurrence of SOS failures in order to be considered as a fault containment unit (FCU)[20]. A FCU is a collection of components that operate correctly regardless of any arbitrary logical or electrical fault outside the region and a fault in a FCU cannot cause hardware outside the region to fail. Therefore the bus guardian should correct or reject the output frames which may result in SOS failures. The correction of output signals or frames will be done by signal reshaping in the value and in the time domain. In order to perform signal reshaping in the time domain the bus guardian should have its own clock synchronization mechanism (it should have its own view of global time, and not the one from the local node). In the current implementation of the TTP/C communication controller, the bus guardian is in the same silicon area with the TTP/C-C1 chip. One bus guardian "guards" both channels and is not totally independent from the TTP/C node (it does not perform clock synchronization). Design alternatives which will eliminate the occurrence of SOS failures in the TTA are: i) the implementation of two independent bus guardians (one for each channel) outside the TTP/C chip connected to each local node having is own clock synchronization algorithm and performing signal reshaping (in time and value) or ii) to use the star topology where two redundant central hubs (each for one channel) have the role of the bus guardian and perform signal reshaping. In both cases the bus guardian will be independent from the node and will have independent power supply and independent oscillators. In the proposed configurations a fault, in any of the fault containment unit will not result into an SOS failure. For example, if a node sends a faulty frame which may cause an SOS failure, the frame will be corrected by the bus guardian (BGs are separate FCUs). If a bus guardian is faulty and makes a frame sent from a node SOS faulty, the frame sent in the another channel (this channel in protected by another bus guardian), will be received as a correct frame. A frame is received correctly, if a node receives correctly one of the frames sent in the redundant channels. Thus an SOS frame in only one channel will not result in an SOS failure. Since one central bus guardian guards only one channel, it will not be considered as a single point of failure. If one central bus guardian fails, the redundant central bus guardian will maintain the communication among the nodes in the redundant channel. A prototype FPGA implementation of a central bus guardian, which performs signal reshaping in the time and value domain, is already finished. First preliminary SWIFI results with the central bus guardian are very promising [4].

7   Conclusion

In this paper we present a methodology for assessment of the error detection mechanisms of the time-triggered architecture. Usually software fault injection tools use complex fault injectors, and the whole fault injection experiment campaigns run in a quite automated fashion, which implies high computing time overhead. We have implemented a set of simple and focused fault injection agents with low timing overhead in order to overcome the problem of temporal intrusiveness. A fault injection tool set for use in experimental assessment of newer chip implementations of the communication controller for the time-triggered architecture has been developed. In the course of development several problems including reducing probe effect, fault distribution, and implementation of the monitoring system for analysis of the SOS failures, were discussed. The TTA with the bus interconnection structure with non-independent local bus guardian is not robust to SOS failures. First preliminary results have shown that the TTA architecture with the star interconnection structure, which uses a centralized bus guardian, is resilient to SOS failures. Validation of the TTA with star topology is in the process of investigation. A future work is to measure the fail silence coverage in the value domain using different end-to-end error detection mechanisms described in Section 2, and to repeat the executed experiments with the newest implementation of the TTP/C communication controller TTP/C-C2.

Acknowledgment

This work has been supported by the European IST project FIT under project No. IST-1999-10748. The Author would like to thank Prof. Hermann Kopetz, the leading architect of the TTA architecture, for his support and valuable suggestions during this work.

References

[1] A. Ademaj. SOS Failures in the TTA Bus Topology. Technical Report 40/2001, Vienna University of Technology, Real-Time Systems Group, Vienna, Austria, 2001. 183

[2] A. Ademaj and G. Bauer. A Note on the Implementation of the Clock Synchronization Algorithm. Technical Report 44/2001, Vienna University of Technology, Real-Time Systems Group, Vienna, Austria, 2001. 183

[3] Buchner at al. Characterization Of Single-Event Upsets In A Flash Analog-To-Digital Converter (AD9058). *Transactions on Nuclear Science,*, 47(6), Dec 2000. 175

[4] G. Bauer, H. Kopetz, and W. Steiner. The Central Guardian Approach to Enforce Fault Isolation in a Time-Triggered System. Research Report 20/2002, Vienna University of Technology, Real-Time Systems Group, Vienna, Austria, 2002. 188

[5] Dodd et al. Single-Event Upset And Snapback In Silicon-On-Insulator Devices and Integrated Circuits. *IEEE Transactions on Nuclear Science*, 47(6), Dec 2000. 175

[6] E. Fuchs. An Evaluation of the Error Detection Mechanisms in MARS using Software-Implemented Fault Injection. In *Second European Dependable Computing Conference (EDCC-2)*, Taormina, Italy, October 1996. 173, 187

[7] N. A. Kanawati G. A. Kanawati and J. A. Abraham. FERRARI: A Tool for the Validation of System Dependability Properties. In *Proc. 22rh Symp. on Fault-Tolerant Computing (FTCS-22)*, Boston, Massachusetts, 1992. 173, 175

[8] Z. Segall J. Barton, E. Czeck and D. Siewiorek. Fault Injection Experiments using FIAT. In *Transactions on Comp*, volume 39, 1990. 175

[9] M. Z. Rela J. C. Cunha and J. G. Silva. Can Software Implemented Fault-Injection be Used on Real-Time Systems? In *Proc. 3rd European Dependable Computing Conference (EDCC-3)*, pages 209–226, Prague, Czech Republic, 1999. 175, 180

[10] H. Madeira J. Carreira and J. G. Silva. Xception: Software Fault Injection and Monitoring in Processor Functional Units. In *IEEE Transactions on Software Engineering*, volume 24 of 2, Feb 1998. 173, 175

[11] J. Arlat Y. Crouzet G. Leber J. Karlsson, P. Folkesson and J. Reisinger. Application of Three Physical Fault Injection Techniques to the Experimental Assessment of the MARS Architecture. *Proc. 5th IFIP Working Conf. on Dependable Computing for Critical Applications, DCCA-5, Urbana-Champaign, IL, USA*, September 1995. 173, 187

[12] H. Kopetz. TTP/C Protocol – Version 0.5. TTTech Computertechnik AG. Available at http://www.ttpforum.org. 173, 174, 175, 181, 182, 183, 184, 185

[13] H. Kopetz. A Comparison of TTP/C and FlexRay. Technical Report 10/2001, Vienna University of Technology, Real-Time Systems Group, Vienna, Austria, 2001. 181

[14] R. Shostak M. Pease and L. Lamport. Reaching Agreement in the Presence of Faults. *Journal of ACM*, (27(2)):228–234, 1980. 182

[15] NASA-JPL. Single Upset Event - Galileo Project http://www.jpl.nasa.gov/galileo/messenger/oldmess/SEU.html. 175

[16] J. Rushby. Bus Architectures For Safety-Critical Embedded Systems. *EMSOFT 2001: First Workshop on Embedded Software*, 47(6), Ocrober 2001. 181

[17] Beth Schroeder. On-line Monitoring: A Tutorial. *IEEE Computer Magazine*, (28), June 1995. 180

[18] TTP/C-C1 Communications Controller Data Sheet. TTTech Computertechnik AG. Available at http://www.ttech.com. 172, 175, 176, 177, 187

[19] TTP/C-C2 Communications Controller Data Sheet. TTTech Computertechnik AG. Available at http://www.ttech.com. 173

[20] A. Steininger and C. Temple. Economic Online Self-Test In The Time-Triggered Architecture. *IEEE Design & Test of Computers*, 16(3):81–89, 1999. 187

[21] C. Temple. Avoiding The Babbling-Idiot Failure In A Time-Triggered Communication System. In *28th Annual International Symposium on Fault-Tolerant Computing*, volume FTCS-28, 1998. 174, 187

[22] Time-Triggered Architecture. http://www.vmars.tuwien.ac.at/projects/tta/. 172

[23] Ravishankar K. Iyer Wei-Lun Kao and Dong Tang. FINE: A Fault Injection and Monitoring Environment for Tracing the UNIX System Behavior under Faults. In *Dependable IEEE Transactions on Software Engineering*, volume 19, Nov 1993. 173

Fast Indulgent Consensus
with Zero Degradation*

Partha Dutta and Rachid Guerraoui

Distributed Programming Laboratory
Swiss Federal Institute of Technology in Lausanne

Abstract. This paper presents a new consensus algorithm for the asynchronous message passing system model augmented with an unreliable failure detector abstraction. Our algorithm (a) matches all known consensus lower bounds on (1) *failure detection, i.e., Ω*, (2) *resilience*, i.e., a majority of correct processes, and (3) *latency*, i.e., two communication steps for a global decision in *nice* runs (when no process crashes and the failure detection is reliable), and (b) has the following *zero degradation* flavor: in every *stable* run of the algorithm (when all failures are initial crashes, and failure detection is reliable), two communication steps are sufficient to reach a global decision.

The zero degradation flavor is particularly important when consensus is used in a repeated form: failures in one consensus instance do not impact performance of future consensus instances.

1 Introduction

1.1 The Motivation

In practice, most runs of a distributed system are *nice*: failures are rare and failure detectors do not usually suspect correct processes to have crashed. Hence, it is important to optimize the performance of distributed algorithms in nice runs. We are interested here in also minimizing the performance degradation of the algorithms in the presence of failures, especially initial failures. To see why this is also important, consider a long-running application using a series of instances of a given distributed algorithm (e.g., an atomic broadcast service using a series of consensus instances [12, 4]). Even if failures are rare, they might occur and one expects a failure to impact the performance of the instance of the algorithm during which the failure occurs. However, it is desirable to minimize the impact of that failure on all subsequent instances of the algorithm. If this impact is nil, then we say that the algorithm has a "zero degradation" flavor.[1]

---

* This work is partially supported by the Swiss National Science Foundation (project number 510-207).

[1] When considering this flavor, we focus on the time complexity of an algorithm, and more precisely on its latency, i.e., the number of communication steps needed for all correct processes to decide (a *global decision*). Aspects like message or memory complexity are outside the scope of this paper.

F. Grandoni (Ed.): EDCC 2002, LNCS 2485, pp. 191–208, 2002.

Our motivation here is to devise a consensus algorithm that, on the one hand, matches all known consensus lower bounds on (1) *failure detection, i.e.,* Ω [3], (2) *resilience*, i.e., a majority of correct processes [4], and (3) *latency*, i.e., two communication steps for a global decision in *nice* runs [10], and on the other hand, provides the zero degradation flavor.

1.2   The Background

The consensus problem consists for a set of processes to decide a common value, among one of the values proposed by the processes. Each process proposes a value v through procedure propose(v). If propose($*$) returns v' at a process, the process is said to have decided v'. Consensus is solved if the following three conditions are ensured: (1) (*validity*) if a process decides v then some process has proposed v, (2) (*uniform agreement*) no two processes decide differently,[2] and (3) (*termination*) every correct process eventually decides.

We consider consensus in a message-passing distributed system model consisting of a set of n processes: $\Pi = \{p_1, p_2, ..., p_n\}$. Processes can fail by crashing and never recover from a crash.[3] A *correct* process is a process that never crashes and executes the deterministic algorithm assigned to it. A process that crashes is said to be *faulty*. Any pair of processes can communicate through *send* and *receive* primitives, which emulate a *reliable* communication channel in the following sense [9]: (1) any message sent to a correct process is eventually received, (2) no message is received more than once, and (3) the channel does not create or alter messages. To solve consensus in this model [6, 5], one needs to consider additional assumptions such as a majority of the processes is correct and the system is "eventually synchronous". The latter assumption can be captured in a modular manner through the abstraction of a failure detector oracle that provides the processes with some (possibly unreliable) information about which process has crashed and which process has not [4].

In this paper, we consider consensus algorithms based on two interesting failure detectors: Ω and $\Diamond \mathcal{S}$. The failure detector Ω outputs at each process, a (leader) process denoted $\Omega.trusted$ such that, eventually, at all correct processes the output is the same correct process. The failure detector $\Diamond \mathcal{S}$ outputs, at each process, a list of suspected processes denoted $\Diamond \mathcal{S}.suspected$ such that: (1) (*strong completeness*) eventually, every crashed process is permanently suspected by every correct process, and (2) (*eventual weak accuracy*) there is a time after which some correct process is never suspected by any correct process.

In [4], Chandra and Toueg presented a consensus algorithm (which we denote by CT) assuming a majority of correct processes and the abstraction of $\Diamond \mathcal{S}$. Independently, Lamport presented in [12] the Paxos consensus algorithm (which

---

[2] Note that we consider the *uniform* consensus problem. In the system model we consider, uniform consensus and consensus are similar [7].

[3] Applying our ideas to the crash-recovery model of [1] is certainly feasible but might distract from the main ideas we are addressing here: achieving zero degradation while matching consensus lower bounds.

we denote by PC) assuming a majority of correct processes and the abstraction of Ω.[4] Both failure detectors were shown to be equivalent in a precise sense and represent the amount of knowledge needed to solve consensus [3], i.e., a *failure detection* lower bound. An inherent characteristic of Ω and $\Diamond\mathcal{S}$ is the *indulgence* of the actual consensus algorithms using them [7]. Roughly speaking, the algorithm is *indulgent* towards its failure detector: even if this failure detector turns out to be completely unreliable and does never provide any useful knowledge about failures (i.e., the system does never provide any synchrony guarantee), the safety properties of consensus (validity and agreement) are preserved. It is shown in [4, 7] that a majority of correct processes is a lower bound for this form of indulgence, i.e., a *resilience* lower bound.

1.3   The Question

Precisely because of the indulgence of algorithms using Ω and $\Diamond\mathcal{S}$, one cannot bound the number of communication steps needed to reach a global decision (*latency*). Fortunately, it is possible to bound this latency when the failure detector does not make mistakes, in particular in *stable* runs. Intuitively, we say that a run is stable if failures are initial (i.e., all failures occurred before the run started) and the failure detector output does not change during the run. More precisely, we say that a run of an Ω-based algorithm is *stable* iff all failures in the run are initial failures and the failure detector outputs same correct process, at all processes, from the very beginning. Similarly, we say that a run of a $\Diamond\mathcal{S}$-based consensus algorithm is stable iff all failures in the run are initial failures, and at all processes, $\Diamond\mathcal{S}.suspected$ is always identical to the set of initially crashed processes. A *nice* run is simply a stable run with no failures.

In nice runs of CT, four communication steps are needed before a consensus decision is reached by all correct processes (global decision). One can easily obtain an optimization of CT that alleviates the need for the first step in a nice run. In every *stable* run of CT, the same number of communication steps (four) are still needed for a global decision. Similarly, in nice runs of PC, five communication steps are needed for a global decision, and a simple optimization of PC alleviates the need for the first two steps in a nice run. In every stable run, still the same number of communication steps (five) are needed. In other words, though the latency in stable runs is relatively high, it does not depend on the identity or the number of the initially failed processes.

Several authors suggested variants of CT where two communication steps are sufficient for a global decision in nice runs [14, 8]: a latency lower bound for these runs [10]. Unlike CT, these algorithms degrade in the presence of (initial) failures; the degradation being more or less graceful depending on algorithm specifics [8].

---

[4] In fact, PC was devised for a system model where channels might lose messages and processes can crash and recover. For the sake of presentation simplicity, we consider a variant of the algorithm in the simpler system model of [4]. In this model, the eventual synchrony assumption of Paxos Consensus can be captured through the failure detector Ω.

More recently, [13] presented two Ω-based consensus algorithms that do not degrade in stable runs. In the first algorithm of [13], three communication steps are required for a global decision in stable runs, thus clearly not optimum in latency. The second algorithm enforces global decision in two communication steps in stable runs but assumes two-third of the processes to be correct: thus clearly not optimum in resilience.

We say that a consensus algorithm is *zero degrading* iff the same number of communication steps are required for achieving a global decision in every stable run (irrespective of the identity or the number of the initially crashed processes). To our knowledge, previous indulgent consensus algorithms that have an optimal latency in nice runs, either are not zero degrading, or are not optimal in terms of resilience. It is legitimate to ask whether we can have the cake and eat it too. This paper shows that the answer is *yes*: we can indeed match (a) the lower bounds on resilience, failure detection, and latency, and (b) yet provide the zero degradation flavor.

1.4   The Contribution

We present a consensus algorithm based on the assumptions of failure detector Ω and a majority of correct processes. In every stable run (whether nice or not), two communication steps are sufficient to reach a global decision. Our algorithm is decentralized: processes exchange consensus *decisions* and *estimates* of the decisions directly, just like in [14, 8, 13]. What makes our algorithm particularly effective is the very fact that processes also exchange their perception about the current leader. Intuitively, they can expedite the decision when they realize that they have the same leader, e.g., in a stable run.

Section 2 gives an overview and then a detailed description of the algorithm with an informal argument for its correctness. The detailed correctness proof of our algorithm is presented in the appendix. We then briefly describe in Section 3 and in Section 4 two additional variants of our algorithm: (1) an Ω-based consensus algorithm such that, given a privileged value PV, one communication step is sufficient to reach consensus in every stable run where all processes propose PV, and (2) a zero degrading $\Diamond S$-based consensus algorithm. Roughly speaking, these variants convey the very fact that our technique to obtain zero degradation can be applied in various indulgent consensus context.

As a side effect of our work, we introduce in Section 5 a performance metric for consensus algorithms which captures the best-case latency of an algorithm (i.e., latency in a nice run) as well as reveals the performance degradation (if any) of the algorithm in the presence of failures. We use this metric to compare our algorithms with previous indulgent consensus algorithms. We point out, finally, the performance gain obtained by our algorithm when consensus is used in a repeated form, with respect to traditional consensus algorithms.

2   The Algorithm

We denote our algorithm by DG_Ω and present it in Figure 1. We give here a description of the algorithm along with an informal argument of its correctness. Detailed correctness proofs are given in the appendix.

2.1   Overview

Our DG_Ω algorithm is round based: every process p_i moves incrementally from one round to the other. Every round consists of two phases; each phase involves exchanging a set of messages. Unless p_i decides (returns from propose($*$)), p_i moves to the next higher round after completing the two phases.

   At each round r, every process queries its Ω failure detector module about the current leader. We say that a process p_i is a *majority-leader* at a round r iff p_i is the current leader at a majority of processes at that round. For a given round r, there can obviously be at most one majority-leader. If the failure detector makes mistakes, then it is possible that there is no majority-leader at a round. In the first phase of a round, processes exchange current leader values; i.e., they exchange the perception about who is the leader. If a process perceives that a majority-leader exists for round r, it adopts the *estimate* of that leader, say value x, as its intermediate *estimate* value, *newEstimate*; otherwise *newEstimate* remains $\perp$. Since there is at most one majority-leader in a round, *newEstimate* at every process is either x or $\perp$.

   Due to the unreliability of the failure detector and process failures, some processes may perceive that a majority-leader exists at round r, whereas some processes may not. Therefore, in the second phase of a round, processes exchange *newEstimate* values. On receiving *newEstimate* values from a majority of processes, if a process receives *newEstimate* $= x$ from all processes in that majority, then the process decides x. If a process receives both *newEstimate* $= x$ and *newEstimate* $= \perp$, then it sets its *estimate* to x. If all received values are $\perp$, then a process does not update its *estimate*. If any process decides x (by receiving a majority of *newEstimate* $= x$), then clearly every process receives at least one message with *newEstimate* $= x$ and hence, updates *estimate* to x. We now give a detailed description of the algorithm.

2.2   Description

The algorithm consists of two parallel tasks: Task 1 and Task 2. When a process proposes a value, it starts both tasks. The execution terminates when the *propose* function returns a value (from Task 1 or from Task 2). We now describe the two tasks.

Task 1: This task proceeds in asynchronous rounds with processes incrementally moving from one round to the other. Each round has two phases: (*phase 1*) exchanging ESTIMATE messages, and (*phase 2*) exchanging NEWESTIMATE messages. Consider any process p_i: p_i maintains (1) the current round number r_i,

---

at process p_i
01: propose(v_i)
02:     **start Task 1; start Task 2**

03:     **Task 1**
04:     $r_i \leftarrow 0$; $estimate_i \leftarrow v_i$; $newEstimate_i \leftarrow \bot$; $leader_i \leftarrow \bot$
05:     **while**($true$)
06:         $leader_i \leftarrow \Omega.trusted$; $newEstimate_i \leftarrow \bot$
07:         send(ESTIMATE, r_i, $estimate_i$, $leader_i$) to Π
08:         **wait until** ((received(ESTIMATE, r_i, $*$, $*$) from $leader_i$ and $\left\lceil \frac{n+1}{2} \right\rceil - 1$ other processes)
                or ($leader_i \neq \Omega.trusted$))
09:         **if** ((received(ESTIMATE, r_i, $*$, $leader_i$) from $leader_i$) **and**
                (received(ESTIMATE, r_i, $*$, $leader_i$) from $\left\lceil \frac{n+1}{2} \right\rceil - 1$ other processes)) **then**
10:             $newEstimate_i \leftarrow$ ($estimate$ received from $leader_i$)
11:         send(NEWESTIMATE, r_i, $newEstimate_i$) to Π
12:         **wait until** received(NEWESTIMATE, r_i, $*$) from $\left\lceil \frac{n+1}{2} \right\rceil$ processes
13:         **if** (received(NEWESTIMATE, r_i, $newEstimate$)
                s.t. $newEstimate \neq \bot$ from $\left\lceil \frac{n+1}{2} \right\rceil$ processes) **then**
14:             $estimate_i \leftarrow$ ($newEstimate$ of any received NEWESTIMATE message)
15:             send(DECIDE, $estimate_i$) to $\Pi \backslash p_i$; return($estimate_i$)   {Decision}
16:         **else if** (received any (NEWESTIMATE, r_i, $newEstimate'$) s.t. $newEstimate' \neq \bot$) **then**
17:             $estimate_i \leftarrow newEstimate'$
18:         $r_i \leftarrow r_i + 1$

19:     **Task 2**
20:     **upon** receiving (DECIDE, x)
21:         send(DECIDE, x) to $\Pi \backslash p_i$
22:         return(x)   {Decision}

Fig. 1. The consensus algorithm DG_Ω

initialized to 0, (2) an estimate of the possible decision value $estimate_i$, which is initialized to the input value of p_i, and (3) an intermediate $newEstimate_i$ value (a possible new value for $estimate_i$), initialized to $\bot$ at the beginning of each round. Further, at the beginning of each round, p_i queries Ω about the current leader and stores the identity of that leader in $leader_i$. Once $leader_i$ is set at the beginning of a round, it does not change inside the round (even if $\Omega.trusted$ changes).

At the beginning of a round, p_i sends ESTIMATE messages to all processes containing $estimate_i$ and $leader_i$. Process p_i waits till it receives ESTIMATE messages from $leader_i$ and $\left\lceil \frac{n+1}{2} \right\rceil - 1$ other processes. It simultaneously keeps on querying Ω. The value of $newEstimate_i$ depends on the output of Ω and the ESTIMATE messages received:

1. If $leader_i \neq \Omega.trusted$ before ESTIMATE message from $leader_i$ is received by p_i, or any of the $\left\lceil \frac{n+1}{2} \right\rceil$ PROPOSAL messages received by p_i has $leader \neq leader_i$, then $newEstimate_i$ remains $\bot$.
2. If p_i received ESTIMATE messages from $leader_i$ and $\left\lceil \frac{n+1}{2} \right\rceil - 1$ other processes, and every received message has $leader = leader_i$, then $newEstimate_i$ is set to the $estimate$ received from $leader_i$.

In the second phase of the round, p_i sends a NEWESTIMATE message, containing $newEstimate_i$, to all processes. Process p_i waits till it receives NEWESTIMATE messages from $\lceil \frac{n+1}{2} \rceil$ processes and then takes one of the following three steps depending on the received messages:

1. If every NEWESTIMATE message received by p_i has $newEstimate \neq \perp$, then p_i adopts any received $newEstimate$ as $estimate_i$. Afterwards, p_i sends a DE-CIDE message with $estimate_i$ as the decision value to all processes different from p_i, and returns $estimate_i$ (i.e., decides $estimate_i$).
2. If any NEWESTIMATE message received by p_i has $newEstimate \neq \perp$, then p_i adopts that $newEstimate$ as $estimate_i$. Afterwards, p_i proceeds to the next round.
3. If every NEWESTIMATE message received by p_i has $newEstimate = \perp$, then p_i proceeds to the next round (without updating $estimate_i$).

Task 2: Upon receiving a DECIDE message with value x, p_i sends a DECIDE message with x as the decision value to all processes different from p_i, and returns x (i.e., decides x).

2.3   Correctness

We now informally argue about the correctness of the algorithm. (The complete proof is given in the appendix.) Validity is straightforward and termination is guaranteed by the presence of an Ω failure detector and a majority of correct processes. The heart of the algorithm deals with agreement.

If some process decides (i.e., returns from propose(*)) then some process must have sent a decision value at line 15. Consider the smallest round, say r, in which some decision value is sent at line 15. Assume process p_i sends decision value v at line 15 of round r. Notice that if some process sends v as the decision value, then it must have received a NEWESTIMATE message with $newEstimate = v$ from some process, say p_j. Let p_l be the *leader* at p_j at round r. By the algorithm, all $\lceil \frac{n+1}{2} \rceil$ ESTIMATE messages received by p_j must have $leader = p_l$. Therefore, every process which receives a majority of ESTIMATE messages must have received at least one message with $leader = p_l$. So, at processes where $leader \neq p_l$, $newEstimate$ remained $\perp$, and at processes where $leader = p_l$, either v was adopted as $newEstimate$ or $newEstimate$ remained $\perp$ (line 9). Therefore, every process which exchanged ESTIMATE messages has $newEstimate \in \{v, \perp\}$ before it sends a NEWESTIMATE message.

Further, before sending decision value v at line 15, p_i must have received $newEstimate = v$ from $\lceil \frac{n+1}{2} \rceil$ processes. Therefore, every process which completes round r must have received $newEstimate = v$ from at least one process (since completion of round r requires receiving NEWESTIMATE messages from a majority). Since, $newEstimate$ values sent at round r are restricted to $\{v, \perp\}$, no NEWESTIMATE message is received with $newEstimate \notin \{v, \perp\}$. Therefore, every process which completes round r adopts v as its $estimate$ (line 17). Similarly, we can show that every decision value sent at round r is v.

Clearly, there are no *estimate* values different from v after round r. Thus, no decision value sent at line 15 of a round higher than r can be different from v. Since r is the smallest round in which some decision value is sent at line 15, then *every decision message has the same value, v.*

2.4   Zero Degradation

Consider any stable run of DG_Ω, i.e., any run where (1) all faulty processes crash before the consensus run starts, and (2) there is a correct process p_c such that, at every correct process, $\Omega.trusted$ is always p_c. Let v be the value proposed by process p_c. Every correct process sends a (ESTIMATE, 0, *, p_c) message to all processes. Correct processes receive (ESTIMATE, 0, *, p_c) from $\lceil \frac{n+1}{2} \rceil$ processes, including a (ESTIMATE, 0, v, p_c) message from p_c. Thus, correct processes adopt v as *newEstimate*. Then, every correct process sends (NEWESTIMATE, 0, v) to all processes. On receiving (NEWESTIMATE, 0, v) from $\lceil \frac{n+1}{2} \rceil$ processes, correct processes send (DECIDE, v) and decide v. Thus, in every stable run of A , all decide events occur in two communication steps. Note that, every nice run is a stable run, and hence, in every nice run of A , all decide events occur in two communication step.

3   One-Step Consensus with Zero Degradation

In a stable period, every run of our consensus algorithm terminates in two communication steps. Can we do better? The answer is "sometimes, yes" . The Ω-consensus lower bound [10] actually means that every Ω-based consensus algorithm has a nice run where at least one correct process needs at least two steps to decide. In fact the lower bound does not preclude the existence of an Ω-based consensus algorithm where, from any starting configuration in a specific non-empty subset of initial configurations, all correct processes need only one step to decide in every nice run.

We briefly describe below a simple variant of our DG_Ω consensus algorithm, denoted DG'_Ω and given in Figure 2. In addition to the assumptions of DG_Ω, we assume for DG'_Ω that all processes have an a priori knowledge of a *privileged value*, PV. Just like for DG_Ω, in every stable run of DG'_Ω, two communication steps are sufficient for all correct processes to decide. Moreover, in all stable runs of DG'_Ω where all correct processes propose PV, one communication step is actually sufficient.

To obtain DG'_Ω, we apply to DG_Ω an idea borrowed from [2]. Only the first round of DG_Ω ($r_i = 0$) is modified. In this first round, if a process p_i receives (ESTIMATE, 0, PV, $leader_i$) messages from $leader_i$ as well as $\lceil \frac{n+1}{2} \rceil - 1$ other processes, p_i sends PV as the decision value to all and decides PV . Otherwise, p_i waits till it receives $\lceil \frac{n+1}{2} \rceil$ ESTIMATE messages, and if p_i received any ESTIMATE message with *estimate* = PV then p_i adopts PV as its *estimate*. This idea is conveyed in lines 11-17 of Figure 2 (the main difference with Figure 1). In a stable run, if all correct processes propose PV, then every process receives *estimate* =

```
at process p_i
01: propose(v_i)
02:    start Task 1; start Task 2

03:    Task 1
04:    r_i ← 0; estimate_i ← v_i; newEstimate_i ← ⊥; leader_i ← ⊥
05:    while(true)
06:       leader_i ← Ω.trusted; newEstimate_i ← ⊥
07:       send(ESTIMATE, r_i, estimate_i, leader_i) to Π
08:       wait until ((received(ESTIMATE, r_i, *, *) from leader_i and ⌈(n+1)/2⌉ − 1 other processes)
                      or (leader_i ≠ Ω.trusted))
09:       if ((received(ESTIMATE, r_i, *, leader_i) from leader_i) and
              (received(ESTIMATE, r_i, *, leader_i) from ⌈(n+1)/2⌉ − 1 other processes)) then
10:          newEstimate_i ← (estimate received from leader_i)
11*:         if (r_i = 0) then
12*:            if (received(ESTIMATE, 0, PV, leader_i)
                   from (leader_i and ⌈(n+1)/2⌉ − 1 other processes)) then
13*:               send(DECIDE, PV) to Π\p_i; return(PV)                            {Decision}
14*:            if (number of (ESTIMATE, 0, *, *) received < ⌈(n+1)/2⌉) then
15*:               wait until (received(ESTIMATE, 0, *, *) from ⌈(n+1)/2⌉ processes)
                                              {Including the messages received at line 8}
16*:            if (received a (ESTIMATE, 0, PV, *)) then
17*:               estimate_i ← PV
18:          send(NEWESTIMATE, r_i, newEstimate_i) to Π
19:          wait until received(NEWESTIMATE, r_i, *) from ⌈(n+1)/2⌉ processes
20:          if (received(NEWESTIMATE, r_i, newEstimate)
                 s.t. newEstimate ≠ ⊥ from ⌈(n+1)/2⌉ processes) then
21:             estimate_i ← (newEstimate of any received NEWESTIMATE message)
22:             send(DECIDE, estimate_i) to Π\p_i; return(estimate_i)               {Decision}
23:          else if (received any (NEWESTIMATE, r_i, newEstimate') s.t. newEstimate' ≠ ⊥) then
24:             estimate_i ← newEstimate'
25:          r_i ← r_i + 1

26:    Task 2
27:    upon receiving (DECIDE, x)
28:       send(DECIDE, x) to Π\p_i
29:       return(x)                                                                 {Decision}
```

Fig. 2. The consensus algorithm DG'_Ω

PV from its *leader* and $\lceil \frac{n+1}{2} \rceil - 1$ other processes in round 0. Thus, all correct processes send (DECIDE, PV) and decide in one communication step. In any stable run, even if all processes do not propose PV, processes decides in two communication steps. Thus, DG'_Ω retains the zero degradation flavor of DG_Ω.

Similar to DG_Ω, the heart of DG'_Ω deals with preserving agreement. The algorithm ensures that if any process sends (DECIDE, v) in round 0, then (i) any process which starts round 1 has $estimate = v$, and (ii) any (DECIDE, v') message at round 0 has $v' = v$. This is sufficient to ensure agreement, since in all subsequent rounds, DG'_Ω is identical to DG_Ω. For space limitations we omit the straightforward proof.

4   A ◇ $\mathcal{S}$-Based Zero Degrading Algorithm

We now discuss how DG_Ω can be transformed to a ◇$\mathcal{S}$-based algorithm $DG_{\diamond\mathcal{S}}$ which retains the zero degradation flavor; i.e., in every stable run, $DG_{\diamond\mathcal{S}}$ achieves a global decision in two communication steps. The algorithm is given in Figure 3. For simplicity of presentation, we assume an independent ◇$\mathcal{S}$-based consensus algorithm C accessed through procedure propose$_C(*)$ which returns the decision value (e.g., the ◇$\mathcal{S}$-based consensus algorithm of [4]). Irrespective of the time complexity of C, $DG_{\diamond\mathcal{S}}$ achieves a global decision in two communication steps in every stable run.

The first round of $DG_{\diamond\mathcal{S}}$ follows nearly the same pattern as that of DG_Ω. If a process is unable to decide in the first round then it invokes propose$_C(*)$ to obtain the decision value (line 17). The primary difference between the first round of $DG_{\diamond\mathcal{S}}$ and that of DG_Ω is in the selection of the current leader. In $DG_{\diamond\mathcal{S}}$, the current leader at a process is the process with the lowest index in Π - ◇$\mathcal{S}$.suspected (line 5). In any stable run, the set Π - ◇$\mathcal{S}$.suspected is precisely the set of correct processes, and hence, the current leader is the same correct process at all correct processes.[5] Using arguments similar to Section 2.4 for DG_Ω, one can easily show that every stable run of $DG_{\diamond\mathcal{S}}$ reaches a global decision in two communication steps.

5   Performance

5.1   Time Complexity Metric

To measure the time complexity of our algorithms and compare it with other consensus algorithms, we introduce a metric denoted $cs_{F,A}$, which captures the number of communication steps of a consensus algorithm A in a given failure pattern F. The metric was informally introduced in [8]. We define it more precisely using a variant of Lamport's logical clock:

- *Modified logical clock:* Consider Lamport's logical clock ([11]), as modified in [14]: (1) send and local events at a process do not change the logical clock, and (2) the time-stamp of a receive(m) event at p_i is: maximum{(time-stamp of send(m) at $sender(m) + 1$), (time-stamp of the event preceding receive(m) at p_i)}.

We then introduce the following notations:

- cs_R: The number of communication steps of a consensus run R is the largest time-stamp of all *decide* events in that run.

---

[5] Obviously, ◇$\mathcal{S}$ does not guarantee that "the process with the lowest index in Π - ◇$\mathcal{S}$.suspected is the same correct process at all correct processes". The claim is true only for stable runs.

at process p_i
01: propose(v_i)
02:    **start Task 1; start Task 2**

03:    **Task 1**
04:    $r_i \leftarrow 0$; $estimate_i \leftarrow v_i$; $newEstimate_i \leftarrow \perp$; $leader_i \leftarrow \perp$
05*: $leader_i \leftarrow$ process with the lowest index in $\{\Pi$ - $\diamond S.suspected\}$; $newEstimate_i \leftarrow \perp$
06:    send(ESTIMATE, r_i, $estimate_i$, $leader_i$) to Π
07*:   **wait until** ((received(ESTIMATE, r_i, *, *) from $leader_i$ and $\left\lceil \frac{n+1}{2} \right\rceil - 1$ other processes)
          or ($leader_i \in \diamond S.suspected$))
08:    **if** ((received(ESTIMATE, r_i, *, $leader_i$) from $leader_i$) **and**
          (received(ESTIMATE, r_i, *, $leader_i$) from $\left\lceil \frac{n+1}{2} \right\rceil - 1$ other processes)) **then**
09:       $newEstimate_i \leftarrow$ ($estimate$ received from $leader_i$)
10:    send(NEWESTIMATE, r_i, $newEstimate_i$) to Π
11:    **wait until** received(NEWESTIMATE, r_i, *) from $\left\lceil \frac{n+1}{2} \right\rceil$ processes
12:    **if** (received(NEWESTIMATE, r_i, $newEstimate$)
          $s.t.\ newEstimate \neq \perp$ from $\left\lceil \frac{n+1}{2} \right\rceil$ processes) **then**
13:       $estimate_i \leftarrow$ ($newEstimate$ of any received NEWESTIMATE message)
14:       send(DECIDE, $estimate_i$) to $\Pi \backslash p_i$; return($estimate_i$)   {**Decision**}
15:    **else if** (received any (NEWESTIMATE, r_i, $newEstimate'$) $s.t.\ newEstimate' \neq \perp$) **then**
16:       $estimate_i \leftarrow newEstimate'$
17*:   return(propose$_C$($estimate_i$))   {**Decision**}

18:    **Task 2**
19:    **upon** receiving (DECIDE, x)
20:       send(DECIDE, x) to $\Pi \backslash p_i$
21:       return(x)   {**Decision**}

Fig. 3. The consensus algorithm $DG_{\diamond S}$

- $cs_{C,F,A}$: The number of communication steps of a consensus algorithm A in a failure pattern F and an initial configuration C,[6] is the smallest cs_R of all runs of A with initial configuration C and failure pattern F.
- $cs_{F,A}$: The number of communication steps of a consensus algorithm A in a failure pattern F, is the largest $cs_{C,F,A}$ of all possible initial configurations of A with failure pattern F.

The $cs_{F,A}$ metric captures the performance of an algorithm in nice runs, as well as the degradation of performance in the presence of failures. By selecting the fastest run among all possible runs with the same initial configuration C and failure pattern F, we eliminate the effect of unreliable failure detection. Further, by choosing the maximum among all $cs_{C,F,A}$ with the same F, the metric does not advantage algorithms that are particularly efficient for specific initial configurations (e.g., our algorithm DG'_Ω).

---

[6] The initial configuration of a distributed system is defined by the initial state of each process and empty communication channels [6]. Here, we are specifically interested in the list of proposed values.

Table 1. $cs_{F,A}$ values

	F0	F1	F2	F3
$\lozenge S$-based consensus algorithms				
CT	3	4	4	4
SC	2	4	6	8
HR	2	3	4	5
$DG_{\lozenge S}$	2	2	2	2
Ω-based consensus algorithms				
PC	3	5	5	5
DPC	2	4	4	4
MR	3	3	3	3
DG_Ω	2	2	2	2

5.2   Performance

Consider algorithms DG_Ω and $DG_{\lozenge S}$. As we show in Section 2.4, there exists runs of each algorithms with initially crashed processes in which all decide events occur within two communication steps, irrespective of the initial configuration. Thus for any failure pattern F in which all faulty processes crash at $t = 0$ (i.e., before the consensus run starts), $cs_{F,DG_\Omega} = cs_{F,DG_{\lozenge S}} = 2$.

In case of DG'_Ω, notice that for every initial configuration C in which no process proposes PV, every run of DG'_Ω which starts from C requires at least two communication steps for global decision. Thus, even though DG'_Ω reaches a global decision in one communication step for some initial configuration, for any failure pattern F, $cs_{F,DG'_\Omega} \geq 2$. (Obviously, for any failure pattern F in which all faulty processes crash at $t = 0$, $cs_{F,DG'_\Omega} = 2$.)

5.3   Comparisons

Table 1 compares the performance of DG_Ω and $DG_{\lozenge S}$ with alternative indulgent consensus algorithms that tolerate a minority of failures. We consider a system of at least 7 processes ($n \geq 7$), and the following failure patterns: (i) *F0*: all processes are correct; (ii) *F1*: Process p_1 crashes at $t = 0$ and all other processes are correct; (iii) *F2*: Processes p_1 and p_2 crash at $t = 0$ and all other processes are correct; and (iii) *F3*: Processes p_1, p_2 and p_3 crash at $t = 0$ and all other processes are correct.

We consider three $\lozenge S$-based algorithms, *CT*: Chandra-Toueg's original $\lozenge S$ consensus algorithm [4], *SC*: early consensus [14], and *HR*: fast consensus [8], and compare them in Table 1 with with our $\lozenge S$-based algorithm, $DG_{\lozenge S}$. The $cs_{F,A}$ values are achieved in any stable run; i.e., when all process crashes are initial and, throughout the run, at every correct process, the suspicion list of the failure detector is identical to the set of initially crashed processes.

Besides our algorithm (DG_Ω), we also consider three Ω-based algorithms; *PC*: Lamport's Paxos Consensus [12], *MR*: the first algorithm in [13] (we do not

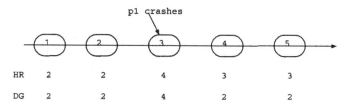

Fig. 4. Repeated consensus performance

consider here the second algorithm of [13] because it assumes at least two-thirds of the processes are correct, and is hence incomparable with other algorithms), and DPC: a decentralized version of PC [12], pointed out in [10]. The $cs_{F,A}$ values are achieved in any stable run, i.e., when all process crashes are initial and, throughout the run, the same correct process remains the leader at every correct process.[7]

The $cs_{F,A}$ values are summarized in Table 1, which clearly conveys the efficiency of DG_Ω and $DG_{\diamond S}$. In short, apart from achieving the failure-free performance of SC and MR ($F0$ failure pattern, i.e., nice runs), DG_Ω and $DG_{\diamond S}$ are immune to the presence of crashed processes in stable runs (zero degradation). It is important to notice here that, similar to the algorithms of [14, 8, 13], the message complexity of DG_Ω and $DG_{\diamond S}$ are $O(n^2)$ when the processes are connected by a point-to-point network, and $O(n)$ in a broadcast network. The original CT and PC algorithms are centralized and have a message complexity of $O(n)$ no matter how the processes are connected.

5.4   Repeated Consensus and Zero Degradation

In practice, the zero degradation property of a consensus algorithm is important in case of repeated consensus based applications. Consider the atomic broadcast

---

[7] A round in the Paxos consensus algorithm (PC) can be divided into three phases: (i) *read phase:* the leader (elected by some leader election service; e.g., Ω) reads whether any *estimate* value might already be locked at a majority of processes, (ii) *write phase:* the leader tries to lock an *estimate* value at majority of processes, and (iii) *decide phase*: the leader disseminates the successfully locked *estimate* as the decision value. The read and the write phase each requires two communication steps (messages sent by the leader to all processes and the processes sending acknowledgments to the leader), and the decide phase requires one communication step. Optimizations can be made along the lines proposed by [10]. In a crash-stop model, the read phase of the algorithm is required only when the leader changes, and hence can be skipped when p_1 is the leader. Further, consider the last two steps in a round: processes sending acknowledgment to the leader (in reply to the *write*) and the subsequent *decision* message sent by the leader. These two steps can be merged into a single step in a decentralized scheme: processes send the acknowledgment to all processes; on receiving acknowledgment from a majority, a process decides immediately. These two optimizations result in the $cs_{F,DPC}$ values presented in Table 1.

algorithm of [4], implemented as a sequence of consensus instances. Further, consider a nice run of the algorithm. If the HR consensus algorithm is used as an underlying consensus module (which is the most efficient $\Diamond \mathcal{S}$-based consensus algorithm we knew of), then each consensus instance takes two communication steps. If $DG_{\Diamond \mathcal{S}}$ consensus algorithm is used instead, still each consensus instance requires two communication steps.

Now, consider a slightly different run, depicted in Figure 4: process p_1 crashes during the third consensus instance (there are no other failures and the failure detector at all processes suspects p_1 after the third consensus instance). The performance of both consensus algorithms (HR and $DG_{\Diamond \mathcal{S}}$) are the same for the first three consensus instances.[8] In the $DG_{\Diamond \mathcal{S}}$ consensus algorithm, even though the crash of process p_1 slows the third consensus instance, other consensus instances are not affected: all subsequent consensus instances still take two communication steps (zero degradation). On the other hand, even in the absence of further failures or false suspicions, every subsequent HR consensus instance takes three communication steps. In long runs of atomic broadcast, this is a significant performance overhead. Similar performance overheads are incurred whenever atomic broadcast uses consensus algorithms which are not zero degrading.

References

[1] M. K. Aguilera, W. Chen, and S. Toueg. Failure detection and consensus in the crash-recovery model. *Distributed Computing*, 13(2):99-125, May 2000. 192

[2] F. Brasileiro, F. Greve, A. Mostefaoui, and M. Raynal. Consensus in one communication step. In *Proceedings of the 6th International Conference on Parallel Computing Technology*, pages 42-50, Novosibirsk, Russia, September 2001. 198

[3] T. D. Chandra, V. Hadzilacos, and S. Toueg. The weakest failure detector for solving consensus. *Journal of the ACM*, 43(4):685-722, 1996. 192, 193

[4] T. D. Chandra and S. Toueg. Unreliable failure detectors for reliable distributed systems. *Journal of the ACM*, 43(2):225-267, 1996. 191, 192, 193, 200, 202, 204

[5] D. Dolev, C. Dwork, and L. Stockmeyer. On the minimal synchrony needed for distributed consensus. *Journal of ACM*, 34(1):77-97, 1987. 192

[6] M. J. Fischer, N. A. Lynch, and M. S. Paterson. Impossibility of distributed consensus with one faulty process. *Journal of the ACM*, 32(2):374-382, 1985. 192, 201

[7] R. Guerraoui. Indulgent algorithms. In *Proceedings of the 19th ACM Symposium on the Principles of Distributed Computing (PODC-19)*, pages 289-298, Portland, OR, July 2000. 192, 193

[8] M. Hurfin and M. Raynal. A simple and fast asynchronous consensus protocol based on a weak failure detector. *Distributed Computing*, 12(4):209-223, 1999. 193, 194, 200, 202, 203

[9] V. Hadzilacos and S. Toueg. Fault-tolerant broadcasts and related problems. In S. Mullender, editor, *Distributed Systems*, ACM Press Books, chapter 5, pages 97-146. Addison-Wesley, second edition, 1993. 192

---

[8] The performance of the third instance may be different: HR may require only 3 steps depending on when exactly p_1 crashes.

[10] I. Keidar and S. Rajsbaum. On the cost of fault-tolerant consensus when there are no faults - a tutorial. Technical Report MIT-LCS-TR-821, MIT, May 2001. 192, 193, 198, 203

[11] L. Lamport. Time, clocks, and the ordering of events in a distributed system. *Communications of the ACM*, 21(7):558-565, July 1978. 200

[12] L. Lamport. The part-time parliament. Technical Report 49, System Research Center, Digital Equipment Corp, Palo Alto, September 1989. A revised version of the paper also appeared in ACM Transaction on Computer Systems, 16(2):133-169, May 1998. 191, 192, 202, 203

[13] A. Mostefaoui and M. Raynal. Leader-based consensus. *Parallel Processing Letters*, 11(1):95-107, March 2001. 194, 202, 203

[14] A. Schiper. Early consensus in an asynchronous system with a weak failure detector. *Distributed Computing*, 10(3):149-157, 1997. 193, 194, 200, 202, 203

Appendix: Correctness of DG_Ω (Figure 1)

Lemma 1: *If a process decides v then some process has sent (*DECIDE, v*) at line 15 of some round.*

Proof: Suppose by contradiction that some process p_i decides v and no process has sent (DECIDE, v) at line 15. Process p_i decides either at line 15 or at line 22 of a round. If p_i decides at line 15 then by the algorithm, p_i must have sent (DECIDE, v) at line 15, a contradiction. Therefore, p_i must have decided at line 22. So, every (DECIDE, v) message which is sent until p_i decides, is sent at line 21, and there is at least one such message. This is a contradiction because every (DECIDE, v) message which is sent at line 21 requires that a distinct (DECIDE, v) message has been sent before it (line 20). □

Proposition 2. *(Validity):* *If a process decides v, then some process has proposed v.*

Proof: If a process decides v, then some process has sent (DECIDE, v) at line 15 of some round (Lemma 1). Assume that (DECIDE, v) was sent at line 15 of round r. Any decision value sent in round r must be the *newEstimate* value of some process at round r (line 14). Further, any *newEstimate* $(\neq \perp)$ value at round r must be the *estimate* of some process at the beginning of round r. Thus, v must be the *estimate* of some process at the beginning of round r. To prove validity, we show: *for any round r, if v is the estimate at some process at the beginning of round r, then v was proposed by some process.* We prove the above statement by induction on round numbers.

- *Base Step*: In round 0, every process sets its *estimate* to its own proposed value at line 4.
- *Induction Hypothesis*: At the beginning of round k, if v is the *estimate* of some process, then v was proposed by some process.
- *Induction Step*: Consider round $k+1$. Every process which executes round $k+1$ must have completed round k. The *estimate* of a process at the beginning of round $k + 1$ is the same as its *estimate* at the end of round k. The

estimate of a process at the end of round k must be the *newEstimate* of some process at round k, and any *newEstimate* $(\neq \perp)$ value must be the *estimate* of some process at the beginning of round k. Thus, any *estimate* value at the beginning of round $k+1$ was an *estimate* value in the beginning of round k. Applying the induction hypothesis, any *estimate* value at the beginning of round $k+1$ is a proposed value. □

Proposition 3 *(Termination): Every correct process eventually decides. (Every correct process eventually returns from the propose($*$) invocation.)*
Proof: We prove the proposition by contradiction. Assume that some correct process never decides. If any correct process decides then it has sent a DECIDE message to all (at line 15 or at line 21) and so every correct processes eventually receives a DECIDE message and decides (recall that messages sent to a correct process is eventually delivered), contradicting our original assumption. Thus, if some correct process never decides then no correct process ever decides. Therefore, by our original assumption, no correct process decides.

If some correct process p_i never decides, then either p_i is blocked forever in a round or is executing an infinite number of rounds. We show both cases to be impossible.

Case 1: Some correct process blocks forever in a round. Let r be the smallest round in which some correct process, say p_i, blocks forever. This can only be possible at some **wait** statement in round r. There are two **wait** statements in a round, at line 8 and at line 12.

Case 1.1: Assume that p_i blocks forever at the **wait** statement of line 8. Since no correct process blocks in any lower round (by definition of r), then every correct process sends an ESTIMATE message in round r. If *leader$_i$* is correct then p_i eventually receives an ESTIMATE message from *leader$_i$*. If *leader$_i$* is faulty then eventually *leader$_i$* $\neq \Omega.trusted$. Further, p_i receive at least $\lceil \frac{n+1}{2} \rceil - 1$ other PROPOSAL messages since there are at least $\lceil \frac{n+1}{2} \rceil$ correct processes. Thus, p_i cannot block forever at line 8.

Case 1.2: Assume that p_i blocks forever at the **wait** statement of line 12. Since no correct process blocks forever at line 8 in round r, then every correct process sends a NEWESTIMATE message. As there are at least $\lceil \frac{n+1}{2} \rceil$ correct processes, p_i receives NEWESTIMATE message from $\lceil \frac{n+1}{2} \rceil$ processes. Thus, p_i cannot block forever at line 12.

Case 2: Assume that all correct processes execute an infinite number of rounds. Consider the smallest time t such that, (i) before t, every faulty process has crashed, and (ii) after t, Ω at every correct process always outputs the same correct process, p_c.[9] By the impossibility of case 1 and the assumption that every correct process executes an infinite number of rounds, there must exist a round r such that, all correct processes start round r after time t. Every correct process sends an ESTIMATE message with *leader* $= p_c$ and receives ESTIMATE messages

---

[9] Time t exists due to the definition of faulty processes and the property of Ω.

from p_c and $\lceil \frac{n+1}{2} \rceil - 1$ correct processes. Correct processes adopt the *estimate* of p_c as its *newEstimate*. Every correct process sends an NEWESTIMATE message with the same *newEstimate* ($\neq \perp$) value. After receiving non-$\perp$ *newEstimate* values from a majority of processes, every correct process sends a DECIDE message and decides at line 15. □

Lemma 4: *For any round, if a process sends a* NEWESTIMATE *message with* newEstimate $= x \neq \perp$, *then all* NEWESTIMATE *messages are sent with* newEstimate $\in \{x, \perp\}$.

Proof: Suppose by contradiction that in some round r, p_i sends a NEWESTIMATE message with *newEstimate* $= x \neq \perp$ and another process p_j sends a NEWESTIMATE message with *newEstimate* $= y \notin \{x, \perp\}$. Process p_i must have received (ESTIMATE, r, x, $leader_i$) message from $leader_i$ and (ESTIMATE, r, $*$, $leader_i$) messages from $\lceil \frac{n+1}{2} \rceil - 1$ other processes. Similarly, process p_j must have received (ESTIMATE, r, y, $leader_j$) message from $leader_j$ and (ESTIMATE, r, $*$, $leader_j$) messages from $\lceil \frac{n+1}{2} \rceil - 1$ other processes. Thus, processes p_i and p_j each received ESTIMATE messages from $\lceil \frac{n+1}{2} \rceil$ processes. Since $x \neq y$, $leader_i \neq leader_j$. As two majorities always overlap, some process must have sent two different ESTIMATE messages in round r; (ESTIMATE, r, $*$, $leader_i$) and (ESTIMATE, r, $*$, $leader_j$): a contradiction. □

Lemma 5 *(Elimination):* *If r is the smallest round in which some* DECIDE *message was sent at line 15, and v is the decision value sent by some process in round r, then (1) every process which completes round r has estimate $= v$ at the end of round r, and (2) every* DECIDE *message sent in round r has the decision value v.*

Proof: Assume that in round r process p_i sends a DECIDE message with value v at line 15. Process p_i must have received (NEWESTIMATE, r, v) messages from $\lceil \frac{n+1}{2} \rceil$ processes. From Lemma 4, all NEWESTIMATE messages are sent with *newEstimate* $\in \{v, \perp\}$. We now prove (1) by contradiction.

(1) Assume process p_j completes round r with *estimate* $\neq v$. Process p_j must have received NEWESTIMATE messages from $\lceil \frac{n+1}{2} \rceil$ processes and hence received at least one (NEWESTIMATE, r, v) message. Since p_j did not adopt v in line 14 or line 17, p_j must have received a NEWESTIMATE message with *newEstimate* $\notin \{v, \perp\}$: a contradiction.

(2) Follows directly from (1). □

Proposition 6 *(Agreement):* *No two processes decide differently.*

Proof: If no process decides, then the proposition is trivially true. If a process decides then some process has sent a DECIDE message at line 15 of some round (Lemma 1). Let r be the smallest round in which some DECIDE message was sent at line 15 and let process p_i sends a decision value v in round r.

Assume that some process decides a value z. Some process must have sent a (DECIDE, z) message at line 15 of some round k (Lemma 1). By definition of

r, $k \geq r$. If $k = r$ then by Lemma 5, $z = v$ (every DECIDE message sent at round r has the decision value v). If $k > r$ then, every process which executes round k must have completed round r. From Lemma 5, every process which completes round r has $estimate = v$ at the end round r. Therefore, no other value can be decided in any subsequent round. Thus, $z = v$.   □

Proposition 7: DG_Ω *(Figure 1) solves consensus.*
Proof: Immediate from propositions 2, 3, and 6.   □

Probabilistic Queries in Large-Scale Networks

Fernando Pedone[1,2], Nelson L. Duarte[3], and Mario Goulart[3]

[1] Hewlett-Packard Laboratories, Software Technology Laboratory
Palo Alto, CA 94304, USA
fernando_pedone@hp.com
[2] Ecole Polytechnique Fédérale de Lausanne (EPFL)
Faculté Informatique & Communications
CH-1015 Lausanne, Switzerland
[3] Mathematics Department, Universidade do Rio Grande
Rio Grande, RS 96200, Brazil
dmtnldf@furg.br
mario@proxy.furg.br

Abstract. Resource location is a fundamental problem for large-scale distributed applications. This paper discusses the problem from a probabilistic perspective. Contrary to deterministic approaches, which strive to produce a precise outcome, probabilistic approaches may sometimes expose users with incorrect results. The paper formalizes the probabilistic resource-location problem with the notion of probabilistic queries. A probabilistic query has a predicate as parameter and returns a set of sites where the predicate is believed to hold. The query is probabilistic because there are some chances that the predicate does not hold in all, or even in any, of the sites returned. To implement probabilistic queries, we introduce PSEARCH, an epidemic-like algorithm that uses basic concepts of Bayesian statistical inference. Among its properties, PSEARCH is able to adapt itself to new system conditions caused, for example, by failures.

1 Introduction

1.1 Motivation and Context

Resource location is a fundamental problem for large-scale distributed applications, and even though finding resources in a network of computers is a problem probably as old as distributed computing itself, different system requirements (e.g., high scalability) and conditions (e.g., unreliable user behavior) of current large-scale applications on the Internet have recently led to a flurry of new approaches to the problem. Good examples of current, and very popular, large-scale applications are peer-to-peer systems such as Gnutella where users find and share information on the Internet (e.g., MP3 music files) [1]. Involving many distributed sites, ability to scale well is a highly-desirable property for such systems. Moreover, since virtually any sites can take part in the system, dealing with unreliable sites is also important.

This paper discusses the problem of finding resources in large distributed systems from a probabilistic perspective. Contrary to deterministic approaches,

F. Grandoni (Ed.): EDCC 2002, LNCS 2485, pp. 209–226, 2002.
© Springer-Verlag Berlin Heidelberg 2002

which strive to produce a precise outcome, this paper discusses an approach in which users may be sometimes presented with incorrect results. Algorithms that provide probabilistic guarantees—also known as *probabilistic algorithms*—have recently been exploited in large-scale distributed systems [11, 13, 6] to improve scalability. To the best of our knowledge, however, this is the first time the approach is used in the context of resource location.

1.2   Probabilistic Queries

We formalize the probabilistic resource-location problem with the notion of *probabilistic queries*. A probabilistic query has a predicate as parameter and returns a set of sites where the predicate is believed to hold. Predicates are application dependent; a predicate could be, for example, "the site stores some music file X," or "the site is equipped with a high-performance CPU." After receiving the result of a query, an application would, in the first case, request file X from one of the sites returned; and, in the second case, send a CPU-bound task for execution to one of such sites. The query is probabilistic because there are some chances that the predicate does not hold in all, or even in any, of the sites returned. Moreover, a resource-locating protocol should not only find sites where a given predicate is satisfied, but highly-available sites where this is true. For example, a site that concentrates many system resources and where most predicates are satisfied is of little use if it is down too often. Therefore, queries should avoid including such sites in their results.

1.3   Psearch Algorithm

To implement probabilistic queries, we introduce PSEARCH, an epidemic-like algorithm that uses basic concepts of Bayesian statistical inference. Briefly, sites exchange information among each other about the execution of previous queries, and use this information to forward queries to the locations where most likely a queried predicate holds. Sites use a gossip technique to exchange these tables among themselves and update entries according to causal relationships between entries and Bayesian statistical inference. PSEARCH is a robust algorithm, which tolerates site crashes and recoveries, message losses, and network partitions. We evaluate the PSEARCH algorithm using a simple analytical model and a simulation model. Our results show that if some of the system sites contain many resources, an assumption that has been found to hold in some environments [10, 12], the results produced by PSEARCH can be very precise.

1.4   Related Work

Traditionally, locating resources and information in a distributed system has been accomplished using mechanisms such as global indexes. There are two fundamental differences between such kinds of mechanisms and PSEARCH: First, mechanisms based on indexes perform *search by references,* while PSEARCH performs *search by content.* Second, index-based mechanisms are normally *deterministic,* while PSEARCH is *probabilistic.* The best example of search by reference is the Internet Domain Name System (DNS) [5], one of the largest name services in use today, but many other systems have also been build based on deterministic mechanisms [2, 8, 9, 14, 19, 20].

Differently from deterministic mechanisms, PSEARCH tries to locate information based on patterns of use: if a certain information can be found at some site, there are some chances that this site stores other interesting information of the same kind—conceptually, this is similar to a cache mechanism. The advantage of PSEARCH over deterministic approaches is that the system can easily evolve to adapt itself to changes in the patterns of use and system failures.

In the context of peer-to-peer networks, some alternative ways of locating resources by content in large-scale networks have emerged. Systems like Gnutella [1] execute brute-force searches: processes propagate queries to their neighbors in order to find the location of files. The work in [3] builds on the assumption that the number of links connecting processes in large-scale networks follows a powerlaw distribution, that is, very few processes are connected to most processes in the system and most processes are connected to a few processes. Based on this observation, decentralized algorithms are proposed which strive to visit first processes with a high number of connections. This approach implicitly assumes that processes with a large number of connections will be also the ones most likely to answer application queries; otherwise, it risks to flood the network with messages. PSEARCH is a more general solution, and if the number of connections is indeed related to the likelihood of successfully resolving queries, PSEARCH will adapt to this situation.

1.5 Summary of Contributions

Summing up, the contributions of the paper are the following:

- We propose a formal definition of *probabilistic queries.* This definition quantifies the result of queries in terms of the probability that they contain useful information and how hard it will be to access this information (i.e., the "quality" of the result).
- We introduce PSEARCH, an epidemic-like probabilistic algorithm. PSEARCH is novel in that it combines standard epidemic techniques with Bayesian statistical inference to adapt to new system conditions (e.g., due to process failures and network partitions).
- We develop an analytical model to reason about PSEARCH, different from traditional epidemic-like analytical models, which would not be appropriate in our context.
- We investigate the performance of PSEARCH by means of simulation, considering various probabilistic data distributions and system failures.

1.6   Roadmap

The remainder of the paper is structured as follows. Section 2 describes our system model. Section 3 formally introduces and discusses the notion of probabilistic queries in the context of large-scale distributed systems. Section 4 presents PSEARCH, an algorithm that solves probabilistic queries using simple concepts from distributed systems and Bayesian statistical inference. Section 5 proposes analytical and simulation models to evaluate the performance of PSEARCH. Section 6 concludes the paper.

2   System Model and Assumptions

2.1   Processes and Failures

We model our distributed system as a set $\Pi = \{p_1, p_2, ...\}$ of processes (or sites) which communicate by message passing. Each process p_i is associated with a unique identifier (e.g., its IP address), and executes a sequence of *steps*, where a step can be a change in the process' local state, sending a message, or receiving a message. A process may crash and subsequently recover. After a process crashes, it does not execute any steps until it recovers. The system is asynchronous, that is, there are no bounds on the time it takes for processes to execute steps nor on the time it takes for messages to be transmitted.

Processes are distinguished between *correct* and *faulty*, according to their behavior with regards to failures. A correct process either is permanently up (i.e., it never crashes) or eventually will be permanently up (i.e., the process crashes and recovers at least once but eventually recovers and no longer crashes). A faulty process may crash and recover an unbounded number of times but eventually crashes and never recovers. All processes, however, whenever up, behave according to their protocol—no Byzantine failures. Furthermore, we do not model processes with a permanent intermittent behavior, that is, processes that keep crashing and recovering forever without ever performing any useful computation. Such processes are problematic from a strict viewpoint since they cannot be satisfactorily distinguished from correct processes that crash and recover an unbounded, but finite, number of times [4].

The correct and faulty abstractions are meant to capture not only real process failures but also the behavior of processes that "join" and "leave" the system spontaneously. This is typically what happens with Internet users with dial-in connections who are online for short periods of time. Moreover, "eventually permanently up" is used to simplify the formal treatment of the problem. In practice, we do not expect correct processes to remain up forever, but "long enough" to perform some useful computation such as participate in the execution of a query. Since it would be complicated to determine how long such processes have to remain up, we simply assume that eventually they remain permanently up (i.e., if they are correct) or down (i.e., if they are faulty).

2.2   Process Timers

Each process is equipped with a *timer*. Timers allow processes to give up waiting for events that may never happen, such as receiving a message sent by a process that has crashed. But timers give no guarantees with respect to processes crashes or message losses—as stated previously, there are no bounds on the time it takes for processes to execute steps nor on the time its takes for messages to be transmitted. For example, if p_i waits for a message from p_j and its timer times out, it can be that p_j has crashed, the message has been lost, the communication link is too slow, or p_i's timer is too fast, and there is no way p_i can distinguish between these cases. The only guarantee provided is that if p_i sets its timer and does not crash, then eventually p_i's timer times out.

2.3   Communication Links

We assume that communication links, defined by the primitives send(m) and receive(m), can duplicate and lose messages but are *fair*, that is, if p_i sends m to p_j a finite number of times, then p_j receives m a finite number of times (e.g., maybe p_j does not receive m at all), but if p_i sends m to p_j an infinite number of times, and p_j is correct, then p_j receives m an infinite number of times (i.e., p_j receives m at least once); furthermore, p_j only receives m if p_i sent m to p_j (i.e., communication links do not create messages). This definition of communication links captures the intuition that if p_i sends m to p_j and both processes do not crash for a "certain period of time," allowing "enough" re-transmissions of m, p_j eventually receives m.

The network is partially connected. The set of neighbors of p_i is denoted by $neighbors(p_i)$. We further assume that there exists a *fair path* connecting any two correct processes p_i and p_j in the system, that is, there is a path $p_i \rightarrow p_{k_1} \rightarrow p_{k_2} \rightarrow ... \rightarrow p_j$ such that every p_{k_l} is correct and every link in the path is fair. Such assumptions admit temporary network partitions, since a process in a unique path between two processes may be temporarily down. However, a fair path between any two correct processes guarantees that network partitions eventually heal since eventually every correct process is permanently up.[1]

3   Probabilistic Queries

3.1   Informal Definition

In this section, we introduce the concept of probabilistic queries. A probabilistic query is a request to find processes in the system in which some local predicate holds. A predicate can be, for example, an assertion about the resources or data available at the process. The query is probabilistic because there is a probability that the result may not contain processes in which the predicate holds and contain processes in which the predicate does not hold.

---

[1] This assumption is not necessary to ensure progress of the execution of the algorithms discussed in this paper, but it allows correct processes to have a convergent view of the system.

3.2   Formal Definition

To execute a query for predicate Σ, p_i calls function $Q(\Sigma)$ and waits for its result. $Q(\Sigma)$ returns a set $\pi \subseteq \Pi$ of processes. When p_i returns from the invocation of $Q(\Sigma)$ with set π, we say that p_i executed query $Q(\Sigma)$. Probabilistic queries are formally defined by properties P1 and P2, presented next, and property P3, presented in the end of the section.

Let π be the result of query $Q(\Sigma)$, executed by some process:

- P1. With probability ϕ_1, there is some p_i in π in which Σ holds.
- P2. With probability ϕ_2, if p_i is in π then Σ holds in p_i.

Probability ϕ_1 represents the percentage of queries, in a sequence of query executions, whose results contain at least one process where the queried predicate holds. Probability ϕ_2 represents the percentage of queries, in a sequence of query executions, whose results do not contain processes in which the queried predicate does not hold. Consider the case in which $\phi_1 = 1$ and $\phi_2 = 1$. From P1, the result of any query should contain at least a process where the queried predicate holds;[2] from P2, the result of any query should not contain processes where the queried predicate does not hold.

In the absence of property P2, queries could be trivially optimized by always returning Π as a result. In the absence of property P1, queries could be trivially optimized by always returning the empty set as a result. Although hardly useful, these cases help explain why one would not be interested in property P1, or P2, alone.

A simple algorithm, which does not incur in any communication overhead among processes, can be used to implement probabilistic queries. Such an algorithm simply chooses a random subset of Π as the result of a query. In Section 4 we present an algorithm that improves the values of ϕ_1 and ϕ_2 by selectively including processes in the result set of a query, trying to avoid processes where the queried predicate does not hold. Such an algorithm, however, requires processes to exchange local information with each other.

3.3   Excluding Faulty Processes

Only finding processes where some predicate holds may not entirely capture the intuitive functionality expected from queries. For example, returning sets of faulty processes is not useful if these process are to be contacted. Therefore, queries should avoid, whenever possible, returning faulty processes. Properties P1 and P2 are only concerned with distinguishing between processes in which some predicate holds and in which it does not. To exclude faulty processes, we introduce property P3.

- P3. Eventually no faulty process is returned in the result of a query.

---

[2] $\phi_1 = 1$ is only possible to achieve if all queried predicates hold in some process in the system, which may not always be the case. When not all queried predicates hold in the system, the maximum ϕ_1 obtainable is smaller than 1.

Actually, one would like to always avoid faulty processes in the result of queries—and not only eventually. It turns out, however, that such a property cannot be achieved satisfactorily [4]. The intuitive reason is that no process can tell in advance whether another process will crash, and if crashed, whether it will recover. Thus, when trying to always avoid faulty processes in the result of queries, processes will inevitably exclude from the query result correct processes that will recover, or include in the query result faulty processes that will crash and never recover, both unwanted results. Nevertheless, by tring to eventually remove faulty processes, queries will always strive to minimize the number of faulty processes returned.

4 The Psearch Algorithm

4.1 Overview of the Algorithm

In this section we introduce PSEARCH, an algorithm that implements probabilistic queries. PSEARCH is a highly-resilient protocol, which guarantees progress in the presence of process crashes, message loses, and network partitions—although such events may affect the results produced by the algorithm (i.e., probabilities ϕ_1 and ϕ_2). In order to achieve this degree of resilience, PSEARCH combines epidemic techniques and basic notions of Bayesian statistical inference.

Queries are executed by a recursive algorithm: Upon receiving a query for execution from the application or from other process, p_i evaluates the queried predicate. If the predicate holds locally, p_i replies immediately to the caller—the application that requested the query or the process it received the query from. If the predicate does not hold locally, p_i forwards the query to other processes and waits for the results; p_i uses the results received from these processes, if any, together with its local estimates about where the queried predicate may hold to reply back to the caller.

To decide where to forward queries, p_i keeps a local list of processes in which p_i believes predicates may hold. This list, denoted s_table, has a collection of entries, each one for a different process (including p_i). Each entry contains a *process id*, an estimate of the probability that a predicate holds at this process, denoted *probability of success*, and a *timestamp* associated with the probability of success. Process p_i continuously updates the entry to itself in its s_table based on the execution of past queries and periodically propagates its s_table to its neighbors; s_tables received by p_i from its neighbors are used to update the entries to other processes in p_i's s_table.

4.2 The Update Algorithm

The update algorithm (see Algorithm 1) is an epidemic-like protocol where processes periodically send their s_tables to their neighbors (according to the network topology). As local s_tables are updated with the information received from other processes, data travels the network, from process to process. When p_i sends its *s_table* to other processes, its entry in the table is more up-to-date, or recent, than any other entries in the table since it is continuously updated by p_i while the other entries have to travel the network, possibly suffering delays.

Algorithm 1 Updating *s_tables* (for process p_i)

1: Initialization:

2:   $s\_table_i \leftarrow \emptyset$ $\{s\_table_i$ *initially empty*$\}$
3:   $I \leftarrow 100$ $\{$*determines the precision of the model*$\}$
4:   **for** $l = 1..I$ **do** $\{$*build table with probabilities and believes*$\}$
5:     $P[B]^l \leftarrow 1/I$ $\{$*initial value of the belief a priori*$\}$
6:     $P[S|B]^l \leftarrow (2l-1)/2I$ $\{$*tentative probabilities of success*$\}$
7:     $P[S|B] \leftarrow P[S|B]^l$ s.t. $P[S|B]^l \in \{P[S|B]^1, ..., P[S|B]^I\}$ $\{$*probability of success*$\}$

8: To update the search table:

9:   **periodically do** $\{$*epidemic propagation:*$\}$
10:    $new\_tmp \leftarrow$ greatest timestamp in $s\_table_i + 1$ $\{$*determine biggest timestamp*$\}$
11:    $s\_table_i \leftarrow s\_table_i \setminus \{[p_i, P[S|B], *]\}$ $\{$*remove own entry, in order to...*$\}$
12:    $s\_table_i \leftarrow s\_table_i \cup \{[p_i, P[S|B], new\_tmp]\}$ $\{$*...include updated entry*$\}$
13:    **for each** $p_j \in neighbors(p_i)$ **do** $\{$*for each neighbor:*$\}$
14:      send s_table_i to p_j $\{$*send s_table$_i$*$\}$

15:    **when** receive s_table_j from p_j $\{$*when receive an s_table$_j$:*$\}$
16:      **for each** $[p_k, P[S|B]_k, tmp_k] \in s\_table_j$ **do** $\{$*for each process...*$\}$
17:        **if** $[p_k, P[S|B]_{k'}, tmp_{k'}] \in s\_table_i$ **then** $\{$*...in both tables...*$\}$
18:          **if** $tmp_{k'} < tmp_k$ **then** $\{$*...take the most up-to-date entry*$\}$
19:            $s\_table_i \leftarrow s\_table_i \setminus \{[p_k, P[S|B]_{k'}, tmp_{k'}]\}$ $\{$*remove old entry for p$_k$*$\}$
20:            $s\_table_i \leftarrow s\_table_i \cup \{[p_k, P[S|B]_k, tmp_k]\}$ $\{$*include new entry for p$_k$*$\}$
21:        **else**
22:          $s\_table_i \leftarrow s\_table_i \cup \{[p_k, P[S|B]_k, tmp_k]\}$ $\{$*include the new entry*$\}$

23:    **while** $|s\_table_i| \geq M$ **do** $\{$*keep table in its right size*$\}$
24:      $oldestEntries \leftarrow \{[p_k, *, tmp_k] \mid [p_k, *, tmp_k]$ is the oldest entry in $s\_table_i\}$

25:      $s\_table_i \leftarrow s\_table_i \setminus oldestEntries$

Processes assign timestamps to their entries using a mechanism similar to Lamport's timestamps [15]. If an entry e is more recent than an entry e' in p_i's *s_table*, the timestamp assigned to e is greater than the timestamp assigned to e' (the converse is not necessarily true). Thus, before sending the *s_table* to its neighbors, p_i updates the timestamp of its entry with a value bigger than any other timestamps in the table.

When p_i receives s_table_j from p_j, it updates its s_table using the entries in s_table_j and taking into account the timestamps associated with the entries. The idea is to try to keep only the most recent entries from both s_tables. For entries in both s_tables related to the same process, p_i can safely determine which one is the most recent (i.e., the one with the biggest timestamp). For entries related to different processes, we face two problems. First, since the relation between entries is a partial order [15], two entries may be not related, and it does not make sense to talk about which one is more recent than the other. Second, from the way timestamps are created, an entry with a timestamp bigger than the timestamp of another entry does not necessarily mean that it is the most recent one [16], if the entries refer to different processes.

The epidemic nature of the algorithm leads to a simple way to handle network partitions. In case of a network partition, s_tables from processes in on partition will fail to reach processes in the other partition. If the partition lasts a long time, the algorithm will tend to make the system converge to a state where s_tables of processes in a partition only contain entries for processes in the same partition. However, since processes keep trying to send their s_tables to all their neighbors, once the partition heals, s_tables will reach processes in both partition, and the system will tend to converge back to the state prior to the partition.

4.3   Executing Queries

To execute query $Q(\Sigma)$ upon request from a local application or from other process, p_i evaluates Σ and depending on the outcome either replies back to the caller or forwards the query to other processes. Each message received from a process with a query also contains a set of *visited processes*. The visited set aims to reduce the chances that the same query will be received more than once by the same processes (this mechanism is similar to the one used by Gnutella [1]). To forward a query, p_i chooses those processes in its s_table with the highest probability of success that are not in the visited set. Before p_i forwards the query, if it decides to do so, it updates the visited set with such processes. The use of a visited set, however, does not completely prevent the reception of duplicated requests.[3]

To limit the diameter of $Q(\Sigma)$, that is, the maximum number of times D—a parameter of the algorithm—that $Q(\Sigma)$ can be forwarded to other processes, a message containing $Q(\Sigma)$ also carries a diameter counter, decremented each time the query is forwarded. If the counter reaches zero at some process p_j and Σ does not hold at p_j, instead of forwarding $Q(\Sigma)$ to another process, p_j returns to the caller a subset of size L—a parameter of the algorithm—of its s_table with the processes in which most probably Σ holds. Once p_i receives the response back from the processes it sent the query to, it determines its own response, based on the probability of success of the entries in its s_table and the probability of success of the results received from other processes.

---

[3] For example, consider that p_1 forwards $Q(\Sigma)$ to p_2 and p_3. Even though p_2 and p_3 will not forward $Q(\Sigma)$ to processes that already received it through p_1, they may both decide to forward $Q(\Sigma)$ to the same process that has not yet received $Q(\Sigma)$.

To execute query $Q(\Sigma)$, p_i calls function $Q(\Sigma, D, \{p_i\})$ (see Algorithm 2). Function $\max_L(set)$ returns a subset of size L containing those processes in set with the highest probability of success.[4] For each query received, p_i calculates the believes a posteriori of each probability of success interval, explained in the next section. The probability of success is taken as the average value of the interval with highest degree of belief.

Algorithm 2 Query execution (for process p_i)

1: **function** $Q(\Sigma)$
2:   return($Q(\Sigma, D, \{p_i\})$)

3: **function** $Q(\Sigma, d, visited)$
4:   **if** Σ holds at p_i **then**
5:     **for** $l = 1 .. I$ **do** $P[B]^l \leftarrow \frac{P[B]^l \times P[S|B]^l}{\sum_k P[B]^k \times P[S|B]^k}$ $\{$update table after success and...$\}$
6:     $result \leftarrow \{[p_i, 1, -]\}$ $\{$...returns result$\}$
7:   **else**
8:     **for** $l = 1 .. I$ **do** $P[B]^l \leftarrow \frac{P[B]^l \times P[\overline{S}|B]^l}{\sum_k P[B]^k \times P[\overline{S}|B]^k}$ $\{$update table after failure$\}$
9:     $bestSet \leftarrow \max_L(s\_table_i \setminus visited)$ $\{$determine best set of processes$\}$
10:    $result \leftarrow \emptyset$ $\{$initially no result is known$\}$
11:    **if** $d > 0$ **then** $\{$if can forward query:$\}$
12:      $visited \leftarrow visited \cup bestSet$ $\{$update current visited processes and...$\}$
13:      **for each** $p_j \in bestSet$ **do** send $Q(\Sigma, d-1, visited)$ to p_j $\{$...forward query$\}$
14:      set timer $\{$...to be ready for failures and message losses$\}$
15:      **wait until** $[(\forall p_j \in bestSet : (receive(response)$ from $p_j))$ **or** timeout$]$
16:      **for each** p_j, received $response_j$ from p_j **do** $\{$for each response received:$\}$
17:        $result \leftarrow \max_L(result \cup response_j)$ $\{$compute its own response$\}$
18:    **else**
19:      $result \leftarrow bestSet$ $\{$return its best guess$\}$

20: $P[S|B] \leftarrow P[S|B]_l$ s.t. $P[B]_l$ is the max in $P[B]_1, P[B]_2, ..., P[B]_I$ $\{$determine new prob. of success$\}$
21: $s\_table_i \leftarrow s\_table_i \setminus \{[p_i, *, *]\}$ $\{$update $s\_table_i\}$
22: $s\_table_i \leftarrow s\_table_i \cup \{[p_i, P[S|B], -]\}$ $\{$done!$\}$

23: return($result$)

24: **when** receive $Q(\Sigma, d, visited)$ from p_j
25:    $response \leftarrow Q(\Sigma, d, visited)$
26:    send $response$ to p_j

---

[4] In line 9 of Algorithm 2, we simplify the notation, denoting the set of processes in entries in s_table that are not in $visited$ by $s\_table \setminus visited$. Thus, "$\setminus$" is not the "standard" set operator since s_table and $visited$ sets are not of the same type.

	$P[B]^l$	$P[S|B]^l$		$P[B|S]^l$ (new $P[B]^l$)	$P[S|B]^l$
$[0.0, 0.2)$	0.2	≈ 0.1	$[0.0, 0.2)$	0.04	≈ 0.1
$[0.2, 0.4)$	0.2	≈ 0.3	$[0.2, 0.4)$	0.12	≈ 0.3
$[0.4, 0.6)$	0.2	≈ 0.5	$[0.4, 0.6)$	0.20	≈ 0.5
$[0.6, 0.8)$	0.2	≈ 0.7	$[0.6, 0.8)$	0.28	≈ 0.7
$[0.8, 1.0]$	0.2	≈ 0.9	$[0.8, 1.0]$	0.36	≈ 0.9

Fig. 1. Initial configuration   **Fig. 2.** Successful query

4.4   The Probability of Success

The probability of success of a process is a local estimate of the likelihood that the next queried predicate received by the process will hold. It is an estimate because the process never knows what the real chances of success are. Processes permanently re-calculate their probabilities of success after executing a query using some heuristics. In PSEARCH, processes use the relation between past successes with respect to the total number of queries locally executed, which roughly means that the more queries the process is able to successfully execute, the higher the chances that future queries will also be successful.

To determine its local probability of success $P[S|B]$, each process keeps a list of probabilities of success intervals $[0, \lambda^1), [\lambda^1, \lambda^2), ..., [\lambda^k, 1]$, where $0 \le \lambda^1 < \lambda^2 < ... < \lambda^k \le 1$, and degrees of belief $P[B]^1, P[B]^2, ..., P[B]^{k+1}$ that $P[S|B]$ lies within each one of these intervals—notice that $\sum_l P[B]^l = 1$. Each interval has an approximate probability of success, $P[S|B]^l$, equal to the average of the values in the interval. Probability $P[S|B]$ is taken as the $P[S|B]^l$ with the highest degree of belief. Figure 1 illustrates an initial configuration with 5 intervals. Since all entries have the same degree of belief, $P[S|B]$ can be any value among 0.1, 0.3, 0.5, 0.7, and 0.9.

Bayesian networks are direct acyclic graphs, where the vertices represent random variables and the edges their relationships. Thus, each process maintains a small Bayesian network $b \to s$, where b is associated to the probability $P[B]^l$ and s is associated to the probability $P[S|B]^l$ [18]. A Bayesian network can be used to make inferences like: "What is the new degree of belief on a probability interval given that the last query was successful?" To compute the new degree of belief on a given interval, $P[B|S]^l$, we use basic conditional probability: $P[B|S]^l \times P[S]^l = P[S|B]^l \times P[B]^l$, and Bayes theorem:

$$P[B|S]^l = \frac{P[S|B]^l \times P[B]^l}{\sum_k P[S|B]^k \times P[B]^k} . \tag{1}$$

Equation (1) is used to compute the belief *a posteriori* on $P[S|B]^l$ (denoted $P[B|S]^l$), which will be the new value of $P[B]^l$ after a query executed at the process holds. If the queried predicate does not hold at the process, a similar equation is used, derived from $P[B|\overline{S}]^l \times P[\overline{S}]^l = P[\overline{S}|B]^l \times P[B]^l$, to re-compute its table. Figure 2 illustrates the new values for $P[B]^l$ when the queried predicate holds. If the heuristic used to determine $P[S|B]$ is effective, then as the execution evolves, $P[S|B]$ becomes the average value of the interval whose belief tends to 1.

4.5 Classes of Resources

We have simplified the discussion about the algorithm by assuming that all possible queried predicates in the system belong to the same "class." Greater accuracy of the results can be obtained by dividing predicates into different classes (e.g., one class could group predicates involving MP3 Bossa Nova music files and another predicates involving MP3 Jazz music files).

While distinguishing between classes will increase the amount of information that processes have to keep locally—each class has to have its own *s_table* and probability of success, we note that not all processes have to keep information about all classes in the system; however, the more information a process has about a class of predicates, the higher the chances that queries executed by this process for predicates in this class will be successful.

Even though a discussion about how predicates can be divided into classes is beyond the scope of this paper (for a discussion, see for example [17]), the propagation and update mechanisms used to execute queries in such contexts are the same ones used for a single class.

5   Psearch Assessment

5.1   Analytical Analysis

In the following, we assess the PSEARCH algorithm by characterizing ϕ_1 and ϕ_2 analytically. We simplify the analysis by considering executions where no processes fail and timers do not time out. Probabilities ϕ_1 and ϕ_2 can be estimated from the local probabilities ϕ_1^i and ϕ_2^i at each p_i:

$$\phi_{1,2} = \sum_i \frac{\text{number of queries executed by } p_i}{\text{total number of queries executed}} \times \phi_{1,2}^i.$$

We model processes and the entries in their *s_tables* with a directed graph $G(\Pi, E)$, where Π is the set of all processes and E the the set of "logical links" between processes: there is a link from p_i to p_j in G if and only if p_j is in p_i's *best_set*. ϕ_1^i is the probability that $Q(\Sigma)$, initiated in p_i with diameter D, can be successfully executed by some process in A_i, the set of all processes that can be returned by the query. We define $C_i^k(d)$, the k-th *simple path*[5] of length d in G with origin in p_i, as $C_i^k(d) = \langle p_{k_0}, p_{k_1}, ..., p_{k_d} \rangle$, where $p_{k_0} = p_i$ and link $\langle p_{k_l}, p_{k_{l+1}} \rangle \in G, 0 \le l < d$ (see Figure 3). The set $C_i(d)$ of all simple paths of length d in G with origin in p_i is defined as $C_i(d) = \cup_k C_i^k(d)$.

We calculate A_i by considering all processes in simple paths of length equal to or smaller than $D+1$ and with origin at p_i in G: $A_i = \cup_{d \le D+1} \cup_{p_j \in C_i(d)} p_j$. ϕ_1^i is the probability that $Q(\Sigma)$ can be solved at some process in A_i:

$$\phi_1^i = 1 - \prod_{p_j \in A_i} P[\overline{S}|B]_j. \tag{2}$$

---

[5] A path is simple if it only contains different processes.

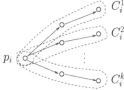

Fig. 3. Paths of length 2   **Fig. 4.** Paths with the same processes

To calculate ϕ_2^i, the probability that Σ holds at all processes returned as the result of query $Q(\Sigma)$, we determine first the probability that Σ does not hold at any process returned by $Q(\Sigma)$. From the PSEARCH algorithm, processes where Σ does not hold can only be returned by processes at distance D. To see why, consider that some process p_j where Σ does not hold receives $Q(\Sigma)$. If p_j is at distance $d < D$ from p_i, p_j forwards $Q(\Sigma)$ to the processes in its *best_set*; if p_j is at distance D from p_i, p_j returns such processes instead. Thus, if p_l is a process returned by $Q(\Sigma)$ in which Σ does not hold, and $C_i^k(D+1)$ is a simple path of length $D+1$ in G from p_i to p_l, then Σ does not hold in any process in $C_i^k(D+1)$, and we say that Σ does not hold in path $C_i^k(D+1)$.

Therefore, the probability that Σ does not hold at some process returned by $Q(\Sigma)$ is the probability that Σ does not hold in some path $C_i^k(D+1)$. Such a probability would be straightforward to calculate if not for the fact that paths are not independent. Consider for example Figure 4 where both paths C_i^k and $C_i^{k'}$ contain processes p_j and $p_{j'}$. When calculating the probability that Σ does not hold at C_i^k and $C_i^{k'}$, we should consider p_i, p_j, and $p_{j'}$ only once.

To solve this problem, we point out that paths C_i^k and $C_i^{k'}$ correspond to the same *events* in the *space of events* determined by paths in G: both C_i^k and $C_i^{k'}$ correspond to the event that Σ fails in p_i, p_j, and $p_{j'}$.[6] Thus, we initially determine the set $\Omega_i = \{e_i^1, e_i^2, ...\}$ of *events of interest*, that is, a subset of the space of events Ω corresponding to all paths in G starting in p_i of length $D+1$ in which Σ fails in all processes in the path and then calculate the probability that these events happen. The probability that event e_i^j happens, denoted $P(e_i^j)$, is calculated as $P(e_i^j) = \omega_{l_1} \times \omega_{l_2} \times ...$, where ω_{l_k} is the probability of success at process p_{l_k} or its converse. Finally, probability ϕ_2^i is determined by:

$$\phi_2^i = 1 - \sum_{e_i^j \in \Omega_i} P(e_i^j). \tag{3}$$

To illustrate our analysis, we consider the simple case of a regular graph where each process has the same number $L-1$ of neighbors and the same probability

---

[6] This case follows directly from the commutative property of intersection: $P[A] \times P[B] = P[B] \times P[A]$. Our solution also works in more complex cases, such as "Y-shaped" paths (e.g., $C_i^k = \langle p_i; p_j; p_k \rangle$ and $C_i^{k'} = \langle p_i; p_j; p_{k'} \rangle$), but for brevity we do not further discuss the issue in this paper.

of success α. Queries are executed with a diameter $D = 0$. In this case, the probability that $Q(\Sigma)$ returns a process where predicate Σ holds is:

$$\phi_1^i = 1 - (1 - \alpha)^L,$$

which is 1 minus the probability that Σ does not hold in any processes among the L involved (i.e., the process where the query originated plus its $L - 1$ neighbors). For the case of a completely connected graph, if $L = n$ then ϕ_1 represents the probability that the "system" can resolve queries. Such a value is the maximum probability achieved by any algorithm—even a deterministic one—when processes have a probability of success equal to α.

The probability that $Q(\Sigma)$ does not return any process where Σ does not hold is:

$$\phi_2^i = 1 - (1 - \alpha) \times (1 - \alpha^{L-1}),$$

which is 1 minus the probability that processes in which Σ does not hold are returned in all paths considered by $Q(\Sigma)$: $(1 - \alpha)$ is the probability that $Q(\Sigma)$ fails at the process where it originated, and $(1 - \alpha^{L-1})$ is the probability that $Q(\Sigma)$ fails in at least one of the remaining $L - 1$ processes (i.e., $L - 1$ paths of length 1).

Figures 5 and 6 show the variations in ϕ_1^i and ϕ_2^i, respectively, with the variation in L and α. As a reference, we have also included a curve with simulation results; details about our simulation are given in the next section. The simulation values shown in Figures 5 and 6 consider a completely connected network and processes with a probability of success equal to 0.1.

For high values of α (i.e., ≥ 0.5), ϕ_1^i quickly tends to 1. For low values of α, and given enough processes, ϕ_1^i can be reasonable high—notice that the probabilities are assumed to be independent. Conversely, ϕ_2^i is much more susceptible to variations in α than to variations in L. Actually, for $L \geq 3$, ϕ_2^i almost only depends on α. From Figures 5 and 6 we can conclude that PSEARCH is effective in scenarios where predicates hold with high probability in a subset of processes, and provided that the system evolves to identify what these processes are.

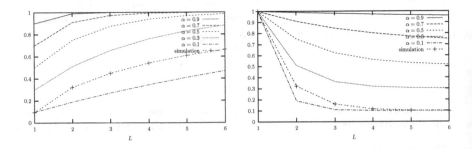

Fig. 5. ϕ_1^i in a fully connected graph   **Fig. 6.** ϕ_2^i in a fully connected graph

5.2   Simulation-Based Analysis

To better understand the behavior of PSEARCH, we have build a simulation model in C++ using the simulation package CSIM [7]. In the beginning of the execution each process is assigned a real probability of success, according to a certain distribution of probability, which determines the chances that a queried predicate holds at the process. This is the probability that processes try to determine using Bayesian statistical inference. Processes generate queries regularly and data starts to be collected once the local probability of success determined by processes become near the real values (i.e., around 5% of difference).

The impact of the probability distribution. Figures 7 and 8 compare different distributions of the real probabilities assigned to processes. To minimize the effects of other parameters, we considered a network completely connected and very large s_tables (i.e., able to store 50 processes). We have conducted experiments where all processes have a real probability of 0.1, a uniform distribution of real probabilities, and a powerlaw distribution of real probabilities. In a powerlaw distribution, a very few processes have a very high real probability of success, and most processes have a low real probability of success (i.e., in our experiments, only three processes have a real probability of success greater than 50%).

For the uniform and the powerlaw distributions, some processes have a high probability of executing queries with success. Such processes eventually end up in the s_tables of all processes, which explains the high values of ϕ_1 and ϕ_2 for these two distributions. Probability ϕ_2 decreases with the increase in the number of processes in the result because there are not so many processes with high probabilities of success, and those with high probability are included first in the result of queries. Therefore, when processes of low probability of success are included ($L \geq 7$) the chances that the queried predicate does not hold in all processes in the result raises.

The effect of failures. In these experiments, we consider a random network: We initially randomly generate links of varying latencies connecting processes and

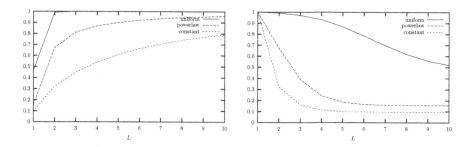

Fig. 7. ϕ_1^i in a fully connected graph   **Fig. 8.** ϕ_2^i in a fully connected graph

then take the biggest connected component as our network—processes not connected to the main component are discarded as are any connections involving them. To achieve a connected component with 100 processes, we interactively increased the initial number of processes until we reached 100 in the main component. The real probabilities of success are generated according to a powerlaw distribution, and each *s_table* can contain 10 processes. In Figures 9 and 10, θ represents the percentage of faulty processes. Faulty processes proceed in cycles: they execute for a certain period of time, crash and lose all the information they gathered, and recover. In the execution, each faulty process spends half of the simulation time up.

Although the effects of process failures is not very significant on the values of ϕ_1 and ϕ_2, even the best case scenario (i.e., no failures) has low values of ϕ_1 and ϕ_2. This happens because with a powerlaw distribution, only very few processes have high real probabilities of success. As all processes periodically forward their *s_tables* to their neighbors, processes with high probability of success never last long in the *s_tables*—notice that in order to be able to get rid of faulty processes, we have to remove processes from *s_tables* based on their timestamps, and not on their probability of success. We discuss in next paragraph a way to improve ϕ_1 and ϕ_2.

Improving ϕ_1 and ϕ_2. To improve ϕ_1 and ϕ_2 and still be able to remove faulty processes, we modified our algorithm as follows: Initially, every process uses the same time interval to forward *s_tables*. After executing a query without success, this value is increased (until it reaches some maximum threshold); after a query is executed with success by the process, the value is decreased (until it reaches some minimum threshold). Therefore, processes with very high probability will send their *s_tables* more frequently than processes with low probability, and so, will dominate the occupancy of *s_tables*. As depicted in Figures 11 and 12, this technique proved to be very effective. Moreover, the impact of failures on ϕ_1 and ϕ_2 is still small.

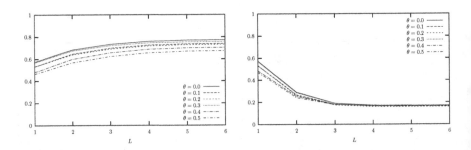

Fig. 9. ϕ_1^i in the presence of failures   **Fig. 10.** ϕ_2^i in the presence of failures

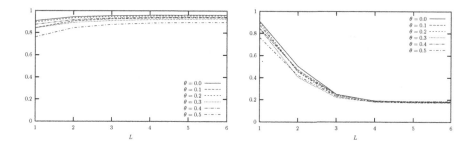

Fig. 11. ϕ_1^i with improved PSEARCH   **Fig. 12.** ϕ_2^i with improved PSEARCH

6   Conclusion

This paper introduced the notion of probabilistic queries, an abstraction used to find resources and information (e.g., data files, processing capabilities) in large-scale systems. Contrary to deterministic solutions to the problem, probabilistic queries admit mistakes. The quality of a probabilistic query algorithm can be measured by two parameters: ϕ_1 and ϕ_2; the former is related to the chances that a query result contains a process of interest and the latter is related to the chances that "useless" processes are returned in the result of the query. Parameters ϕ_1 and ϕ_2 are complementary. Without ϕ_2, optimal queries could return all processes in the system; without ϕ_1, optimal queries could return no processes at all. The paper also presents PSEARCH, an algorithm that implements probabilistic queries using basic concepts of Bayesian statistical inference.

Preliminary results, by analytical and simulation models, show that if the system contains processes that concentrate most of the resources, an assumption that has been observed in some environments [10, 12], PSEARCH can be reasonable precise. PSEARCH is a promising way of dealing with the location problem in distributed system. Part of its power comes from its ability to adapt to system changes, that is, if the patterns of use chance over time, with some resources being more requested than others or some processes being more able to respond to request than others, PSEARCH adapts itself to new demands. We are currently working on a large set of experiments whose goal is to better understand the behavior of PSEARCH under various system loads and network partitions.

References

[1] *Peer-to-peer: Harnessing the Benefits of a Disruptive Technology*. O'Reilly & Associates, Inc., 2001. 209, 211, 217

[2] K. Aberer. P-grid: A self-organizing access structure for p2p information systems. In *9th International Conference on Cooperative Information Systems*, volume 2172 of *Lecture Notes in Computer Science*. Springer, 2001. 211

[3] L. A. Adamic, R. M. Lukose, A. R. Puniyani, and B. A. Huberman. Search in power-law networks. Technical report, Hewlett-Packard Laboratories, 2001. 211

[4] M. K. Aguilera, W. Chen, and S. Toueg. Failure detection and consensus in the crash-recovery model. In *Proceedings of the International Symposium on Distributed Computing (DISC'98)*, pages 231–245, September 1998. 212, 215

[5] P. Albitz and C. Liu. *DNS and BIND*. O'Reilly & Associates, 3rd edition, 1998. 211

[6] K. Birman, M. Hayden, O. Ozkasap, Z. Xiao, M. Budiu, and Y. Minsky. Bimodal multicast. *ACM Transactions on Computer Systems*, 17(2):41–88, May 1999. 210

[7] *CSIM 18 simulation engine (C++ version)*. Mesquite Software, Inc. 3925 W. Braker Lane, Austin, TX 78755-0306. 223

[8] F. Dabek, E. Brunskill, M. F. Kaashoek, D. Karger, R. Morris, I. Stoica, and H. Balakrishnan. Building peer-to-peer systems with chord, a distributed lookup service. In *8th IEEE Workshop on Hot Topics in Operating Systems*, May 2001. 211

[9] M. J. Demmer and M. P. Herlihy. The arrow distributed directory protocol. *Lecture Notes in Computer Science*, 1499, 1998. 211

[10] M. Faloutsos, P. Faloutsos, and C. Faloutsos. On power-law relationships of the internet topology. *Computer Communication Review*, 29(4), 1999. 210, 225

[11] I. Gupta, T. D. Chandra, and G. S. Goldszmidt. On scalable and efficient distributed failure detectors. In *Proceedings of the 20th ACM Symposium on Principles of Distributed Computing (PODC'2001)*, August 2001. 210

[12] B. A. Huberman and L. A. Adamic. Growth dynamics of the World-Wide Web. *Nature*, 401(6749), September 1999. 210, 225

[13] K. P. Birman I. Gupta, R. van Renesse. Scalable fault-tolerant aggregation in large process groups. In *Proceedings of the International Conference on Dependable Systems and Networks (DSN'2001)*, July 2001. 210

[14] J. Kubiatowicz, D. Bindel, P. Eaton, Y. Chen, D. Geels, R. Gummadi, S. Rhea, W. Weimer, C. Wells, H. Weatherspoon, and B. Zhao. OceanStore: An architecture for global-scale persistent storage. *ACM SIGPLAN Notices*, 35(11):190–201, November 2000. 211

[15] L. Lamport. Time, clocks, and the ordering of events in a distributed system. *Communications of the ACM*, 21(7):558–565, July 1978. 216, 217

[16] F. Mattern. Virtual time and global states of distributed systems. In M. Cosnard et al., editor, *Proceedings of the International Workshop on Parallel and Distributed Algorithms*. Elsevier Science Publishers, 1989. 217

[17] Open Directory Project. http://dmoz.org. 220

[18] D. S. Sivia. *Data Analysis: A Bayesian Tutorial*. Oxford Science Publications, 1996. 219

[19] A. S. Tanenbaum, R. van Renesse, H. van Staveren, G. J. Sharp, S.J. Mullender, J. Jansen, and G. van. Rossum. Experiences with the amoeba distributed operating system. *Communications of the ACM*, 33(12), December 1990. 211

[20] S. Q. Zhuang, B. Y. Zhao, A. D. Joseph, R. H. Katz, and J. D. Kubiatowicz. Bayeux: an architecture for scalable and fault-tolerant wide-area data dissemination. In *International Workshop on Network and Operating System Support for Digital Audio and Video*, 2001. 211

Towards Information Society Dependability Initiative in FP6: Roadmapping Activities in Dependability

Luca Simoncini

University of Pisa

Abstract. The Information Society Dependability Initiative (ISDI) is a proposed major initiative encompassing RTD and education and training on the various aspects of dependability (reliability, safety, security, survivability, etc.) together with means for encouraging dependability best practice.

1   Need and Relevance

Various recent EU publications have, either implicitly or explicitly, testified to the need for much higher, and more cost-effective levels of system dependability than is typically achieved by many of today's complex ICT systems. For example, the Presidency Conclusions of the Lisbon European Council (23 and 24 March 2000) and the action plan for eEurope envisage a Europe which by 2010 will be making widespread use of computer systems for many highly demanding and complex tasks. These documents stress the need for the information infrastructure, and the systems dependent on this infrastructure, to be adequately secure (and, more generally, dependable), and to be worthy of the high levels of trust and confidence that governments and citizens will have to place in them.

What will matter to governments, industries, and citizens will be the overall dependability of the systems on which they are relying. They will need an appropriate balance of the various facets of dependability, together with appropriate levels of performance and usability, and they will need this from the systems as a whole, not just from isolated subsidiary components of these systems and their infrastructure.

Many of the goals of the eEurope Action Plan (e.g. increase security of electronic transactions while protecting citizens' privacy; enhance user confidence in e-commerce; provide a quality telematics infrastructure for healthcare, to prevent disease and assist elderly and other people with special needs; use IT to improve transportation safety and decrease negative environmental effects) cannot be fully attained unless we are able to make much more effective use of existing dependability-related processes and mechanisms than is normally achieved, and in some areas by achieving significant technical advances over even the best current practice.

The use of computer-based artifacts to improve social well-being — or to more effectively meet economic challenges — is forever increasing society's dependence on such technology, inducing new risks, especially social risks concerning privacy and safety of the citizen. Indeed, one pervasive theme that has been discussed in fora such

F. Grandoni (Ed.): EDCC 2002, LNCS 2485, pp. 227-233, 2002.

as the ACM Risks Forum over more than a decade has been the "ubiquity of systemic vulnerabilities relating to security, reliability, availability, and overall survivability, with respect to human enterprises, society at large, and to systems, applications, and enterprises based on information technologies" illustrating the need for an integrated approach that addresses both technological issues and their possible consequences on our human values and constitutional foundations.

The vulnerabilities of concern span computer systems embedded within appliances and vehicles to those that control critical national and international infrastructure such as communication, energy and water supply. Due to their ubiquity, embedded computer systems have a great impact on the socio-economy and affect our everyday life in many respects. Their dependability is therefore of vital interest for human society at large, and acceptance by the public can only be achieved if dependability is clearly demonstrated. Moreover, the dependency of ever more functions of daily life on embedded systems implies a severe threat to people in case of accidental failure or deliberate attack.

Vulnerabilities in systems at the other end of the spectrum are also frightening. In the U.S., the President's Commission on Critical Infrastructure Protection of the previous U.S. administration has identified serious vulnerabilities in telecommunications, electric power and other energy sources, transportation, financial services, emergency services and government continuity. It also noted how interdependent these critical infrastructures are, and how they are all related to information technologies. It also observed a general lack of public awareness of these vulnerabilities and a lack of taking proper actions to avert possible risks in time.

Such vulnerabilities may be, and to a certain extent nowadays are, exploited for criminal acts against civil society and its institutions. This has triggered prolific legislative activity at the level of both international and national organizations. The resulting law enforcement actions, while necessary in order to counter such new forms of crimes, may result themselves in "counter-threats" to civil liberties and privacy, being often based on widespread global surveillance and the use of technology that is not mature enough. It is a specific duty of the dependability community to, on the one hand, provide suitable technological solutions required by proper legislation and law enforcement authorities and, on the other hand, provide such authorities and the public at large with clear and complete information on such technologies, including their intrinsic limitations and the risks which may arise from their improper use.

So, while information technology has enormous potential to assist the Community in reaching its social and economic objectives, this potential will not be exploitable unless we devote significant attention to improving the dependability of computer-based systems so that citizens may have a justified confidence in them, especially when deployed in critical applications. Many recent developments and announcements provide evidence of the great need to define and plan a broader and more fully-integrated set of dependability-related activities for IST FWP6 than has proved possible in FWP5. (Here we are, of course, using the term dependability to encompass such system attributes as reliability, availability, safety, security, survivability, etc., and are allowing for the fact that what is invariably needed is some cost-effective balance of several such attributes.)

Many recent major system failures have proven to be due to management failing to pay adequate attention to socio-technical problems, rather than to lack of adequate technology. (This fact has led to the establishment by the UK EPSRC of a major six year inter-disciplinary research collaboration on the Dependability of Computer-Based Systems.) Moreover, the various different stake-holders involved with a major computing system may well have conflicting polices (e.g., concerning the balance between privacy versus accountability) which need careful resolution. Thus the ISDI RTD programme must be a broad multi-disciplinary R&D one that encompasses socio-technical R&D (e.g., concerning how best to divide responsibility for complex tasks between computers and humans, and on risk perception and management), and covering ethical-legal issues (e.g., concerning the status of virtual identities and privacy), as well as purely technical R&D.

The information infrastructure, and many of the systems and the dependability problems that will exist in years to come, will be global in nature. Hence there are on-going negotiations regarding EU-US cooperation on dependability. These are being conducted within the framework of the EU-USA Science & Technology agreement, via a number of joint workshops. It is now evident that, whilst Europe has many social, political and technological approaches that are at variance with the US, both parties recognise that they exist in a global interconnected and interdependent ambient network and have more to gain by cooperation on 'dependability' than pure coexistence. The Information Society Dependability Initiative will encompass measures aimed at facilitating national, European and international cooperation, including those likely to be set up as a result of the current negotiations.

2   Scale of Ambition and Critical Mass

The broad aim of the Information Society Dependability Initiative (ISDI), is simply stated: to contribute significantly to the provision of the many and varied highly critical computing and communication systems and services, and of the highly-trained personnel, that will be required for the achievement of the ambitious plans for eEurope and the Information Society in the decade to come. The Information Society Dependability Initiative will also involve itself, whenever appropriate, in the consideration of existing and emerging industrial, national government, and EU policies that are of direct relevance to information infrastructure dependability issues, and in attempts to analyse how these policies could and should influence, and be influenced by, current and likely future technological and socio-technological dependability developments and research plans, both within the EU and elsewhere.

In order that FWP6 can have the envisaged coherent managed portfolio of industrial and long term research and of accompanying measures in dependability and closely allied subjects ISDI might for example take the form of a single large Dependability IP, and accompanying NoEs. Another alternative might be based on some sort of "steering group", either inside or outside the IST Directorate, which coordinates a set of more focussed IPs and NoEs, so as to achieve a similar effect. In either case, it will be important to ensure that ISDI, as well as coordinating activities that centre on dependability *per se*, also provides concrete support to activities, in all probability in various other IPs, related to particular types of system and application, in which dependability is but one of a number of crucial issues that have to be addressed. Moreover, its activities regarding education and training, and technical awareness, should relate to the needs of Europe generally, and not just the organizations who are taking part in FWP6.

Thus the aims of the ISDI include:

- the setting-up of a large-scale programme of education & training, and of technical awareness activities, aimed especially at industry.
- the establishing of means, allied to this programme, of calibrating an organisation's abilities with respect to the processes, skills and tools involved in creating and deploying critical computing systems, in effect a dependability-oriented version of the Software Engineering Institute's "Capability Maturity Model" (CMM) scheme.
- the creation of effective mechanisms for encouraging and enabling sector-specific and application-oriented IST RTD projects to pay due attention to dependability issues, and to try to gain full benefit from state-of-the-art dependability tools and practices.
- the initiation of a well-planned programme of research (both industrially-oriented, and long term) that responds to the challenges posed by novel and highly ambitious applications, upcoming technology developments (such as ambient networking, dependable application services, and computation grids), and the ever-increasing threats to dependability, e.g., from hackers and corrupt insiders.

(This list is in fact just an initial definition of the scope of the envisaged Information Society Dependability Initiative – it will, undoubtedly, be refined and extended through the extensive industrial involvement that is planned in the Accompanying Measure in System Dependability's work on road-mapping and on constituency and consensus building.)

3   Integration

The intellectual integration that is aimed for will strive to bring together most, if not all, the following technology areas: Biometrics, Cryptography, Dependability and Fault Tolerance, Dependable Embedded Systems, Early Warning and Information Sharing, eConfidence, Evidence/Forensics, Interdependencies (technological and sociological), IT & Law (European and International), Privacy and Identity Management, Smart Cards, and Trust in e-Business.

The starting point will be to establish the following groupings based on the needs of business and society at large: (i) Information Infrastructure Interdependencies and Vulnerability, (ii) Privacy and Identity Management, (iii) Trust and Security in e-business processes (including e-confidence), and (iv) Dependable embedded systems, together with the various underpinning technologies and competence streams such as: early warning and information sharing, fault tolerance, crypto, biometrics, smart cards, IT & law, risk management, and evidence & forensics. It will attempt to integrate the results of the road-mapping activities currently being undertaken by the various different communities within the overall dependability arena, taking as our conceptual framework the taxonomies and classifications of dependability that have been developed over many years by the IFIP Working Group on Dependability and Fault Tolerance.

Such an integration will enable overlaps, synergies, and gaps among the various existing dependability-related research projects and communities, and facilitate the establishment of a number of more broadly-based teams, and the mounting of a more effective attack on the present and likely future dependability challenges that face eEurope and the Information Society.

4   Roadmap Projects

In the domain of interest, several Roadmap projects address issues around securing infrastructures, securing mobile services, dependability, personal trusted devices, privacy and basic security technologies. In this panel we have invited presentations of the following Roadmap projects.

AMSD - IST-2001-37553: Accompanying Measure System Dependability

This project addresses the need for a coherent major initiative in FP6 encompassing a full range of dependability-related activities, e.g. RTD on the various aspects of dependability per se; (reliability, safety, security, survivability, etc.), education and training; and means for encouraging and enabling sector-specific IST RTD projects to use dependability best practice. It is aimed at initiating moves towards the creation of such an Initiative, via road- mapping and constituency and consensus building undertaken in co-operation with groups, working in various dependability-related topic areas, who are already undertaking such activities for their domains. The results will be an overall dependability road-map that considers dependability in an adequately holistic way, and a detailed road-map for dependable embedded systems.

Contact point :   Tom Anderson, University of Newcastle
                    tom.anderson@ncl.ac.uk

PAMPAS - IST-2001-37763: Pioneering Advanced Mobile Privacy and Security

An accompanying measure is proposed that aims to ensure that future mobile services and systems satisfy security, privacy and identity management requirements. This is seen as indispensable for broad user acceptance and market success. To this end, the project will produce a coherent framework for future research in this area and issue recommendations for European research within FP6. The approach taken is to start from likely developments in mobile systems and applications, and to identify their security and privacy requirements. Building upon this analysis, available technologies (e.g. cryptography, privacy-enhancing technologies, PKI, DRM) will be investigated and mapped onto an application / technology matrix. Besides open research aspects, the concluding assessment will also identify needs with respect to standardisation and regulation.

Contact point :   Axel Busboom, Ericsson Eurolab Deutschland GmbH
                    axel.busboom@eed.ericsson.se

ACIP - IST-2001-37257: Analysis & Assessment for Critical Infrastructure Protection

Developed societies have become increasingly dependent on ICT and services. Infrastructures such as IC, banking and finance, energy, transportation, and others are relying on ICT and are mutually dependent. The vulnerability of these infrastructures to attacks may result in unacceptable risks because of primary and cascading effects. The investigation of cascading and feedback effects in highly complex, networked systems requires massive support by computer-based tools. The aim of ACIP is to provide a roadmap for the development and application of modelling and simulation, gaming and further adequate methodologies for the following purposes:

- identification and evaluation of the state of the art of CIP;
- analysis of mutual dependencies of infrastructures and cascading effects;
- investigation of different scenarios in order to determine gaps, deficiencies, and robustness of CIS;
- identification of technological development and necessary protective measures for CIP.

Contact point :   Reinhard Hutter, Industrieanlagen-Betriebsgesellschaft mbH
hutter@iabg.de

RAPID - IST-2001-38310 : Roadmap for Advanced Research in Privacy and Identity Management

RAPID aims at developing a strategic roadmap for applied research in the area of privacy and identity management. The project will build a robust platform of leading experts and stakeholders and provide a forum in which these stakeholders can develop a detailed technology roadmap for RTD activities in FWP6. These experts are drawn from industry players, academic and research institutions and civil rights organisations and cover the domains of privacy enhancing technologies, IT security , law & IT and socio-economic issues. In order to preserve its overall relevance, RAPID has set itself the ambitious goal to complete its work plan in 12 months. To support this aim, RAPID will put in place a dedicated project management and scientific co-ordination structure by combining human resources and skills and state of the art quality assurance techniques.

Contact point :   Otto Vermeulen, PricewaterhouseCoopers N.V
otto.vermeulen@nl.pwcglobal.com

DDSI – IST-2001-29202 : Dependability Development Support Initiative

The goal of DDSI is to support the development of dependability policies across Europe. The overall aim of this project is to establish networks of interest, and to provide baseline data upon which a wide spectrum of policy-supporting activities can be undertaken both by European institutions and by public and private sector stakeholders across the EU and in partner nations. By convening workshops, bringing together key experts and stakeholders in critical infrastructure dependability, DDSI facilitates the emergence of a new culture of transnational collaboration in this field, which is of global interest, and global concern. In order to make rapid progress in the area, the outcomes of the workshops as well as the information gathered in order to prepare for the workshops will be actively disseminated towards a wider, but still targeted community of interest, including policy makers business, decision makers, researchers and other actors already actively contributing to this field today.

The outcomes of this 18 month project will be: a network of experts and stakeholders; a clear "bottom line" in terms of information on the current status (status reports), policy road maps on 4 elements, the outcomes of the 4 workshops, and a web site making all this information accessible to a wider audience and for use of future actors in this field.

Contact point :   Maarten Botterman, Stichting RAND Europe
                   m.bottermann@randeurope.org
                   url : www.DDSI.org

The Design of a COTS
Real-Time Distributed Security Kernel*

Miguel Correia, Paulo Veríssimo, and Nuno Ferreira Neves

Faculdade de Ciências da Universidade de Lisboa
Bloco C5, Campo Grande, 1749-016 Lisboa, Portugal
{mpc,pjv,nuno}@di.fc.ul.pt

Abstract. This paper describes the design of a security kernel called
TTCB, which has innovative features. Firstly, it is a distributed sub-
system with its own secure network. Secondly, the TTCB is real-time,
that is, a synchronous subsystem capable of timely behavior. These two
characteristics together are uncommon in security kernels. Thirdly, the
TTCB can be implemented using only COTS components.
We discuss essentially three things in this paper: (1) The TTCB is a
simple component providing a small set of basic secure services. It aims
at building a new style of protocols to achieve intrusion tolerance, which
for the most part execute in insecure, arbitrary failure environments, and
resort to the TTCB only in crucial parts of their operation. (2) Besides,
the TTCB is a synchronous device supplying functions that may be an
enabler of a new generation of timed secure protocols, until now known to
be fragile due to attacks on timing assumptions. (3) Finally, we present
a design methodology that establishes our hybrid failure assumptions in
a well-founded manner. It helps us to achieve a robust design, despite
using exclusively COTS components, with the advantage of allowing the
security kernel to be easily deployed on widely used platforms.

1 Introduction

This paper describes the design of a security kernel called Trusted Timely Computing Base (TTCB). A security kernel [2] is a fail-controlled subsystem trusted
to execute a few functions correctly, albeit immersed in an environment subjected to malicious faults. In the past, security kernels have mainly been used as
intrusion prevention devices, by supporting the mediation/protection of all system interactions, and/or all accesses to system resources. The reference monitor
paradigm is such an example [8]. Alternatively, we argue that a security kernel
can be used as an *intrusion tolerance device*. The idea is to consider that most
of the system runs in an environment prone to attacks, but there is a secure
subsystem, the security kernel, that is used to run crucial phases of execution
allowing a collection of entities to *tolerate* intrusions in some of them. Think for

---

* This work was partially supported by the EC, through project IST-1999-11583
(MAFTIA), and by the FCT, through the Large-Scale Informatic Systems Laboratory (LASIGE) and the project POSI/1999/CHS/33996 (DEFEATS).

F. Grandoni (Ed.): EDCC 2002, LNCS 2485, pp. 234–252, 2002.

example in a web server with several replicas. A security kernel can run some steps of an intrusion tolerant protocol that provides correct results, even if some replicas are intruded and behave maliciously (i.e., try to break the protocol). Intrusion tolerance is the approach taken in the MAFTIA project, under which the TTCB is being developed [15][1]. The TTCB assists the implementation of some of the intrusion-tolerant middleware components, whose architecture and general design principles have been described elsewhere [20]. The formal verification of the TTCB is on-going work in the context of the MAFTIA project, and will be the subject of future reports.

The TTCB has some innovative features. Firstly, it is a *distributed* subsystem with its own secure channel/network – the control channel/network (see Figure 1). A distributed security kernel represents a "hard-core" component, offering trusted services to a collection of participants[2], despite the fact that the latter reside in different nodes, and that their normal communication is through an insecure network – the payload network (see figure). In consequence, the collection of participants can achieve some degree of distributed trust, for low-level facts reported to/by the TTCB for/to all (and thus agree on them), without having to explicitly communicate. That is, protocol participants essentially exchange their messages in a world full of threats, some of them may even be malicious and cheat, but there is an oracle that correct participants can trust, and a channel that they can use to get in touch with each other, even if for rare moments. Moreover, this oracle also acts as a checkpoint that malicious participants have to synchronize with, and this limits their potential for Byzantine actions (inconsistent value faults).

Secondly, the TTCB is synchronous (or real-time), in the sense of having reliable clocks and being able to execute timely functions, and obviously do it in a distributed way: the control channel provides timely (synchronous) inter-module communication. As such, it is capable, for example, of telling the time, measuring durations of distributed operations, and detecting timing failures.

Thirdly, the TTCB can be implemented using only COTS components, hardware and operating system. In consequence, all the design guidelines and the mechanisms we describe in the paper are reproducible and useable in open settings. As a matter of fact, a prototype of the TTCB that runs in mainstream PCs with RT-Linux, a real-time brand of Linux [3], is currently available for free non-commercial use.

The paper discusses essentially three things about our distributed security kernel. First, it presents the TTCB model (Section 3), describes the services provided by the TTCB and their implementation, with special emphasis on the security services (Section 4). Next it shows how resilience to intruders can be enforced in the proposed COTS-based implementation. The TTCB follows a design methodology based on a *composite fault model*, that clearly identifies

---

[1] More information is available at the sites www.navigators.di.fc.ul.pt and www.maftia.org.

[2] Throughout the paper we use interchangeably the words *entity* and *participant* to denominate any software component that uses the TTCB services.

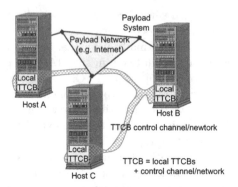

Fig. 1. The architecture of a system with a TTCB

the malicious faults that have to be processed in order to prevent intrusions in the TTCB (Section 5). To conclude, the paper motivates the design of intrusion tolerant systems using the TTCB (Section 6).

2   Related Work

The TTCB is a distributed security kernel which is radically different from the classic Trusted Computing Base (TCB) [11] or the Network Trusted Computing Base (NTCB), composed by a set of interconnected TCBs [12]. The objective of both the TCB and the NTCB is to provide *intrusion prevention* for all critical software in the host, i.e., to prevent that attacks against a host have success. The TTCB, on the contrary, is supposed to be the only secure component of a host, and to provide a set of simple services that assist processes (or other software components) to tolerate attacks. Even if some processes are attacked with success, the TTCB assists the collection of processes to go on delivering their service correctly. In another paper we show how the TTCB can be used to execute intrusion tolerant protocols [4]. We are not aware of any distributed security kernel with the above mentioned characteristics of the TTCB. We are also not aware of any real-time security kernel.

The TTCB builds on the Timely Computing Base work [19]. The objective of this distributed component it to assist the implementation of timed operations and to detect timing failures. It assumes a benign failure model, i.e., on the contrary to the TTCB it is not resilient to malicious faults. The TTCB provides not only all the functionality of the Timely Computing Base, but also additional security-related services.

There is some other work on the design of secure devices to assist the execution of secure applications. The Trusted Computing Platform Alliance (TCPA) is defining a secure *subsystem* that provides some local security services to applications, e.g., persistent storage and platform authentication [17]. Project Dyad explored the use of the Citadel secure coprocessor to implement a number of secure distributed applications, e.g., electronic payment [18]. Several papers describe the use of SmartCards with the same generic purpose [7, 16]. Although this paper describes the implementation of the TTCB in COTS PCs and OS, it could also be implemented inside devices like secure coprocessors or Smart-Cards. Moreover, the TTCB is a distributed component and therefore it can support and assist distributed applications in a more effective way. In fact, the protocols proposed in [4] can tolerate any number of faulty participants, which is an exciting result. The TTCB is also real-time, so it can assist the execution of applications with time requirements.

3   The TTCB

The TTCB is a secure real-time distributed component that aims to assist the execution of applications. The architecture of a system with a TTCB is suggested in Figure 1. An architecture with a TTCB has a local module in some hosts, called the *local TTCB*. These modules are interconnected by a *control channel* or *control network*, depending on the implementation. This set up of local TTCBs interconnected by the control channel/network is collectively called *the* TTCB. The TTCB is used to assist protocols/applications running between participants in the hosts concerned, on any usual distributed system architecture, encompassing a set of hosts interconnected by a network (e.g., the Internet). We call the latter the *payload system and network*, to differentiate from the TTCB part.

Conceptually, a *local TTCB* should be considered to be a *module* inside a host, with a well defined interface, and separated from the OS. In practice, this conceptual separation between the local TTCB and the OS can be achieved in several ways: (1) the local TTCB can be implemented in a separate, tamper-proof hardware module —coprocessor, PC board, etc.— and so the separation is physical; (2) the local TTCB can be implemented on the native hardware, with a virtual separation and shielding implemented in software, between the former and the OS processes. The direction followed was the second, the one based on COTS components (hardware and software). This design of the TTCB is discussed later in the paper.

The local TTCBs are assumed to be fail-silent (they fail by crashing). The TTCB cannot produce erroneous interactions or results (even on account of attacks). Every local TTCB has a clock and the clocks are synchronized.

The TTCB control channel has well-defined characteristics, specified in Table 1 as a set of abstract network properties, on which the design of the internal protocols relies. In this way the control channel does not have to rely on a specific network technology: the abstract network can be mapped onto different networks with the assistance of simple adaptation mechanisms.

The TTCB offers two sets of services, listed in Table 2, which any component (protocol, application) in the local host can use [13].

Table 1. Abstract Network (AN) properties

AN1 Broadcast – The AN has an unreliable packet broadcast primitive
AN2 Integrity – Nodes can detect if packets were corrupted in the network. Corruptions are converted to omission failures
AN3 Omission degree – No more than Od omissions may occur in a given interval of time
AN4 Bounded delay – Any correct packet is received within a maximum delay T_{send} from the send request
AN5 Partition free – The network does not get partitioned
AN6 Broadcast Degree – If a broadcast is received by any local TTCB other than the sender, then it is received by at least Bd local TTCBs
AN7 Confidentiality – The content of network traffic cannot be read by unauthorized users
AN8 Authenticity – Nodes can detect if a packet was broadcast by a correct node

Table 2. TTCB Services

Security services	
Local authentication	For an entity to authenticate the TTCB and establish a secure channel with it.
Trusted block agreement	Achieves agreement on a small, fixed size, data block.
Trusted random numbers	Generates trustworthy random numbers.
Time services	
Trusted timely execution	Executes operations securely and within a certain interval of time.
Trusted duration measurement	Measures the duration of an operation execution.
Trusted timing failure detection	Checks if an operation is executed in a time interval.
Trusted absolute timestamping	Provides globally meaningful timestamps.

4   TTCB Services

This section presents the TTCB security-related services and their design. The design is generic since it relies on an abstraction of the control network (Table 1).

4.1   TTCB Local Security Services

This section describes the local (non-distributed) security-related services of the TTCB, Local Authentication Service and Random Number Generation Service.

Local Authentication Service The purpose of this service is to allow the entity to authenticate and establish a *secure channel* with a local TTCB. The need for this service derives from the fact that, in general, the communication

		Action	Description
1	P → T	$\langle E_u(K_{et}, X_e) \rangle$	The entity sends the TTCB the new key K_{et} and a challenge X_e, both encrypted with the local TTCB public key K_u
2	T → P	$\langle S_r(X_e) \rangle$	TTCB sends the entity the signature of the challenge obtained with its private key K_r

Fig. 2. Local Authentication Service protocol

path between the entity and the local TTCB is not trustworthy. For instance, that communication is probably made through the operating system that may be corrupted and behave maliciously. We assume that the entity–local TTCB communication can be subject to passive and active attacks [9]. A call to the TTCB is composed of two messages, a request and a reply, that can be read, modified, reordered, deleted, and replayed.

Every local TTCB has an asymmetric key pair (K_u, K_r) that is used to authenticate it. The entity that calls the Local Authentication Service is assumed to have a trusted copy of the local TTCB public key K_u. These public keys can be distributed, for instance, manually or using a Public Key Infrastructure (PKI). The private key K_r is assumed to be known only by the local TTCB. A secure channel is obtained establishing a shared symmetric key K_{et} between the entity and the local TTCB, that is later used to secure their communication.

The protocol to establish the shared key has to be an *authenticated key establishment protocol* with local TTCB authentication. The protocol is presented in Figure 2. The formal properties of the protocol and the proof that it verifies those properties can be found in [5].

The shared key K_{et} has to be generated by the entity, not by the TTCB. We would desire it to be the other way around, but the only key they share initially is the local TTCB public key, that can be used by the entity to protect information that can be read only by the local TTCB (that has the corresponding private key) but not the contrary. K_{et} has to be generated by the entity in such a way that a malicious OS cannot guess or disclose it. The generation of a random key requires sources of randomness (timing between key hits and interrupts, mouse position, etc.), sources that in mainstream computers are controlled by the OS. This means that when an entity gets allegedly random data from those sources, it may get either data given or known by a potentially malicious OS. Therefore, there is the possibility of a malicious OS being able to guess the random data that will be used by the entity to generate the key, and consequently, the key itself. This problem is hard to solve, however, a set of practical criteria can help to mitigate it: (1) the entity should use as much as possible sources of random data not controlled by the OS. (2) The entity should use as many different sources of random data as possible. Even if an intruder manages to corrupt the OS, it will probably not be able to corrupt its code in many different places and in such a synchronized way, so that it may guess the random number. (3) The entity must use a *strong mixing function*, i.e., a function that produces an output whose bits are uncorrelated to the input bits [6]. An example is a hash function such as MD4 or MD5. For similar reasons, the protocol challenge, X_e, has to be generated by the entity using the same approach.

The Local Authentication Service protocol is implemented in the TTCB API as a single call with the following syntax:

eid, chlg_sign ← **TTCB_localAuthentication**(key, protection, challenge)

The input parameters are the key, the communication protection to be used, and the challenge. The output parameters are the entity identification –*eid*– used to identify the entity in the subsequent calls, and the signature of the challenge.

Random Number Generation Service This service supplies uniformly distributed random numbers, which can be used as nonces or keys for cryptographic primitives such as distributed authentication protocols. The TTCB provides this service for efficiency since the method described in the previous section can be slow.

The interface of the service is a single function that returns a random number:

number ← **TTCB_getRandom**()

In a future version of the TTCB, based on an appliance board, we envisage the use of a hardware random number generator. In the current RT-Linux TTCB, the random numbers are given by the Linux random number generator. This generator works with an entropy pool that collects random data from several inputs: device driver noise, timing between key hits, timing between some interrupts, mouse position, timing between disk accesses, etc. When a random number is requested, a hash of the entropy poll is calculated using MD5.

4.2   TTCB Distributed Security Service

Distributed services are services that require the cooperation of several local TTCBs for their execution. This section describes the only TTCB distributed security-related service— the Trusted Block Agreement Service— but a fundamental one. The remainder distributed services are time-related (see [13]).

The Trusted Block Agreement Service This service (Agreement Service for short) performs agreement protocols between sets of entities. These protocols, which for instance, multicast a number of bytes or reach to a consensus with a majority decision, are executed in a secure and timely fashion since the service runs inside the TTCB. The service is not intended to replace agreement protocols in the payload system: it works with "small" blocks of data (currently 160 bits), and the TTCB has limited resources to execute it.

The Agreement Service is formally defined in terms of the three functions *TTCB_propose*, *TTCB_decide* and *decision*. An entity *proposes a value* when it calls *TTCB_propose*. An entity *decides a result* when it calls *TTCB_decide* and receives back a result. The function *decision* calculates the result in terms of the inputs of the service. Formally, the Agreement Service is defined by the following properties:

- *AS1 Termination.* Every correct entity eventually decides a result.
- *AS2 Integrity.* Every correct entity decides at most one result.
- *AS3 Agreement.* If a correct entity decides *result*, then all correct entities eventually decide *result*.
- *AS4 Validity.* If a correct entity decides *result* then *result* is obtained applying the function *decision* to the values proposed.
- *AS5 Timeliness.* Given an instant *tstart* and a known constant $T_{agreement}$, a process can decide by $tstart+T_{agreement}$.

The TTCB is a timely component in a payload system with uncertain timeliness. Therefore, the Timeliness property is valid only at the TTCB interface. An entity can only decide with the timeliness the payload system permits.

The interface of the Agreement Service has two functions: an entity calls *TTCB_propose* to propose its value and *TTCB_decide* to try to decide a result (*TTCB_decide* is non-blocking and returns an error if the agreement did not terminate).

```
out  ← TTCB_propose(eid, elist, tstart, decision, value)
result ← TTCB_decide(eid, tag)
```

An agreement is uniquely identified by three parameters: *elist* (the list of entities involved in the agreement), *tstart* (a timestamp), and *decision* (a constant identifying the decision function). The service terminates at most $T_{agreement}$ after it "starts", i.e., after either: (1) the last entity in *elist* proposed or (2) after *tstart*, which of the two happens first. That shows the meaning of *tstart*: it is the instant at which an agreement "starts" despite the number of entities in *elist* that proposed. If the TTCB receives a proposal after *tstart* it returns an error.

The other parameters of *TTCB_propose* are: *eid* is the unique identification of an entity before the TTCB, obtained using the Local Authentication Service; *value* is the block the entity proposes; *out* is a structure with two fields, *error*, an error code and *tag*, an unique identifier of the agreement before a local TTCB. An entity calls *TTCB_decide* with the *tag* that identifies the agreement that it wants to decide. *result* is a record with four fields: (1) *error*, an error code; (2) *value*, the value decided; (3) *proposed-ok*, a mask with one bit per entity in *elist*, where each bit indicates if the corresponding entity proposed the value that was decided; (4) *proposed-any*, a similar mask that indicates which entities proposed any value. Two *decision* functions currently available are: *TTCB_TBA_RMULTICAST*, that returns the value proposed by the first entity in *elist* (therefore the service works as a reliable multicast); *TTCB_TBA_MAJORITY*, that returns the most proposed value. Both return the two masks.

Trusted Block Agreement Service Protocol The internal protocol that implements the Agreement Service is time-triggered: *TTCB_propose* is called asynchronously, and gives the TTCB data that is stored in tables; periodically that data is broadcast to all local TTCBs, including the sender, and, also periodically, data is read from the network and processed.

The protocol uses two tables (Figure 3). The *dataTable* stores all agreements data. Each record has the state of one agreement with the format: *(tag, elist,*

For each local TTCB

propose routine
```
1  when entity calls TTCB_propose(eid, elist, tstart, decision, value) do
2    if (entity already proposed) or (eid ∉ elist) or (clock() > tstart) then return error;
3    insert (elist, tstart, decision, eid, value) in sendTable;
4    get R ∈ dataTable : R.elist = elist ∧ R.tstart = tstart ∧ R.decision = decision;
5    if (R = ⊥) then R := (get_tag(), elist, tstart, decision, ⊥); insert R in dataTable;
6    return R.tag;
```
broadcast routine
```
7  when clock() = round_s × T_s do
8    repeat Od + 1 times do broadcast(sendTable);
9    sendTable := ⊥; round_s := round_s + 1;
```
receive routine
```
10 when clock() = round_r × T_r do
11   while (read(M) ≠ error) do
12     foreach (elist, tstart, decision, eid, value) ∈ M.sendTable do
13       get R∈ dataTable : R.elist = elist ∧ R.tstart = tstart ∧ R.decision = decision;
14       if (R = ⊥) then R := (get_tag(), elist, tstart, decision, ⊥); insert R in dataTable;
15       insert value in R.vtable;
16   round_r := round_r + 1;
```
decide routine
```
17 when entity calls TTCB_decide(eid, tag) do
18   get R ∈ dataTable : R.tag = tag;
19   if (R≠⊥) and [(clock()>R.tstart+T_agreement) or (all entities proposed a value)] then
20     return (calculate result using function R.decision and values in R.vtable);
21   else return error;
```

Fig. 3. Agreement Service internal protocol. Instance at a local TTCB

tstart, decision, vtable). All fields have the usual meaning except *vtable*, which is a table with the values proposed (one per entity in *elist*). *sendTable* stores data to be broadcast to all local TTCBs. Every record is a proposal with the format: *(elist, tstart, decision, eid, value).* The agreement is identified by *(elist, tstart, decision), eid* identifies the entity that proposed and *value* is the value proposed.

The protocol has four routines. The *propose routine* is executed when an entity calls the TTCB function *TTCB_propose* (Lines 1-6). The routine begins by doing some tests: if the entity already proposed a value for this agreement; if the entity that calls the service is in *elist*; if *tstart* already expired (Line 2). Other tests, are also made but are not represented since they are not so related to the algorithm functionality. If the propose is accepted, its data is inserted in sendTable and dataTable, and the *tag* is returned (Lines 3-6). The *broadcast routine* broadcasts data to all local TTCBs every T_s (the period) either if there is data in sendTable or not (Lines 7-9). Every message is broadcasted $Od + 1$ times in order to tolerate omissions in the network (Od is the omission degree). After the broadcast, sendTable is cleaned. The *receive routine* reads and processes messages every T_r (Lines 10-16). Since each message is broadcasted $Od + 1$ times, copies of the same message have to be discarded by the function *read* (Line 11). For each message received, the data in each record of sendTable is inserted in dataTable (Lines 12-15). The *decide routine* is executed when an entity calls the function *TTCB_decide*. The routine searches dataTable for the agreement identified by the tag and returns an error if it does not exists. If the instant $tstart + T_{agreement}$ passed or the local TTCB has the values proposed by all entities in *elist*, the result is obtained and returned.

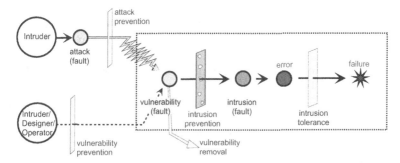

Fig. 4. The Composite Fault Model of MAFTIA

The above protocol can be proved correct if communication is done using a reliable broadcast primitive. This primitive and the proof can be found in [5].

5 The TTCB Design: Enforcing Resilience to Intruders

A system design addresses both functional and non-functional aspects. The functional aspects are concerned with the algorithms and protocols that make the system perform its service, mostly presented in the previous section. This section is concerned with the non-functional design of the COTS-based TTCB.

5.1 Design Methodology

Composite Fault Model with Hybrid Failure Assumptions The organization of assumptions in terms of a composite fault model [20] underpins our design philosophy. In MAFTIA, we say that the impairments that may occur to a system, security-wise, have to do with a wealth of causes, which range from internal faults (i.e., vulnerabilities), to external, interaction faults (i.e., attacks) which activate those vulnerabilities, producing faults (i.e., intrusions) that can directly lead to component failure.

The composite fault model is shown in Figure 4. The figure also shows where to apply different techniques to prevent the system from failing. Because we differentiated the several fault classes, we can apply these techniques selectively, and in a structured way. Note for example, that an intrusion cannot occur unless there is a vulnerability to be activated by a corresponding attack (it makes no sense to prevent an attack for which there is no vulnerability, or vice-versa).

A *composite fault model with hybrid failure assumptions* is one where the presence and severity of vulnerabilities, attacks and intrusions varies from component to component. Consider a component or sub-system like the TTCB, for which a given controlled failure assumption was made. How can we achieve coverage of such an assumption, given the unpredictability of attacks and the elusiveness of vulnerabilities?

The first-line techniques are vulnerability prevention (e.g., using correct coding practices), and then attack prevention (e.g., physically isolating an access point) and vulnerability removal (e.g., patching the OS and removing absolute privileges from the root account).

All these techniques contribute to intrusion prevention. However, after this step there may still be attack-vulnerability combinations to fear from (illustrated in the figure, by the holes in the intrusion prevention barrier). The design must then be complemented with the necessary intrusion tolerance measures, for example, using intrusion detection and recovery or masking, until we justifiably achieve confidence that the component behaves as assumed, failing in the assumed controlled manner, i.e., the component is trustworthy. The measure of its trustworthiness is the coverage of the controlled failure assumption.

Note that there is a body of research on *hybrid failures* for consensus and diagnosis algorithms, assuming failure type distributions for different participants [10, 22]. For instance, some participants are assumed to behave arbitrarily while others are assumed to fail only by crashing. The present work might best be described as *architectural hybridization*, in the lines of works such as [14, 21], where failure assumptions are in fact enforced by the architecture and construction of the system components, and thus well-founded. Hybrid behavior occurs component-wise: components in general are assumed to fail arbitrarily, but can use the services of a fail-controlled component, the TTCB.

The Methodology The design of the TTCB with regard to the non-functional properties follows the principles underlined above. The design methodology has four steps. It makes sense to perform several iterations until the final result.

1. Define the desired system (TTCB) architecture and failure modes
2. Define the environment assumptions and the adaptation mechanisms that enforce these assumptions
3. Design the mechanisms and protocols that enforce the system failure modes
4. Assess the system design

Step one is the definition of the TTCB architecture and failure modes. The TTCB architecture was presented in Section 3 but is more detailed below in Section 5.2. The architecture itself can prevent some attacks against specific components. For example, the control network being physically inaccessible to hackers. About the failure modes, recall that we consider the local TTCBs to be fail-silent, and consider the inter-TTCB communication also to be fail-silent.

Step two is about the system's *environment*, i.e., about whatever is external to the system but that interacts with it: host hardware and OS, networks, intruders, etc. The environment is characterized in terms of a set of assumptions that, in practice, have to be enforced using adaptation mechanisms. The environment assumptions and the adaptation mechanisms are presented in the section 5.3.

Step three deals with constructing the mechanisms and protocols which enforce the fail-silent behavior of the TTCB, on the assumed environment and architecture. This resumes to make the TTCB resilient to attacks and intrusions.

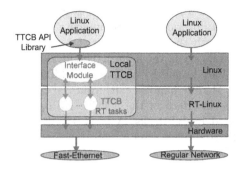

Fig. 5. The architecture of a host for the COTS-based TTCB

The design methodology may recursively be applied to the internal components of the TTCB as part of this step. This is discussed in Section 5.4.

Step four consists in assessing the system design, or in this case, the TTCB subsystem. On the one hand, determining whether the coverage of the design assumptions is acceptably high. On the other hand, determining whether given the assumptions, the algorithmics and their implementation provide the specified services. The verification and assessment of the TTCB design is on-going work on the context of project MAFTIA.

5.2   System Architecture

The general architecture of the TTCB was presented in Sections 1 and 3. It was also mentioned that our current implementation is based on common PCs with RT-Linux. To pursue the COTS strategy, our implementation is based on Fast-Ethernet, for campus-wide systems: we provide each host having a TTCB with an extra LAN adapter. We envisage future designs based on tamperproof hardware and wide-area networks such as an ISDN Virtual Private Network (VPN)[3]. A VPN provides a private channel, if we assume that the public telecommunications network is not eavesdropped. Additional security can be obtained using secure channels, e.g., encrypting the TTCB communication.

RT-Linux is an engineering of Linux, which was modified in order that a real-time executive takes control of the hardware, to enforce real-time behavior of some real-time (RT) tasks. RT tasks were defined as special Linux loadable kernel modules (LKMs), so they run inside the kernel. The scheduler was changed to handle these tasks in a preemptive way and to be configurable to different scheduling disciplines. Linux runs as the lowest priority task and its interruption scheme was changed to be intercepted by RT-Linux.

Real-time FIFOs are the basic mechanism for communication between and with RT tasks.

---

[3] ISDN is a public digital network technology for data and telephony that provides connections with guaranteed bandwidth in multiples of 64 Kbps (128 Kbps, 1 Mbps...).

The COTS-based *local TTCB* architecture is detailed in Figure 5. The API functions are defined in libraries and communicate with the local TTCB using RT-Linux FIFOs. Currently there is one library for applications in C and another for Java (TTCB API Library in the figure). The local TTCB is implemented by an LKM (Interface Module) and by a number of RT tasks (TTCB RT Tasks). The TTCB Interface Module handles calls from the entities. It is not real-time since it is part of the interface of the TTCB. All operations with timeliness constrains are executed by RT tasks. A local TTCB has always at least two RT tasks that handle communication: one to send messages to the other local TTCBs and another to receive and process incoming messages.

5.3   Environment Assumptions and Adaptation Mechanisms

The environment assumptions are shown in Table 3. The environment includes the PCs with RT-Linux (the *host*), the payload network and the control network.

RT-Linux and Protection From the point of view of security, RT-Linux is very similar to Linux. Its main vulnerability is the ability a superuser has to control any resource in the system. This vulnerability is usually reasonably easy to exploit, e.g., using race conditions. Recently, several Linux extensions try to compartmentalize the power of the superuser. Linux *capabilities* [1], already part of the kernel, are privileges or access control lists associated with processes, allowing a fine grain control on how they use certain objects. Currently, though, the practical way of using this mechanism is quite basic. There is a system wide *capability bounding set* that bounds the capabilities that can be held by any system process. Removing a capability from that set disables the ability to use an object. Although basic, this mechanism fits our needs.

Enforcing Environment Assumptions Assumptions A1 and A2 impose the only limits on what the intruder can do inside a host. Otherwise, we assume that it can access the host, run software there, and become root or run processes with superuser privileges.

Table 3. Environment assumptions

A1 The host protection mechanisms are not reconfigured by any intruder.
A2 The host kernel memory is not read or written by any intruder.
A3 The control channel access point is not read or written by any intruder.
A4 The data on the control channel is not read or written by any intruder.
A5 Given a known interval of time, the control channel does not corrupt more than k packets.
A6 There are no partitions in the control channel.

The protection mechanisms mentioned in A1 are basically a set of commands in a script that remove a set of Linux capabilities from the capability bounding set. This script is executed when the host is rebooted. Therefore, assumption A1 is secured preventing hackers from rebooting the system. This can be done either protecting the access to the host or using a reboot password[4].

Assumption A2 protects the working space of both the RT-Linux kernel and the modules that support the TTCB. If the intruder manages to modify the kernel memory, he has a dramatic potential for damage, which ranges from modifying kernel or TTCB code or state, to arbitrarily controlling any of the system components, since code in the kernel memory can execute privileged CPU instructions. Assumption A2 is enforced by removing two vulnerabilities:

- *Loadable kernel modules insertion:* LKMs allow a hacker that gained superuser privileges to insert code in the kernel. The vulnerability is disabled removing the capability CAP_SYS_MODULE off the capability bounding set.
- */dev/mem and /dev/kmem devices:* these devices can be used to read and modify the system memory, including the kernel. This vulnerability is removed taking CAP_SYS_RAWIO off the capability bounding set.

Assumptions A3 through A6 refer to the control channel. Assumption A3 stipulates that an intruder cannot access the control network adapter from inside the host, and in consequence, he/she can neither send to, nor read and/or intercept packets from, the control network. This can be enforced modifying the relevant LAN controller.

Assumption A4, on the other hand, is secured by ensuring that an intruder does not have physical access to the control network medium devices (cables, switches, etc.). The assumption makes sense if we consider that it is a short-range, inside-premises closed network, connecting a set of servers inside a single institution, with no other connection. We are assuming that the intruder comes from the Internet, through the payload network, without physical access to the servers or control network hardware. Long-range solutions also use technologies such as ISDN VPN, that are hard for the common Internet intruder to tamper with in conjunction with an attack through the payload network. Note however that assumption A4 can still be enforced for a more powerful hacker who can eavesdrop on the control channel, by using cryptographic schemes in the inter-TTCB communication.

In the just assumed absence of active attacks on the control channel, assumptions A5 and A6 establish limits to the events that may affect the timeliness of communication on the former, so that known bounds can be derived on message delivery delays, and failure detection can be accurately performed. Networks can be tested in order to find out the maximum number of packets they may corrupt in an interval of time, the omission degree. Likewise, short-range LANs have negligible partitioning, which can be further improved by using redundant channels, a must to enforce A6 in wider-area networks.

---

[4] This discussion concerns the environment during runtime. We also assume that the kernel and the local TTCB binaries are not corrupted by an intruder or, at least, corruption is detected during reboot.

5.4   Enforcing System Failure Modes

The composite fault model in Figure 4 shows that different techniques can be used to make a system resilient to intrusions. The *intruder* in the figure is part of the environment, so its behavior is modelled by the environment assumptions in Table 3. Now, look at assumptions A1 through A4 in the table: they impose restrictions to the behavior of the intruder. Hypothesizing about limits to the behavior of malicious entities, such as hackers or viruses is, of course, not acceptable. Therefore, in the previous section we devised mechanisms that impose these restrictions in practice, i.e., that enforce the assumptions despite the potential arbitrary behavior of the intruder.

Assumptions A1 through A4 effectively do attack prevention (see Figure 4): it is an assumption that the intruder is not able to attack either the TTCB software modules or the control channel. Therefore, at this stage there is no need to enforce the system resilience to intruders. Handling the attacks/intrusions at step two (environment assumptions) is the same as doing it at step three. If we made RT-Linux part of the system then it would be the system that would be preventing or tolerating the faults, instead of the environment, i.e., protection would be made in step three instead of two. However, in this particular case, the way it is done seems more intuitive.

What remains to be defined at this stage is how the abstract network properties (Table 1) are obtained on top of the real network, taking in account the environment assumptions.

Property AN1 is available in the Ethernet and can be simulated with IP multicast or with several message sends in other networks. Property AN2 is imposed by most networks, through the *cyclic redundancy check* (CRC), if no attacks on the network are considered (assumptions A3/A4). If there are attacks, message integrity checks (MICs) can be used instead. Property AN3 is guaranteed by the environment assumption A5. For property AN4 to be guaranteed in a dedicated switched Fast-Ethernet, packet collisions have to be avoided, since they would cause unpredictable delays. This requires that: (1) only one host can be connected to each switch port (hubs cannot be used); and (2) the traffic load has to be controlled. The first requirement is obvious. The second is solved by an access control mechanism, that accepts or rejects the execution of a service taking in account the availability of resources (buffers and bandwidth). Property AN5 is guaranteed by the assumption A6. For property AN6, in a switched Fast-Ethernet Bd can easily exceed half of the nodes. Properties AN7 and AN8 are guaranteed by the assumptions A3 and A4 and could be enhanced using common cryptographic schemes.

6   Intrusion Tolerance with the TTCB

After delving into the discussion of the TTCB services and design, a pertinent question at this stage is: *What is the TTCB good for?* This question is best answered after explaining the failure assumptions followed in the MAFTIA architecture.

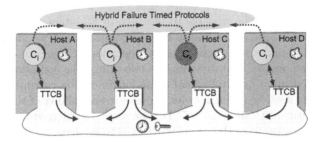

Fig. 6. Intrusion Tolerance with a TTCB

6.1 Fault Model

A crucial aspect of any fault-tolerant architecture is the fault model upon which the system architecture is conceived, and component interactions are defined. Hybrid assumptions, combining different kinds of failure assumptions, are followed in our work. This is because controlled failure assumptions have the problem of coverage in case of malicious faults, and arbitrary failure assumptions, on the other hand, are costly in terms of timeliness and complexity. With hybrid assumptions some parts of the system would be justifiably assumed to exhibit fail-controlled behavior, whilst the remainder of the system would still be allowed an arbitrary behavior. However, such an approach is only feasible when the fault model is well-founded, otherwise the system becomes easy prey to hackers. In consequence, the implementation of the TTCB discussed in Section 5 combines different techniques and methods tackling different classes of faults, in order to achieve the postulated behavior (fail-silent) with high coverage.

6.2 Strategy for Intrusion Tolerance

With the TTCB, we can implement intrusion-tolerance mechanisms, on a hybrid of arbitrary-failure (the payload system) and fail-silent (the TTCB) components. The TTCB is designed to assist crucial steps of the operation of middleware protocols. We use the word "crucial" to stress the tolerance aspect: unlike classical, prevention-based approaches (e.g., Reference Monitor), the component does not stand in the way of all resources and operations. As a matter of fact, protocols run in an untrusted environment, local participants only trust interactions with the security kernel, single components can be intruded, and correct service provision is built on distributed fault tolerance mechanisms, for example through agreement and replication amongst collections of participants in several hosts.

Observe Figure 6: software components C_i interact through protocols which run on the payload system (the top arrows). However, they can locally access the TTCB in some steps of their execution (for example, to be informed whether a message just received was or not corrupted). The white color is used to mean a trusted environment (the TTCB). The key means the environment is cryptographically secure. The grey colors for the payload system mean untrusted.

Trusting the TTCB security kernel means that it is not feasible to subvert the TTCB, but it may be possible to interfere in its interaction with entities. In similar terms, whilst we let a local host be compromised, we must make sure that it does not undermine fault-tolerant operation of the protocols amongst distributed components. The above implies two things: the operation of protocols can be intruded upon and individual components can be corrupted (e.g., C_k); and special care must be taken in order to preserve the validity of the interactions of a correct entity with its local TTCB. The reader is referred to [4], where we give a practical example of the use of the TTCB to implement intrusion-tolerant protocols.

In order to understand the assumptions on timeliness of our system, let us analyze Figure 6 again: the clock inside the TTCB area is meant to suggest it is a fully synchronous (or hard real-time) component. On the other hand, the warped clock in the payload area suggests that it has uncertain timeliness, or partial synchronism. It can even be asynchronous.

Constructing secure timed protocols in these environments is a hard task, due to the risk of attacks on the timing assumptions. For that reason, most known secure broadcast or byzantine agreement protocols are of the asynchronous class. However, certain services, if provided in a trusted way (by the TTCB, which has thus to be a synchronous— real-time— component) can provide invaluable help.

6.3   Example Applications with a TTCB

This section exemplifies the use of the TTCB in two different settings. Figure 7(a) shows a web server replicated inside a facility, a company or another institution. Clients call the server using an intrusion tolerant protocol. This protocol uses the TTCB to perform some crucial steps, but otherwise runs in the payload system. If a subset of replicas is corrupted and behave maliciously, the server will still provide correct results, tolerating these malicious faults. An inside-facility TTCB can be the version described in the paper. This solution requires an extra Fast-Ethernet adapter per host and an extra network switch, an affordable price.

Several Internet authentication schemes rely on highly secure and distributed servers. For instance, Public Key Infrastructures have Certification Authorities (CAs) with these characteristics. Figure 7(b) shows a TTCB distributed over a wide area, that allows the execution of intrusion tolerant protocols over such an extension. The TTCB control channel has to be a highly secure and wide channel, with guaranteed bandwidth (e.g., the above mentioned ISDN VPN).

7   Conclusions and Future Work

The paper describes the design of a security kernel – the TTCB – with innovative features: first, it is distributed, with local parts in hosts connected by a control channel; second, it is real-time, capable of timely behavior; and third, it can be constructed using only COTS components. The paper also presents the services of the TTCB and gives an intuition on how these services can be used to

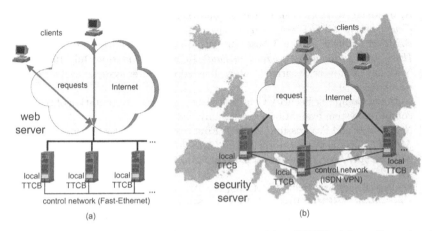

Fig. 7. Examples of intrusion tolerant systems with a TTCB: (a) replicated web server; (b) distributed security server

support the construction of a new generation of intrusion tolerant protocols [4]. The currently available implementation of the TTCB is based on common hardware running a real-time operating system, RT-Linux, and on a Fast-Ethernet network. By applying our design methodology, we expect that the existing implementation exhibits a good coverage of the assumptions, acceptable to most applications. This solution has one extra added advantage – the TTCB can be tested and used in open settings.

References

[1] Linux Capabilities FAQ 0.2.
   ftp://ftp.guardian.no/pub/free/linux/capabilities/ capfaq.txt,   2000.
   246
[2] S. Ames, M. Gasser Jr., and R. Schell. Security kernel design and implementation: An introduction. *IEEE Computer*, 16(7):14–22, 1983.   234
[3] M. Barabanov. A Linux-based real-time operating system. Master's thesis, New Mexico Institute of Mining and Technology, June 1997.   235
[4] M. Correia, L. C. Lung, N. F. Neves, and P. Veríssimo. Efficient byzantine-resilient reliable multicast on a hybrid failure model. In *Proc. of the 21th IEEE Symposium on Reliable Distributed Systems*, October 2002.   236, 237, 250, 251
[5] M. Correia, P. Veríssimo, and N. F. Neves. The design of a COTS real-time distributed security kernel (extended version). DI/FCUL TR 01–12, Department of Computer Science, University of Lisbon, 2001.   239, 243
[6] D. Eastlake, S. Crocker, and J. Schiller. Randomness recommendations for security. IETF Network Working Group, Request for Comments 1750, December 1994.   240
[7] N. Itoi and P. Honeyman. Smartcard integration with Kerberos v5. In *Proc. of the USENIX Workshop on Smartcard Technology*, May 1999.   237
[8] B. Lampson. Protection. *Operating Systems Review*, 8(1):18–24, 1974.   234

[9] A. J. Menezes, P. C. Van Oorschot, and S. A. Vanstone. *Handbook of Applied Cryptography.* CRC Press, 1997. 239

[10] F. Meyer and D. Pradhan. Consensus with dual failure modes. In *Proc. of the 17th IEEE International Symposium on Fault-Tolerant Computing,* July 1987. 244

[11] National Computer Security Center. Trusted computer systems evaluation criteria, August 1983. 236

[12] National Computer Security Center. Trusted network interpretation of the trusted computer system evaluation criteria, July 1987. 236

[13] N. F. Neves and P. Veríssimo, editors. *First Specification of APIs and Protocols for MAFTIA Middleware. Project MAFTIA IST-1999-11583 deliverable D24.* August 2001. http://www.research.ec.org/maftia/deliverables/d24final.pdf. 237, 240

[14] D. Powell, editor. *Delta-4 - A Generic Architecture for Dependable Distributed Computing.* ESPRIT Research Reports. Springer-Verlag, November 1991. 244

[15] D. Powell and R. J. Stroud, editors. *MAFTIA: Conceptual Model and Architecture. Project MAFTIA IST-1999-11583 deliverable D2.* November 2001. http://www.research.ec.org/maftia/deliverables/D2fin.pdf. 235

[16] T. Stabell-Kulø, R. Arild, and P. H. Myrvang. Providing authentication to messages signed with a smart card in hostile environments. In *Proc. of the USENIX Workshop on Smartcard Technology,* May 1999. 237

[17] Trusted Computing Platform Alliance (TCPA). Main specification version 1.1a. Technical report, TCPA, December 2001. http://www.trustedpc.org/. 236

[18] J. D. Tygar and B. S. Yee. Dyad: A system for using physically secure coprocessors. In *Workshop on Technological Strategies for the Protection of Intellectual Property in the Network Multimedia Environment,* April 1993. 237

[19] P. Veríssimo, A. Casimiro, and C. Fetzer. The Timely Computing Base: Timely actions in the presence of uncertain timeliness. In *Proc. of the International Conference on Dependable Systems and Networks,* pages 533–542, June 2000. 236

[20] P. Veríssimo, N. F. Neves, and M. Correia. The middleware architecture of MAFTIA: A blueprint. In *Proc. of the IEEE Third Information Survivability Workshop,* October 2000. 235, 243

[21] P. Veríssimo, L. Rodrigues, and A. Casimiro. Cesiumspray: a precise and accurate global clock service for large-scale systems. *Journal of Real-Time Systems,* 12(3):243–294, 1997. 244

[22] C. Walter, N. Suri, and M. Hugue. Continual on-line diagnosis of hybrid faults. In *Proc. of the 4th IFIP International Working Conference on Dependable Computing for Critical Applications,* 1994. 244

Wrapping Real-time Systems
from Temporal Logic Specifications

Manuel Rodríguez, Jean-Charles Fabre and Jean Arlat

LAAS-CNRS, 7 Avenue du Colonel Roche, 31077 Toulouse Cedex 4 — France
E-mail: {rodriguez, fabre, arlat}@laas.fr

Abstract. This paper defines a methodology for developing wrappers for real-time systems starting from temporal logic specifications. Error confinement wrappers are automatically generated from the specifications of the target real-time system. The resulting wrappers are the executable version of the specifications, and account for both timing and functional constraints. They are executed on-line by a runtime checker, a sort of virtual machine that interprets temporal logic. A reflective approach is used to implement an observation layer placed between the runtime checker and the target system. It allows the wrappers to obtain the necessary event and data items from the target system so as to perform at runtime the checks defined by the temporal logic specifications. The proposed method has been applied to the use of real-time microkernels in dependable systems. Fault injection is used to assess the detection coverage of the wrappers and analyze trade-offs between performance and coverage.

1. Introduction

A wrapper can be defined in general terms as a software component that sits around a target component or system. Traditionally, wrappers have been used in the security domain (e.g., [1]) to enforce security policies through firewalls.

The notion of wrapper was initially defined by the DARPA Information Science and Technology working group, as a software entity composed of two parts: an *adapter*, providing additional services to applications, and an *encapsulation mechanism*, responsible for linking components. This definition is mostly related to interfacing heterogeneous systems.

As far as dependability is concerned, the definition of error confinement wrappers is a crucial issue. The notion of *error confinement wrapper* was defined by Voas [2, 3] in relation with the use of COTS (Commercial Off-The-Shelf) components in the design and implementation of dependable systems. The author distinguishes between input wrappers, which filter syntactically incorrect inputs, and output wrappers, which submit outputs to an acceptance test. An example of such a type of input wrappers for Windows-NT applications is provided in [4].

Error confinement wrappers are built from *executable assertions* [5-7]. Executable assertions can be used during software development, to aid developers in finding faults in the system [5], but also when the system is in operation, as part of fault-tolerance mechanisms [6]. As an example of the latter, the work reported in [8] defines an efficient platform for running wrappers based on executable assertions of COTS microkernels.

When executable assertions are derived from formal specifications of the target system, we talk of *runtime verification* [9-13]. In these works, a monitor checks system constraints at runtime against an executable formal description of the system. The wrapping approach proposed in this paper is related to runtime verification for error confinement.

F. Grandoni (Ed.): EDCC 2002, LNCS 2485, pp. 253–270, 2002.

Although the notion of wrapping is well established today, the means available to support the implementation of wrappers remain very limited. In particular, executable assertions do provide a nice paradigm to implement error confinement. However, no wrapping framework has been defined to specify and integrate portable wrappers to various real-time executive software components.

The aim of this work is to provide a methodology, an implementation framework and supporting tools, to improve the dependability of real-time executive systems by means of error confinement wrappers. The methodology aims at translating formal specifications of system requirements into error confinement wrapping code, and supports the verification of properties at runtime for a given target executive software. The benefits of the wrapping are then evaluated by fault injection techniques.

In our framework, the expected behavior of real-time systems is expressed using temporal logic specifications. Error confinement wrappers are automatically generated by a compilation process from early defined temporal logic specifications of the target real-time system services. The wrappers are the executable version of the specifications, and account for both timing and functional constraints. They are executed on-line by a runtime checker, a sort of virtual machine that interprets temporal logic. A reflective approach is then used to implement an observation layer placed between the runtime checker and the target system. Such a layer allows the wrappers to obtain the necessary event and data items from the target system so as to perform at runtime the checks defined by the temporal logic specifications. Fault injection is then used to evaluate the efficiency of the selected wrappers.

The proposed method has been applied to the use of real-time microkernels in dependable systems. We use software implemented fault injection (SWIFI) to characterize the error detection coverage and the tradeoff between performance and coverage of a set of wrappers generated from the microkernel specifications provided in [14]. The target real-time system used is composed of the Chorus microkernel [15] and the mine drainage control system application [16].

Significant research has been done in the field of runtime verification [9-13, 17]. The work in [9] proposes the concept of *observer* for designing self-checking distributed systems. The observer is an on-line monitor that checks the system behavior against an executable model of the system. In the paper, the observer concept is developed for formal models based on Petri nets and LAN based distributed systems built on a broadcast service. The approach is applied to a virtual ring MAC protocol, the Link and Transport layers in an industrial LAN, and the OSI layering in an open system architecture. Many works have used Real Time Logic (RTL) to monitor timing constraints of real-time tasks at runtime. For instance, in the work reported in [11], timing properties of tasks are modeled in RTL and an efficient runtime monitor is derived from the defined set of constraints. The objective is to detect timing violations as early as possible. The system is viewed as a sequence of event occurrences triggered by tasks and sent to the monitor. The latter detects timing violations by resolving constraints with the actual timestamps of events. The work reported in [12] defines an out-of-time supervisor for programs whose requirements specifications consist of nondeterministic SDL models. The system is viewed as a set of input and output signals that are processed by the supervisor an arbitrary amount of time after their occurrence (i.e., out-of-time). The approach is exemplified with a simple telecom application.

A recent work [18] proposes an interesting approach to translate a past time linear temporal logic formula into an executable algorithm based on dynamic programming.

By analyzing the execution trace of a running program, this algorithm can determine whether the program behavior conforms to its specification. The objective was to monitor the execution of Java programs as part of the NASA PathExplorer project.

The paper is structured as follows. Section 2 provides an overview of the proposed wrapping framework. Section 3 presents briefly some notions about temporal logic and describes the runtime checker as well as the process of translating temporal logic specifications into error confinement wrappers. In Section 4, a reflective approach is defined to provide the wrappers with the information they need so as to check the behavior of a real-time microkernel-based system. In Section 5, fault injection is used to characterize a real-time system encapsulated with a set of microkernel wrappers. Section 6 sketches the conclusion to the paper.

2. Wrapping Framework

The proposed framework is composed of four elements: i) the *reference*, which is the formal description of the system requirements, ii) the *wrapping*, which comprises the wrappers and the runtime checker, iii) the *observation*, which characterizes how the behavior of the system is perceived by the wrappers, and iv) the *Target Software Component* (TSC), which consists of the target component of the system that is to be wrapped. Fig. 1 provides an overall description of this framework. It is worth noting that while this framework is generic and can be used with any TSC, our work focuses on its application to real-time microkernel-based systems.

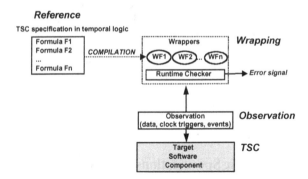

Fig. 1. Overall framework

The reference consists of the *specification* of a set of temporal and functional properties of the TSC that are to be verified at runtime (NB. the issue of proving the specification correct is out of the scope of the paper). This specification is given as a set of formulas (*F1, F2, ..., Fn* in the figure) expressed in future time linear temporal logic [19], which has proved to be a suitable logic for specifying properties of reactive and concurrent systems. The formulas of the specification are written in the form of assertions (i.e., *antecedent* ⇒ *consequent*, which means that the consequent is not checked until the antecedent is true). We have extended some temporal operators of standard temporal logic to manage clock ticks and asynchronous events explicitly. The so-extended temporal logic has been called CETL (see Section 3.1).

A salient feature of our approach is that the wrapping software is divided into two layers, consisting of the *runtime checker* and the *wrappers* (Section 3). The runtime checker is a sort of virtual machine in charge of executing the wrappers (*WF1, WF2, ..., WFn* in Fig. 1). Essentially, the runtime checker is an interpreter of temporal logic that raises an error signal whenever the consequent of an assertion is evaluated to false. Conversely, the wrappers are the executable version of the specification. Their role is to detect timing and value failures of the TSC operation at runtime. We have developed a compiler that automatically translates each assertion into a single wrapper in C language (e.g., *F1* into *WF1*, *F2* into *WF2*, etc.). The compilation process mechanizes the task of writing wrappers from specifications, so it helps make the wrapper code more robust.

The *observation* layer is in charge of providing the necessary TSC information to the runtime checker and the wrappers. Such an information may consist of messages [9], event occurrences [11], signals [12], or states [13]. Indeed, it depends very much on the formalism used to describe the TSC requirements. In our case, temporal logic is built from predicates that describe the internal state of the TSC at different instants of time signaled by clock triggers and event occurrences. Accordingly, the type of information we need to observe correspond to internal TSC data, clock triggers and asynchronous events, as indicated in Fig. 1. Note also that the observation layer makes the runtime checker and the wrappers independent from the particular implementation of the underlying TSC. In other words, when different implementations of the same TSC are to be tested (e.g., different implementations of the same POSIX interface), only the observation layer must be modified. We have used a *reflective* approach [20] to develop such an observation layer, which is described in Section 4.2 in the framework of real-time microkernels.

Finally, note that the wrapping code (wrappers and runtime checker) can run either in a separate machine or in the same target machine. In the first case, the wrapping code does not introduce any temporal overhead, and can also run asynchronously with the target component. In this paper, we deal with the second case, which is, in our opinion the most complex situation, given that the temporal overhead introduced by the wrapping code has to be considered. During the testing phase (see Section 5.1), we eliminate such an overhead by means of the evaluation tool used (MAFALDA-RT). In this way, the original execution times of the system are preserved, and it is possible to obtain precise evaluation measurements. During the operational phase, however, the wrapping overhead must be taken into account so as to check whether task deadlines are met (see Section 5.2).

3. From Temporal Logic Specifications to Error Confinement Wrappers

This section describes the way temporal logic specifications are translated into wrappers. First, we introduce the extensions done to standard future time linear temporal logic. Wrappers are executed on-line by the runtime checker. Accordingly, we then describe this important component of our approach. Finally, we illustrate with a simple example the process of translating an assertion into an error confinement wrapper.

3.1. The Temporal Logic CETL

Linear temporal logic is built on the notion of sequence of states, and does not take into account the type of event that originates a state change. As we are interested in differentiating several types of events triggering a state change, we have extended some of the standard operators of linear temporal logic (i.e., operators *next* ($\bigcirc$) and *sometime* ($\Diamond$)) in order to deal with two types of events: *clock triggers* and *asynchronous events*. Clock triggers (or *ticks*) correspond to the interrupts triggered by the clock of a real-time system (normally, every 10 ms.). Asynchronous events correspond to specific actions leading to state changes in an asynchronous way (for instance, system calls issued by real-time tasks or interrupts triggered by external events, signals or messages). The extended operators that we are considering are the following: $\mathbf{O}$ (next state triggered by a clock trigger), $\odot$ (next state triggered by an asynchronous event), $\Diamond[e]$ (some future state triggered by the asynchronous event called e), $\Diamond[e]^{<k}$ (some future state triggered by the asynchronous event called e before the occurrence of k clock triggers).

The linear temporal logic extended with these temporal operators is referred to in the paper as CETL, for *Clock and Event driven Temporal Logic*. Note that this type of extension is a common practice in the domain of runtime verification. For instance, in [18], past time linear temporal logic is extended with four new temporal operators (called *monitoring operators*), which are more intuitive and compact than the standard temporal operators. The authors call this extended logic *ptLTL*. In the domain of static verification, the work reported in [21] extends operator *until* of future time linear temporal logic to operator *during*, which is more appropriate to check temporal properties of fault tolerant circuits. The so-extended temporal logic is called *TL*.

Our main objective in this paper is to show how executable algorithms (i.e., the wrappers), that are derived from specifications can be efficiently run by a runtime checker, in order to check system properties on-line. Thus, we mainly focus on the practical issues of our approach. Due to space limitation, the complete definitions and semantics of CETL are not included in this paper; the interested reader can refer to [22]. Nevertheless, it is worth noting that an important property of CETL is that the extended operators are equivalent to the standard ones, as long as information concerning the type and the number of triggered states is available.

As any temporal logic, CETL is built from *temporal operators* (e.g., see the operators previously identified) and a *first order logic*. The first order logic is built from Boolean predicates combined with logical operators ($\wedge, \neg$, etc.), predicates which in turn are built from variables combined with relational ($<, \leq$, etc.) and arithmetic ($+, -$, etc.) operators. Moreover, in temporal logic a difference is usually made between *state variables* and *constant variables*. State variables refer to the current state of the target system, and hence their value can vary between states. However, the value of a constant variable is fixed all time, and there exists a (implicit) universal quantification over all the constant variables defined in a formula.

3.2. Runtime Checker

Essentially, the runtime checker supports the execution of the wrappers by interpreting the temporal logic CETL. Accordingly, the runtime checker provides an interface to the wrappers with services for managing the temporal operators (Table 1a), the predicates of the antecedent and the consequent of an assertion (Table 1b), and the constant variables (Table 1c). Note that, an error is signaled by the runtime checker, when a predicate of the consequent of an assertion is evaluated to false (service *ASSERT*).

The wrappers are executed concurrently by the runtime checker. Concurrency is made possible thanks to the functional decomposition of a wrapper into several tasks that are to be run at different instants. Internally, the runtime checker maintains a sort of *process context block* for each wrapper, which characterizes the state of the execution of the wrapper at different instants. Such an information is referred to as *wrapper context*, and corresponds to the values of the constant variables of a formula for such a particular execution of the wrapper. The related services are listed in Table 1c.

Services (C language)	Meaning
a) Management of temporal operators (F is a CETL formula, and e is an event identifier)	
NEXT (k, F, context);	$\bigcirc^k(F)$, F is true at the kth state
NEXT_CLOCK (k, F, context);	$\mathbf{O}^k(F)$, F is true at the kth state triggered by a tick
NEXT_EVENT (k, F, context);	$\circledcirc^k(F)$, F is true at the kth state triggered by an event
SOMETIME (e, F, context);	$\diamondsuit[e](F)$, F is true in a future state triggered by event e
K_SOMETIME (e,k,F,context);	$\diamondsuit[e]^{<k}(F)$, F is true in a future state triggered by event e, before the occurrence of k ticks
b) Management of predicates	
CONDITION (predicates);	*Evaluates predicates of the antecedent*
ASSERT (predicates);	*Evaluates predicates of the consequent and signals an error when false*
c) Management of the wrapper context	
NEW_CONTEXT ();	*Creates a context from a static memory pool*
CONTEXT_SET(value, context, index);	*Assigns parameter value to context[index]*
CONTEXT_GET (context, index)	*Returns the contents of context[index]*
DELETE_CONTEXT (context);	*Deletes a wrapper context*

Table 1. Services provided by the runtime checker

3.3. Error Confinement Wrappers

The translation of a CETL assertion into an algorithm is based on a simple *rewriting* process. Indeed, the original CETL assertion is just rewritten into an algorithm that can be effectively executed by the runtime checker. This rewriting process is carried out by a compiler, which automatically translates a CETL assertion into its corresponding wrapper. The compiler has been developed using PCCTS, a C version of ANTRL [23]. Instead of giving the long and tedious list of the rewriting rules used by the compiler, we illustrate the rewriting process by means of a simple example. Our objective here is that the reader has a general but precise idea of how the global rewriting process works.

Table 2 shows the rewriting of a CETL assertion into an error confinement wrapper. Let us consider assertion AS defined in Table 2a. The antecedent of assertion AS is represented by the term $\diamondsuit[e](a=t \wedge a=u)$, while its consequent corresponds to $\circledcirc(a<u \wedge \mathbf{O}^2(a>u))$. Variable a is a constant integer number. Note that this way of specifying constant variables is a standard notation in temporal logic.

Assertion AS verifies that, it is always true ($\square$) that, whenever event e occurs and system variable t is equal to system variable u, at the next occurrence of an asynchronous event, the old value of t (represented by variable a) is lower than u, and two clock triggers later, it is higher than u. The pseudo algorithm in Table 2b implements assertion AS by using runtime checker services. Note that symbol $\Rightarrow$ does not correspond to the standard logical implication, but it means that the consequent of an assertion is not checked until the antecedent is true. For didactic reasons, we provide an equivalent pseudo algorithm in Table 2c that illustrates the behavior of the runtime checker services when executing algorithm in Table 2b. The rewriting process works globally as follows. In the pseudo algorithm shown in Table 2b, each temporal operator of assertion AS is substituted by a call to a temporal operator service of the runtime checker (*SOMETIME, NEXT_EVENT, NEXT_CLOCK*); the actual values of the variables are obtained by executing a *get_* instruction (*get_t, get_u*); predicates of the antecedent are assessed by service *CONDITION*, while those of the consequent are evaluated by service *ASSERT*. Note the particular case of variable a, which is assigned the value of variable t and is never modified in the sequel.

a) Assertion AS
$\forall a \in Z \, \square(\lozenge[e](a = t \wedge a = u) \Rightarrow \circledcirc(a < u \wedge O^2(a > u)))$

b) Pseudo algorithm with runtime checker services	c) Plain pseudo algorithm equivalent to assertion AS of a)

```
Function AS                          Function AS
int a, u;                            int a, u;
loop                                 loop
    /* Antecedent */                     /* Antecedent */
    SOMETIME (e);                         wait_event (e);
    a = get_t ();                         a = get_t ();
    t = get_t ();                         t = get_t ();
    CONDITION (a == t);                   if (a == t)
    u = get_u ();                            u = get_u ();
    CONDITION (a == u);                      if (a == u)
    /* Consequent */                             /* Consequent */
    NEXT_EVENT (1);                              wait_event (any);
    u = get_u ();                                u = get_u ();
    ASSERT ⌐(a < u);                             if not ⌐(a < u)
    NEXT_CLOCK (2);                                  signal_error ()
    u = get_u ();                                else
    ASSERT ⌐(a > u);                                 wait_clock_triggers (2);
end loop                                             u = get_u ⌐();
                                                     if not ⌐(a > u)
                                                        signal_error ()
                                                     end if
                                                 end if
                                         end if
                                     end if
                                 end loop
```

d) Error confinement wrapper (C language)

```
int start () {return SOMETIME (e, ANT, null) ;}
   /* Antecedent */
   int ANT (Context* context) {
   int a = get_t ();
   int t = get_t ();
   CONDITION (a == t);
   int u = get_u ();
   CONDITION (a == u);
   context = NEW_CONTEXT ();
   CONTEXT_SET (a, context, 1);
   return NEXT_EVENT (1, CON_1, context);
   }
   /* Consequent */
int CON_1 (Context* context) {
   int a = CONTEXT_GET (context, 1);      /* Retrieve data from the context */
   int u = get_u (⌐);                              /* Obtain TSC data */
   ASSERT (a < u);                      /* Request the evaluation of predicates */
   return NEXT_CLOCK (2, CON_2, context);    /*Set the next temporal operator*/
   }
int CON_2 (Context* context) {
   int a = CONTEXT_GET (context, 1);
   int u = get_u (⌐);
   ASSERT (a >⌐u);
   DELETE_CONTEXT ();
}
```

Table 2. From a CETL assertion to a wrapper

To handle concurrent evaluations of wrappers at runtime (in a similar way to the concurrent execution of real-time tasks), algorithm in Table 2b must be divided into several routines, one for each temporal operator defined in assertion AS. The resulting algorithm is provided in Table 2d, and corresponds to the error confinement wrapper for assertion AS. Routine *ANT* represents the antecedent, routines *CON_1* and *CON_2* represent the consequent, plus the initialization function *start*). In each routine, a group of predicates is to be checked together against the state of the system at a given instant. Note that the wrapper in Table 2d introduces the notion of wrapper context. The wrapper context is composed of the set of constant variables defined by a formula. Thus, the wrapper context for assertion AS is composed of constant variable *a*. The wrapper context is retrieved at the beginning of each routine (e.g., see routines

CON_1 and *CON_2*), and extended (when applicable) at the end of the routine. The exception to this is the first routine of the antecedent (routine *ANT*), where the wrapper context is not retrieved but created for the first time. The last routine of the consequent (routine *CON_2*) deletes the context. Note that the context can be deleted before by the runtime checker, if a predicate is evaluated to false.

The runtime checker executes a wrapper according to the algorithm shown in Fig. 2. For example, a run of routine *CON_1* in Table 2d is as follows:

- Upon receipt of any event, routine *CON_1* executes and retrieves the wrapper context, composed of variable *a* (*int a = CONTEXT_GET (context, 1)*).
- The value for variable *u* is obtained from the TSC (*int u = get_u ()*).
- Predicate *a < u* is evaluated (*ASSERT (a < u)*).
- Finally, the subsequent temporal operator is set (*NEXT_CLOCK (2, CON_2, context)*).

---

1. *Upon receipt of either a clock trigger or an event occurrence, check whether a wrapper is waiting for it.*
2. *If not, return control to the TSC.*
3. *If yes, for each wrapper:*
   3.1. *Let the wrapper retrieve the context (if applicable).*
   3.2. *Let the wrapper obtain the data needed for the assessment of the predicates from the TSC.*
   3.3. *Evaluate the predicates.*
      3.3.1. *If a predicate part of the antecedent is false, finish the wrapper instance (no error signal is raised).*
      3.3.2. *If a predicate part of the consequent is false, raise an error signal and finish the wrapper instance.*
   3.4. *Let the wrapper extend the context (or create or destroy it when applicable).*
   3.5. *Set up the subsequent temporal operator (if applicable).*
4. *Return control to the TSC.*

Fig. 2. Execution steps carried out by the runtime checker

4. Wrapping Real-Time Microkernel-Based Systems

A microkernel is an essential component of a system responsible for providing basic services to upper layers, such as scheduling, synchronization, process management or time management. This section describes how microkernel services specified in CETL can be verified *in practice* by means of error confinement wrappers. A simple example illustrates all the steps described in Fig. 1 when the TSC is a real-time microkernel. We first introduce a simple kernel specification and its corresponding error confinement wrapper. Then, we describe the approach used to observe the internal state of the microkernel. Finally, we exemplify how wrappers execute with the help of the runtime checker.

4.1. Compiling kernel Specifications into Wrappers: Example

Let consider a typical kernel service, namely *Create* (Fig. 3). Fig. 3a gives the CETL specification for the creation of higher priority tasks by means of service *Create*. A comprehensive temporal logic specification of real-time microkernels can be found in [14]. Fig. 3b provides the wrapper generated by the CETL compiler for assertion *Create*. The interpretation of assertion *Create* is as follows. When the running task, represented by *tha*, requests the creation of a higher priority task *thb*, the kernel routine corresponding to service *Create* is then executed (indicated by event ↑*Create*). Some time later, the kernel inserts the newly created task *thb* into the ready queue (event ↑*signal*). As the child task has a higher priority than its parent, the latter is preempted after a context switch operation (event ↓*context_switch*). As a result, child task *thb* is elected to run (predicate *running = thb*), while parent task *tha* is inserted back into the ready queue (predicate *tha ∈ ready (prio(tha))*).

$\forall tha, thb \in Z \; \square(\lozenge[\uparrow Create] \; (created\_th = thb \wedge running = tha \wedge prio(thb) > prio(tha)$
$\wedge \lozenge[\uparrow signal] \; (signaled\_th = thb \wedge running = tha))$
$\Rightarrow \circledcirc(event = \downarrow context\_switch \wedge running = thb \wedge tha \in ready \, (prio(tha))))$

a) Assertion Create

```
int start () {
        return SOMETIME (ev_begin_Create, ANT_1, null);
}
int ANT_1 (Context* context) {
        int created_th = get_created_th ();
        int thb = get_created_th ();
        CONDITION (created_th == thb);
        int running = get_running ();
        int tha = get_running ();
        CONDITION (running == tha);
        CONDITION (prio(thb) > prio(tha));
        context = NEW_CONTEXT ();
        CONTEXT_SET (thb, context, 1);
        CONTEXT_SET (tha, context, 2);
        return SOMETIME (ev_begin_signal, ANT_2, context);
}
int ANT_2 (Context* context) {
        int thb = CONTEXT_GET (context, 1);
        int tha = CONTEXT_GET (context, 2);
        int signaled_th = get_signaled_th ();
        CONDITION (signaled_th == thb);
        int running = get_running ();
        CONDITION (running == tha);
        return NEXT_EVENT (1, CON, context);
}
int CON (Context* context) {
        int thb = CONTEXT_GET (context, 1);
        int tha = CONTEXT_GET (context, 2);
        int event = get_event ();
        ASSERT (event == ev_end_context_switch);
        int running = get_running ();
        ASSERT (running == thb);
        ASSERT (isInQueue (tha, ready (prio(tha))));
}
```

b) Wrapper Create

Fig. 3. Assertion *Create* and its associated wrapper

4.2. Using Reflection to observe the Target System

We describe now how the internal state of a microkernel can be observed using *reflection* [20]. In a reflective approach, the target system delivers events to the wrappers (*reification*) and the wrappers get the necessary information from the target system (*introspection*). In addition, reflection also allows the behavior of the target system to be controlled using mechanisms based on the concept of *intercession*. These notions are refined in the next paragraphs.

In a reflective system [24, 25], a clear distinction is made between the so-called *base-level*, running the target system, and the *metalevel*, responsible for controlling and updating the behavior of the target system. Information is provided from the base-level to the metalevel, that becomes *metalevel data* or *metainformation*. Any change in the metainformation is reflected to the base-level. The distinction made between the base-level and the metalevel provides a clear separation of concerns between the functional aspects handled at the base-level and the non-functional aspects (here, error detection and error confinement) handled at the metalevel.

Fig. 4 illustrates the various layers, components and mechanisms that make up the reflective framework. This framework complies with and extends the principles introduced in [8]. Here, the base-level is the real-time microkernel, while the metalevel (the *metakernel)* is composed of both the wrappers and the runtime checker. The association of both layers leads to the notion of *reflective real-time microkernel.*

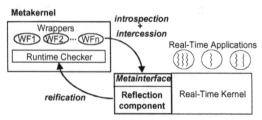

Fig. 4. Reflective framework

The kernel provides the necessary observation through the so-called *reflection component*, which is a special component added to the target microkernel. The reflection component is responsible for the management of the intercepted events (i.e., reification), the observation of internal items (i.e., introspection), and the required actions down into the real-time kernel (i.e., intercession). The reified events are delivered as *upcalls* to the metakernel, whereas introspection and intercession are provided by the reflection component through the so-called *metainterface*. The metainterface is defined as a set of services providing access to the necessary information from and actions into the real-time kernel. It is worth noting, however, that the metainterface we define in this section only considers introspection services.

Reification is carried out using *upcalls*, a jump instruction inserted into the kernel that diverts the execution flow from the kernel to the metakernel, thus not triggering any context switch. For example, assertion *Create* defines event ↑*Create*, which corresponds to the start of the kernel service that carries out the execution of system call *Create*. Accordingly, an upcall is inserted at the beginning of the *Create* routine of the kernel, which takes as an input parameter the identifier of event ↑*Create*. When the kernel enters routine `service_create`, the upcall is executed and diverts execution to the runtime checker. Events ↑*signal* and↓*context_switch* of assertion *Create* are reified in a similar way — see hereafter (left).

```
service_create (...) {            clock_handler (...) {
        upcall (ev_begin_create);         upcall (clock_trigger);
    ...                               ...
}                                 }
```

Clock triggers can also be reified by inserting an upcall at the beginning of the `clock handler` routine of the kernel as shown above (right).

On the other hand, introspection consists in obtaining the necessary information through the metainterface. The definition of the metainterface is directly derived from the kernel specification. Indeed, the specification points out the necessary events, data structures and functions of the kernel that must be observed and controlled. To illustrate this point, Table 3 lists the set of services of the metainterface corresponding to assertion *Create*.

Temporal logic	Metainterface		
created_th	int	`get_created_th`	`()`
running	int	`get_running`	`()`
signaled_th	int	`get_signaled_th`	`()`
event	int	`get_event_id`	`()`
prio(th)	int	`prio`	`(int th)`
ready (level)	int	`ready`	`(int level)`
th ∈ queue	int	`isInQueue`	`(int th, int queue)`

Table 3. Metainterface necessary to wrapper *Create*

Porting the kernel wrappers to other systems depends on the ability of supplying the microkernel with the adequate reflection component. Indeed, the reflection component makes both the wrappers and the runtime checker independent from the underlying kernel. The specification of the reflection component, comprising both the metainterface and the identified upcalls, remains the same whenever the same set of assertions is used. For instance, the reflection component for assertion *Create* is fully defined by services in Table 3 plus the associated upcalls. Therefore, to port wrapper *Create* to another system it is only necessary to recompile the runtime checker on the new system, as long as the target kernel provides the corresponding reflection component.

4.3. Executing the Error Confinement Wrappers

This section illustrates the execution of error confinement wrappers and the checks they perform on the target system. The target system is represented in Fig. 5 by a set of real-time tasks executing concurrently and requesting kernel service *Create*. Fig. 5a represents the original execution of such tasks together with the events triggered into the microkernel, while Fig. 5b represents the same set of tasks extended with the runtime checker, which executes wrapper *Create*. The horizontal axis represents the pass of time. The vertical axis represents real-time tasks with respect to their priority (τ_1 has higher priority than τ_2, and so on). A white box represents the execution of a task in user mode, while a pattern box represents its execution in kernel mode. A task that enters ready state is represented by a circle on the bottom left corner of the box; a circle on the top right corner means that the task leaves the ready state (e.g., task τ_3 is ready to run during the whole interval represented in Fig. 5a).

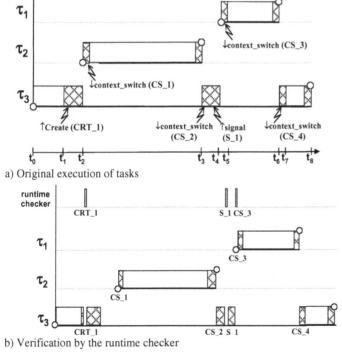

a) Original execution of tasks

b) Verification by the runtime checker

Fig. 5. Execution of wrapper *Create* by the runtime checker

t_0	Task τ_3 is running in user mode.
t_1	τ_3 requests the creation of a higher priority task (τ_1) by means of system call *Create*. Event CRT_1 is triggered when task τ_3 enters service *Create* in kernel mode.
t_2	A higher priority task τ_2 preempts tasks τ_3. Task τ_2 obtains the processor after a context switch (event CS_1).
t_2-t_3	Task τ_2 executes.
t_3	Task τ_2 suspends and task τ_3 is given the processor after a context switch (event CS_2). Task τ_3 continues execution of service *Create* in kernel mode.
t_4	Creation of task τ_1 is completed (event S_1).
t_5	Because priority of τ_1 is higher than priority of τ_3, the latter is preempted by its child, which obtains the processor after a context switch (event CS_3).
t_5-t_6	Child task executes.
t_6	Child task ends execution. Its parent obtains the processor after a context switch (event CS_4).
t_7	Task τ_3 finishes executing service *Create* in kernel mode, and continues execution in user mode.
t_8	Task τ_3 ends execution.

Table 4. Original execution of tasks

The detailed behavior of the original set of tasks represented in Fig. 5a is described in Table 4. Wrapper *Create* is executed by the runtime checker during the intervals represented in Fig. 5b, labeled by the kernel event at the origin of the activation of the runtime checker. Remember that the runtime checker is a sort of virtual machine in charge of executing wrappers, which is activated after the occurrence of an event triggered within the target system. Note also that the runtime checker does not preempt, but simply interrupts, the task executing at the moment of its activation, so no context switch is triggered.

In other words, the runtime checker executes at the highest priority on behalf of the running task. In consequence, checks carried out by the wrappers by means of the runtime checker do not modify the original scheduling of tasks, as shown in Fig. 5b. However, the time needed for the wrappers to execute have to be taken into account during the operational phase of the system, in order to check that task deadlines are not violated because of the additional temporal overhead introduced by the wrappers (see Section 5.2).

Each activation of the runtime checker leads thus to the execution of one or several wrappers concurrently. The steps followed by the runtime checker to execute wrapper *Create*, as well as the checks performed by this wrapper, are detailed in Table 5.

Events		Runtime checker actions				
Activated	Expected	Wrapper	Routine	Cxt	Expressions checked by services CONDITION and ASSERT	Result
...	CRT					
CRT_1	CRT	Create	ANT_1		created_th == τ1	TRUE
					running == τ3	TRUE
					prio(τ1) > prio(τ3)	TRUE
CS_1	S, CRT					
CS_2	S, CRT					
S_1	S, CRT	Create	ANT_2	c1	signaled_th == τ1	TRUE
					running == τ3	TRUE
CS_3	Any	Create	CON	c1	event == CS	TRUE
					running == τ1	TRUE
					isInQueue (τ3, ready (prio(τ3)))	TRUE
CS_4	CRT					
...	CRT					

Table 5. Event occurrences and actions carried out by the runtime checker to verify *Create*

Column *Activated event* contains the various events triggered during the execution of the system, while column *Expected event* corresponds to the events waited for by the runtime checker at a given moment. Columns *Wrapper*, *Routine* and *Ctx* refer respectively to the name of the wrapper activated, to the wrapper routine executed, and to the wrapper context used. Column *Expressions checked* reports the verifications performed by the wrappers by means of services *CONDITION* and *ASSERT* of the runtime checker. Note that constant variables *tha* and *thb* have been substituted by the task identifier they represent (τ_1, τ_2, etc.), depending on the information contained into the corresponding wrapper context.

– Initially, given that *Create* is the only wrapper installed, the single event expected by the runtime checker is ↑*Create* (CRT).
– At the occurrence of event CRT_1, routine ANT_1 of wrapper *Create* is executed. As the child task has higher priority than its parent, event ↑*signal* (S) is programmed. Context c1 is then allocated with information *tha* = τ_3 and *thb* = τ_1. Next, the runtime checker suspends and waits for events ↑*Create* and ↑*signal*.
– Events CS_1 and CS_2 are ignored since they are not expected.
– Event S_1 triggers routine ANT_2 of wrapper *Create* under wrapper context c1. The antecedent of *Create* is then evaluated to true, since the task signaled during the execution of τ_3 is indeed τ_1. The runtime checker waits then for any event.
– At the occurrence of the next event (CS_3), the consequent of *Create* is evaluated under context c1. It is verified that: the event triggered is a context switch, the running task is τ_1, and task τ_3 has been preempted into the ready queue. Since this expression evaluates to true, assertion *Create* succeeds and no error is thus signaled.
– Finally, event CS_4 is ignored and the running checker waits for event ↑*Create*.

5. Assessment by Fault Injection

We characterize the failure coverage and the performance of wrappers in a real-time system consisting of the *Chorus* microkernel [15] and the *mine drainage control application* [16]. The Chorus kernel was protected by a set of error confinement wrappers derived from an extended kernel specification (see [14]). Note that we first translated these specifications into CETL before compiling them into wrappers. In total, 31 wrappers were used, corresponding to 18 scheduling assertions, 2 timer assertions and 11 synchronization assertions.

The mine drainage control application [16] was used by a number of authors (e.g., [26, 27]). Table 6 shows the main attributes of the tasks of this application. The objective is to pump to the surface mine water collected in a sump at the bottom of the shaft. The main safety requirement is that the pump should not be operated when the level of methane gas in the mine reaches a high value to avoid an explosion. The level of methane is monitored by task CH4 Sensor. Other environment parameters monitored are the level of carbon monoxide (task CO Sensor) and the flow of air in the mine (task Air-Flow Sensor). The flow of water in the pipes of the pump is checked by task Water-Flow Sensor, whereas the water levels in the sump are detected by task Hlw Handler.

Task	Type	Deadline (ms)	Period (ms)	Priority
CH4 Sensor	Periodic	30	80	10
CO Sensor	Periodic	60	100	8
Air-Flow Sensor	Periodic	100	100	7
Water-Flow Sensor	Periodic	40	1000	9
Hlw Handler	Sporadic	200	6000	6

Table 6. Attributes of tasks

MAFALDA-RT [28, 29] was used to assess the error detection coverage and the performance of the kernel wrappers. The tool has been developed to encompass the assessment by fault injection of both hard and soft real-time systems. It provides a facility to eliminate time intrusiveness by controlling the hardware clock of the target system. Such a facility was used to eliminate the temporal overhead introduced both by the tool itself and by the error confinement wrappers. Therefore, tasks were not aware neither of the execution of tool nor of the wrappers from a temporal viewpoint. Note that we are using the wrappers in a testbed system, not in the final system; we are thus interested in evaluating wrapper coverage and wrapper performance without increasing the original execution time of the tasks.

5.1. Error detection Coverage

Table 7 briefly describes the three different fault injection campaigns carried out with and without wrappers. MAFALDA-RT selects randomly the injection target (bits, parameters, etc.) and checks whether the corrupted element is accessed during the experiment, i.e., whether the fault is activated (only activated faults are considered).

↓ Target components Injected fauts →	Bit-flip	Specific (Table 8)
Priority Ceiling Protocol (PCP)	pPCP (parameters of PCP system calls)	—
Timers (TIM)	mTIM (code segment of TIM)	sTIM

Table 7. Target components and types of injected faults for the three campaigns carried out

The targets of the injected faults were the Priority Ceiling Protocol component (PCP) and the timers component (TIM) of the microkernel. Faults based on bit-flips were uniformly injected over the memory image of the PCP parameters stack (campaign pPCP) and of the timers code segment (campaign mTIM). The specific faults considered in campaign sTIM are specified in Table 8.

#1	Random corruption by single bit-flip of the expiration time of a randomly selected sporadic timer.
#2	Avoiding once the insertion of a randomly selected sporadic timer into the timeout queue.
#3	Avoiding once the deletion of a randomly selected timer from the timeout queue.
#4	Random corruption by single bit-flip of the expiration time of a randomly selected periodic timer.
#5	Avoiding once the insertion of a randomly selected periodic timer into the timeout queue.
#6	Avoiding once the expiration of a randomly selected timer.

Table 8. Specific high-level faults injected in sTIM (only one fault injected by experiment)

Fig. 6 reports both the *first* fault manifestations observed for the standard kernel (campaigns pPCP, mTIM, sTIM), and the corresponding wrapper detection coverage observed for the wrapped version of the kernel (campaigns wrap-pPCP, wrap-mTIM, wrap-sTIM). Few errors impaired the system when the parameters of the synchronization system calls were corrupted (campaign pPCP), because of the high ratio of correct experiments observed (79.7%). This is mostly due to the corruption of unused bits within parameters (random selection by the fault injection tool). Conversely, the consistency checks implemented within the API (represented by class *error status*) detected most errors (19.4%). Few errors (0.9%) could thus propagate and lead to the failure of the application (classes *deadline missed, incorrect results, application hang* and *system hang*). In the wrapped version of the kernel (campaign wrap-pPCP), the wrappers detected the same class of errors previously detected by means of an error status with a shorter latency. All of them were related to the corruption of a parameter handling a critical section identifier. Obviously, wrappers cannot improve here error detection coverage, since it was already good in the standard kernel.

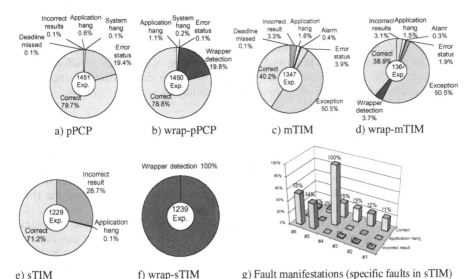

a) pPCP

b) wrap-pPCP

c) mTIM

d) wrap-mTIM

e) sTIM

f) wrap-sTIM

g) Fault manifestations (specific faults in sTIM)

- The most critical situation occurs when an error propagates to the application, making it fail either in the time or in the value domain. Timing failures are represented by classes *Deadline missed*, *Application hang* and *System hang*, while value failures are represented by class *Incorrect result*.
- The error detection mechanisms of the microkernel are represented by classes *Alarm*, *Error status* and *Exception*.
- Class *Wrapper detection* represents timing and value errors detected by the wrappers.
- Class *Correct* represents the case when both the time production and the value of the application results are correct.

Fig. 6. *First* fault manifestations and wrapper detection coverage

However, if wrappers are to be used as a support to recovery actions, a wrapper profile as the one represented in Fig. 6b can result interesting.

When the code segment of the timers component was subjected to injection (campaign mTIM), more failures occurred (5.4%) than in campaign pPCP. Still, the majority of the errors were detected by means of an exception (50.5%). Indeed, the kind of errors induced by bit-flips affecting code segment cells corresponds very frequently to low-level errors readily detectable by exceptions (e.g., incorrect operation codes, segmentation faults, etc.). This is the main reason why the wrappers were little activated (3.7%) in campaign wrap-mTIM (also because only first detections are reported). Indeed, the used wrappers have been developed from a high level specification (see [14]), and the type of problems they detect are accordingly also complex. Since most bit-flips were intercepted by exceptions, they could not propagate and originate complex errors.

For that reason, we carried out a new fault injection campaign, sTIM, where the injected faults corresponded to the specific set of high level errors specified in Table 8. As shown by Fig. 6e, 28.7% of the injections led the application to issue incorrect results. Here, the injected faults are out of reach of the exception mechanism. Fig. 6g indicates that 97% of the failures were caused by fault types #5 and #6. Indeed, both of them prevented a periodic task, required for the correct computation of results, from being released. Interestingly, the wrappers avoided all the failures, but also caught all errors that did not previously lead to any observable abnormal situation (Fig. 6f).

In summary, we observed that the error detection mechanisms embedded in the standard kernel provided a high detection coverage with regard to errors caused by bit-flips in system call parameters and in code segment cells. It was thus expected that the improvement provided by error confinement wrappers be either redundant (as in campaign wrap-pPCP) or poor (as in campaign wrap-mTIM). However, using a different fault model, the standard kernel was unable to avoid the propagation of errors to upper layers that provoked an important rate of application failures. The coverage of the error confinement wrappers was then demonstrated, since they systematically prevented the application from misbehaving.

5.2. Worst Case Performance Measurements

Measuring the execution time of the wrappers is of primary importance to determine the feasibility of the wrappers with respect to the timing requirements of the real-time application. During the fault injection experiments carried out with MAFALDA-RT, the execution time of the wrappers could be eliminated (see Section 5.1 and [28]). However, when wrappers are to be integrated into the final system, their execution times must be explicitly taken into account.

Each release of the runtime checker leads to the concurrent execution of several instances of the wrappers. The maximum number of such wrapper instances running concurrently at any time was 9, even though a peak of 47 wrapper instances ready to run was observed. Table 9 shows the worst case overhead (OVH) and the worst case number of releases (REL) of the runtime checker observed in a task instance (i.e., interval between two consecutive releases of a task). The target system used was based on a Pentium running at 75Mhz.

Task	OVH (ms)	REL	OVH/REL
CH4 Sensor	18.119	32	0.566
CO Sensor	6.909	15	0.461
Air-Flow Sensor	6.884	15	0.459
Water-Flow Sensor	6.814	15	0.445
Hlw Handler	13.327	28	0.476

Table 9. Overhead (OVH), releases (REL) and ratio (OVH/REL)

The overhead depends on the number of releases of the runtime checker, i.e., the higher the number of runtime checker releases, the higher the overhead. Conversely, the higher the number of wrapped kernel services requested by a task, the higher the number of releases of the runtime checker. For instance, task CH4 Sensor presents the maximum overhead because it involves more wrapped operations than the other tasks. This means that the runtime checker overhead does not depend on the duration of a task, but rather on its behavior profile, i.e., the type and number of services the task requests to the kernel. For instance, the total overhead introduced by the runtime checker would be the same for two tasks with different computation times but with the same type and number of wrapped services requested. Hence, the overhead of the runtime checker is independent from the execution time of the tasks. This is supported by the low variation of ratio OVH/REL (Table 9). This indicates that a single release of the runtime checker always incurs a similar overhead, no matter the task on behalf of which it is executed. As a result, since the worst case execution times of the wrappers and the runtime checker can be known a priori (e.g., using static code analysis), the exact overhead induced by a given wrapped task can be determined beforehand by analyzing its behavior profile. The overhead can thus be tuned either by selecting the minimum set of wrappers that minimize the ratio between the overhead and the error detection coverage, or by deciding *on-the-fly*, whether enough spare time is available in the system to wrap a service requested by a task. The latter approach is similar to the way aperiodic servers accept or reject the execution of aperiodic tasks [30].

6. Conclusion

This paper proposed a methodology, a framework and supporting tools (e.g., fault injector, temporal logic compiler, etc.) for wrapping real-time systems from temporal logic specifications. System specifications expressed in linear temporal logic are automatically translated by a compiler into error confinement wrappers. Temporal logic provides a consistent way (few operators and state variables in the predicates) for describing the specifications of traditional executive functions. The case study illustrated this feature by considering complex functions, such as scheduling of real-time tasks.

A relevant attribute of our approach is that the wrappers are executed concurrently by a runtime checker, a sort of virtual machine that interprets temporal logic. The reflective approach provides the wrappers with the information they need to check the system behavior at runtime. The reflective software layer makes both the wrappers and the runtime checker independent from the underlying system: only this layer must be modified when different implementations of the same system are to be checked (e.g., different implementations of the same POSIX interface).

This methodology was applied to the wrapping of real-time microkernel-based systems. The behavior of the wrappers and the runtime checker was illustrated with a significant example, based on the verification of a well-known microkernel service (task creation and scheduling). It showed that the execution of the wrappers does not alter the original scheduling of the real-time tasks running on the target system.

The MAFALDA-RT tool was used to evaluate by fault injection (both bit flips and specific faults) a real-time system composed of the Chorus microkernel and a mine drainage control application. In that case, the error detection mechanisms embedded in the original kernel provided already good detection coverage. Accordingly, the wrappers used to protect the kernel could not significantly improve such coverage. However, when a different fault model based on high-level faults was used, most generated errors propagated and provoked the failure of the application. Such failures were systematically avoided by the wrappers. In addition, the performance measures reported showed that the overhead of the wrappers is bounded and can be tuned (e.g., by selecting the minimum set of wrappers minimizing the rate overhead–coverage, or by deciding *on-the-fly* whether enough time is available to execute a wrapper).

It is worth noting that the applicability of the proposed wrapping approach goes beyond real-time kernel functions, and can be of high benefit for various software components and applications. Indeed, it would also benefit embedded real-time systems that cannot accommodate massive redundancy due to weight and/or power constraints.

As a future work, we are currently extending the wrappers with error recovery mechanisms for real-time microkernel-based systems. The objective is not only to detect errors, but also to be able to recover from errors in a bounded time.

Acknowledgement. Manuel Rodríguez has been supported by THALES. The work reported in this paper was partially carried out in the framework of LIS[1] and is currently partially financed by the DSoS project (IST-1999-11585). Our thanks go to Prof. Scott Hazelhurst (Wits University, Joannesburgh, South Africa) for his useful insights on the temporal logic used in this work. The constructive comments made by the anonymous reviewers and by Prof. András Pataricza (Budapest University of Technology and Economics, Hungary) are gratefully acknowledged.

---

[1] Located at LAAS, the Laboratory for Dependability Engineering (LIS) was a Cooperative Laboratory between five industrial companies (Airbus France, Astrium, Électricité de France, Technicatome, THALES) and LAAS-CNRS.

References

[1] W. R. Cheswick and S. M. Bellovin, *Firewalls and Internet Security*, Addison-Wesley, 1994.

[2] J. Voas, K. Miller, *Interface Robustness for COTS-Based Systems*, Digest no. 97/013, Colloquium on COTS and Safety Critical Systems, IEE, Computing and Control Division, pp. 7/1-7/12, 1997.

[3] J. M. Voas, "Certifying Off-the-Shelf Software Components", *Computer*, pp. 53-59, 1998.

[4] A. K. Ghosh, M. Schmid, F. Hill, "Wrapping Windows NT Software for Robustness", in *Proc. 29th Int. Symp. on Fault-Tolerant Computing*, Madison, WI, USA, pp. 344-347, 1999.

[5] A. Mahmood, D. M. Andrews, E. J. McCluskey, "Executable Assertions and Flight Software", in *Proc. 6th Digital Avionics Systems Conf.*, Baltimore, MD, USA, pp. 346-351, 1984.

[6] C. Rabéjac, J.-P. Blanquart, J.-P. Queille, "Executable Assertions and Timed Traces for On-Line Software Error Detection", in *Proc. 26th Int. Symp. on Fault-Tolerant Computing*, Sendai, Japan, pp. 138-147, 1996.

[7] M. Hiller, "Executable Assertions for Detecting Data Errors in Embedded Control Systems", in *Proc. Int. Conf. on Dependable Systems and Networks*, New York, NY, USA, pp. 24-33, 2000.

[8] F. Salles, M. Rodríguez, J.-C. Fabre, J. Arlat, "Metakernels and Fault Containment Wrappers", in *Proc. 29th Int. Symp. on Fault-Tolerant Computing Systems*, Madison, WI, USA, pp. 22-29, 1999.

[9] M. Diaz, G. Juanole, J.-P. Courtiat, "Observer — A Concept for Formal On-Line Validation of Distributed Systems", *IEEE Trans. on Software Engineering*, vol. 20, no. 12, pp. 900-913, 1994.

[10] F. Jahanian, R. Rajkumar, S. Raju, "Runtime Monitoring of Timing Constraints in Distributed Real-Time Systems", *Real-Time Systems*, vol. 7, no. 3, pp. 247-274, 1994.

[11] A. K. Mok, G. Liu, "Efficient Run-Time Monitoring of Timing Constraints", in *Proc. 3rd Real-Time Technology and Applications Symp.*, Montreal, Canada, pp. 252-262, 1997.

[12] T. Savor, R. E. Seviora, "An Approach to Automatic Detection of Software Failures in Real-Time Systems", *Ibid.*, pp. 136-146, 1997.

[13] Enforceable Security Policies, TR98-1664, Dept. Comp. Science, Cornell Univ., Ithaca, NY (USA), 1998.

[14] M. Rodríguez, J.-C. Fabre, J. Arlat, "Formal Specification for Building Robust Real-time Microkernels", in *Proc. 21st Real-Time Systems Symp*, Orlando, FL, USA, pp. 119-128, 2000.

[15] Chorus Systems, "CHORUS/ClassiX release 3 - Technical Overview", TR CS/TR-96-119.12, Chorus Systems, 1997 (www.sun.com/chorusos).

[16] A. Burns, A. J. Wellings, *Real-time Systems and their Programming Languages*, Addison-Wesley, 1997.

[17] I. Majzik, J. Jávorszky, A. Pataricza E. Selényi, "Concurrent Error Detection of Program Execution Based on Statechart Specification", in *Proc. 10th European Workshop on Dependable Computing*, Vienna, Austria, pp. 181-185, 1999.

[18] K. Havelund, G. Rosu, "Synthesizing Monitors for Safety Properties", in *Proc. Int. Conf. on Tools and Algorithms for Construction and Analysis of Systems*, Grenoble, France, pp. 342-256, 2002.

[19] B. C. Moszkowski, *Executing Temporal Logic Programs*, Cambrige University Press, 1987.

[20] P. Maes, "Concepts and Experiments in Computational Reflection", in *Proc. Conf. on Object-Oriented Programming, Systems and Aplications*, Orlando, FL (USA), pp. 147-155, 1987.

[21] S. Hazelhurst, J. Arlat, "Specifying and Verifying Fault Tolerant Hardware", in *Proc. Designing Correct Circuits*, Grenoble, France, 2002.

[22] M. Rodríguez Moreno, "Wrapping Technology for the Dependability of Real-Time Systems", Doctoral Dissertation, National Polytechnic Institute, Toulouse, France, July 2002. (in French).

[23] ANTLR, *ANTLR Complete Language Translation Solutions*, http://www.antlr.org.

[24] G. Kiczales, J. D. Rivières, D. G. Bobrow, *The Art of the Metaobject Protocol*, MIT Press, 1991.

[25] J.-C. Fabre, T. Pérennou, "A Metaobject Architecture for Fault Tolerant Distributed Systems: The FRIENDS Approach", *IEEE Trans. on Computers*, pp. 78-95, 1998.

[26] A. Burns, A. M. Lister, "A Framework for Building Dependable Systems", *The Computer Journal*, vol. 34, no. 2, pp. 173-181, 1991.

[27] M. Joseph, *Real-Time Systems: Specification, Verification and Analysis*, Prentice-Hall, 1996.

[28] M. Rodríguez, A. Albinet, J. Arlat, "MAFALDA-RT: A Tool for Dependability Assessment of Real-Time in *Proc. Int. Conf. on Dependable Systems and Networks*, Washington, DC, USA, pp. 267-272, 2002.

[29] M. Rodríguez, J.-C. Fabre and J. Arlat, "Assessment of Real-Time Systems by Fault-Injection", in *Proc. European Safety and Reliability Conference*, Lyon, France, pp. 101-108, 2002.

[30] J. A. Stankovic, M. Spuri, K. Ramamritham, G. C. Buttazzo, *Deadline Scheduling for Real-Time Systems: EDF and Related Algorithms*, Kluwer Academic Publishers, 1998.

Model-Based Dependability Evaluation Method for TTP/C Based Systems*

Pavel Herout[1], Stanislav Racek[1], and Jan Hlavička[2]

[1] Department of Computer Science, University of West Bohemia, Univerzitni 22
306 14 Plzen, Czech Republic
{herout,stracek}@kiv.zcu.cz
[2] Department of Computer Science and Engineering
Czech Technical University, Karlovo namesti 13
121 35 Praha 2, Czech Republic
hlavicka@cslab.felk.cvut.cz

Abstract. This paper presents a simulation model of the Time-Triggered Protocol (TTP/C) based embedded computer system as a tool for evaluation of system capability to tolerate a chosen category of faults. The model, being written in ANSI-C, is portable and machine-independent. Its structure is modular and flexible, so that the system to be studied and the experiment setting can easily be changed. The functionality of this model is demonstrated on a set of fault injection experiments aimed mainly to evaluate the correctness of the TTP/C specification. These experiments were done within the EU/IST FIT (Fault Injection for Time triggered architecture) project solution.

1 Introduction

Simulation is one of the standard methods of fault tolerance (FT) evaluation. The main advantage of simulation is above all the fact that it is flexible and can easily be adapted to an environment, which is near to real. Fault injection (FI) can be performed on a simulation model of the system to be evaluated, on a prototype, or on the system itself. Each of these approaches has its advantages and disadvantages (flexibility and ease of implementation in the first case, more convincing results in the last case). Here we consider a discrete-time process-oriented simulation method at the level of distributed system processes, messages and/or services (i.e., not at the level of electronic modules and/or signals).

The EC/IST project Fault Injection for Time Triggered Architecture (FIT) includes several forms of FI, like hardware induced FI, software implemented FI (SWIFI), heavy-ion impacts on the chip, etc [3]. One of the SWIFI approaches is based on the use of a C language based simulation model of the TTP/C protocol created using a proprietary simulation tool C-Sim [2] suitable for building large

---

* The research was in part supported by a grant of 5th Framework Program Information Societies Technology: IST-1999-10748 Fault Injection for Time Triggered Architecture (FIT).

F. Grandoni (Ed.): EDCC 2002, LNCS 2485, pp. 271–282, 2002.

and portable simulation programs. C-Sim has the form of a library of basic object types and operations on them, which enables these types to be enhanced with new attributes and methods fulfilling the needs of a concrete model. C-Sim is in fact an extension of the C language that provides SIMULA-like functions.

The simulation model was built on the basis of the TTP/C protocol specification [14]. There are some previous works, which provide formal proofs of the correctness of individual specified TTP/C properties and services (e.g., [13], [12]). The simulation-based experimental testing of TTP/C properties can extend the correctness verification for more complex situations, including even non-stable states of the TTP/C protocol state machine.

The rest of the paper is organized as follows: section 2 briefly describes the properties of the system under test. The structure of the simulation model is presented in section 3 together with some workload applications. Section 4 describes the fault injection experiment organization. Experimental results are presented in section 5 and conclusion is in section 6.

2   System to Be Evaluated

A distributed system for real-time applications has been developed on the basis of time-triggered architecture (TTA) [9]. Its special feature is fixed partitioning of the time slots on the bus, which guarantees a predictable time behavior of the nodes connected to the bus. The method of access to the bus is then TDMA (Time Division Multiple Access) instead of more common CSMA (Carrier Sense Multiple Access).

One of the possible implementations of the TDMA method is the so-called TTP/C protocol, which is a real-time communication protocol for the interconnection of electronic modules of distributed fault-tolerant real-time systems (C indicates that it meets the requirements for SAE class C automotive applications), because this kind of TTP/C based applications seems to be very promising (see, e.g., [5]). Nodes connected to the bus form the so-called TTP/C cluster. Each node (module) is treated as the *smallest replaceable unit* (SRU). Every node consists of three main parts – see Fig. 1:

- host processor, which executes an application program (and has its own I/O interface to the controlled process),
- dual-port CNI (Computer Network Interface) memory, which serves as interface between the controller and the host,
- communication controller, which executes the TTP/C protocol.

The basic period of the bus communication activity is a TDMA round. Within this round every node has its own slot assigned to transmit its messages. The TTP/C protocol has been designed to tolerate any single physical fault in any one of its constituent parts (communication controllers, bus) without any impact on the operation of a properly configured cluster (single fault hypothesis). As long as an external fault impacts only a single TTP/C node, the TTP/C cluster should tolerate such a fault.

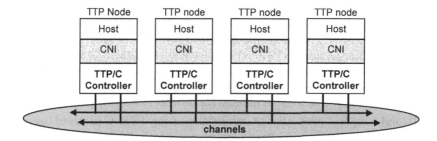

Fig. 1. Structure of a TTP/C cluster

3 Structure of the Simulation Model

3.1 TTP/C Protocol C-Reference Model

The definition of the TTP/C protocol is given in printed form in the Specifications [14]. This document should serve as a basis for any silicon implementation of the TTP/C protocol, i.e., for a communication chip (C1 and C2 chips have been designed by TTTech company so far).

To have a more precise (silicon implementation independent) description of the TTP/C protocol data and functionality, we first built in co-operation with TU Vienna and TTTech Vienna a C-language coded specification, which was denoted as the *TTP/C protocol C-reference model*. This model itself is not executable, but the data types contain all the necessary information and the defined set of procedures covers as much of the protocol functionality as possible. A C-language based functional specification need not necessarily be executable – it is useful as a more precise description of the protocol/controller function than the verbal form. Moreover, it can serve as source data for a software tool making a (semi)automatic chip design from its C-language based functional description. The C-reference model describes two main TTP/C protocol data structures:

- CNI (Computer Network Interface) – used as data interface between the node communication controller and the node host processor,
- MEDL (MEssage Descriptor List) – used as constant-like information describing the node communication controller activity.

These data structures have their layout in accordance with [14], but are treated as abstract data types, i.e., with implementation (data layout) independent interface procedures, so a simple change of data layout has no influence on the description of the C-reference model functionality. The C-reference model includes some more data types, e.g. types of frames, which are transmitted on the bus.

3.2 C-Sim Based Simulation Model of TTP/C Cluster

The simulation model of the TTP/C cluster is based on the C-reference model of the TTP/C protocol as its basic abstract layer. The model is based on the principle of process-oriented discrete simulation (i.e., simulation using pseudo-parallel processes) and implemented by means of the C-Sim tool [2]. The principles and software structure of the model are described on the web page [3]. The source code of the C-Sim based simulation model embeds the code of C-reference model functions into a discrete-time simulation process program, which describes the activity of a TTP/C protocol single instance (i.e., the activity of an abstract TTP/C controller). The form of simulation process enables us:

- To add temporal properties of an instance of the TTP/C protocol computation using a global model-time concept usual with discrete simulation.
- To run several instances (processes) of the TTP/C protocol with their activity "interleaved" in the global model time with regard to local time flow of protocol instances.

The process-oriented simulation environment further enables other activity processes to be added (without any influence on the temporal properties of the protocol instances), e.g. one instance (per node) of bus guardian activity, or one instance of the FI process. The FI process generates disturbances of the "normal" TTP/C activity in order to test its correctness and/or robustness.

The actual version of the simulation model C-language code has a clear and well-defined SW modular structure, which is based on two-dimensional layering of SW modules. This structure is in more details described in [3]. Experience with the FIT project solution identifies three main application areas of the C-language based simulation model:

- *Evaluation of protocol specification (and its possible modifications) correctness.* Thus we can test a TTP/C cluster communication framework using instances of an abstract TTP/C controller (C-language coded functional model of a real controller) and a synthetic testing application (see below).
- *Evaluation of a TTP/C based real-world application, using its C-language source codes.* As the C-Sim based model enables C-language coded application SW modules to be incorporated, it is generally possible to use the C-Sim based and PC station executed development (evaluation) system instead of the TTP/C cluster.
- *Verification of a given fault hypothesis* using SW implemented FI either into CNI data structures or into a specific application data item.

3.3 Testing Applications

In order to evaluate the TTP/C protocol based system dependability, two main categories of testing applications (i.e. applications executed on the TTP/C cluster undergoing the test) were used:

- A "synthetic" application which is constructed to represent a wide class of TTP/C cluster utilization cases in order to enable experimental verification of a given abstract hypothesis and to enable the test results to be generalized.
- A "realistic" application, which is as close as possible to a chosen safety-critical real-time embedded application. Such an application clearly enables

us to test thoroughly some specific property (e.g., a chosen output variable behavior under the influence of transient faults), but a generalization of the test results is more difficult.

So far the following set of applications has been developed and is ready for use (apart from the last one) for fault tolerance testing purposes:

- *Dummy application* (synthetic), which only keeps the cluster communication activity "alive" and does no useful work. It only transmits the TTP/C N-frames containing the node ID. This type of application is quite sufficient when testing only the TTP/C protocol temporal domain properties (see tested hypotheses in part 4.2) and can be configured for any number of TTP/C nodes between 4 and 64.

- *Sine-wave application* (synthetic). This application uses the TTP/C cluster composed of four nodes, all of them performing the same activity: repeated read of an external (sine-wave) signal value and making instances of their own "image" of the read value. Three nodes form a TMR-type fault-tolerant unit (FTU) which uses SW voting to issue one common output value. The fourth node serves as a reference (golden) node. This application is suitable to verify all the hypotheses stated below (see part 4.2). With some caution, the test results can be generalized for any problem from the class of stateless applications (i.e., applications without H-state – see [9]) which uses a similar organization of the TTP/C cluster and performs a similar endless read-compute-write cycle.

- *Single-wheel brake-by-wire (BBW) application.* This application from a "semi-realistic" category was designed by the Volvo company and accepted by the FIT project partners as a standard TTP/C cluster testing workload. The BBW source code has been delivered in the form of C-language modules, so it can be either compiled and loaded into real HW or incorporated into C-language based simulation framework (as we have done). A run of BBW application emulates a car braking (ABS) control system for one wheel.

- *Four-wheel brake-by-wire (BBW-4W)*, also designed by Volvo, uses up to ten TTP/C nodes. This application belongs to the "true realistic" category in the sense that after thorough testing using the TTP/C evaluation cluster and/or the simulation model, it could be passed with minor changes to a real car control system. The incorporation of this application into the C-Sim based simulation framework is currently in progress.

4 Fault Injection Experiment Organization

4.1 Fault Model

Within the FIT project, a transient fault model has been accepted. This applies to heavy ion impact, short-time change of a pin signal level, bit flip in real CNI using the SWIFI method and also to the C-Sim model. We can also inject a permanent fault using a very dense stream of transient CNI bit flip faults. As the simulation model was built from TTP/C specifications [14], we injected transient faults attacking only data structures which are exactly defined there (e.g., CNI, local image of CNI, RAM copy of MEDL). A distortion of the transmitted frames can be injected either into the data area of a given CNI or directly into the data structure of the transmitted frame.

We introduced a hierarchical model of information-damaging transient fault types (for definitions see also [10]), where a higher-level type can degenerate (for specific values of the parameters) into a lower-level type:

Single-bit fault is *a random setting of a bit within a RAM located bit array.* We recognize three types of single-bit faults: setting to logical 0, setting to logical 1, and bit flip (setting to the opposite value). The attributes of a single-bit fault are: memory array identification (process, array, bit offset), fault mask indicating which bits should not be affected, discrete probability function of fault type (e.g., $\{1/3, 1/3, 1/3\}$ means that every type of single-bit fault can occur with the same probability).

m-**bit fault** is *a set of m single-bit faults within a given bit array* which is located inside a single error containment region – see [9]. All single-bit faults are injected at the same time. Every bit of the array has the same probability to be (successively) chosen as a subject of fault injection. The value of m should be less than or equal to the length of the given bit array, and for $m = 1$ we get a single-bit fault. The attributes of the m-bit fault are: single bit fault attributes and the number m of bits, which are influenced by the fault, denoted as *dimension of m-bit fault.*

Burst of simultaneous faults is *a stochastic stream of k m-bit faults*, where the time between single events (faults) within the stream has a given probability density function. The attributes of a burst are: simultaneous fault attributes, mean frequency of faults within the stream (λ_c), and number k of faults in the burst, denoted as *length of the burst of faults*. For $k = 1$ we get one m-bit fault, etc.

Stream of bursts is *a stochastic stream of events*, where one event means one burst of faults. The number of events within a stream is not limited. The attributes of a stream are: burst attributes, mean frequency of events within the stream (λ_s), and minimal gap g between two successive events within the stream. For $k = 1, m = 1$ we get a stream of single-bit faults.

4.2 Tested Hypotheses

The fault-tolerant properties of the (simulated) TTP/C cluster can be described by means of a hierarchical set of hypotheses. Every "higher level" hypothesis assumes that the "lower level" hypotheses are valid. The used set of hypotheses is as follows.

4.2.1 TTP/C Single-Fault Hypothesis in the Time Domain. The TTP/C protocol has been designed to tolerate any single permanent physical fault in any one of its constituent parts, like the TTP/C cluster nodes denoted as SRUs in [14]. *Tolerating a single fault means that a failed node is "fail silent", i.e., that*

the failure does not propagate outside of the node and moreover all other nodes within the TTP/C cluster are able to recognize the failed node no later than after one TDMA round. As for the transient fault influencing one SRU, [14] stipulates that for its duration shorter than one SRU slot, the TTP/C based system should tolerate such a fault, assuming that the next fault will not come before the attacked SRU reintegrates.

4.2.2 Single-Fault Hypothesis in the Value Domain. When the TTP/C time domain hypothesis is valid, it is possible to design TTP/C systems which fulfill the so-called *value domain single-fault tolerance hypothesis*, which means that *the system never delivers a bad value at any of its outputs.* The basic way to achieve this property is to use node-level redundancy, i.e., to construct groups of nodes representing Fault Tolerant Units (FTUs).

4.2.3 Transient-Fault Robustness in the Time Domain. To reveal as many inconsistencies in the TTP/C specification as possible, we extended the tests "beyond specification" and formulated the so-called transient fault robustness hypothesis in the time domain in the following way: *No sequence of transient faults which disturb the TTP/C level single node volatile (register or RAM located) information can result in a permanent cluster fault, i.e., the attacked node always reintegrates once the sequence of faults is stopped and no other node is influenced (no fault propagation occurs).*

4.2.4 Transient-Fault Robustness in the Value Domain. The TTP/C specification [14] states that: *The resilience of a TTP/C cluster with respect to multiple failures depends on the application specific configuration. Many multiple internal faults will be tolerated under normal operating conditions.*

To have a possibility to test the stated property, we formulated the following hypothesis: *No sequence of transient faults which disturb TTP/C level cluster-wide volatile (i.e., register or RAM located) information can result in a permanent cluster fault. Thus the cluster executing an application always recovers its correct output(s) once the sequence of faults is stopped.* This hypothesis should be made valid (by a proper cluster design) with a sufficient probability, especially for stateless applications.

4.3 FI Experiment Methodology

The described simulation method of TTP/C based system fault tolerance evaluation is flexible enough to enable a broad spectrum of FI experiments organization. Using the testing applications characterized above (which are typically capable of non-stop activity) and the transient fault types described above, we mostly use the following FI experiment scenario:

- One experiment is a run of the simulation program for a set of chosen values of the parameters.
- The experiment simulates a given duration of TTP/C cluster activity (e.g., 1 million TDMA rounds).

- Cluster activity is disturbed by a chosen stream of transient faults, and statistics on the influence of the faults is collected. The stream of faults can be either synchronized with the modeled cluster activity (when testing hypotheses 1 or 2) or quite asynchronous (hypotheses 3, 4).
- A violation of the tested hypothesis can bring the simulation experiment run to an end (depending on the hypothesis).

As the execution of the program that simulates the TTP/C system activity is deterministically serialized (it uses pseudo-random number generators which are always started from the same value), it is possible to analyze which reason led to the violation of the tested hypothesis during the given simulation experiment.

4.4 FI Tools

Due to the nature of the experimental testing it is necessary to perform many simulation experiments to reach a sufficient reliability of results of the type *"the tested hypothesis is valid"*. Obviously, a single experiment with negative result suffices to confirm the inverse statement: *"the tested hypothesis is not valid"*. To be able to repeat many simulation experiments, we designed and implemented a special SW tool.

Fault Injection Module (FIM) is a flexible tool for FI in the C-Sim simulation environment. It has a wide range of possible ways to prepare the simulation-based fault injection experiments, run them and analyze their results. The main characteristics of the tool:

- It enables a huge set (thousands) of experiments to be prepared (described), each with one or several streams of faults. The experiment is one run of the simulation program using one set of parameters.
- It controls a run of the whole set of experiments. It uses pseudo-random fault injection disturbing RAM-located information according to the description of the set.
- It enables experiments with "interesting results" (i.e., those leading to an arbitrary error) to be selected automatically.
- It runs these selected experiments for a second time. During this run it also continually writes each fault record (number of the affected node, time, type of faults and fault location).

With this tool the entire RAM-located information can be induced very effectively and quickly, and the results can be analyzed, including repeated experiment run. For more information see [3].

5 Fault Injection Experimental Results

A large set of FI experiments has been performed so far within the FIT project solution, testing **all the hypotheses** stated above in 4.2. The limited space of this paper doesn't allow to report all of them, so we will try to give a comprehensive overview. Moreover, not all the tests have been finished to the date of this paper printing.

We started with tests aimed to reveal the simulation model bugs and to validate the simulation model. This process was repeated many times during the C-Sim based simulation model building, so the C-Sim based simulation model of the TTP/C cluster activity was tested thoroughly. It is necessary to emphasize that from the methodological point of view every simulation experiment means a test both of the given hypothesis and also of the testing tool. Due to the deterministic nature of the model itself it is possible to analyze if an unexpected result was caused by a program bug or by an out-of-specification modeled system behavior. Several inconsistencies in the protocol specifications were discovered and subsequently corrected during construction of the model.

To evaluate the model validity, the most important set of comparable FI experiments was executed in parallel in Vienna and in Prague, during which two different forms of SWIFI (software implemented fault injection) were used. TU Vienna used as the object of FI a real TTP/C system, whereas at TU Prague the faults were injected into its model coded in C. The organization of the FI experiments was the same, with the exception of some slight differences which were due to different implementation. All of the 526 bits of the CNI control area were a subject to bit-flip injection. The results of the comparison have shown a conformance of 98.9 %, while the cause of the unmatched results can be easily explained by slight differences in experiment organization [1].

5.1   Systematic CNI Bits Injection

For this group of experiments we used the injected node (F-node) CNI data area as the target of FI. The goal of the experiments was to validate the first and second hypotheses given above in 4.2.1 and 4.2.2. The choice of CNI has (at least) three good reasons:

- CNI structure is exactly defined by the TTP/C specification, so the model built directly from this specification makes the FI into specified bits easy.
- We can assume that a majority of internal errors (caused either by TTP/C controller or by an application) will propagate as a corrupted CNI item.
- Data exchanged among the TTP/C cluster nodes is stored in the F-node CNI, so the coordination at application level can be disturbed as well.

All bits of the control area of CNI were successively tested (result tables are accessible at [3]), using mainly sine-wave application. *Systematic injection was synchronous in the sense that the fault injection process was synchronized with the TTP/C cluster activity.* Thus the injected fault is applied within a chosen time point (slot) of the TDMA round, only within the "application" state of the TTP/C protocol state machine activity. It means that the assumption of single-fault is valid, i.e. the fault influences only one SRU and the next fault cannot come before the F-node reintegration.

Single-Fault Hypothesis in the Time Domain. This group of FI experiments was aimed to test the first given hypothesis (fail-silence in time domain). The following reactions were observed:

a) Fault propagation from the injected F-node: *no propagation, i.e., no violation of the TTP/C single fault hypothesis in the temporal domain was observed.*

b) Malfunction of the affected F-node: *no malfunction was observed, the node always recovered* (returned into the "application" state).

It means that no violation of the TTP/C single-fault hypothesis in the time domain was observed within this group of extensive tests (for more details see [3]), what is not surprising so much, because the correctness of TTP/C protocol within its steady-state processing has been proven formally, e.g. [12], [13].

Single-Fault Hypothesis in Value Domain. When the first tested hypothesis is valid (or at least not denied), a fault-tolerant TTP/C application can be designed using node replication. Such an application, if properly constructed, can fulfill the single-fault hypothesis in the value domain. We used at first the sine-wave testing application, where three nodes (including the injected F-node) form a TMR-based FTU. We repeated all the tests as within the previous group comparing the FTU's and R-node (reference node) output. No mismatches were observed during these tests, what means that *the single-fault hypothesis in the value domain was not violated.* As the result is application dependent, only the following conclusion can be drawn:

- TTP/C cluster is a framework that enables to construct an application that tolerates a single fault (i.e. does not give a bad output value).
- The sine-wave application is constructed properly in the sense that it does not violate single-fault value-domain hypothesis.

Moreover we tested the value-domain hypothesis using both BBW applications. These tests were not concluded yet. Some preliminary results concerning BBW time behavior (both without and with FI) can be observed at [3].

5.2   Randomly Induced CNI Bits Injection

Random CNI bits injection can be described as a stationary stochastic process, which at randomly chosen time points randomly chooses a CNI bit (or several bits for multiple bit-flips) whose value is to be injected. *This means that the injection process is asynchronous with the process of TTP/C cluster activity.* When a chosen rate of events (the mean frequency of single injections) within the injection process is dense enough (say, approximately the same as the basic frequency of repeating the TDMA rounds), a fault can be injected before the simulated controller activity has recovered from a previous fault, so faults are generally incoming in every state of the TTP/C protocol state machine activity. Thus the ability of the controller to integrate itself into the cluster activity (when faults are disturbing the process of integration) has also been verified.

Transient-Fault Robustness in the Time Domain. We made a large set of experiments with randomly induced CNI bit injections using the FIM tool. These tests were mostly aimed to test the ability of TTP/C abstract controller reintegration even when the process of reintegration is disturbed with a successive fault. The most important result is that *the transient-fault robustness hypothesis as stated in 4.2.3 does not generally apply*, what is not so surprising, because we are "out of TTP/C specification", especially out of single-fault assumption. For a "heavy" injection with dense stochastic stream of CNI bit injections we observed some percentage of fault propagations and cluster errors.

As an example we can introduce one set of experiments which was done using the sine-wave testing application. Each of the 526 CNI bits was injected with several fault types (0, 1, bit-flip) and the bit-injection stream parameters were changed. Total number of experiments executed was 6 192, length of each of them was 200 000 TDMA rounds, one round has 4 slots per 2.5 ms. There were 112 experiments that led to a fault propagation (1.8 %).

Experiment results like those given above can be utilized in two ways. At first the robustness property related to a certain fault type can be evaluated by means of a probability value. Thus, e.g., the estimated probability that the modeled cluster will not "survive" a transient fault of the type "dense stream of CNI bits injection, length 1 second" is (related to the modeled 350 hours of the cluster function time) about 1.4×10^{-6}.

The second way, how to use the experiment results is to analyze the reasons which led to a cluster fault and try to improve the TTP/C protocol state machine (the abstract TPP/C controller) behavior in order to prevent fault propagation.

Transient-Fault Robustness in the Value Domain. This property (as defined in 4.2.4) relies on the previous one (4.2.3). It is not surprising, that both properties can be reached only with a certain probability (e.g. reliability value), because they are "out of TTP/C specification". We tested the transient-fault robustness property using the sine-wave application whose all four nodes were "attacked" with a dense stream of CNI bit-flip bursts, every bit of the CNI is endangered with the same probability. The tests done so far were described in [4]. The preliminary results show, that e.g. for the length of burst 16 TDMA rounds, mean period of bursts 128 TDMA rounds and "dimension" of burst varying from 1 to 1 000 bit-flips, there is the probability of about 10^{-3} that the modeled cluster output does not recover, i.e. that the burst of transient faults is transformed into the permanent fault. This value is clearly application dependent (and fault-type dependent as well), what means that a model-based test of this type should be done at a final stage of the application design.

6   Conclusions

The method presented in this paper uses C-language coded protocol specification as a basic abstract layer of discrete-time simulation model of TTP/C system (cluster) that is executing an application. The method enables us to inject various kinds of faults and to evaluate their influence (i.e., to test different hypotheses concerning fault tolerance). The simulation model can be executed on an ordinary PC station and the simulation model-time speed is comparable with the TTP/C evaluation cluster real-time speed. The simulation model validity was tested in cooperation with TU Vienna by comparison with the SWIFI method applied to real HW. This comparison revealed a very high degree of coincidence of the results. The method enables an evaluation of protocol specification correctness and of a TTP/C based real-world application, using its C-language source code as a part of the simulation program. The results obtained so far are based on the tests of TTP/C protocol specified properties (the corresponding hypotheses were confirmed). The tests using the "abstract controller" (SW based, built from specification) also significantly contributed to an improvement of TTP/C protocol specification quality. Further results were obtained by testing the TTP/C protocol robustness verifying the resilience of a TTP/C cluster with respect to multiple faults. We found that many multiple internal faults will be tolerated under normal operating conditions, and a TTP/C based system can successfully survive even in very severe conditions.

References

[1] Ademaj, A., Grillinger, P., Herout, P., Hlavicka, J.: Fault Tolerance Evaluation using two SWIFI Methods. In: Proceedings of IEEE IOLTW 2002, Isle of Bendor (France), 8–10. 7. 2002 (in print)   279
[2] http://www.c-sim.zcu.cz   271, 274
[3] http://www.fit.zcu.cz   271, 274, 278, 279, 280
[4] Grillinger, P., Racek, S.: Transient faults robustness evaluation of safety critical systems using simulation. In: Proceedings of BEC 2002 (Baltic Electronic Conference), Tallinn, Oct. 2002 (in print)   281
[5] Heiner, G., Thurner, T.: Time-triggered architecture for safety-related distributed real-time systems in transportation systems. In: Proceedings of FTCS-28, Munich, Germany (1998) 402–407   272
[6] Hlavicka, J., Racek, S., Smrha, P.: Functional validation of fault-tolerant asynchronous algorithms. In: Proceedings of Euromicro, Prague, Czech Republic (1996) 143–150
[7] Hlavicka, J., Racek, S., Herout, P.: Analysis and testing of process controller dependability. In: Proceedings of Ninth IEEE European Workshop on Dependable Computing, Gdansk, Poland (1998) 7-11
[8] Hlavicka, J., Racek, S., Herout, P.: Evaluation of Process Controller Fault Tolerance Using Simulation. Simulation Practice and Theory, Vol. 7, Nr. 8, March 2000, 769–790
[9] Kopetz, H.: Real-Time Systems, Design Principles for Distributed Embedded Applications. Kluwer Academic Publishers, 1997, p. 338   272, 275, 276
[10] Laprie, J. C. (ed.): Dependability: Basic concepts and terminology. Springer-Verlag Wien, New York, 1992, p. 265   276
[11] Manzone, A. et al.: Fault tolerant automotive systems: An overview. In: Proceedings of 7th Int'l On-Line Testing Workshop, Taormina, Italy, 9–11. 7. 2001, 117–121
[12] Pfeifer, H., Schwier, D., Henke, F. W.: Formal Verification for Time-Triggered Clock Synchronization. Published in Dependable Computing and Fault-Tolerant Systems, Vol. 12, C. B. Weinstock and J. Rushby, eds., 207–226, IEEE Computer Society   272, 280
[13] Rushby, J.: Systematic Formal Verification for Fault-Tolerant Time-Triggered Algorithms. IEEE Transactions for SW Engineering, Vol. 25, No.5, Sept/Oct 1999, 651–661   272, 280
[14] TTP/C Protocol – Specification of the protocol. Version 1.0 of 1. Feb. 1999. TTTech Computertechnik GmbH, http://www.tttech.com   272, 273, 276, 277

Author Index

Lecture Notes in Computer Science

For information about Vols. 1–1234

please contact your bookseller or Springer-Verlag